About ESource

ESource—The Prentice Hall Engineering Source —www.prenhall.com/esource

ESource—The Prentice Hall Engineering Source gives professors the power to harness the full potential of their text and their first-year engineering course. More than just a collection of books, ESource is a unique publishing system revolving around the ESource website—www.prenhall.com/esource. ESource enables you to put your stamp on your book just as you do your course. It lets you:

Control You choose exactly what chapter or sections are in your book and in what order they appear. Of course, you can choose the entire book if you'd like and stay with the authors' original order.

Optimize Get the most from your book and your course. ESource lets you produce the optimal text for your students needs.

Customize You can add your own material anywhere in your text's presentation, and your final product will arrive at your bookstore as a professionally formatted text.

ESource ACCESS

Starting in the fall of 2000, professors who choose to bundle two or more texts from the ESource series for their class, or use an ESource custom book will be providing their students with complete access to the library of ESource content. All bundles and custom books will come with a student password that gives web ESource ACCESS to all information on the site. This passcode is free and is valid for one year after initial log-on. We've designed ESource ACCESS to provides students a flexible, searchable, on-line resource.

ESource Content

All the content in ESource was written by educators specifically for freshman/first-year students. Authors tried to strike a balanced level of presentation, an approach that was neither formulaic nor trivial, and one that did not focus too heavily on advanced topics that most introductory students do not encounter until later classes. Because many professors do not have extensive time to cover these topics in the classroom, authors prepared each text with the idea that many students would use it for self-instruction and independent study. Students should be able to use this content to learn the software tool or subject on their own.

While authors had the freedom to write texts in a style appropriate to their particular subject, all followed certain guidelines created to promote a consistency that makes students comfortable. Namely, every chapter opens with a clear set of **Objectives**, includes **Practice Boxes** throughout the chapter, and ends with a number of **Problems**, and a list of **Key Terms**. **Applications Boxes** are spread throughout the book with the intent of giving students a real-world perspective of engineering. **Success Boxes** provide the student with advice about college study skills, and help students avoid the common pitfalls of first-year students. In addition, this series contains an entire book titled ***Engineering Success*** by Peter Schiavone of the University of Alberta intended to expose students quickly to what it takes to be an engineering student.

Creating Your Book

Using ESource is simple. You preview the content either on-line or through examination copies of the books you can request on-line, from your PH sales rep, or by calling 1-800-526-0485. Create an on-line outline of the content you want, in the order you want, using ESource's simple interface. Either type or cut and paste your own material and insert it into the text flow. You can preview the overall organization of the text you've created at anytime (please note, since this preview is immediate, it comes unformatted.), then press another button and receive an order number for your own custom book. If you are not ready to order, do nothing—ESource will save your work. You can come back at any time and change, re-arrange, or add more material to your creation. You are in control. Once you're finished and you have an ISBN, give it to your bookstore and your book will arrive on their shelves six weeks after they order. Your custom desk copies with their instructor supplements will arrive at your address at the same time.

To learn more about this new system for creating the perfect textbook, go to www.prenhall.com/esource. You can either go through the on-line walkthrough of how to create a book, or experiment yourself.

Supplements

Adopters of ESource receive an instructor's CD that contains professor and student code from the books in the series, as well as other instruction aides provided by authors. The website also holds approximately **350 Powerpoint transparencies** created by Jack Leifer of Univ. of Kentucky—Paducah available to download. Professors can either follow these transparencies as pre-prepared lectures or use them as the basis for their own custom presentations.

Introduction to Visual Basic 6.0

David I. Schneider
University of Maryland

Prentice Hall
Upper Saddle River, NJ 07458

Library of Congress Cataloging-in-Publication Data
Schneider, David I.
Introduction to Visual Basic 6.0 / David I. Schneider.
p. cm.
ISBN 0-13-026813-5
1. Microsoft Visual BASIC. 2. BASIC (Computer program language) I. Title.

QA76.73.B3 S3595 2000
005.26'8—dc21

00.026322

Vice-president of editorial development, ECS: **MARCIA HORTON**
Acquisitions editor: **ERIC SVENDSEN**
Associate editor: **JOE RUSSO**
Vice-president of production and manufacturing: **DAVID W. RICCARDI**
Executive managing editor: **VINCE O' BRIEN**
Managing editor: **DAVID A. GEORGE**
Editorial/production supervisor: **LAKSHMI BALASUBRAMANIAN**
Cover director: **JAYNE CONTE**
Manufacturing buyer: **PAT BROWN**
Editorial assistant: **KRISTEN BLANCO**
Marketing manager: **DANNY HOYT**

Upper Saddle River, New Jersey 07458

Reprinted with corrections July, 2001.

Printed in the United States of America.

10 9 8 7 6 5 4

ISBN 0-13-026813-5

Prentice-Hall International (UK) Limited, *London*
Prentice-Hall of Australia Pty. Limited, *Sydney*
Prentice-Hall Canada, Inc., Toronto
Prentice-Hall Hispanoamericana, S.A., *Mexico*
Prentice-Hall of India Private Limited, *New Delhi*
Prentice-Hall of Japan, Inc., *Tokyo*
Pearson Education (Singapore) Pte. Ltd., *Singapore*
Editoria Prentice-Hall do Brasil, Ltda., *Rio de Janeiro*

Titles in the ESource Series

Introduction to UNIX
0-13-095135-8
David I. Schwartz

Introduction to AutoCAD 2000
0-13-016732-0
Mark Dix and Paul Riley

Introduction to Maple
0-13-095133-1
David I. Schwartz

Introduction to Word
0-13-254764-3
David C. Kuncicky

Introduction to Excel, 2/e
0-13-016881-5
David C. Kuncicky

Introduction to Mathcad
0-13-937493-0
Ronald W. Larsen

Introduction to AutoCAD, R. 14
0-13-011001-9
Mark Dix and Paul Riley

Introduction to the Internet, 3/e
0-13-031355-6
Scott D. James

Design Concepts for Engineers
0-13-081369-9
Mark N. Horenstein

Engineering Design—A Day in the Life of Four Engineers
0-13-085089-6
Mark N. Horenstein

Engineering Ethics
0-13-784224-4
Charles B. Fleddermann

Engineering Success
0-13-080859-8
Peter Schiavone

Mathematics Review
0-13-011501-0
Peter Schiavone

Introduction to C
0-13-011854-0
Delores Etter

Introduction to C++
0-13-011855-9
Delores Etter

Introduction to MATLAB
0-13-013149-0
Delores Etter with David C. Kuncicky

Titles in the ESource Series

Introduction to FORTRAN 90
0-13-013146-6
Larry Nyhoff and Sanford Leestma

Introduction to Java
0-13-919416-9
Stephen J. Chapman

Introduction to Engineering Analysis
0-13-016733-9
Kirk D. Hagen

Introduction to PowerPoint
0-13-040214-1
Jack Leifer

Graphics Concepts
0-13-030687-8
Richard M. Lueptow

Graphics Concepts with Pro/ENGINEER®
0-13-014154-2
Richard M. Lueptow, Jim Steger, and Michael T. Snyder

Graphics Concepts with SolidWorks
0-13-014155-0
Richard M. Lueptow and Michael Minbiole

Introduction to Visual Basic 6.0
0-13-026813-5
David I. Schneider

Introduction to Mathcad 2000
0-13-020007-7
Ronald W. Larsen

www.prenhall.com/esource/

About the Authors

No project could ever come to pass without a group of authors who have the vision and the courage to turn a stack of blank paper into a book. The authors in this series worked diligently to produce their books, provide the building blocks of the series.

Delores M. Etter is a Professor of Electrical and Computer Engineering at the University of Colorado. Dr. Etter was a faculty member at the University of New Mexico and also a Visiting Professor at Stanford University. Dr. Etter was responsible for the Freshman Engineering Program at the University of New Mexico and is active in the Integrated Teaching Laboratory at the University of Colorado. She was elected a Fellow of the Institute of Electrical and Electronics Engineers for her contributions to education and for her technical leadership in digital signal processing. In addition to writing best-selling textbooks for engineering computing, Dr. Etter has also published research in the area of adaptive signal processing.

Sanford Leestma is a Professor of Mathematics and Computer Science at Calvin College, and received his Ph.D. from New Mexico State University. He has been the long-time co-author of successful textbooks on Fortran, Pascal, and data structures in Pascal. His current research interest are in the areas of algorithms and numerical computation.

Larry Nyhoff is a Professor of Mathematics and Computer Science at Calvin College. After doing bachelor's work at Calvin, and Master's work at Michigan, he received a Ph.D. from Michigan State and also did graduate work in computer science at Western Michigan. Dr. Nyhoff has taught at Calvin for the past 34 years—mathematics at first and computer science for the past several years. He has co-authored several computer science textbooks since 1981 including titles on Fortran and C++, as well as a brand new title on Data Structures in C++.

Acknowledgments: We express our sincere appreciation to all who helped in the preparation of this module, especially our acquisitions editor Alan Apt, managing editor Laura Steele, developmental editor Sandra Chavez, and production editor Judy Winthrop. We also thank Larry Genalo for several examples and exercises and Erin Fulp for the Internet address application in Chapter 10. We appreciate the insightful review provided by Bart Childs. We thank our families—Shar, Jeff, Dawn, Rebecca, Megan, Sara, Greg, Julie, Joshua, Derek, Tom, Joan; Marge, Michelle, Sandy, Lory, Michael—for being patient and understanding. We thank God for allowing us to write this text.

Mark Dix began working with AutoCAD in 1985 as a programmer for CAD Support Associates, Inc. He helped design a system for creating estimates and bills of material directly from AutoCAD drawing databases for use in the automated conveyor industry. This system became the basis for systems still widely in use today. In 1986 he began collaborating with Paul Riley to create AutoCAD training materials, combining Riley's background in industrial design and training with Dix's background in writing, curriculum development, and programming. Dix and Riley have created tutorial and teaching methods for every AutoCAD release since Version 2.5. Mr. Dix has a Master of Education from the University of Massachusetts. He is currently the Director of Dearborn Academy High School in Arlington, Massachusetts.

Paul Riley is an author, instructor, and designer specializing in graphics and design for multimedia. He is a founding partner of CAD Support Associates, a contract service and professional training organization for computer-aided design. His 15 years of business experience and 20 years of teaching experience are supported by degrees in education and computer science. Paul has taught AutoCAD at the University of Massachusetts at Lowell and is presently teaching AutoCAD at Mt. Ida College in Newton, Massachusetts. He has developed a program, Computer-aided Design for Professionals that is highly regarded by corporate clients and has been an ongoing success since 1982.

www.prenhall.com/esource/

Scott D. James is a staff lecturer at Kettering University (formerly GMI Engineering & Management Institute) in Flint, Michigan. He is currently pursuing a Ph.D. in Systems Engineering with an emphasis on software engineering and computer-integrated manufacturing. Scott decided on writing textbooks after he found a void in the books that were available. "I really wanted a book that showed how to do things in good detail but in a clear and concise way. Many of the books on the market are full of fluff and force you to dig out the really important facts." Scott decided on teaching as a profession after several years in the computer industry. "I thought that it was really important to know what it was like outside of academia. I wanted to provide students with classes that were up to date and provide the information that is really used and needed."
Acknowledgments: Scott would like to acknowledge his family for the time to work on the text and his students and peers at Kettering who offered helpful critiques of the materials that eventually became the book.

Charles B. Fleddermann is a professor in the Department of Electrical and Computer Engineering at the University of New Mexico in Albuquerque, New Mexico. All of his degrees are in electrical engineering: his Bachelor's degree from the University of Notre Dame, and the Master's and Ph.D. from the University of Illinois at Urbana-Champaign. Prof. Fleddermann developed an engineering ethics course for his department in response to the ABET requirement to incorporate ethics topics into the undergraduate engineering curriculum. *Engineering Ethics* was written as a vehicle for presenting ethical theory, analysis, and problem solving to engineering undergraduates in a concise and readily accessible way.
Acknowledgments: I would like to thank Profs. Charles Harris and Michael Rabins of Texas A & M University whose NSF sponsored workshops on engineering ethics got me started thinking in this field. Special thanks to my wife Liz, who proofread the manuscript for this book, provided many useful suggestions, and who helped me learn how to teach "soft" topics to engineers.

David I. Schwartz is an Assistant Professor in the Computer Science Department at Cornell University and earned his B.S., M.S., and Ph.D. degrees in Civil Engineering from State University of New York at Buffalo. Throughout his graduate studies, Schwartz combined principles of computer science to applications of civil engineering. He became interested in helping students learn how to apply software tools for solving a variety of engineering problems. He teaches his students to learn incrementally and practice frequently to gain the maturity to tackle other subjects. In his spare time, Schwartz plays drums in a variety of bands.
Acknowledgments: I dedicate my books to my family, friends, and students who all helped in so many ways. Many thanks go to the schools of Civil Engineering and Engineering & Applied Science at State University of New York at Buffalo where I originally developed and tested my UNIX and Maple books. I greatly appreciate the opportunity to explore my goals and all the help from everyone at the Computer Science Department at Cornell. Eric Svendsen and everyone at Prentice Hall also deserve my gratitude for helping to make these books a reality. Many thanks, also, to those who submitted interviews and images.

Ron Larsen is an Associate Professor of Chemical Engineering at Montana State University, and received his Ph.D. from the Pennsylvania State University. He was initially attracted to engineering by the challenges the profession offers, but also appreciates that engineering is a serving profession. Some of the greatest challenges he has faced while teaching have involved non-traditional teaching methods, including evening courses for practicing engineers and teaching through an interpreter at the Mongolian National University. These experiences have provided tremendous opportunities to learn new ways to communicate technical material. He tries to incorporate the skills he has learned in non-traditional arenas to improve his lectures, written materials, and learning programs. Dr. Larsen views modern software as one of the new tools that will radically alter the way engineers work, and his book *Introduction to Mathcad* was written to help young engineers prepare to meet the challenges of an ever-changing workplace.
Acknowledgments: To my students at Montana State University who have endured the rough drafts and typos, and who still allow me to experiment with their classes—my sincere thanks.

Peter Schiavone is a professor and student advisor in the Department of Mechanical Engineering at the University of Alberta, Canada. He received his Ph.D. from the University of Strathclyde, U.K. in 1988. He has authored several books in the area of student academic success as well as numerous papers in international scientific research journals. Dr. Schiavone has worked in private industry in several different areas of engineering including aerospace and systems engineering. He founded the first Mathematics Resource Center at the University of Alberta, a unit designed specifically to teach new students the necessary *survival skills* in mathematics and the physical sciences required for success in first-year engineering. This led to the Students' Union Gold Key Award for outstanding contributions to the university. Dr. Schiavone lectures regularly to freshman engineering students and to new engineering professors on engineering success, in particular about maximizing students' academic performance. He wrote the book *Engineering Success* in order to share the *secrets of success in engineering study*: the most effective, tried and tested methods used by the most successful engineering students.

Acknowledgements: Thanks to Eric Svendsen for his encouragement and support; to Richard Felder for being such an inspiration; to my wife Linda for sharing my dreams and believing in me; and to Francesca and Antonio for putting up with Dad when working on the text.

Mark N. Horenstein is a Professor in the Department of Electrical and Computer Engineering at Boston University. He has degrees in Electrical Engineering from M.I.T. and U.C. Berkeley and has been involved in teaching engineering design for the greater part of his academic career. He devised and developed the senior design project class taken by all electrical and computer engineering students at Boston University. In this class, the students work for a virtual engineering company developing products and systems for real-world engineering and social-service clients. Many of the design projects developed in his class have been aimed at assistive technologies for individuals with disabilities.

Acknowledgments: I would like to thank Prof. James Bethune, the architect of the Peak Performance event at Boston University, for his permission to highlight the competition in my text. Several of the ideas relating to brainstorming and teamwork were derived from a workshop on engineering design offered by Prof. Charles Lovas of Southern Methodist University. The principles of estimation were derived in part from a freshman engineering problem posed by Prof. Thomas Kincaid of Boston University.

Kirk D. Hagen is a professor at Weber State University in Ogden, Utah. He has taught introductory-level engineering courses and upper-division thermal science courses at WSU since 1993. He received his B.S. degree in physics from Weber State College and his M.S. degree in mechanical engineering from Utah State University, after which he worked as a thermal designer/analyst in the aerospace and electronics industries. After several years of engineering practice, he resumed his formal education, earning his Ph.D. in mechanical engineering at the University of Utah. Hagen is the author of an undergraduate heat transfer text. Having drawn upon his industrial and teaching experience, he strongly believes that engineering students must develop effective analytical problem solving abilities. His book, *Introduction to Engineering Analysis*, was written to help beginning engineering students learn a systematic approach to engineering analysis.

Richard M. Lueptow is the Charles Deering McCormick Professor of Teaching Excellence and Associate Professor of Mechanical Engineering at Northwestern University. He is a native of Wisconsin and received his doctorate from the Massachusetts Institute of Technology in 1986. He teaches design, fluid mechanics, and spectral analysis techniques. "In my design class I saw a need for a self-paced tutorial for my students to learn CAD software quickly and easily. I worked with several students a few years ago to develop just this type of tutorial, which has since evolved into a book. My goal is to introduce students to engineering graphics and CAD, while showing them how much fun it can be." Rich has an active research program on rotating filtration, Taylor Couette flow, granular flow, fire suppression, and acoustics. He has five patents and over 40 refereed journal and proceedings papers along with many other articles, abstracts, and presentations.

Acknowledgments: Thanks to my talented and hard-working co-authors as well as the many colleagues and students who took the tutorial for a "test drive." Special thanks to Mike Minbiole for his major contributions to Graphics Concepts with SolidWorks. Thanks also to Northwestern University for the time to work on a book. Most of all, thanks to my loving wife, Maiya, and my children, Hannah and Kyle, for supporting me in this endeavor. (Photo courtesy of Evanston Photographic Studios, Inc.)

Jack Leifer is an Assistant Professor in the Department of Mechanical Engineering at the University of Kentucky Extended Campus Program in Paducah, and was previously with the Department of Mathematical Sciences and Engineering at the University of South Carolina—Aiken. He received his Ph.D. in Mechanical Engineering from the University of Texas at Austin in December 1995.

His current research interests include the modeling of sensors for manufacturing, and the use of Artificial Neural Networks to predict corrosion.

Acknowledgements: I'd like to thank my colleagues at USC—Aiken, especially Professors Mike May and Laurene Fausett, for their encouragement and feedback; Eric Svendsen and Joe Russo of Prentice Hall, for their useful suggestions and flexibility with deadlines; and my parents, Felice and Morton Leifer, for being there and providing support (as always) as I completed this book.

David C. Kuncicky is a native Floridian. He earned his Baccalaureate in psychology, Master's in computer science, and Ph.D. in computer science from Florida State University. He has served as a faculty member in the Department of Electrical Engineering at the FAMU–FSU College of Engineering and the Department of Computer Science at Florida State University. He has taught computer science and computer engineering courses for over 15 years. He has published research in the areas of intelligent hybrid systems and neural networks. He is currently the Director of Engineering at Bioreason, Inc. in Sante Fe, New Mexico.

Acknowledgments: Thanks to Steffie and Helen for putting up with my late nights and long weekends at the computer. Thanks also to the helpful and insightful technical reviews by Jerry Ralya, Kathy Kitto, Avi Singhal, Thomas Hill, Ron Eaglin, Larry Richards, and Susan Freeman. I appreciate the patience of Eric Svendsen and Joe Russo of Prentice Hall for gently guiding me through this project. Finally, thanks to Susan Bassett for having faith in my abilities, and for providing continued tutelage and support.

Jim Steger is currently Chief Technical Officer and cofounder of an Internet applications company. He graduated with a Bachelor of Science degree in Mechanical Engineering from Northwestern University. His prior work included mechanical engineering assignments at Motorola and Acco Brands. At Motorola, Jim worked on part design for two-way radios and was one of the lead mechanical engineers on a cellular phone product line. At Acco Brands, Jim was the sole engineer on numerous office product designs. His Worx stapler has won design awards in the United States and in Europe. Jim has been a Pro/Engineer user for over six years.

Acknowledgments: Many thanks to my co-authors, especially Rich Lueptow for his leadership on this project. I would also like to thank my family for their continuous support.

David I. Schneider holds an A.B. degree from Oberlin College and a Ph.D. degree in Mathematics from MIT. He has taught for 34 years, primarily at the University of Maryland. Dr. Schneider has authored 28 books, with one-half of them computer programming books. He has developed three customized software packages that are supplied as supplements to over 55 mathematics textbooks. His involvement with computers dates back to 1962, when he programmed a special purpose computer at MIT's Lincoln Laboratory to correct errors in a communications system.

Michael T. Snyder is President of Internet startup Appointments123.com. He is a native of Chicago, and he received his Bachelor of Science degree in Mechanical Engineering from the University of Notre Dame. Mike also graduated with honors from Northwestern University's Kellogg Graduate School of Management in 1999 with his Masters of Management degree. Before Appointments123.com, Mike was a mechanical engineer in new product development for Motorola Cellular and Acco Office Products. He has received four patents for his mechanical design work. "Pro/Engineer was an invaluable design tool for me, and I am glad to help students learn the basics of Pro/Engineer."

Acknowledgments: Thanks to Rich Lueptow and Jim Steger for inviting me to be a part of this great project. Of course, thanks to my wife Gretchen for her support in my various projects.

Stephen J. Chapman received a BS in Electrical Engineering from Louisiana State University (1975), an MSE in Electrical Engineering from the University of Central Florida (1979), and pursued further graduate studies at Rice University. Mr. Chapman is currently Manager of Technical Systems for British Aerospace Australia, in Melbourne, Australia. In this position, he provides technical direction and design authority for the work of younger engineers within the company. He is also continuing to teach at local universities on a part-time basis.

Mr. Chapman is a Senior Member of the Institute of Electrical and Electronics Engineers (and several of its component societies). He is also a member of the Association for Computing Machinery and the Institution of Engineers (Australia).

Reviewers

ESource benefited from a wealth of reviewers who on the series from its initial idea stage to its completion. Reviewers read manuscripts and contributed insightful comments that helped the authors write great books. We would like to thank everyone who helped us with this project.

Concept Document

Naeem Abdurrahman *University of Texas, Austin*
Grant Baker *University of Alaska, Anchorage*
Betty Barr *University of Houston*
William Beckwith *Clemson University*
Ramzi Bualuan *University of Notre Dame*
Dale Calkins *University of Washington*
Arthur Clausing *University of Illinois at Urbana –Champaign*
John Glover *University of Houston*
A.S. Hodel *Auburn University*
Denise Jackson *University of Tennessee, Knoxville*
Kathleen Kitto *Western Washington University*
Terry Kohutek *Texas A&M University*
Larry Richards *University of Virginia*
Avi Singhal *Arizona State University*
Joseph Wujek *University of California, Berkeley*
Mandochehr Zoghi *University of Dayton*

Books

Stephen Allan *Utah State University*
Naeem Abdurrahman *University of Texas, Austin*
Anil Bajaj *Purdue University*
Grant Baker *University of Alaska—Anchorage*
Betty Burr *University of Houston*
William Beckwith *Clemson University*
Haym Benaroya *Rutgers University*
Tom Bledsaw *ITT Technical Institute*
Tom Bryson *University of Missouri, Rolla*
Ramzi Bualuan *University of Notre Dame*
Dan Budny *Purdue University*
Dale Calkins *University of Washington*
Arthur Clausing *University of Illinois*
James Devine *University of South Florida*
Patrick Fitzhorn *Colorado State University*
Dale Elifrits *University of Missouri, Rolla*
Frank Gerlitz *Washtenaw College*
John Glover *University of Houston*
John Graham *University of North Carolina—Charlotte*
Malcom Heimer *Florida International University*
A.S. Hodel *Auburn University*
Vern Johnson *University of Arizona*
Kathleen Kitto *Western Washington University*
Robert Montgomery *Purdue University*
Mark Nagurka *Marquette University*
Romarathnam Narasimhan *University of Miami*
Larry Richards *University of Virginia*
Marc H. Richman *Brown University*
Avi Singhal *Arizona State University*
Tim Sykes *Houston Community College*
Thomas Hill *SUNY at Buffalo*
Michael S. Wells *Tennessee Tech University*
Joseph Wujek *University of California, Berkeley*
Edward Young *University of South Carolina*
Mandochehr Zoghi *University of Dayton*
John Biddle *California State Polytechnic University*
Fred Boadu *Duke University*
Harish Cherukuri *University of North Carolina –Charlotte*
Barry Crittendon *Virginia Polytechnic and State University*
Ron Eaglin *University of Central Florida*
Susan Freeman *Northeastern University*
Frank Gerlitz *Washtenaw Community College*
Otto Gygax *Oregon State University*
Donald Herling *Oregon State University*
James N. Jensen *SUNY at Buffalo*
Autar Kaw *University of South Florida*
Kenneth Klika *University of Akron*
Terry L. Kohutek *Texas A&M University*
Melvin J. Maron *University of Louisville*
Soronadi Nnaji *Florida A&M University*
Michael Peshkin *Northwestern University*
Randy Shih *Oregon Institute of Technology*
Neil R. Thompson *University of Waterloo*
Garry Young *Oklahoma State University*

Contents

ABOUT ESOURCE iii

ABOUT THE AUTHORS vii

1 AN INTRODUCTION TO COMPUTERS AND VISUAL BASIC 1

1.1 An Introduction to Computers 1
1.2 An Introduction to Visual Basic 4
1.2.1 Why Windows, and Why Visual Basic? 5
1.2.2 How You Develop a Visual Basic Application 6
1.2.3 The Different Versions of Visual Basic 7
1.3 Programming Tools 7
1.3.1 Flowcharts 8
1.3.2 Pseudocode 10
1.3.3 Hierarchy Charts 11
1.3.4 Direction of Numbered NYC Streets Algorithm 12
1.3.5 Comments 14

2 FUNDAMENTALS OF PROGRAMMING IN VISUAL BASIC 15

2.1 Visual Basic Objects 15
2.1.1 Invoking Visual Basic 6.0 15
2.1.2 Text Boxes 17
2.1.3 Labels 17
2.1.4 Command Buttons 17
2.1.5 Picture Boxes 17
2.1.6 Comments 24
2.2 Visual Basic Events 27
2.2.1 An Event Procedure Walkthrough 28
2.2.2 Comments 32
2.3 Numbers 34
2.3.1 Arithmetic Operations 34
2.3.2 Scientific Notation 36
2.3.3 Variables 37
2.3.4 Print Method 39
2.3.5 Relational Operators 40
2.3.6 Numeric Functions: Sqr, Int, Round 41
2.3.7 Comments 42
2.4 Strings 44
2.4.1 Variables and Strings 45
2.4.2 Concatenation 46
2.4.3 Declaring Variable Types 46
2.4.4 Scope of Variables 47
2.4.5 Using Text Boxes for Input and Output 48
2.4.6 ANSI Character Set 49
2.4.7 String Relationships 51
2.4.8 String Functions: Left, Mid, Right, UCase, Trim 51

2.4.9 String-Related Numeric Functions: Len, InStr 52
2.4.10 Format Functions 53
2.4.11 Comments 54
2.5 **Input and Output 57**
2.5.1 Reading Data from Files 57
2.5.2 Input from an Input Box 60
2.5.3 Formatting Output with Print Zones 61
2.5.4 Tab Function 62
2.5.5 Using a Message Box for Output 63
2.5.6 Line Continuation Character 63
2.5.7 Output to the Printer 64
2.5.8 Internal Documentation 64
2.5.9 Comments 65
2.6 **Built-in Functions 67**
2.6.1 Algebraic Functions 67
2.6.2 Trigonometric Functions 69
2.6.3 Miscellaneous Functions 72
2.6.4 Types of Numeric Variables 72
2.6.5 Comments 73
2.7 **Programming Projects 74**

3 **CONTROLLING PROGRAM FLOW 97**

3.1 **General Procedures 97**
3.1.1 Sub procedures 97
3.1.2 Variables and Expressions as Arguments 102
3.1.3 Passing Values Back from Sub procedures 104
3.1.4 Function Procedures 106
3.1.5 Comments 108
3.2 **Decision Structures 110**
3.2.1 Select Case Blocks 114
3.2.2 Logical Operators 118
3.2.3 Comments 119
3.3 **Do Loops 121**
3.3.1 Bisection Method for Finding a Zero of a Function 124
3.3.2 Derivatives 127
3.3.3 Comments 130
3.4 **For...Next Loops 132**
3.4.1 Comments 138
3.5 **Case Study: Numerical Integration 139**
3.5.1 Designing the Numerical Integration Program 143
3.5.2 Pseudocode for the Numerical Integration Program 144
3.5.3 Writing the Numerical Integration Program 145
3.6 **Programming Projects 147**

4 **ARRAYS 175**

4.1 **Creating and Accessing Arrays 175**
4.1.1 Two-Dimensional Arrays 184
4.1.2 Vectors and Matrices 185
4.1.3 Comments 186
4.2 **Sorting and Searching 187**
4.2.1 Ordered Arrays 187
4.2.2 Bubble Sort 189
4.2.3 Searching 193
4.2.4 Comments 196

4.3 Arrays and Sequential Files 197
4.3.1 Creating a Sequential File from Visual Basic 197
4.3.2 Adding Items to a Sequential File 198
4.3.3 Comment 202
4.4 Programming Projects 203

5 ADDITIONAL FEATURES OF VISUAL BASIC 217

5.1 Graphics 217
5.1.1 Specifying a Viewing Window 217
5.1.2 Drawing Graphs of Functions 219
5.1.3 Comments 225
5.2 Four Additional Controls 226
5.2.1 The Frame Control 227
5.2.2 The Check Box Control 227
5.2.3 The Option Button Control 229
5.2.4 The List Box Control 231
5.3 Visual Basic Debugging Tools 234
5.3.1 The Three Program Modes 235
5.3.2 The Immediate Window 235
5.3.3 The Watch Window 236
5.3.4 The Locals Window 236
5.3.5 Stepping Through a Program 237
5.3.6 Six Walkthroughs 237
5.3.7 Stepping Through a Program Containing a General Procedure 239
5.3.8 Communication Between Arguments and Parameters 240
5.3.9 Stepping Through Programs Containing Decision Structures 240
5.3.10 Select Case Blocks 241
5.3.11 Stepping Through a Program Containing a Do Loop 242
5.4 Programming Projects 243

A ANSWERS TO SELECTED PROBLEMS 249

INDEX 265

1

An Introduction to Computers and Visual Basic

Sections

- 1.1 An Introduction to Computers
- 1.2 An Introduction to Visual Basic
- 1.3 Programming Tools

Objectives

After reading this chapter, you should be able to:

- Understand some general computer terminology and concepts.
- Know the difference between Visual Basic and BASIC.
- Be familiar with three programming tools used to help convert algorithms to programs.

1.1 AN INTRODUCTION TO COMPUTERS

Introduction to Visual Basic 6.0 Programming is a book about problem solving with computers. The programming language used is Visual Basic, but the principles taught apply to many modern programming languages. The examples and exercises present a sampling of the ways that computers are used in society.

Computers are so common today that you certainly have seen them in use and heard some of the terminology applied to them. Here are some of the questions that you might have about computers and programming.

Question:

What is meant by a personal computer?

Answer:

The word "personal" does not mean that the computer is intended for personal, as opposed to business, purposes. Rather, it indicates that the machine is operated by one person at a time instead of by many people.

Question:

What are the main components of a personal computer?

Answer:

The visible components are shown in Figure 1.1. Instructions are entered into the computer by typing them on the keyboard or by reading them from a diskette in a diskette drive or from a hard disk. Characters normally appear on the monitor as they are typed. Information processed by the computer can be displayed on the monitor, printed on the printer, or recorded on a diskette or hard drive. Hidden from view inside the system unit are the microprocessor and the memory of the computer. The microprocessor, which can be thought of as the brain of the computer, carries out all computations. The memory stores the instructions and data that are processed by the computer.

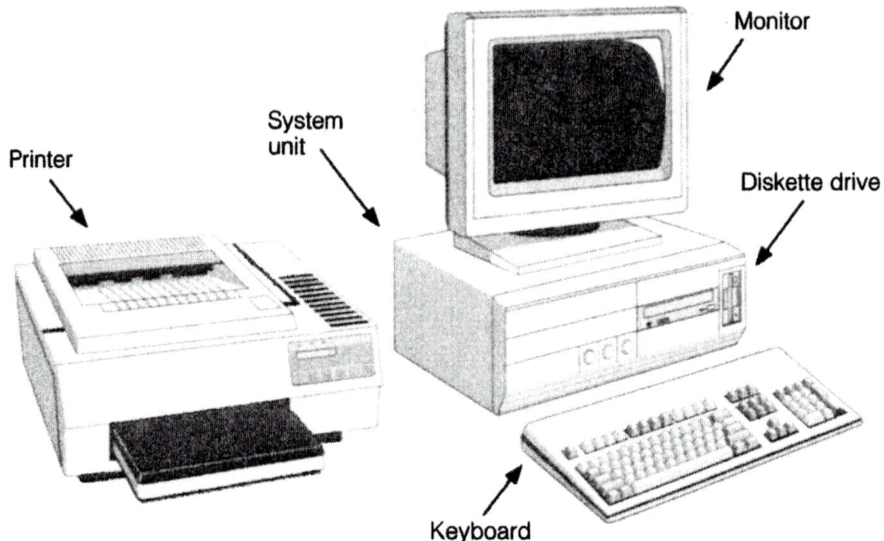

Figure 1.1. Components of a personal computer

Question:

What are some uses of computers in our society?

Answer:

Whenever we make a phone call, a computer determines how to route the call and calculates the cost of the call. Banks store all customer transactions on computers and process these data to revise the balance for each customer. Airlines record all reservations into computers. This information, which is said to form a database, can be accessed to determine the status of any flight. NASA uses computers to calculate the trajectories of satellites. Business analysts use computers to create line and bar charts that give visual impact to data.

Question:

What are some topics covered in this text that students can use immediately?

Answer:

Computer files can be created to hold lists of names, addresses, and phone numbers, which can be alphabetized and printed in their entirety or selectively. Line graphs or attractive tables can be created to enhance the data in a term paper. Mathematical computations can be carried out for science, business, and engineering courses. Personal financial transactions, such as bank deposits and loans, can be recorded, organized, and analyzed.

Question:

How do we communicate with the computer?

Answer:

Many languages are used to communicate with the computer. At the lowest level (the level closest to the computer), there is machine language, which is understood directly by the microprocessor but is awkward for humans. Visual Basic is an example of a higher-level (closer to people) language. It consists of instructions people can relate to, such as Print, Input, and Do. The Visual Basic software translates Visual Basic programs into machine-language programs.

Question:

How do we get computers to perform complicated tasks?

Answer:

Tasks are broken down into a sequence of instructions that can be expressed in a computer language. (This text uses the language Visual Basic.) The sequence of instructions is called a **program**. Programs range in size from two or three instructions to tens of thousands. Instructions are typed on the keyboard and stored in the computer's memory. (They also can be stored permanently on a diskette or hard disk.) The process of executing the instructions is called *running the program.*

Question:

Are there certain features that all programs have in common?

Answer:

Most programs do three things: take in data, manipulate them, and give desired information. These operations are referred to as input, processing, and output. The input data might be held in a portion of the program, reside on a diskette or hard drive, or be provided by the computer operator in response to requests made by the computer while the program is running. The processing of the input data occurs inside the computer and can take from a fraction of a second to many hours. The output data are displayed on the screen, printed on the printer, or recorded onto a disk. As a simple example, consider a program that computes sales tax. An item of input data is the cost of the thing purchased. The processing consists of multiplying the cost by a certain percentage. An item of output data is the resulting product, the amount of sales tax to be paid.

Question:

What are the meanings of the terms *hardware* and *software*?

Answer:

The term *hardware* refers to the physical components of the computer, including all peripherals, central processing unit, disk drives, and all mechanical and electrical devices. Programs are referred to as *software*.

Question:

What are the meanings of the terms *programmer* and *user*?

Answer:

A *programmer* is a person who solves problems by writing programs on a computer. After analyzing the problem and developing a plan for solving it, he or she writes and tests the program that instructs the computer how to carry out the plan. The program might be run many times, either by the programmer or by others. A *user* is any person who uses a program. While working through this text, you will function both as a programmer and as a user.

Question:

What is meant by *problem solving*?

Answer:

Problems are solved by carefully reading them to determine what data are given and what outputs are requested. Then a step-by-step procedure is devised to process the given data and produce the requested output. This procedure is called an *algorithm*. Finally, a computer program is written to carry out the algorithm. Algorithms are discussed in Section 1.3.

Question:

What types of problems are solved in this text?

Answer:

Carrying out computations, creating and maintaining records, alphabetizing lists, and graphing functions are some of the types of problems we will solve.

Question:

What is the difference between standard BASIC and Visual Basic?

Answer:

In the early 1960s, two mathematics professors at Dartmouth College developed BASIC to provide their students with an easily learned language that could tackle complicated programming projects. As the popularity of BASIC grew, refinements were introduced that permitted structured programming, which increases the reliability of programs. Visual Basic is a version of BASIC that was written by Microsoft Corporation to incorporate object-oriented programming into BASIC and to allow easy development of Windows applications.

1.2 AN INTRODUCTION TO VISUAL BASIC

Visual Basic is one of the most exciting developments in programming in many years. Visual Basic is the latest generation of BASIC, and is designed to make user-friendly programs easier to develop. Before the creation of Visual Basic, developing a user-friendly program usually required teams of programmers using arcane languages like "C" that came in 10-pound boxes with thousands of pages of documentation. Now it can be done by a few people using a language that is a direct descendant of BASIC—the language most accessible to beginning programmers.

Visual Basic 6.0 requires the Microsoft Windows operating system. Although you don't need to be an expert user of Microsoft Windows, you do need to know the basics before you can master Visual Basic—that is, you need to be comfortable with manipulating a mouse, you need to know how to manipulate a window, and you need to know how to use Notepad and My Computer. However, there is no better way to master Microsoft Windows than to write applications for it—and that is what Visual Basic is all about.

1.2.1 Why Windows, and Why Visual Basic?

What people call *graphical user interfaces*, or GUIs (pronounced "gooies"), have revolutionized the microcomputer industry. Instead of the cryptic C:\> prompt that DOS users have long seen (and that some have long feared), users are presented with a desktop filled with little pictures called icons. Icons provide a visual guide to what the program can do.

Accompanying the revolution in how programs look was a revolution in how they feel. Consider a program that requests information for a database. Figure 1.2 shows how such a DOS-based BASIC program gets its information. The program requests the six pieces of data one at a time, with no opportunity to go back and alter previously entered information. After the program requests the six pieces of data, the screen clears and the six inputs are again requested one at a time. Figure 1.3 shows how an equivalent Visual Basic program gets its information. The boxes may be filled in any order. When the user clicks on a box with the mouse, the cursor moves to that box. The user can either type in new information or edit the existing information. When the user is satisfied that all the information is correct, he or she just clicks on the Write to Database button. The boxes will clear and the data for another person can be entered. After all names have been entered, the user clicks on the Exit button. In Figure 1.2, the program is in control; in Figure 1.3, the user is in control!

```
Enter Name (Enter EOD to terminate): Mr. President
Enter Address: 1600 Pennsylvania Avenue
Enter City: Washington
Enter State: DC
Enter Zipcode: 20500
Enter Phone Number: 202-395-3000
```

Figure 1.2. Input screen of a DOS-based BASIC program to fill a database.

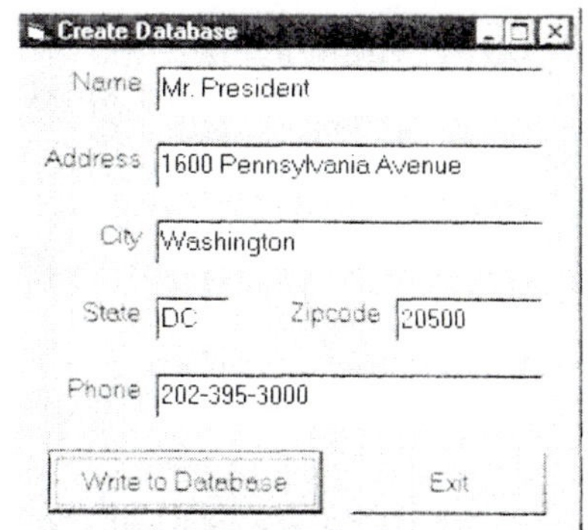

Figure 1.3. Input screen of a Visual Basic program to fill a database.

1.2.2 How You Develop a Visual Basic Application

A key element of planning a Visual Basic application is deciding what the user sees—in other words, designing the screen. What data will he or she be entering? How large a window should the application use? Where will you place the command buttons—the "buttons" the user clicks on to activate the applications? Will the applications have places to enter text (text boxes) and places to display output? What kind of warning boxes (message boxes) should the application use? In Visual Basic, the responsive objects a program designer places on windows are called controls.

Two features make Visual Basic different from traditional programming languages:

1. You literally draw the user interface, much like using a paint program.
2. When you're done drawing the interface, the command buttons, text boxes, and other objects that you have placed in a blank window will automatically recognize user actions such as mouse movements and button clicks. That is, the sequence of procedures executed in your program is controlled by "events" that the user initiates, rather than by a predetermined sequence of procedures in your program.

In any case, only after you design the interface does anything like traditional programming occur. Objects in Visual Basic recognize events like mouse clicks; how the objects respond to them depends on the instructions you write. You always need to write instructions in order to make controls respond to events. This makes Visual Basic programming fundamentally different from conventional programming.

Programs in conventional programming languages run from the top down. For conventional programming languages, execution starts from the first line and moves with the flow of the program to different parts as needed. A Visual Basic program works completely differently. The core of a Visual Basic program is a set of independent groups of instructions that are activated by the events they have been told to recognize. This is a fundamental shift. Instead of doing what the programmer thinks should happen, the program gives the user control.

Most of the programming instructions in Visual Basic that tell your program how to respond to events like mouse clicks occur in what Visual Basic calls *event procedures*. Essentially, anything executable in a Visual Basic program is either in an event procedure or is used by an event procedure to help the procedure carry out its job. In fact, to stress that Visual Basic is fundamentally different from traditional programming languages, Microsoft uses the term *project*, rather than *program*, to refer to the combination of programming instructions and user interface that makes a Visual Basic application possible.

Here is a summary of the steps you take to design a Visual Basic application:

1. Decide how the windows that the user sees will look.
2. Determine which events the objects on the window should recognize.
3. Write the event procedures for those events.

Now here is what happens when the program is running:

1. Visual Basic monitors the window and the objects in the window to detect any event that an object can recognize (mouse movements, clicks, keystrokes, and so on).
2. When Visual Basic detects an event, it examines the program to see if you've written an event procedure for that event.
3. If you have written an event procedure, Visual Basic executes the instructions that make up that event procedure and goes back to Step 1.
4. If you have not written an event procedure, Visual Basic waits for the next event and goes back to Step 1.

These steps cycle continuously until the application ends. Usually, an event must happen before Visual Basic will do anything. Event-driven programs are more reactive than active—and that makes them more user friendly.

1.2.3 The Different Versions of Visual Basic

Visual Basic 1.0 first appeared in 1991. It was followed by Version 2.0 in 1992, Version 3.0 in 1993, Version 4.0 in 1995, Version 5.0 in 1997, and Version 6.0 in 1998. Because Microsoft has publicly announced that Visual Basic is a key product for the company, Microsoft will continue to add further enhancements to the language. For example, Microsoft is using versions of Visual Basic to control all its applications, such as Microsoft Office. Master Visual Basic and you will be well prepared for almost any office computer environment.

Visual Basic 6.0 comes in four editions—Learning, Professional, Enterprise, and Working Model Edition. All editions require either Windows 95, Windows 98, or Windows NT (4.0 or later). You can use any edition of Visual Basic 6.0 with this textbook.

1.3 PROGRAMMING TOOLS

An *algorithm* is a logical sequence of steps that solve a problem. This section discusses some specific algorithms and develops three tools used to convert algorithms into computer programs: flowcharts, pseudocode, and hierarchy charts.

Probably without knowing it, you use algorithms every day to make decisions and perform tasks. For instance, whenever you mail a letter, you must decide how much postage to put on the envelope. One rule of thumb is to use one stamp for every five sheets of paper or fraction thereof. Suppose a friend asks you to determine the number of stamps to place on an envelope. The following algorithm will accomplish the task.

1. Request the number of sheets of paper; call it Sheets. *(input)*
2. Divide Sheets by 5. *(processing)*
3. Round the quotient up to the next highest whole number; call it Stamps. *(processing)*
4. Reply with the number Stamps. *(output)*

The preceding algorithm takes the number of sheets (Sheets) as input, processes the data, and produces the number of stamps needed (Stamps) as output. We can test the algorithm for a letter with 16 sheets of paper.

1. Request the number of sheets of paper; Sheets = 16.
2. Dividing 5 into 16 gives 3.2.
3. Rounding 3.2 up to 4 gives Stamps = 4.
4. Reply with the answer: 4 stamps.

This problem-solving example can be pictured by

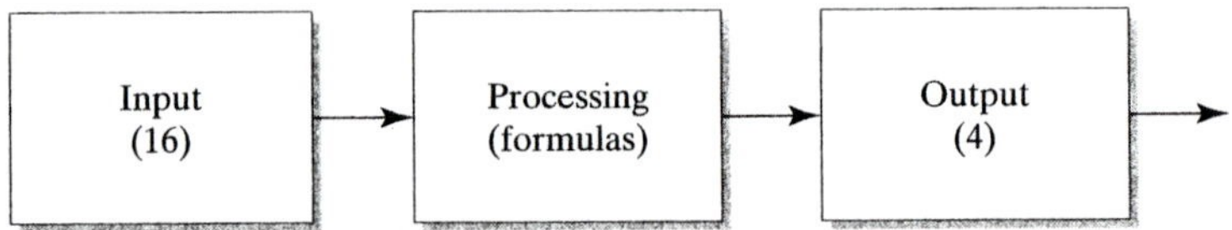

Of the program design tools available, the three most popular are the following:

***Flowcharts*:** Graphically show the logical steps to carry out a task and show how the steps relate to each other.

***Pseudocode*:** Uses English-like phrases with some Visual Basic terms to outline a task.

***Hierarchy charts*:** Show how the different parts of a program relate to each other.

1.3.1 Flowcharts

A *flowchart* consists of special geometric symbols connected by arrows. Within each symbol is a phrase presenting the activity at that step. The shape of the symbol indicates the type of operation that is to occur. For instance, the parallelogram denotes input or output. The arrows connecting the symbols, called *flowlines*, show the progression in which the steps take place. Flowcharts should "flow" from the top of the page to the bottom. Although the symbols used in flowcharts are standardized, no standards exist for the amount of detail required within each symbol.

A table of the flowchart symbols adopted by the American National Standards Institute (ANSI) follows. Figure 1.4 shows the flowchart for the postage stamp problem.

Symbol	Name	Meaning
	**Flowline**	Connects symbols and indicates the flow of logic.
	Terminal	Represents the beginning (Start) or the end (End) of a task.
	Input/Output	Stands for input and output operations, such as reading and printing. The data to be read or printed are described inside.
	Processing	Represents arithmetic and data-manipulation operations. The instructions are listed inside the symbol.
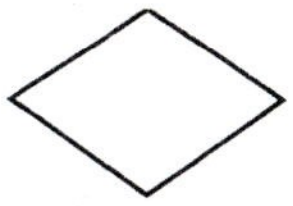	**Decision**	Used for any logic or comparison operations. Unlike the input/output and processing symbols, which have one entry and one exit flowline, the decision symbol has one entry and two exit paths. The path chosen depends on whether the answer to a question is "yes" or "no."
	**Connector**	Joins different flowlines.
	**Offpage Connector**	Indicates that the flowchart continues to another page.
	Predefined Process	Represents a group of statements that perform one processing task.
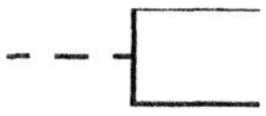	**Annotation**	Provides additional information about another flowchart symbol.

The main advantage of using a flowchart to plan a task is that it provides a pictorial representation of the task, which makes the logic easier to follow. We can see clearly every step and how each step is connected to the next. The major disadvantage with flowcharts is that when a program is large, the flowcharts may continue for many pages, making them difficult to follow and modify.

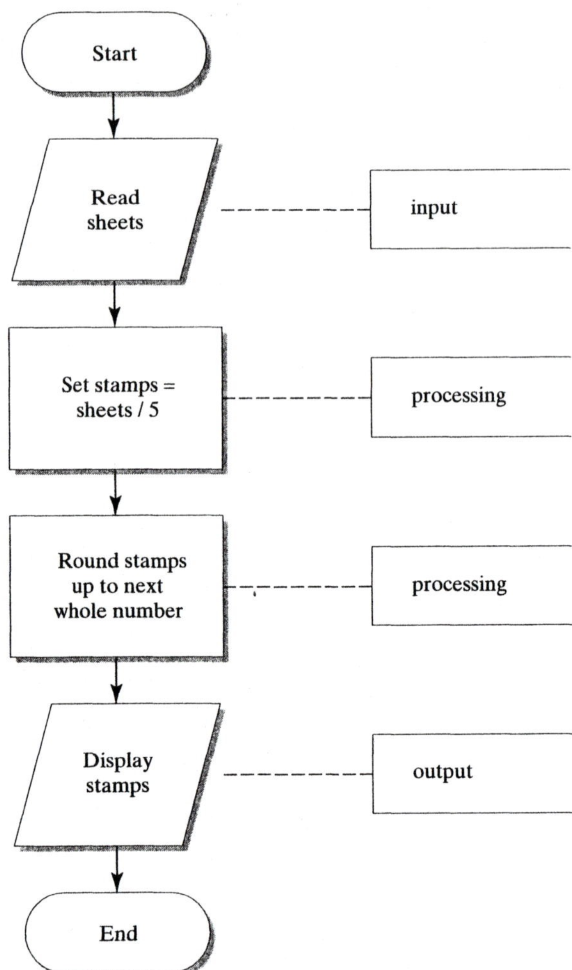

Figure 1.4. Flowchart for the postage stamp problem.

1.3.2 Pseudocode

Pseudocode is an abbreviated version of actual computer code (hence, *pseudocode*). The geometric symbols used in flowcharts are replaced by English-like statements that outline the process. As a result, pseudocode looks more like computer code than does a flowchart. Pseudocode allows the programmer to focus on the steps required to solve a problem rather than on how to use the computer language. The programmer can describe the algorithm in Visual Basic-like form without being restricted by the rules of Visual Basic. When the pseudocode is completed, it can be easily translated into the Visual Basic language.

Here is pseudocode for the postage stamp problem:

Program: Determine the proper number of stamps for a letter
Read Sheets *(input)*
Set the number of stamps to Sheets / 5 *(processing)*
Round the number of stamps up to the next whole number *(processing)*
Display the number of stamps *(output)*

Pseudocode has several advantages. It is compact and probably will not extend for many pages as flowcharts commonly do. Also, the plan looks like the code to be written and so is preferred by many programmers.

1.3.3 Hierarchy Charts

The last programming tool we'll discuss is the *hierarchy chart*, which shows the overall program structure. Hierarchy charts are also called structure charts, HIPO (Hierarchy plus Input-Process-Output) charts, top-down charts, or VTOC (Visual Table of Contents) charts. All these names refer to planning diagrams that are similar to a company's organization chart.

Hierarchy charts show the organization of a program but leave out the specific processing logic. They describe what each part, or *module*, of the program does, and they show how the modules relate to each other. The details on how the modules work, however, are omitted. The chart is read from top to bottom and from left to right. Each module may be subdivided into a succession of submodules that branch out under it. Typically, after the activities in the succession of submodules are carried out, the module to the right of the original module is considered. A quick glance at the hierarchy chart reveals each task performed in the program and where it is performed. Figure 1.5 shows a hierarchy chart for the postage stamp problem.

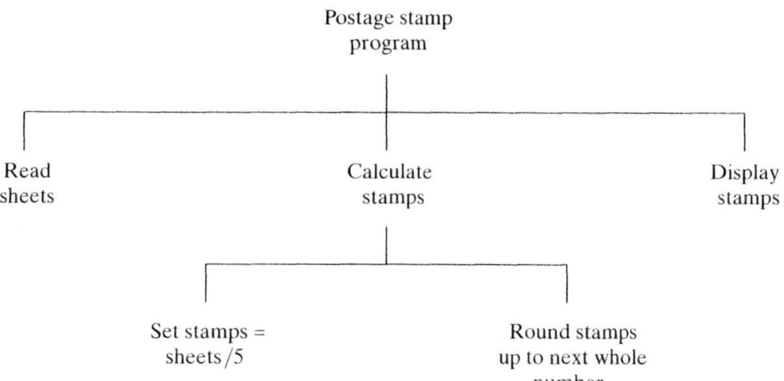

Figure 1.5. Hierarchy chart for the postage stamp problem.

The main benefit of hierarchy charts is in the initial planning of a program. We break down the major parts of a program so we can see what must be done in general. It is easy to spot mistakes in our thinking at this general level, and simpler to correct our approach than at more detailed levels. When we're satisfied with the hierarchy chart, we can then refine each module into more detailed plans using flowcharts or pseudocode. This process is called the *divide-and-conquer* method.

The postage stamp problem was solved by a series of instructions to read data, perform calculations, and display results. Each step was in a sequence; that is, we moved from one line to the next without skipping over any lines. This kind of structure is called a *sequence structure*. Many problems, however, require a decision to determine whether a series of instructions should be executed. If the answer to a question is "Yes,"

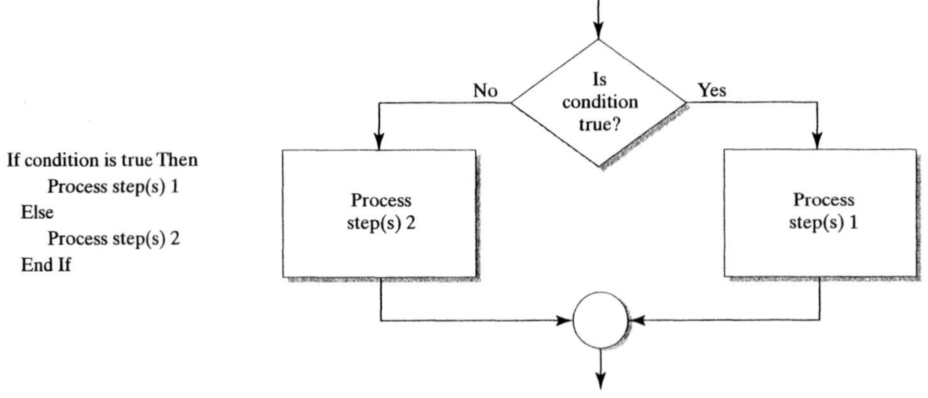

Figure 1.6. Pseudocode and flowchart for a decision structure.

then one group of instructions is executed. If the answer is "No," then another is executed. This structure is called a *decision structure*. Figure 1.6 contains the pseudocode and flowchart for a decision structure.

```
If condition is true Then
  Process step(s) 1
Else
  Process step(s) 2
End If
```

The sequence and decision structures are both used to solve the next problem:

1.3.4 Direction of Numbered NYC Streets Algorithm

Problem: Given a street number of a one-way street in New York, decide the direction of the street, either eastbound or westbound.

Discussion: There is a simple rule to tell the direction of a one-way street in New York: Even-numbered streets run eastbound. Odd-numbered streets run westbound.

Input: Street number

Processing: Decide if the street number is divisible by 2.

Output: "Eastbound" or "Westbound"

Figure 1.7 through Figure 1.9 show the flowchart, pseudocode, and hierarchy chart for the New York numbered streets problem.

Program: Determine the direction of a numbered NYC street.

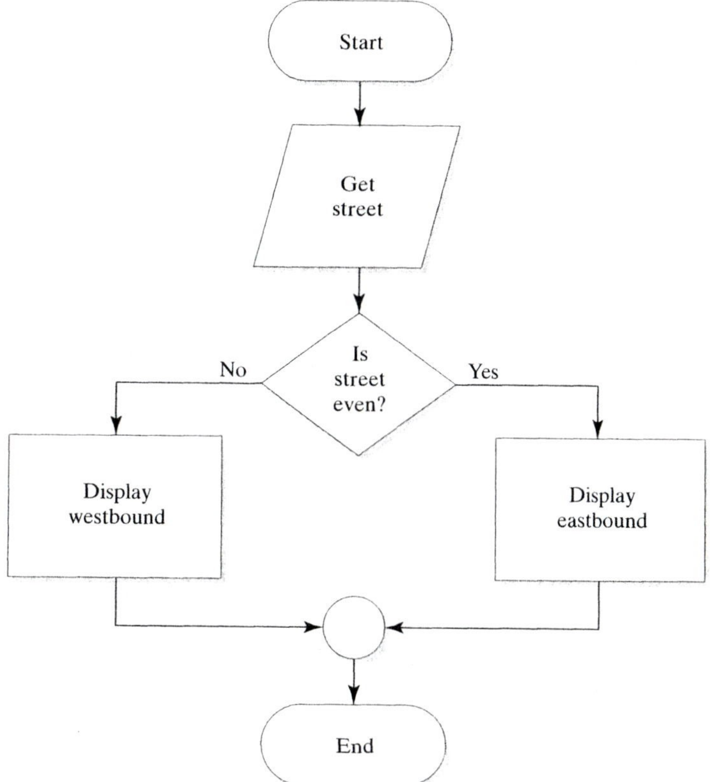

Figure 1.7. Flowchart for the New York numbered streets problem.

```
Get Street
If Street is even Then
    Display Eastbound
  Else
    Display Westbound
```

Figure 1.8. Pseudocode for the New York numbered streets problem.

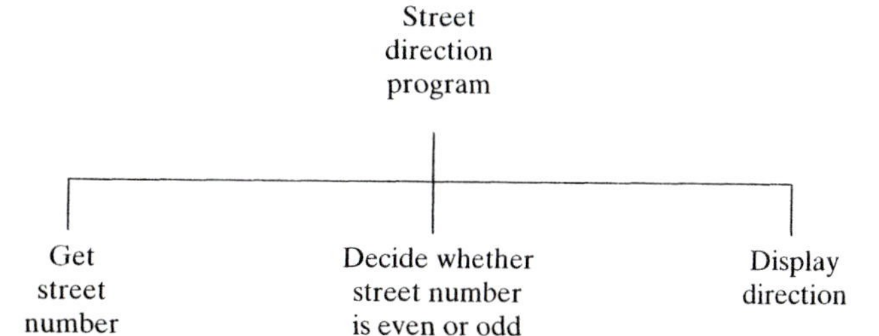

Figure 1.9. Hierarchy chart for the New York numbered streets problem.

1.3.5 Comments

1. Tracing a flowchart is like playing a board game. We begin at the Start symbol and proceed from symbol to symbol until we reach the End symbol. At any time, we will be at just one symbol. In a board game, the path taken depends on the result of spinning a spinner or rolling a pair of dice. The path taken through a flowchart depends on the input.
2. The algorithm should be tested at the flowchart or pseudocode stage before being coded into a program. Different data should be used as input, and the output checked. This process is known as *desk checking*. The test data should include nonstandard data as well as typical data.
3. Flowcharts, pseudocode, and hierarchy charts are universal problem-solving tools. They can be used to construct programs in any computer language, not just Visual Basic.
4. Flowcharts are used throughout this text to provide a visualization of the flow of certain programming tasks and Visual Basic control structures. Major examples of pseudocode and hierarchy charts appear in the case studies.
5. There are four primary logical programming constructs: sequence, decision, loop, and unconditional branch. Unconditional branch, which appears in some languages as Goto statements, involves jumping from one place in a program to another. Structured programming uses the first three constructs but forbids the fourth. One advantage of pseudocode over flowcharts is that pseudocode has no provision for unconditional branching and thus forces the programmer to write structured programs.
6. Flowcharts are time-consuming to write and difficult to update. For this reason, professional programmers are more likely to favor pseudocode and hierarchy charts. Because flowcharts so clearly illustrate the logical flow of programming techniques, however, they are a valuable tool in the education of programmers.
7. There are many styles of pseudocode. Some programmers use an outline form, whereas others use a form that looks almost like a programming language. The pseudocode appearing in this book focuses on the primary tasks to be performed by the program and leaves many of the routine details to be completed during the coding process. Several Visual Basic keywords, such as, Print, If, Do, and While, are used extensively in the pseudocode appearing in this book.
8. Many people draw rectangles around each item in a hierarchy chart. In this book, rectangles are omitted to encourage the use of hierarchy charts by making them easier to draw.

KEY TERMS

Algorithm	Flowline	Programmer
Control	Graphical User Interface (GUI)	Pseudocode
Decision structure	Hardware	Sequence structure
Desk checking	Hierarchy chart	Software
Divide-and-conquer method	Module	
Flowchart	Program	

2

Fundamentals of Programming in Visual Basic

2.1 VISUAL BASIC OBJECTS

Visual Basic programs display a Windows style screen (called a *form*) with boxes into which users type (and edit) information and buttons that they click to initiate actions. The boxes and buttons are referred to as *controls*. Forms and controls are called *objects*. In this section, we examine forms and four of the most useful Visual Basic controls.

2.1.1 Invoking Visual Basic 6.0

To invoke Visual Basic, click the Start button, point to Programs, point to Microsoft Visual Basic 6.0, and click on Microsoft Visual Basic 6.0 in the final list.

With all versions of Visual Basic 6.0, the center of the screen will contain the New Project window of Figure 2.1 The main part of the window is a tabbed dialog box with three tabs—New, Existing, and Recent. (If the New tab is not in the foreground, click on it to bring it to the front.) The number of project icons showing are either 3 (with the Working Model and Learning Editions) or 13 (with the Professional and Enterprise Editions).

Double-click the Standard EXE icon to bring up the initial Visual Basic screen in Figure 2.2 The appearance of this screen varies slightly with the different editions of Visual Basic.

The *Toolbar* is a collection of icons that carry out standard operations when clicked. For example, the fifth icon, which looks like a diskette, can be used to save the current program to a disk. To reveal the function of a Toolbar icon, position the mouse pointer over the icon for a few seconds.

SECTIONS

- 2.1 Visual Basic Objects
- 2.2 Visual Basic Events
- 2.3 Numbers
- 2.4 Strings
- 2.5 Input and Output
- 2.6 Built-in Functions
- 2.7 Programming Projects

OBJECTIVES

After reading this chapter, you should be able to:

- Understand what Visual Basic objects are and how they are created.
- Recognize Visual Basic events and know some ways to handle them.
- Be familiar with the ways Visual Basic handles numbers.
- Know what strings are and how to manipulate them.
- Perform various input and output operations in Visual Basic.

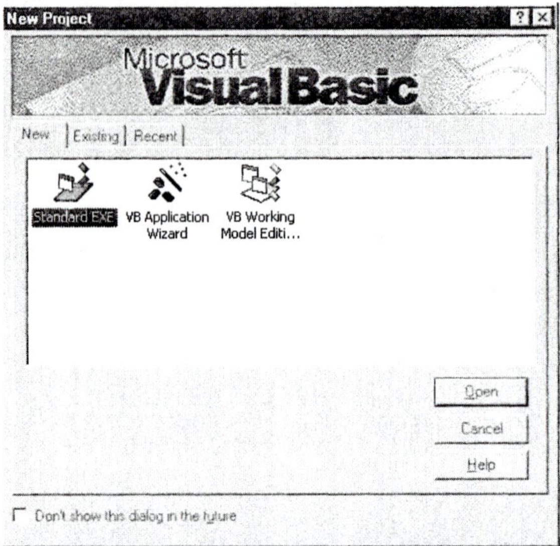

Figure 2.1. New Project window from Working Model Edition of VB 6.0.

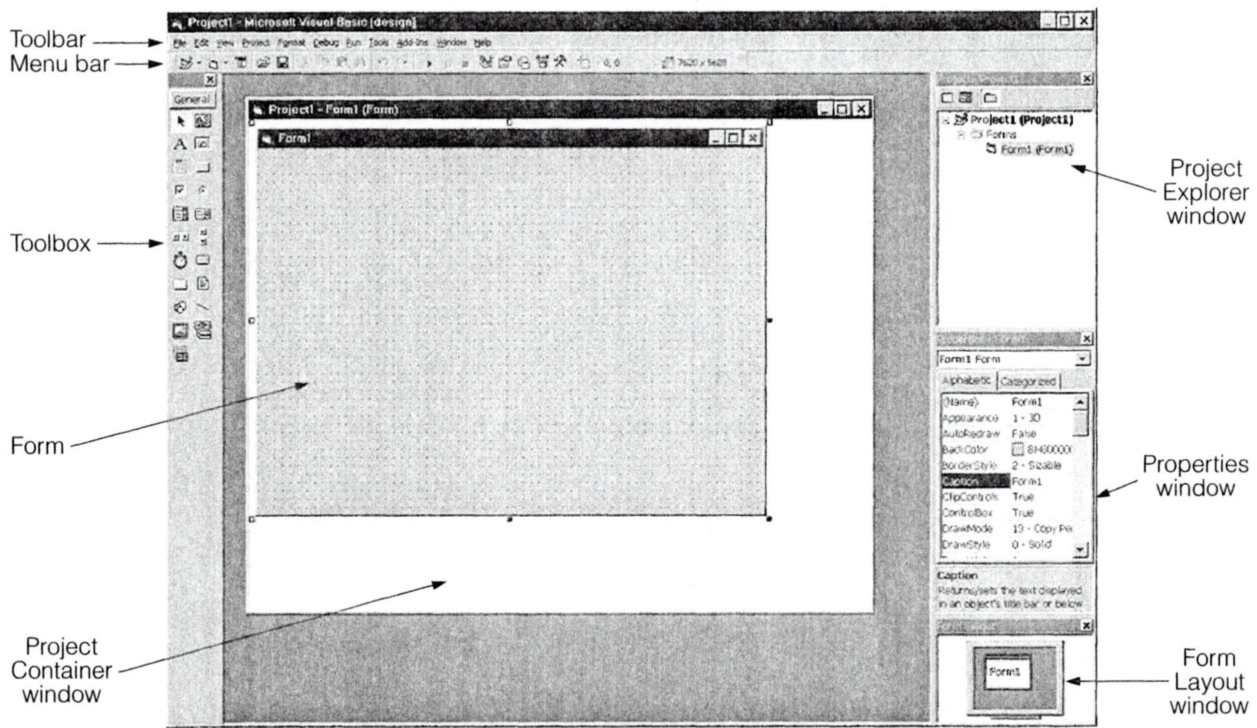

Figure 2.2. The initial Visual Basic screen.

The *Menu bar* of the Visual Basic screen displays the commands you use to work with Visual Basic. Some of the menus, like File, Edit, View, and Window, are common to most Windows applications. Others, such as Project, Format, and Debug, provide commands specific to programming in Visual Basic.

The large stippled *Form window,* or *form* for short, becomes a Windows window when a program is executed. Most information displayed by the program appears on the form. The information usually is displayed in controls that have been placed on the form. The *Form Layout window* allows you to position the location of the form at run time relative to the entire screen using a small graphical representation of the screen.

The Project Explorer window is not needed for our purposes. The *Properties window* is used to change how objects look and react.

The icons in the *Toolbox* represent controls that can be placed on the form. The four controls discussed in this chapter are text boxes, labels, command buttons, and picture boxes.

2.1.2 Text Boxes

You use a text box primarily to get information, referred to as *input*, from the user.

2.1.3 Labels

You place a label to the left of a text box to tell the user what type of information to enter into the text box. You also use labels to display output.

2.1.4 Command Buttons

The user clicks a command button to initiate an action.

2.1.5 Picture Boxes

You use a picture box to display text or graphics output.

A Text Box Walkthrough

1. Double-click on the text box icon. (The text box icon consists of the letters ab and a vertical bar cursor inside a rectangle, and is the fourth icon in the Toolbox.) A rectangle with eight small squares, called sizing handles, appears at the center of the form (Figure 2.3).

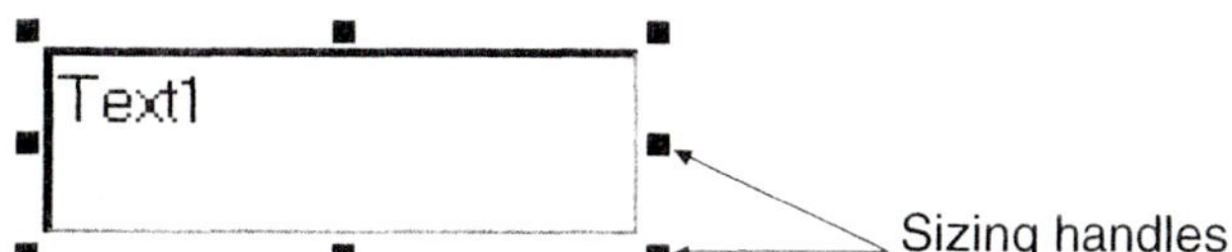

Figure 2.3. A text box with sizing handles.

2. Click anywhere on the form outside the rectangle to remove the handles.
3. Click on the rectangle to restore the handles. An object showing its handles is (said to be) *selected.* A selected object can have its size altered, location changed, and other properties modified.
4. Move the mouse arrow to the handle in the center of the right side of the text box. The cursor should change to a double arrow (↔). Hold down the left mouse button, and move the mouse to the right. The text box is stretched to the right. Similarly, grabbing the text box by one of the other handles and moving the mouse stretches the text box in another direction. For instance, you use the handle in the upper-left corner to stretch the text box up and to the left. Handles also can be used to make the text box smaller.
5. Move the mouse arrow to any point of the text box other than a handle, hold down the left mouse button, and move the mouse. You can now drag the text box to a new location. Using Steps 4 and 5, you can place a text box of any size anywhere on the form.

Note: The text box should now be selected; that is, its sizing handles should be showing. If not, click anywhere inside the text box to select it.

6. Press the delete key, Del, to remove the text box from the form. Step 7 gives an alternative way to place a text box of any size at any location on the form.
7. Click on the text box icon in the Toolbox. Then move the mouse pointer to any place on the form. (When over the form, the mouse pointer becomes a pair of crossed thin lines.) Hold down the left mouse button, and move the mouse on a diagonal to generate a rectangle. Release the mouse button to obtain a selected text box. You can now alter the size and location as before.

   Note: The text box should now be selected; that is, its sizing handles should be showing. If not, click anywhere inside the text box to select it.

8. Press F4 to activate the Properties window. (You can also activate the properties window by clicking on it or clicking on the Properties Window icon in the Toolbar.) See Figure 2.4 The first line of the Properties window (called the *Object box*) reads "Text1 TextBox." Text1 is the current name of the text box. The two tabs permit you to view the list of properties either alphabetically or grouped into categories. Text boxes have 43 properties that can be grouped into 7 categories. Use the up- and down-arrow keys (or the up- and

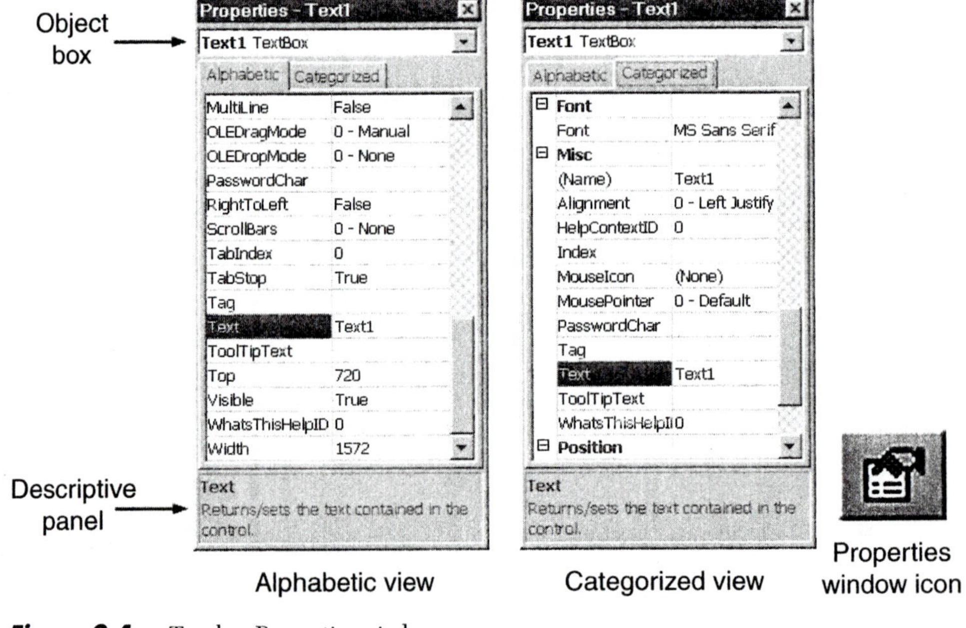

Figure 2.4. Text box Properties window.

down-scroll arrows) to glance through the list. The left column gives the property and the right column gives the current setting of the property. We discuss four properties in this walkthrough.

9. Move to the Text property with the up- and down-arrow keys. (Alternatively, scroll until the property is visible and click on the property.) The Text property is now highlighted. The Text property determines the words in the text box. Currently, the words are set to "Text1" in the *Settings box* on the right.

10. Type your first name. As you type, your name replaces "Text1" in both the Settings box and the text box (Figure 2.5). (Alternatively, you could have clicked on the Settings box and edited its contents.)

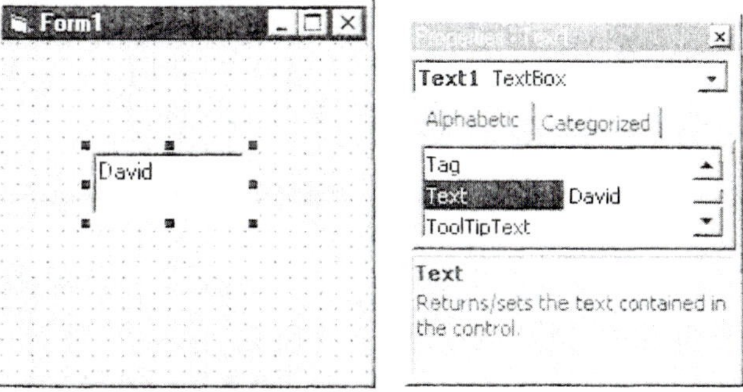

Figure 2.5. Setting the text property to David.

11. Click at the beginning of your name in the Settings box and add your title, such as Mr., Ms., or The Honorable. (If you mistyped your name, you can easily correct it now.)
12. Press Shift+Ctrl+F to move to the first property that begins with the letter F. Now use the down-arrow key or the mouse to highlight the property ForeColor. The foreground color is the color of the text.
13. Click on the down arrow in the right part of the Settings box, and then click on the Palette tab to display a selection of colors (Figure 2.6). Click on one of the solid colors, such as blue or red. Notice the change in the color of your name.

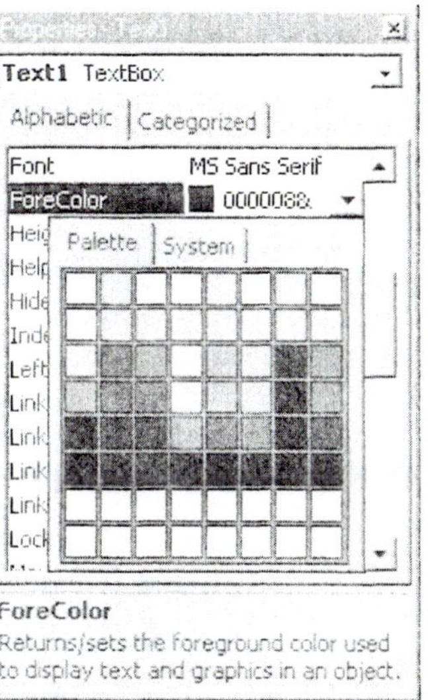

Figure 2.6. Setting the ForeColor property.

14. Highlight the Font property with a single click of the mouse. The current font is named MS Sans Serif.
15. Click on the ellipsis (...) box in the right part of the Settings box to display a dialog box (Figure 2.7). The three lists give the current name (MS Sans Serif Rom), current style (Regular), and current size (8) of the font. You can

change any of these attributes by clicking. Click on Bold in the style list, and click on 12 in the size list. Now click on the OK button to see your name displayed in a larger bold font.

16. Click on the text box and resize it to be about 3 inches wide and 1 inch high. Visual Basic programs consist of three parts—interface, values of properties, and code. Our interface consists of a form with a single object, a text box. We have set a few properties for the text box—the text (namely, your name), foreground color, font style, and font size. Visual Basic endows certain capabilities to programs that are independent of any code. We will now run the existing codeless program and experience these capabilities.

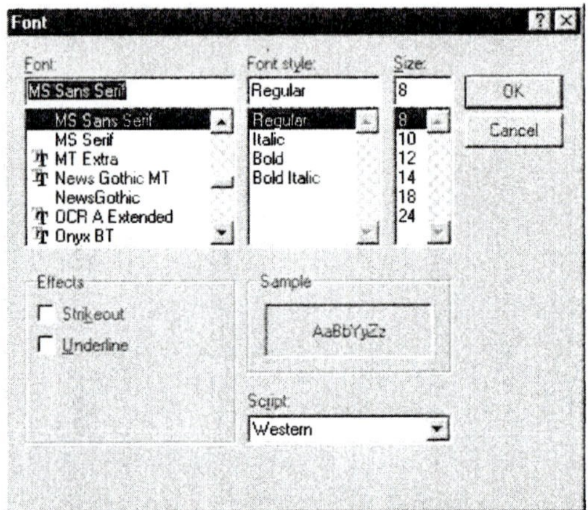

Figure 2.7. The Font dialog box.

17. Press F5 to run the program. (Alternatively, you can run a program from the menu by pressing Alt/R/S or by clicking on the Start icon, the 12th icon on the Toolbar.) Notice that the dots have disappeared from the form.

18. The cursor is at the beginning of your name. Press the End key to move the cursor to the end of your name. Now type in your last name, and then keep typing. Eventually, the words will scroll to the left.

19. Press Home to return to the beginning of the text. You have a full-fledged word processor at your disposal. You can place the cursor anywhere you like to add or delete text. You can drag the cursor across text to create a block, place a copy of the block in the clipboard with Ctrl+C, and then duplicate it anywhere with Ctrl+V.

20. To terminate the program, press Alt+F4. Alternatively, you can end a program by clicking on the End icon, the 14th icon on the Toolbar, or clicking on the form's close button.

21. Select the text box, activate the Properties window, select the MultiLine property, click on the down-arrow button, and finally click on True. The MultiLine property has been changed from False to True.

22. Run the program, and type in the text box. Notice that now words wrap around when the end of a line is reached. Also, text will scroll up when it reaches the bottom of the text box.

23. End the program.

24. Press Alt/F/V or click on the Save Project icon to save the work done so far. A Save File As dialog box appears (Figure 2.8). Visual Basic creates two disk files to store a program. The first, with the extension .frm, is entered into the Save File As dialog box and the second, with the extension .vbp, into a Save Project As dialog box. Visual Basic refers to programs as *projects*.

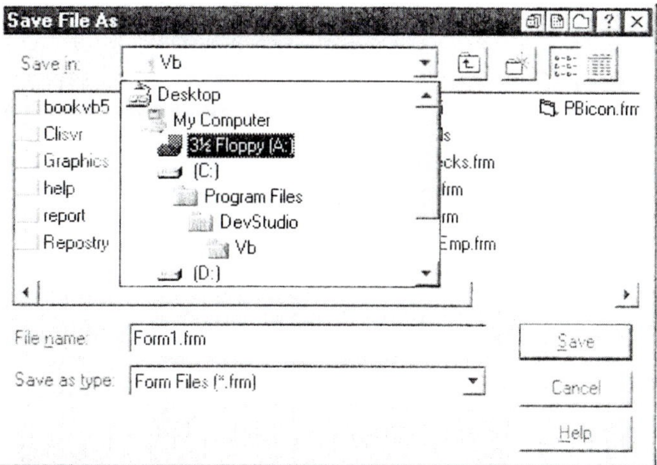

Figure 2.8. The Save File As dialog box.

25. Type a file name, such as *testprog*, into the "File name" box. The extension .frm automatically will be appended to the name. Do not press the Enter key yet. (Pressing the Enter key has the same effect as clicking Save.) The selection in the "Save in" box tells where your program will be saved. Alter it as desired. (*Suggestion:* If you are using a computer in a campus computer lab, you probably should use a diskette to save your work. If so, place the diskette in a drive, say, the A drive, and select 3 1/2 Floppy (A:) in the "Save in" box.)

26. Click the Save button when you are ready to go on. (Alternatively, press Tab several times until the Save button is highlighted and then press Enter.) The Save Project As dialog box appears.

27. Type a file name into the File name box. You can use the same name, such as *testprog*, as before. Then proceed as in Steps 25 and 26. (The extension .vbp will be added.)

28. Press Alt/F/N to begin a new program. (As before, select Standard EXE.)

29. Place three text boxes on the form. (Move each text box out of the center of the form before creating the next.) Notice that they have the names Text1, Text2, and Text3.

30. Run the program. Notice that the cursor is in Text1. We say that Text1 has the *focus*. (This means that Text1 is the currently selected object and any keyboard actions will be sent directly to this object.) Any text typed will display in that text box.

31. Press Tab once. Now, Text2 has the focus. When you type, the characters appear in Text2.

32. Press Tab several times, and then press Shift+Tab a few times. With Tab, the focus cycles through the objects on the form in the order the objects were created. With Shift+Tab, the focus cycles in the reverse order.
33. End the program.
34. Press Alt/F/O, or click on the Open Project icon to reload your first program. When a dialog box asks if you want to save your changes, click the No button or press N. An Open Project dialog box appears on the screen. Click on the Recent tab to see a list of the programs most recently opened or saved. Your first program and its location should appear at the top of the list. (*Note:* You can also find any program by clicking on the Existing tab and using the dialog box to search for the program.) Click on the name of your first program and then click on the Open button. Alternatively, double-click on the name. (You also have the option of typing the name into the "File name" box and then clicking the Open button.)

Note: Whenever you open a program that has been saved, you will not see the program's form. To view the form, select Object from the View menu by pressing Alt/V/B. If the word "Object" is grayed, run the program, terminate the program, and then try Alt/V/B again.

A Command Button Walkthrough

1. Press Alt/F/N and double-click on Standard EXE to start a new program. There is no need to save anything.
2. Double-click on the command button icon to place a command button in the center of the form. (The rectangular-shaped command button icon is the sixth icon in the Toolbox.)
3. Activate the Properties window, highlight the Caption property, and type "Please Push Me" (Figure 2.9). Notice that the letters appear on the command button as they are typed. The button is too small.

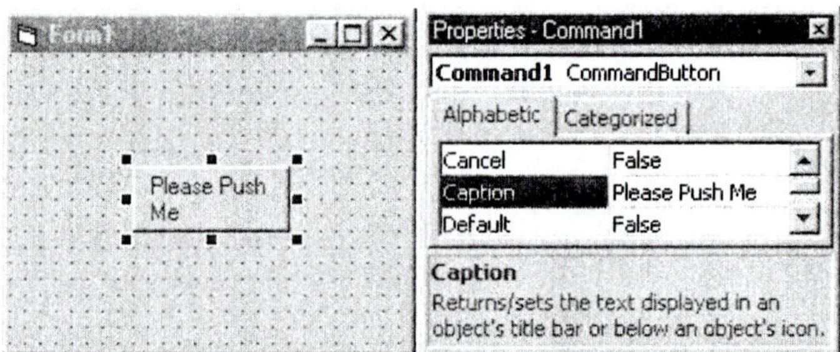

Figure 2.9. Setting the Caption property.

4. Click on the command button to select it, and then enlarge it to accommodate the phrase "Please Push Me" on one line.
5. Run the program, and click on the command button. The command button appears to move in and then out. (We can write code that is activated when a command button is pushed.)
6. End the program, and select the command button.
7. From the Properties window, edit the Caption setting by inserting an ampersand (&) before the first letter, P. Notice that the ampersand does not show on the button. However, the letter following the ampersand is now

underlined (Figure 2.10). Pressing Alt+P while the program is running executes the same code as clicking the command button. Here, P is referred to as the *access key* for the command button. (The access key is always specified as the character following the ampersand.)

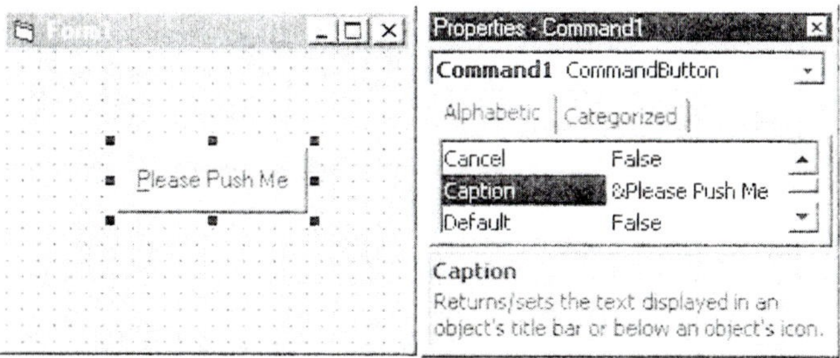

Figure 2.10. Designating P as an access key.

A *A Label Walkthrough*

1. Press Alt/F/N and double-click on Standard EXE to start a new program. There is no need to save anything.
2. Double-click on the label icon to place a label in the center of the form. (The label icon, a large letter A, is the third icon in the Toolbox.)
3. Activate the Properties window, highlight the Caption property, and type "Enter Your Phone Number." Such a label would be placed next to a text box into which the user will enter a phone number.
4. Click on the label to select it, and then widen it until all words are on the same line.
5. Make the label narrower until the words occupy two lines.
6. Activate the Properties window, and double-click on the Alignment property. Double-click two more times and observe the label's appearance. The combination of sizing and alignment permits you to design a label easily.
7. Run the program. Nothing happens, even if you click on the label. Labels just sit there. The user cannot change what a label displays unless you write code to allow the change.
8. End the program.

A Picture Box Walkthrough

1. Press Alt/F/N, and double-click on Standard EXE to start a new program. There is no need to save anything.
2. Double-click on the picture box icon to place a picture box in the center of the form. (The picture box icon is the second icon in the Toolbox. It contains a picture of the sun shining over a desert.)
3. Enlarge the picture box.
4. Run the program. Nothing happens and nothing will, no matter what you do. Although picture boxes look like text boxes, you can't type in them. However, you can display text in them, you can draw lines and circles in them, and you can insert pictures into them.

5. End the program and click the picture box to select it.
6. Activate the Properties window, and double-click on the Picture property. A Load Picture dialog box appears (Figure 2.11).

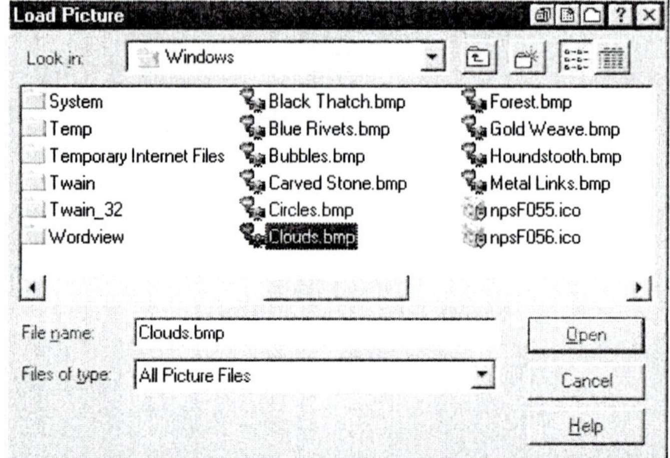

Figure 2.11. The Load Picture dialog box.

7. Select the Windows folder and then double-click on one of the picture files. Good candidates are Clouds.bmp (Figure 2.12), and Setup.bmp.
8. Click on the picture box and press Del to remove the picture box.

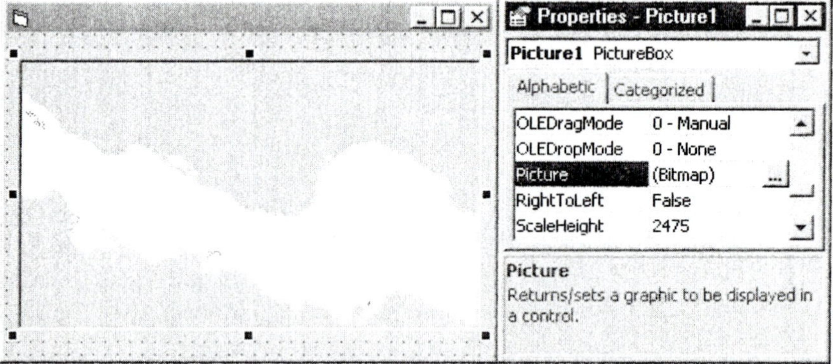

Figure 2.12. A picture box filled with the Clouds.bmp picture.

2.1.6 Comments

1. When selecting from a list, double-clicking has the same effect as clicking once and pressing Enter.
2. On a form, the Tab key cycles through the objects that can get the focus, and in a dialog box, it cycles through the items.
3. The form itself is also an object and has properties. For instance, you can change the text in the title bar with the Caption property. You can move the form by dragging the title bar of its ProjectContainer window.
4. The name of an object is used in code to refer to the object. By default, objects are given names like Text1 and Text2. You can use the Properties window to change the Name property of an object to a more suggestive name. (The Name property is always the first property in the list of proper-

ties. An object's Name must start with a letter and can be a maximum of 40 characters. It can include numbers and underline (_) characters, but can't include punctuation or spaces.) Also, Microsoft recommends that each name begin with a three-letter prefix that identifies the type of the control. See the table below.

OBJECT	PREFIX	EXAMPLE
command button	cmd	cmdComputeTotal
form	frm	frmPayroll
label	lbl	lblInstructions
picture box	pic	picClouds
text box	txt	txtAddress

5. The Name and Caption properties of a command button are both initially set to something like Command1. However, changing one of these properties does not affect the setting of the other property. The same is true for the Name and Caption properties of forms and labels, and for the Name and Text properties of text boxes.
6. The color settings appear as strings of digits and letters preceded by &H and trailed with &. Don't concern yourself with this notation.
7. Here are some fine points on the use of the Properties window.

   a. Press Shift+Ctrl+*letterkey* to highlight the first property that begins with that letter. Successive pressings highlight successive properties that begin with that letter.
   b. To change the selected object from the Properties window, click on the down-arrow icon at the right of the Object box of the Properties window. Then select the new object from the drop-down list.

8. Some useful properties that have not been discussed are the following:

   a. BorderStyle: Setting the BorderStyle to "0 – None" removes the border from an object.
   b. Visible: Setting the Visible property to False hides an object when the program is run. The object can be made to reappear with code.
   c. BackColor: Specifies the background color for a text box, label, picture box, or form. Also specifies the background color for a command button having the Style property set to "1 – Graphical." (Such a command button can display a picture.)
   d. BackStyle: The BackStyle property of a label is opaque by default. The rectangular region associated with the label is filled with the label's background color and caption. Setting the background style of a label to transparent causes whatever is behind the label to remain visible; the background color of the label essentially becomes "see through."
   e. Font: Can be set to any of Windows' fonts, such as Courier or Times New Roman. Two unusual fonts are Symbol and Wingdings. For instance, with the Wingdings font, pressing the keys for %, &, ', and J yield a bell, a book, a candle, and a smiling face, respectively. To view the character sets for the different Windows' fonts, click on the Start

button, and successively select Programs, Accessories, and Character Map. Then click on Character Map or press the Enter key. After selecting a font, hold down the left mouse button on any character to enlarge it and obtain the keystroke that produces that character.

9. When you click on a property in the Properties window, a description of the property appears just below the window. With the Learning, Professional, and Enterprise Editions of VB 6.0 you can obtain very detailed (and somewhat advanced) information about a property by clicking on the property and pressing F1 for Help.
10. Most properties can be set or altered with code as the program is running instead of being preset from the Properties window. For instance, a command button can be made to disappear with a line such as Command1.Visible = False.
11. The BorderStyle and MultiLine properties of a text box can be set only from the Properties window. You cannot alter them during run time.
12. Of the objects discussed in this section, only command buttons have true access keys.
13. If you inadvertently double-click on an object in a form, a window containing two lines of text will appear. (The first line begins Private Sub.) This is a code window and is discussed in the next section. To remove this window, click on its Close button.
14. To enlarge (or decrease) the Project Container window, position the mouse cursor anywhere on the right or bottom edge and drag the mouse. To enlarge (or decrease) the form, select the form and drag one of its sizing handles. Alternatively, you can enlarge either the Project Container window or the form by clicking on its Maximize button.
15. We will always be selecting the Standard EXE icon from the New Project window.

PRACTICE!

1. What is the difference between the Caption and the Name of a command button?
2. Suppose in an earlier session you created an object that looks like an empty rectangle. It might be a picture box, a text box with Text property set to nothing (blanked out by deleting all characters), or a label with a blank caption and BorderStyle property set to Fixed Single. How might you determine which it is?

Solutions

1. The Caption is the text appearing on the command button, whereas the Name is the designation used to refer to the command button. Initially, they have the same value, such as Command1. However, they can each be changed independently of the other.
2. Click on the object to select it, and then press F4 to activate its Properties window. The Object box gives the Name of the object (in bold letters) and its type, such as Label, TextBox, or PictureBox.

We have examined only four of the objects from the Toolbox. To determine the type of one of the other objects, hold the mouse pointer over it for a few seconds.

2.2 VISUAL BASIC EVENTS

When a Visual Basic program is run, a form and its controls appear on the screen. Normally, nothing happens until the user takes an action, such as clicking a control or pressing the Tab key. Such an action is called an *event*.

The three steps to creating a Visual Basic program are as follows:

1. Create the interface; that is, generate, position, and size the objects.
2. Set relevant properties for the objects.
3. Write the code that executes when the events occur.

This section is devoted to Step 3.

Code consists of statements that carry out tasks. Visual Basic has a repertoire of over 200 statements. In this section, we limit ourselves to statements that change properties of objects while a program is running.

Properties of an object are changed in code with statements of the form

```
objectName.property = setting
```

where *objectName* is the name of the form or a control, *property* is one of the properties of the object, and *setting* is a valid setting for that object. Such statements are called *assignment statements*. They assign values to properties. Here are three other assignment statements.

The statement

```
txtBox.Font.Size = 12
```

sets the size of the characters in the text box named txtBox to 12.

The statement

```
txtBox.Font.Bold = True
```

converts the characters in the text box to boldface.

The statement

```
txtBox.Text = ""
```

clears the contents of the text box; that is, it invokes the blank setting.

Most events are associated with objects. The event *clicking cmdButton* is different from the event *clicking picBox*. These two events are specified cmdButton_ Click and picBox_Click. The statements to be executed when an event occurs are written in a block of code called an *event procedure*. The structure of an event procedure is

```
Private Sub objectName_event()
    statements
End Sub
```

The word Sub in the first line signals the beginning of the event procedure, and the first line identifies the object and the event occurring to that object. The last line signals the termination of the event procedure. The statements to be executed appear between these two lines. (*Note:* The word Private indicates that the event procedure cannot be invoked by an event from another form. This will always be the case in this text. The word *Sub* is an abbreviation of *Subprogram*.) For instance, the event procedure

```
Private Sub cmdButton_Click()
    txtBox.Text = ""
End Sub
```

clears the contents of the text box when the command button is clicked.

2.2.1 An Event Procedure Walkthrough

The form in Figure 2.13, which contains a text box and a command button, will be used to demonstrate what event procedures are and how they are created. Three event procedures will be used to alter the appearance of a phrase that is typed into the text box. The event procedures are txtPhrase_LostFocus, txtPhrase_GotFocus, and cmdBold_Click.

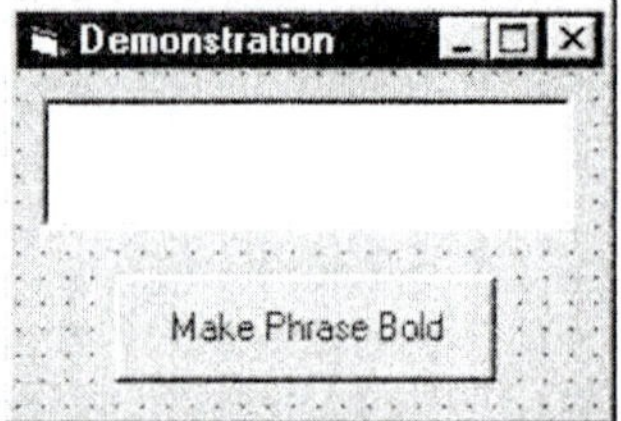

Figure 2.13. The interface for the event procedure walkthrough.

OBJECT	PROPERTY	SETTING
frmWalkthrough	Caption	Demonstration
txtPhrase	Text	(blank)
cmdBold	Caption	Make Phrase Bold

1. Create the interface in Figure 2.13 The Name properties of the form, text box, and command button should be set as shown in the Object column. The Caption property of the form should be set to Demonstration, the Text property of the text box should be made blank, and the Caption property of the command button should be set to Make Phrase Bold.
2. Double-click on the text box. A window, called a *code window*, appears (Figure 2.14). Just below the title bar are two drop-down list boxes. The left box is called the *Object box* and the right box is called the *Procedure box*. (When you position the mouse pointer over one of these list boxes, its type appears.)

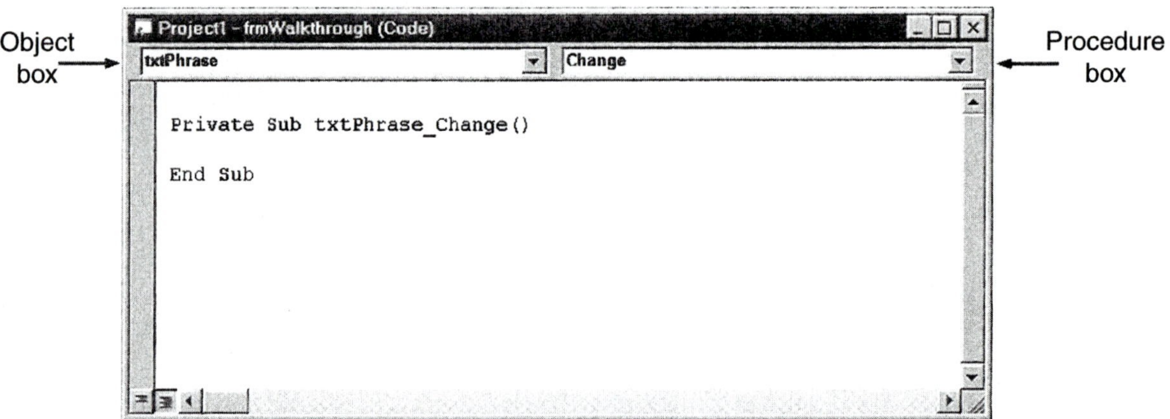

Figure 2.14. A code window.

3. Click on the down-arrow button to the right of the Procedure box. The drop-down menu that appears contains a list of all possible event procedures associated with text boxes (Figure 2.15).

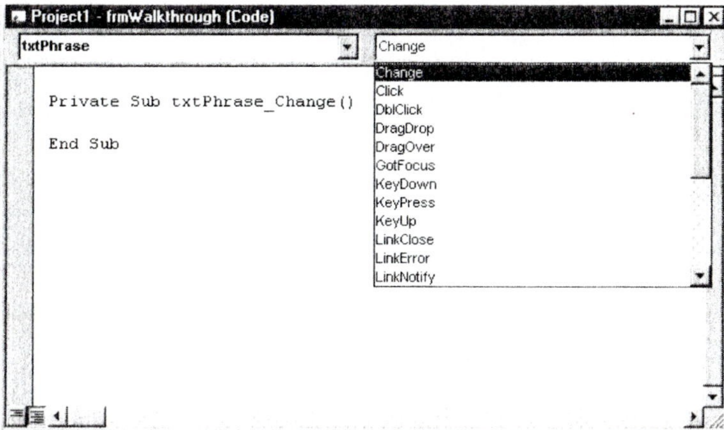

Figure 2.15. Drop-down menu of event procedures.

4. Scroll down the list of event procedures and click on LostFocus. (LostFocus is the 14th event procedure.) The lines

```
Private Sub txtPhrase_LostFocus()

End Sub
```

appear in the code window with a blinking cursor poised at the beginning of the blank line.

5. Type the line

```
txtPhrase.Font.Size = 12
```

between the existing two lines. (We usually indent lines inside procedures.) (After you type each period, the editor displays a list containing possible choices of items to follow the period (Figure 2.16). This feature is called "List Properties/Methods." In Figure 2.16, instead of typing the word "Size," you can double-click on "Size" in the displayed list or highlight the word "Size" and press Tab.) The screen appears as in Figure 2.17. We have now created an event procedure that is activated whenever the text box loses the focus.

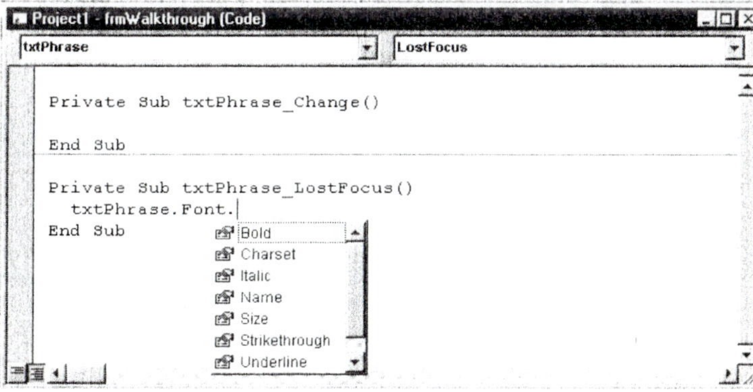

Figure 2.16. A LostFocus event procedure.

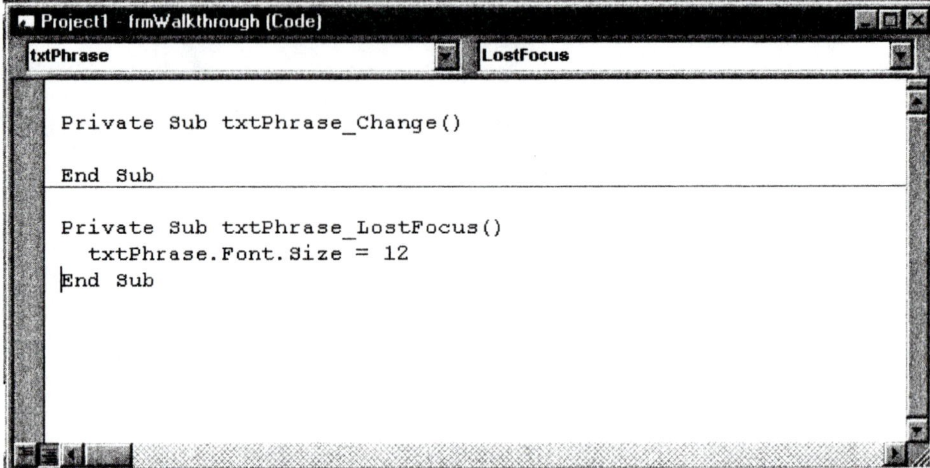

Figure 2.17. A LostFocus event procedure.

6. Let's create another event procedure for the text box. Click on the down-arrow button to the right of the Procedure box, scroll up the list of event procedures, and click on GotFocus. Then type the lines

```
txtPhrase.Font.Size = 8
txtPhrase.Font.Bold = False
```

   between the existing two lines (Figure 2.18).

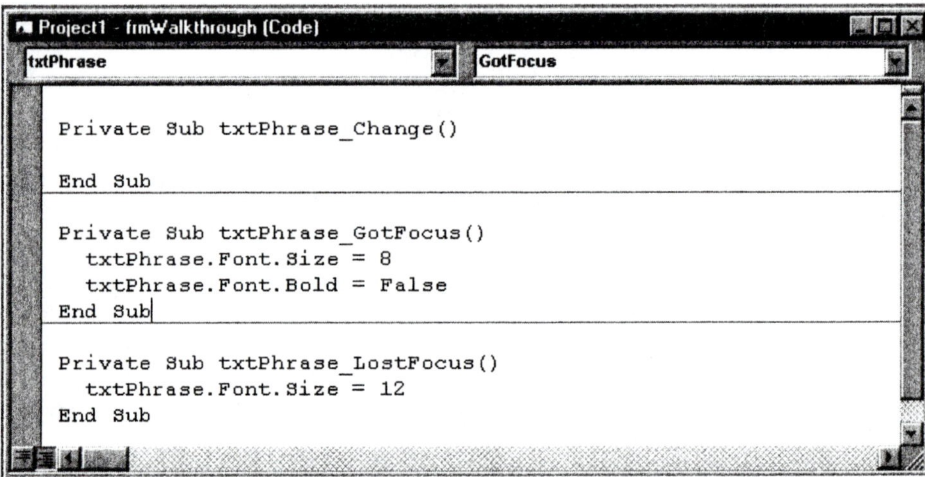

Figure 2.18. A GotFocus event procedure.

7. The txtPhrase_Change event procedure in Figure 2.18 was not used and can be deleted. To delete the procedure, highlight it by dragging the mouse across the two lines of code, and then press the Del key.

8. Let's now create an event procedure for the command button. Click on the down-arrow button to the right of the Object box. The drop-down menu contains a list of the objects, along with a mysterious object called (General), which will be discussed later (Figure 2.19).

```
Project1 - frmWalkthrough (Code)
txtPhrase                         GotFocus
(General)
cmdBold
Form
txtPhrase                         ()
  txtPhrase.Font.Bold = False
End Sub

Private Sub txtPhrase_LostFocus()
  txtPhrase.Font.Size = 12
End Sub
```

Figure 2.19. List of objects.

9. Click on cmdBold. The event procedure cmdBold_Click is displayed. Type in the line

```
txtPhrase.Font.Bold = True
```

The screen appears as in Figure 2.20, and the program is complete.

```
Project1 - frmWalkthrough (Code)
cmdBold                           Click

Private Sub cmdBold_Click()
  txtPhrase.Font.Bold = True
End Sub

Private Sub txtPhrase_GotFocus()
  txtPhrase.Font.Size = 8
  txtPhrase.Font.Bold = False
End Sub

Private Sub txtPhrase_LostFocus()
  txtPhrase.Font.Size = 12
End Sub
```

Figure 2.20. The three event procedures.

10. Now run the program by pressing F5.
11. Type something into the text box. In Figure 2.21, the words "Hello Friend" have been typed. (A text box has the focus whenever it is ready to accept typing; that is, whenever it contains a blinking cursor.)

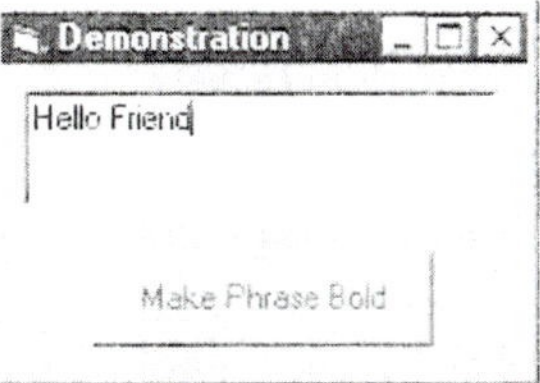

Figure 2.21. Text box containing input.

12. Press the Tab key. The contents of the text box will be enlarged as in Figure 2.22 When Tab was pressed, the text box lost the focus; that is, the event LostFocus happened to txtPhrase. Thus, the event procedure txtPhrase_LostFocus was called, and the code inside the procedure was executed.

Figure 2.22. Text box after it has lost the focus.

13. Click on the command button. This calls the event procedure cmdBold_Click, which converts the text to boldface (Figure 2.23).

Figure 2.23. Text box after the command button has been clicked.

14. Click on the text box or press the Tab key to move the cursor (and, therefore, the focus) to the text box. This calls the event procedure txtPhrase_GotFocus, which restores the text to its original state.
15. You can repeat Steps 11 to 14 as many times as you like. When you are finished, end the program by pressing Alt+F4, clicking the End icon on the Toolbar, or clicking the Close button (X) on the form.

2.2.2 Comments

1. To hide the code window, press the right mouse button and click on Hide. You can also hide it by clicking on the icon at the left side of the title bar and clicking on Close. To view a hidden code window, press Alt/View/Code. To hide a form, close its container. To view a hidden form, press Alt/View/ Object.
2. The form is the default object in Visual Basic code. That is, code such as

```
Form1.property = setting
```

can be written as

```
property = setting
```

Also, event procedures associated with Form1 appear as

```
Form_event()
```

rather than

```
Form1_event()
```

3. Another useful command is SetFocus. The statement

```
object.SetFocus
```

moves the focus to the object.

4. We have ended our programs by clicking the End icon or pressing Alt+F4. A more elegant technique is to create a command button, call it cmdQuit, with caption Quit and the event procedure:

```
Private Sub cmdQuit_Click()
    End
End Sub
```

5. Certain words, such as Sub, End, and False, have special meanings in Visual Basic and are referred to as *keywords* or *reserved words*. The Visual Basic editor automatically capitalizes the first letter of a keyword and displays the word in blue.

6. Visual Basic can detect certain types of errors. For instance, consider the line

```
txtPhrase.Font.Bold = False
```

from the walkthrough. Suppose you neglected to type the word False to the right of the equal sign before leaving the line. Visual Basic would tell you something was missing by displaying the left message box that follows. (Also, the line would turn red.) On the other hand, suppose in the cmdBold. Click event procedure you misspell the keyword "Bold" as "bolt." You might notice something is wrong when the letter "b" is not capitalized. If not, you will certainly know about the problem when the program is run because Visual Basic will display the right message box that follows when you click on the command button. After you click on Debug, the line containing the offending word will be highlighted.

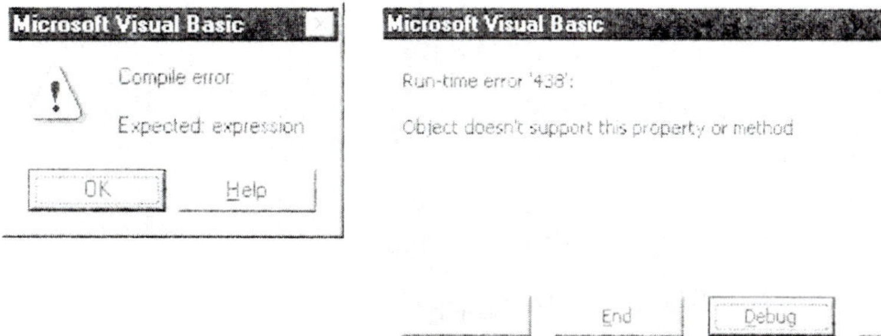

7. At design time, colors are selected from a palette. At run time, the eight most common colors can be assigned with the color constants vbBlack, vbRed, vbGreen, vbYellow, vbBlue, vbMagenta, vbCyan, and vbWhite. For instance, the statement

```
picBox.BackColor = vbYellow
```

gives picBox a yellow background.

8. For statements of the form *object.property* = *setting*, with properties Caption, Text, or Font.Name, the setting must be surrounded by quotes. (For instance, lblTwo.Caption = "Name," txtBox.Text = "Fore," and picBox.Font.Name =

"Courier.") When the words True or False appear to the right of the equal sign, they should *not* be surrounded by quotation marks.

9. Code windows have many features of word processors. For instance, the operations cut, copy, paste, find, undo, and redo can be carried out with the 6th through 11th icons of the Toolbar. These operations, and several others, also can be initiated from the Edit menu.

10. Names of existing event procedures associated with an object are *not* automatically changed when you rename the object. You must change them yourself and also change any references to the object. Therefore, you should finalize the names of your objects before you put any code into their event procedures.

11. If you find the automatic List Properties/Methods feature distracting, you can turn it off by pressing Alt/Tools/Options, selecting the Editor page, and deselecting Auto List Members. If you do so, you can still display a list manually at the appropriate time by pressing Ctrl+J.

12. Earlier versions of Visual Basic used the property FontSize instead of Font.Size. Although Font.Size is preferred, FontSize is allowed for compatibility. Similarly, properties such as FontBold, FontItalic, and FontName have been included for compatibility with earlier versions of Visual Basic.

13. Assignment statements can be written preceded with the keyword Let. For instance, txtBox.Text = "Hello," also can be written Let txtBox.Text = "Hello." Therefore, assignment statements are also known as Let statements.

PRACTICE!

1. You can always locate an existing event procedure by searching through the code window with the Pg Up and Pg Dn keys. Give another way.

Solution

1. With the code window showing, click on the arrow to the right of the Object box and then select the desired object. Then click on the arrow to the right of the Procedure box, and select the desired event procedure.

2.3 NUMBERS

Much of the data processed by computers consists of numbers. In "computerese," numbers are often called *numeric constants*. This section discusses the operations that are performed with numbers and the ways numbers are displayed.

2.3.1 Arithmetic Operations

The five arithmetic operations in Visual Basic are addition, subtraction, multiplication, division, and exponentiation. Addition, subtraction, and division are denoted in Visual Basic by the standard symbols +, –, and /, respectively. However, the notations for multiplication and exponentiation differ from the customary mathematical notations.

Mathematical notation	Visual Basic Notation
$a \cdot b$ or $a \times b$	a*b
a^r	a^r

(The asterisk [*] is the upper character of the 8 key. The caret [^] is the upper character of the 6 key.) *Note:* In this book, the proportional font used for text differs from the fixed-width font used for programs. In the program font, the asterisk appears as a five-pointed star (*).

One way to show a number on the screen is to display it in a picture box. If *n* is a number, then the instruction

```
picBox.Print n
```

displays the number *n* in the picture box. If the picBox.Print instruction is followed by a combination of numbers and arithmetic operations, it carries out the operations and displays the result. Print is a reserved word and the Print operation is called a *method*. Another important method is Cls. The statement

```
picBOx.Cls
```

erases all text and graphics from the picture box picBox.

The following program applies each of the five arithmetic operations to the numbers 3 and 2. Notice that 3/2 is displayed in decimal form. Visual Basic never displays numbers as common fractions. *Note1:* The star in the fifth and eighth lines is the computer-font version of the asterisk. *Note 2:* The word "Run" in the phrasing [Run ...] indicates that F5 should be pressed to execute the program. *Note 3:* All programs appearing in examples and case studies are provided on the CD accompanying this book. See the discussion of the CD near the end of the book for details.

Below is the form design and a table showing the names of the objects on the form and the settings, if any, for properties of these objects. This form design is also used in the discussion and examples in the remainder of this section.

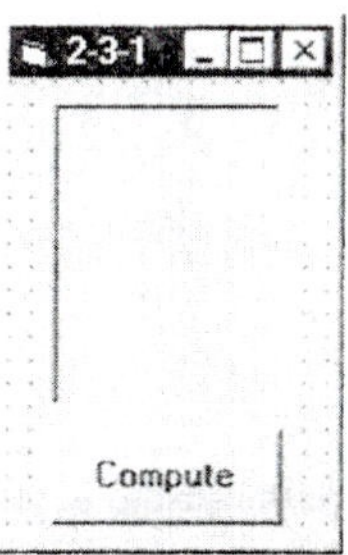

OBJECT	PROPERTY	SETTING
frm2_3_1	Caption	2-3-1
picResults		
cmdCompute	Caption	Compute

```
Private Sub cmdCompute_Click()
    picResults.Cls
    picResults.Print 3 + 2
    picResults.Print 3 - 2
    picResults.Print 3 * 2
    picResults.Print 3 / 2
    picResults.Print 3 ^ 2
    picResults.Print 2 * (3 + 4)
End Sub
```

```
[Run, and then click the command button.]
```

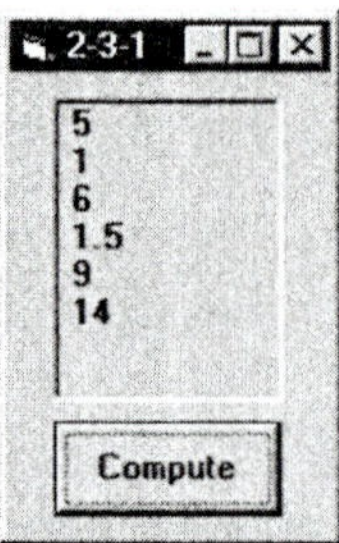

2.3.2 Scientific Notation

Let's quickly review powers of 10 and scientific notation. Our method of decimal notation is based on a systematic use of exponents.

$10^1 = 10$	$10^{-1} = 1/10 = .1$
$10^2 = 100$	$10^{-2} = .01$
$10^3 = 1000$	$10^{-3} = .001$
•	•
•	•
•	•
$10^n = \underbrace{1000\ldots0}_{n \text{ zeros}}$	$10^{-n} = \underbrace{.000\ldots01}_{n \text{ digits}}$

Scientific notation provides a convenient way of writing numbers by using powers of 10 to stand for zeros. Numbers are written in the form $b \times 10r$, where b is a number from 1 up to (but not including) 10, and r is an integer. For example, it is much more convenient to write the diameter of the sun (1,400,000,000 meters) in scientific notation: 1.4×10^9 meters. Similarly, rather than write .0000003 meters for the diameter of a bacterium, it is simpler to write 3×10^{-7} meters.

Any acceptable number can be entered into the computer in either standard or scientific notation. The form in which Visual Basic displays a number depends on many factors, with size being an important consideration. In Visual Basic, $b \times 10r$ is usually written as bEr. (The letter E is an abbreviation for *exponent*.) The following forms of the numbers just mentioned are equivalent.

1.4*10^9	1.4E+09	1.4E+9	1.4E9	1400000000
3*10^-7	3E-07	3E-7	.0000003	

The computer displays r as a two-digit number, preceded by a plus sign if r is positive and a minus sign if r is negative.

Here is a program that illustrates scientific notation. The computer's choice of whether to display a number in scientific or standard form depends on the magnitude of the number.

```
Private Sub cmdCompute_Click()
    picResults.Cls
    picResults.Print 1.2 * 10 ^ 34
    picResults.Print 1.2 * 10 ^ 8
    picResults.Print 1.2 * 10 ^ 3
    picResults.Print 10 ^ -20
    picResults.Print 10 ^ -2
End Sub
```

```
[Run, and then click the command button.]
```

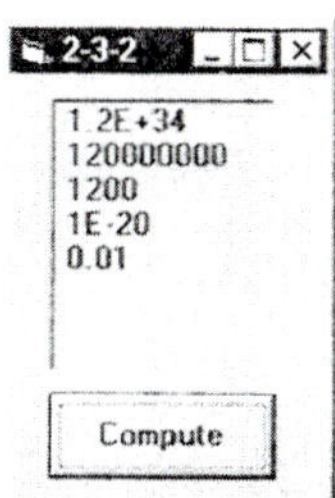

2.3.3 Variables

In applied mathematics problems, quantities are referred to by names. For instance, consider the following high school algebra problem. "If a car travels at 50 miles per hour, how far will it travel in 14 hours? Also, how many hours are required to travel 410 miles?" The solution to this problem uses the well-known formula

```
distance = speed × time elapsed
```

Here's how this problem would be solved with a computer program.

```
Private Sub cmdCompute_Click()
    picResults.Cls
    speed = 50
    timeElapsed = 14
    distance = speed * timeElapsed
    picResults.Print distance
    distance = 410
    timeElapsed = distance / speed
    picResults.Print timeElapsed
End Sub
```

```
[Run, and then click the command button. The following is
displayed in the picture box.]

700
8.2
```

The third line of the event procedure sets the speed to 50, and the fourth line sets the time elapsed to 14. The fifth line multiplies the value for the speed by the value for the time elapsed and sets the distance to this product. The next line displays the answer to the first question. The three lines before the End Sub statement answer the second question in a similar manner.

The names *speed, timeElapsed*, and *distance*, which hold numbers, are referred to as *variables*. Consider the variable *timeElapsed*. In the fourth line, its value was set to 14. In the eighth line, its value was changed as the result of a computation. On the other hand, the variable *speed* had the same value, 50, throughout the program.

In general, a variable is a name that is used to refer to an item of data. The value assigned to the variable may change during the execution of the program. In Visual Basic, variable names can be up to 255 characters long, must begin with a letter, and can consist only of letters, digits, and underscores. (The shortest variable names consist of a single letter.) Visual Basic does not distinguish between uppercase and lowercase letters used in variable names. Some examples of variable names are *total, numberOfCars, taxRate_1998*, and *n*. As a convention, we write variable names in lowercase letters except for the first letters of additional words (as in *numberOfCars*).

If *var* is a variable and *num* is a constant, then the statement

var = *num*

assigns the number *num* to the variable *var*. (Such a statement is another example of an assignment statement.) Actually, the computer sets aside a location in memory with the name *var* and places the number *num* in it. The statement

```
picBox.Print var
```

looks into this memory location for the value of the variable and displays the value in the picture box.

A combination of constants, variables, and arithmetic operations that can be evaluated to yield a number is called a *numeric expression*. Expressions are evaluated by replacing each variable by its value and carrying out the arithmetic. Some examples of expressions are 2*distance+7, n+1, and (a+b)/3.

This program displays the value of an expression.

```
Private Sub cmdCompute_Click()
    picResults.Cls
    a = 5
    b = 4
    picResults.Print a * (2 + b)
End Sub
```

```
[Run, and then click the command button. The following is
displayed in the picture box.]

30
```

If *var* is a variable, then the statement

var = *expression*

first evaluates the expression on the right and *then* assigns its value to the variable. For instance, the event procedure in Example 3 can be written as

```
Private Sub cmdCompute_Click()
    picResults.Cls
    a = 5
    b = 4
    c = a * (2 + b)
    picResults.Print c
End Sub
```

The expression a * (2 + b) is evaluated to 30 and then this value is assigned to the variable *c*.

Because the expression on the right side of an assignment statement is evaluated *before* an assignment is made, a statement such

$$n = n + 1$$

is meaningful. It first evaluates the expression on the right (that is, it adds 1 to the original value of the variable *n*), and then assigns this sum to the variable *n*. The effect is to increase the value of the variable *n* by 1. In terms of memory locations, the statement retrieves the value of *n* from *n*'s memory location, uses it to compute $n + 1$, and then places the sum back into *n*'s memory location.

2.3.4 Print Method

Consider the following event procedure.

```
Private Sub cmdDisplay_Click()
     picResults.Cls
     picResults.Print 3
     picResults.Print -3
End Sub

[Run, and then click the command button.]
```

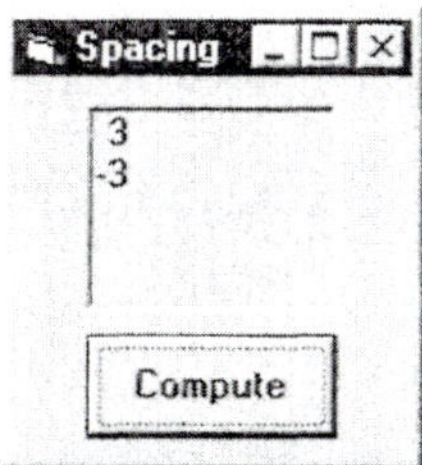

Notice that the negative number –3 begins directly at the left margin, whereas the positive number 3 begins one space to the right. The Print method always displays nonnegative numbers with a leading space. The Print method also displays a trailing space after every number. Although the trailing spaces are not apparent here, we will soon see evidence of their presence.

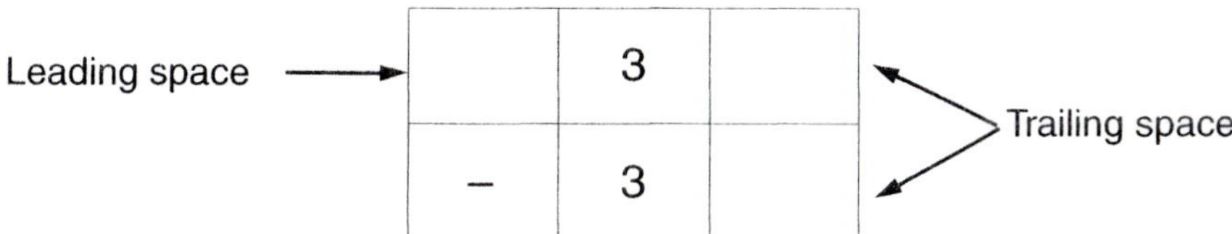

The Print methods used so far display only one number per line. After displaying a number, the cursor moves to the leftmost position and down a line for the next display. Borrowing from typewriter terminology, we say that the computer performs a carriage return and a line feed after each number is displayed. The carriage return and line feed, however, can be suppressed by placing a semicolon at the end of the number.

The following program illustrates the use of semicolons in Print methods. The output reveals the presence of the space trailing each number. For instance, the space trailing –3 combines with the leading space of 99 to produce two spaces between the numbers.

```
Private Sub cmdDisplay_Click()
    picResults.Cls
    picResults.Print 3;
    picResults.Print -3;
    picResults.Print 99;
    picResults.Print 100
End Sub
```

[Run, and then click the command button.]

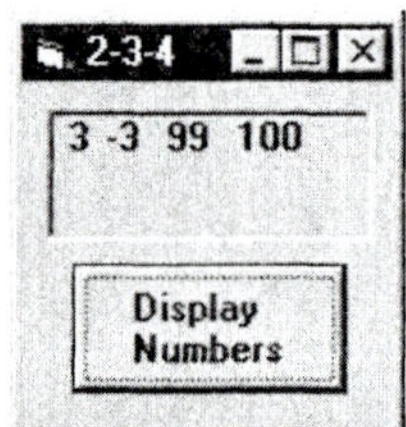

Semicolons can be used to display several numbers with one Print method. If *m*, *n*, and *r* are numbers, a line of the form

```
picBox.Print m; n; r
```

displays the three numbers, one after another, separated only by their leading and trailing spaces. For instance, the Print methods in preceding Example 4 can be replaced by the single line

```
picResults.Print 3; -3; 99; 100
```

2.3.5 Relational Operators

Relational operators compare the size of two numbers. Table 2-1 shows the different mathematical relational operators, their representations in Visual Basic, their meanings, and examples. A *condition* is an expression involving relational operators that is either true or false.

TABLE 2-1 Relational operators.

MATHEMATICAL NOTATION	VISUAL BASIC NOTATION	MEANING	EXAMPLE
=	=	equal to	2 = 2
≠	<>	unequal to	1 <> 2
<	<	less than	2 < 3
>	>	greater than	1.6 > 1
≤	<=	less than or equal to	2 <= 3
≥	>=	greater than or equal to	5 >= 5

EXAMPLE 2.1:

1. Determine whether each of the following conditions is true or false.

(a) $1 <= 1$ (c) $-2 <> 2$
(b) $1 < 1$ (d) $-2 < -3$

SOLUTION

a. True. The notation < = means "less than *or* equal to." That is, the condition is true provided either of the two circumstances holds. The second one (equal to) holds.

b. False. The notation < means "strictly less than" and no number can be strictly less than itself.

c. True. Two numbers are equal only if they are identical. Because −2 is different from 2, they are not equal.

d. False. The relationship $a < b$ holds only if the number a is to the left of the number b on the number line.

EXAMPLE 2.2:

1. Suppose the value of *num1* is 4 and the value of *num2* is 3. Is the condition (*num1* + *num2*) < 2 * *num1* true or false?

SOLUTION

1. The value of *num1* + *num2* is 7 and the value of 2 * *num1* is 8. Since 7 < 8, the condition is true.

2.3.6 Numeric Functions: Sqr, Int, Round

Visual Basic has a number of built-in functions that greatly extend its mathematical capability. *Functions* associate with one or more values, called the *input*, and a single value, called the *output*. The function is said to *return* the output value.

The function Sqr calculates the square root of a number. The function Int finds the greatest integer less than or equal to a number. Therefore, Int discards the decimal part of positive numbers. The value of Round(n, r) is the number n rounded to r decimal places. The parameter r can be omitted. If so, n is rounded to a whole number. Some examples follow:

Sqr(9) is 3.	Int(2.7) is 2.	Round(2.7) is 3.
Sqr(0) is 0.	Int(3) is 3.	Round(2.317, 2) is 2.32.
Sqr(2) is 1.414214.	Int(−2.7) is −3.	Round(2.317, 1) is 2.3.

The terms inside the parentheses can be either numbers (as shown), numeric variables, or numeric expressions. Expressions are first evaluated to produce the input.

The following program evaluates each of the functions for a specific input given by the value of the variable n.

```
Private Sub cmdEvaluate_Click()
    picResults.Cls
    n = 6.76
    root = Sqr(n)
    picResults.Print root; Int(n), Round(n, 1)
End Sub
```

```
[Run, and then click the command button. The following is
displayed in the picture box.]

2.6 6 6.8
```

This program evaluates each of the preceding functions at an expression.

```
Private Sub cmdEvaluate_Click()
    picResults.Cls
    a = 2
    b = 3
    picResults.Print Sqr(5 * b + 1); Int(a ^ b); Round(a / b, 3)
End Sub
```

```
[Run, and then click the command button. The following is
displayed in the picture box.]
```

```
4 8 0.667
```

2.3.7 Comments

1. Numbers must not contain commas, dollar signs, or percent signs. Also, mixed numbers, such as 8 1/2, are not allowed.
2. Parentheses should be used when necessary to clarify the meaning of an expression. When there are no parentheses, the arithmetic operations are performed in the following order: (1) exponentiations; (2) multiplications and divisions; and (3) additions and subtractions. In the event of ties, the leftmost operation is carried out first. Table 2-2 summarizes these rules.

TABLE 2-2 Level of precedence for arithmetic operations.

()	Inner to outer, left to right
^	Left to right in expression
* /	Left to right in expression
+ -	Left to right in expression

3. Restricted keywords cannot be used as names of variables. For instance, the statements "print = 99" and "end = 99" are not valid. Some other common keywords are Call, If, Select, and Sub. If a keyword is used as a variable name, you will soon be warned that somethings wrong. As soon as the cursor is moved from the line, an error message will appear, and the line will turn red. The use of some other keywords (such as Error, Height, Name, Rate, Time, Val, Width, and Year) as variable names does not trigger an immediate warning, but generates an error message when the program is run. Although there is a way to get Visual Basic to accept this last group of keywords as variable names, we will never use keywords as variable names. You can tell immediately when you inadvertently use a reserved word as a variable in an assignment statement because Visual Basic automatically capitalizes the first letter of keywords. For instance, if you type "rate = 50" and press the Enter key, the line will change to "Rate = 50."
4. Grammatical errors, such as misspelling or incorrect punctuation, are called *syntax errors*. Certain types of syntax errors are spotted by the smart editor when they are entered, whereas others are not detected until the program is

executed. When Visual Basic spots an error, it displays a dialog box. Some incorrect statements and their errors are given below.

STATEMENT	REASON FOR ERROR
picBox.Primt 3	Misspelling of keyword
picBox.Print 2 +	No number follows the plus sign
9W = 5	9W is not a valid variable name

5. Errors detected while a program is running are called *run-time errors*. Although some run-time errors are due to improper syntax, others result from the inability of the computer to carry out the intended task. For instance, if the value of *numVar* is 0, then the statement

```
numVarInv = 1/numVar
```

interrupts the program with the run-time error "Division by zero." If the file Data.txt is not in the root folder of the C drive, then a statement that refers to the file by the filespec "C:\Data.txt" produces the run-time error "File not found."

The dialog box generated by a run-time error states the type of error and has a row of four command buttons captioned Continue, End, Debug, and Help. If you click on the Debug command button, Visual Basic will highlight in yellow the line of code that caused the error. (*Note:* After a run-time error occurs, the program is said to be in break mode. See the first page of Section 5.4 for a discussion of the three program modes.)

6. A third type of error is the so-called *logical error*. Such an error occurs when a program does not perform the way it was intended. For instance, the line

```
ave = firstNum + secondNum / 2
```

is syntactically correct. However, the missing parentheses in the first line are responsible for an incorrect value being generated.

7. The omission of the asterisk to denote multiplication is a common error. For instance, the expression a(b+c) is not valid. It should read a*(b+c).

8. When *n* is a number that is halfway between two successive whole numbers (such as 1.5, 2.5, 3.5, and 4.5), then *n* is rounded by Round(*n*) to the nearest even number. That is, half the time *n* is rounded up and half the time it is rounded down. For instance, Round(2.5) is 2 and Round(3.5) is 4. Similar results hold for any number whose decimal part ends in 5. For instance, Round(3.65, 1) is 3.6 and Round(3.75, 1) is 3.8.

9. When you first open a program that has been saved on disk, the Code window may not appear. If so, run and then terminate the program to see the Code window. To see the Form window, click on Object in the View menu or press Shift+F7. To return to the Code window, click on Code in the View window or press F7.

PRACTICE!

1. Evaluate 2+3*4.
2. Complete the table by filling in the value of each variable after each line is executed.

	a	b	c
`Private Sub cmdCompute_Click()`			
`a = 3`	3	—	—
`b = 4`	3	4	—
`c = a + b`			
`a = c * a`			
`picResults.Print a - b`			
`b = b * b`			
`End Sub`			

Solutions

1. Multiplications are performed before additions. If the intent is for the addition to be performed first, the expression should be written (2+3)*4.

	a	b	c
`Private Sub cmdCompute_Click()`	—	—	—
`a = 3`	—	—	
`b = 4`	4	—	
`c = a + b`	3	4	7
`a = c * a`	21	4	7
`picResults.Print a - b`	21	4	7
`b = b * b`	21	16	7
`End Sub`	—	—	—

2. Each time an assignment statement is executed, only one variable has its value changed (the variable to the left of the equal sign).

2.4 STRINGS

Visual Basic can process two primary types of data: numbers and strings. Sentences, phrases, words, letters of the alphabet, names, telephone numbers, addresses, and social security numbers are all examples of strings. Formally, a *string constant* is a sequence of characters that is treated as a single item. Strings can be assigned names with assignment statements, can be displayed with Print methods, and can be combined by an operation called concatenation (denoted by &).

2.4.1 Variables and Strings

A *string variable* is a name used to refer to a string. The allowable names of string variables are identical to those of numeric variables. The value of a string variable is assigned or altered with assignment statements and displayed with Print methods just like the value of a numeric variable.

The following code shows how assignment statements and Print are used with strings. The string variable *today* is assigned a value by the fourth line, and this value is displayed by the fifth line. The quotation marks surrounding each string constant are not part of the constant and are not displayed by the Print method. (The form design for Examples 1 through 5 consists of a command button and picture box.)

```
Private Sub cmdButton_Click()
    picBox.Cls
    picBox.Print "hello"
    today = "9/17/99"
    picBox.Print today
End Sub
```

```
[Run, and then click the command button. The following is
displayed in the picture box.]
```

```
hello
9/17/99
```

If *x*, *y*, ..., *z* are characters and *strVar1* is a string variable, then the statement

```
strVar1 = "xy...z"
```

assigns the string constant *xy...z* to the variable, and the statement

```
picBox.Print "xy...z"
```

or

```
picBox.Print strVar1
```

displays the string *xy...z* in a picture box. If *strVar2* is another string variable, then the statement

```
strVar2 = strVar1
```

assigns the value of the variable *strVar1* to the variable *strVar2*. (The value of *strVar1* will remain the same.) String constants used in assignment or picBox.Print statements must be surrounded by quotation marks, but string variables are never surrounded by quotation marks.

As with numbers, semicolons can be used with strings in picBox.Print statements to suppress carriage returns and line feeds. However, picBox.Print statements do not display leading or trailing spaces along with strings.

Here is a program that illustrates the use of the assignment statement and Print method with text.

```
Private Sub cmdShow_Click()
    picOutput.Cls
    phrase = "win or lose that counts."
    picOutput.Print "It's not whether you "; phrase
    picOutput.Print "It's whether I "; phrase
End Sub
```

```
[Run, and then click the command button. The following is
displayed in the picture box.]

It's not whether you win or lose that counts.
It's whether I win or lose that counts.
```

This program has strings and numbers occurring together in a picBalance.Print instruction.

```
Private Sub cmdCompute_Click()
    picBalance.Cls
    interestRate = 0.0655
    principal = 100
    phrase = "The balance after a year is"
    picBalance.Print phrase; (1 + interestRate) * principal
End Sub
```

[Run, and then click the command button. The following is displayed in the picture box.]

```
The balance after a year is 106.55
```

2.4.2 Concatenation

Two strings can be combined to form a new string consisting of the strings joined together. The joining operation is called *concatenation* and is represented by an ampersand (&). For instance, "good" & "bye" is "goodbye." A combination of strings and ampersands that can be evaluated to form a string is called a *string expression*. The assignment statement and Print method evaluate expressions before assigning them to variables or displaying them.

Here is a program that illustrates concatenation.

```
Private Sub cmdDisplay_Click()
    picQuote.Cls
    quote1 = "The ballgame isn't over,"
    quote2 = "until it's over."
    quote = quote1 & quote2
    picQuote.Print quote & " Yogi Berra"
End Sub
```

```
[Run, and then click the command button. The following is
displayed in the picture box.]

The ballgame isn't over, until it's over. Yogi Berra
```

2.4.3 Declaring Variable Types

So far, we have not distinguished between variables that hold strings and variables that hold numbers. There are several advantages to specifying the type of values, string or numeric, that can be assigned to a variable. A statement of the form

```
Dim variableName As String
```

specifies that only strings can be assigned to the named variable. A statement of the form

```
Dim variableName As Single
```

specifies that only numbers can be assigned to the named variable. The term Single derives from *single-precision real number*. After you type the space after the word "As," the editor displays a list of all the possible next words. In this text we use only a few of the items from this list.

A Dim statement is said to *declare* a variable. From now on we will declare all variables. However, all the programs will run correctly even if the Dim statements are omitted. Declaring variables at the beginning of each event procedure is regarded as good programming practice because it makes programs easier to read and helps prevent certain types of errors.

This rewrite of an earlier program declares all variables.

```
Private Sub cmdCompute_Click()
    Dim interestRate As Single
    Dim principal As Single
    Dim phrase As String
    picBalance.Cls
    interestRate = 0.0655
    principal = 100
    phrase = "The balance after a year is"
    picBalance.Print phrase; (1 + interestRate) * principal
End Sub
```

Several Dim statements can be combined into one. For instance, the first three Dim statements of the last program in Section 2.4.1 can be replaced by

```
Dim interestRate As Single, principal As Single, phrase As String
```

Visual Basic actually has several different types of numeric variables. So far, we have used only single-precision numeric variables. Single-precision numeric variables can hold numbers of magnitude from as small as $1.4 \times 10 - 45$ to as large as 3.4×10^{38}. Another type of numeric variable, called *Integer*, can hold only whole numbers from –32768 to 32767. Integer-type variables are declared with a statement of the form

```
Dim intVar As Integer
```

The Integer data type uses less memory than the Single data type and statements using the Integer type execute faster. (This is only useful in programs with many calculations, such as the programs that use For...Next loops.) Of course, Integer variables are limited because they cannot hold decimals or large numbers. Integer variables are used extensively with For...Next loops and occasionally when the data clearly consist of small whole numbers.

Other types of numeric variables are Long, Double, and Currency. We do not use them in this text. Whenever we refer to a numeric variable without mentioning a type, we mean Single or Integer.

2.4.4 Scope of Variables

As soon as a variable is declared inside an event procedure with a Dim statement, it is assigned a *default value*. The default value for numeric variables is 0. The default value for string variables is the *null string* "", the string containing no characters. After the event procedure is exited (that is, when End Sub is reached) the variable ceases to exist. The next time the event procedure is invoked, the variable again initially will assume its default value. Such a variable is said to have *local scope*. If two different event procedures have local variables of the same name, these variables are treated as separate entities; they have absolutely no relationship to each other.

There is another way to declare a variable so that its value persists and so that the variable can be recognized by every event procedure associated with the form. Such a variable is said to have *form-level scope*. To declare a form-level variable, place its Dim statement at the top of the code window in the (Declarations) section of (General). Also, do not include a Dim statement for that variable inside any event procedure.

In the next program, x is a form-level variable and y is a local variable.

```
Dim x As Single

Private Sub cmdOne_Click()
    Dim y As Single
    x = x + 1
    y = y + 1
    picBox.Print "x ="; x; " y ="; y
End Sub

Private Sub cmdTwo_Click()
    Dim y As Single
    x = x + 1
    y = y + 1
    picBox.Print "x ="; x; " y ="; y
End Sub

[Run, click the first command button twice, and click the
second command button. The following is displayed in the
picture box.]

                 x = 1       y = 1
                 x = 2       y = 1
                 x = 3       y = 1
```

2.4.5 Using Text Boxes for Input and Output

The content of a text box is always a string. Therefore, statements such as

```
strVar = txtBox.Text
```

and

```
txtBox.Text = strVar
```

can be used to assign the contents of the text box to the string variable *strVar* and vice versa.

Numbers are stored in text boxes as strings. Therefore, they should be converted to numbers before being assigned to numeric variables. If *str* is a string representation of a number, then

```
Val(str)
```

is that number. Conversely, if *num* is a number, then

```
Str(num)
```

is a string representation of the number. Therefore, statements such as

```
numVar = Val(txtBox.Text)
```

and

```
txtBox.Text = Str(numVar)
```

can be used to assign the contents of the text box to the numeric variable *numVar* and vice versa. *Note:* When a nonnegative number is converted to a string with Str, its first character (but not its last character) is a blank space.

Here is a program that converts miles to furlongs and vice versa. *Note:* A furlong is one-eighth of a mile.

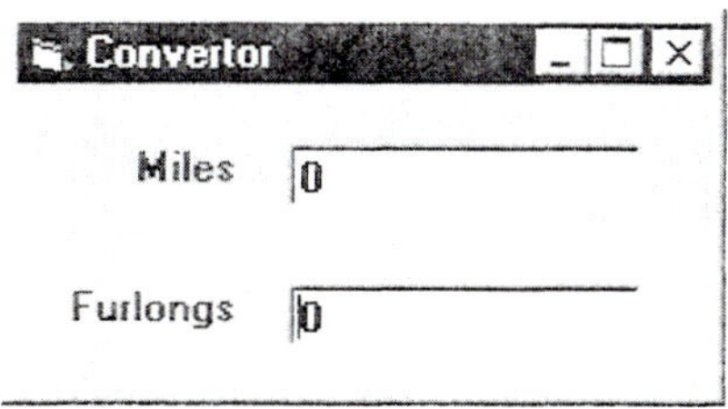

OBJECT	PROPERTY	SETTING
frmConvertor	Caption	Convertor
lblMile	Caption	Miles
txtMile	Text	0
lblFurlong	Caption	Furlongs
txtFurlong	Text	0

The two text boxes have been named txtMile and txtFurlong. With the Event procedures shown, typing a number into a text box and pressing Tab results in the converted number being displayed in the other text box.

```
Private Sub txtMile_LostFocus()
    txtFurlong.Text = Str(8 * Val(txtMile.Text))
End Sub

Private Sub txtFurlong_LostFocus()
    txtMile.Text = Str(Val(txtFurlong.Text) / 8)
End Sub
```

2.4.6 ANSI Character Set

Each of the 47 different keys in the center typewriter portion of the keyboard can produce two characters, for a total of 94 characters. Adding 1 for the space character produced by the space bar makes 95 characters. These characters, which have numbers ranging from 32 to 126 associated with them, are called ANSI (or ASCII) characters.

Most of the best-known fonts, such as Ariel, Courier, Helvetica, and Times New Roman, are essentially governed by the ANSI standard, which assigns characters to most of the numbers from 32 to 255. See Table 2-3.

If *n* is a number between 32 and 255, then

Chr(*n*)

is the string consisting of the character with ANSI value *n*. If *str* is any string, then

TABLE 2-3 ANSI values

Ansi value	Char	Ansi value	Char	Ansi value	Char	Ansi value	Char	Ansi value	Char	Ansi value	Char	Ansi value	Char
32		64	@	96	`	128	€	160		192	À	224	à
33	!	65	A	97	a	129	□	161	¡	193	Á	225	á
34	"	66	B	98	b	130	‚	162	¢	194	Â	226	â
35	#	67	C	99	c	131	ƒ	163	£	195	Ã	227	ã
36	$	68	D	100	d	132	„	164	¤	196	Ä	228	ä
37	%	69	E	101	e	133	…	165	¥	197	Å	229	å
38	&	70	F	102	f	134	†	166	¦	198	Æ	230	æ
39	'	71	G	103	g	135	‡	167	§	199	Ç	231	ç
40	(	72	H	104	h	136	ˆ	168	¨	200	È	232	è
41	)	73	I	105	i	137	‰	169	©	201	É	233	é
42	*	74	J	106	j	138	Š	170	ª	202	Ê	234	ê
43	+	75	K	107	k	139	‹	171	«	203	Ë	235	ë
44	,	76	L	108	l	140	Œ	172	¬	204	Ì	236	ì
45	-	77	M	109	m	141	□	173	-	205	Í	237	í
46	.	78	N	110	n	142	□	174	®	206	Î	238	î
47	/	79	O	111	o	143	□	175	¯	207	Ï	239	ï
48	0	80	P	112	p	144	□	176	°	208	Ð	240	ð
49	1	81	Q	113	q	145	‘	177	±	209	Ñ	241	ñ
50	2	82	R	114	r	146	’	178	²	210	Ò	242	ò
51	3	83	S	115	s	147	“	179	³	211	Ó	243	ó
52	4	84	T	116	t	148	”	180	´	212	Ô	244	ô
53	5	85	U	117	u	149	•	181	µ	213	Õ	245	õ
54	6	86	V	118	v	150	–	182	¶	214	Ö	246	ö
55	7	87	W	119	w	151	—	183	·	215	×	247	÷
56	8	88	X	120	x	152	˜	184	¸	216	Ø	248	ø
57	9	89	Y	121	y	153	™	185	¹	217	Ù	249	ù
58	:	90	Z	122	z	154	š	186	º	218	Ú	250	ú
59	;	91	[	123	{	155	›	187	»	219	Û	251	û
60	<	92	\	124	|	156	œ	188	¼	220	Ü	252	ü
61	=	93	]	125	}	157	□	189	½	221	Ý	253	ý
62	>	94	^	126	~	158	□	190	¾	222	Þ	254	þ
63	?	95	_	127	□	159	Ÿ	191	¿	223	ß	255	ÿ

Asc(*str*)

is the ANSI value of the first character of *str*. For instance, the statement

```
txtBox.Text = Chr(65)
```

displays the letter A in the text box and the statement

```
picBox.Print Asc("Apple")
```

displays the number 65 in the picture box.

Concatenation can be used with Chr to obtain strings using the higher ANSI characters. For instance, with one of the fonts that conforms to the ANSI standard, the statement

```
txtBox.Text = "32" & Chr(176) & " Fahrenheit"
```

displays 32° Fahrenheit in the text box.

2.4.7 String Relationships

The string *a* is said to be less than the string *b* if *a* precedes *b* alphabetically when using the ANSI (or ASCII) table to alphabetize their values. For instance, "cat" < "dog", "cart" < "cat", and "cat" < "catalog". Digits precede uppercase letters, which precede lowercase letters. Two strings are compared left to right, character by character, to determine which one should precede the other. Therefore, "9W" < "bat", "Dog" < "cat", and "Sales-98" < "Sales-retail".

Table 2-4 shows the different relational operators, their representations in Visual Basic, their meanings, and examples.

TABLE 2-4 Relational operators.

MATHEMATICAL NOTATION	VISUAL BASIC NOTATION	MEANING	EXAMPLE
=	=	identical to	"a" = "a"
≠	<>	different from	"a" <> "A"
<	<	precedes alphabetically	"a" < "b"
>	>	follows alphabetically	"b" > "a"
≤	<=	precedes alphabetically or is identical to	"A" <= "B"
≥	>=	follows alphabetically or is identical to	"b" >= "a"

EXAMPLE 2.3:

1. A relationship (or condition) between two strings is either true or false. Determine whether each of the following conditions is true or false.

(a) "G" <= "a" (c) "bar" < "bat"
(b) "A" <= "G" (d) "Bat" < "bat"

SOLUTION

a. True. The uppercase letters come before the lowercase letters in the ANSI table.

b. True. The symbol <= means less than *or* equal. Of course, the condition "A" < "G" is also true.

c. True. The characters of the strings are compared one at a time working from left to right. Because the first two match, the third character decides the order.

d. True. The first character of "Bat" precedes the first character of "bat" in the ANSI table.

2.4.8 String Functions: Left, Mid, Right, UCase, Trim

The functions Left, Mid, and Right are used to extract characters from the left end, middle, and right end of a string. Suppose *str* is a string and *m* and *n* are positive integers. Then Left(*str*, *n*) is the string consisting of the first *n* characters of *str* and Right(*str*, *n*) is the string consisting of the last *n* characters of *str*. Mid(*str*, *m*, *n*) is the string consisting of *n* characters of *str*, beginning with the *m*th character. UCase(*str*) is the string *str* with all of its lowercase letters capitalized. Trim(*str*) is the string *str* with all leading and trailing spaces removed. Some examples are as follows:

Left("fanatic", 3) is "fan".
Right("fanatic", 3) is "tic".
Left("12/15/99", 2) is "12".
Right("12/15/99", 2) is "99".
Mid("fanatic", 5, 1) is "t".
Mid("12/15/99", 4, 2) is "15".
UCase("Disk") is "DISK".
UCase("12three") is "12THREE".
Trim(" 1 2 ") is "1 2".
Trim("–12 ") is "–12".

The strings produced by Left, Mid, and Right are referred to as *substrings* of the strings from which they were formed. For instance, "fan" and "t" are substrings of "fanatic". The substring "fan" is said to begin at position 1 of "fanatic" and the substring "t" is said to begin at position 5.

Like the numeric functions discussed in Section 2.3, Left, Mid, Right, UCase, and Trim also can be evaluated for variables and expressions.

This program evaluates the functions above for variables and expressions. Note that spaces are counted as characters.

```
Private Sub cmdEvaluate_Click()
    Dim str1 As String, str2 As String
    picResults.Cls
    str1 = "Quick as "
    str2 = "a wink"
    picResults.Print Left(str1, 7)
    picResults.Print Mid(str1 & str2, 7, 6)
    picResults.Print UCase(str1 & str2)
    picResults.Print "The average "; Right(str2, 4);
       " lasts .1 second."
    picResults.Print Trim(str1); str2
End Sub

[Run, and then click the command button. The following is
displayed in the picture box.]

Quick a
as a w
QUICK AS A WINK
The average wink lasts .1 second.
Quick asa wink
```

2.4.9 String-Related Numeric Functions: Len, InStr

The functions Len and InStr operate on strings but produce numbers. The function Len gives the number of characters in a string. The function InStr searches for the first occurrence of one string in another and gives the position at which the string is found. Suppose *str1* and *str2* are strings. The value of Len(*str1*) is the number of characters in *str1*. The value of InStr(*str1*, *str2*) is 0 if *str2* is not a substring of *str1*. Otherwise, its value is the first position of *str2* in *str1*. Some examples of Len and InStr follow:

Len("Shenandoah") is 10.
InStr("Shenandoah", "nand") is 4.
Len("Just a moment") is 13.
InStr("Just a moment", " ") is 5.
Len(" ") is 1.
InStr("Croissant", "ist") is 0.

Here is a program that evaluates functions at variables and expressions. The eighth line locates the position of the space separating the two names. The first name will end one position to the left of this position and the last name will consist of all but the first *n* characters of the full name.

```
Private Sub cmdAnalyze_Click()
    Dim nom As String
    Dim n As Integer
    Dim first As String
    Dim last As String
    picResults.Cls
    nom = txtFullName.Text
    n = InStr(nom, " ")
    first = Left(nom, n - 1)
    last = Right(nom, Len(nom) - n)
    picResults.Print "Your first name is "; first
    picResults.Print "Your last name has"; Len(last);
      "letters."
End Sub

[Run, type John Doe into the text box, and then click the
command button.]
```

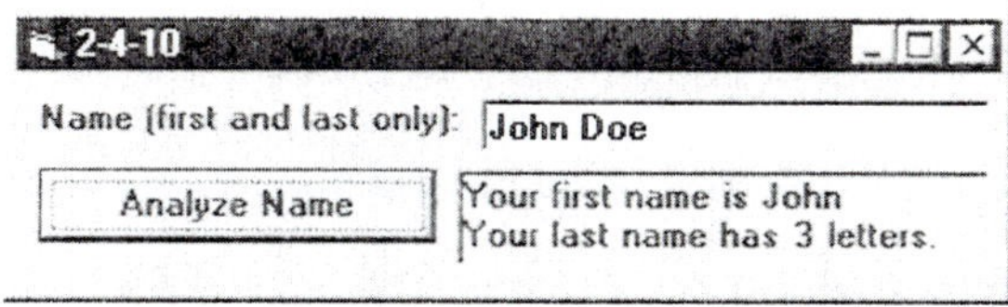

2.4.10 Format Functions

The Format functions are used to display numbers and dates in familiar forms and to right-justify numbers. Here are some examples of how numbers are converted to strings with Format functions.

FUNCTION	STRING VALUE
FormatNumber(12345.628, 1)	12,345.6
FormatCurrency(12345.628, 2)	$12,345.63
FormatPercent(0.185, 2)	18.50%

The value of FormatNumber(*n*, *r*) is the string containing the number *n* rounded to *r* decimal places and displayed with commas every three digits to the left of the decimal point. The value of FormatCurrency(*n*, *r*) is the string consisting of a dollar sign followed by the value of FormatNumber(*n*, *r*). FormatCurrency uses the accountant's convention of using surrounding parentheses to denote negative amounts. The value of FormatPercent(*n*, *r*) is the string consisting of the number *n* displayed as a percent and rounded to *r* decimal places.

With all three functions, *r* can be omitted. If so, the number is rounded to 2 decimal places. Strings corresponding to numbers less than 1 in magnitude have a zero to the left of the decimal point. Also, *n* can be a number, a numeric expression, or even a string corresponding to a number.

FUNCTION	STRING VALUE
FormatNumber(1 + Sqr(2), 3)	2.414
FormatCurrency(−1000)	($1,000.00)
FormatPercent(".005")	0.50%

If *dateString* represents a date in a form such as 7-4-1999, 7-4-99, or 7/4/99, then the value of FormatDateTime(*dateString*, vbLongDate) is a string giving the date in a form such as Sunday, July 04, 1999.

FUNCTION	STRING VALUE
FormatDateTime("9-15-99", vbLongDate)	Wednesday, September 15, 1999
FormatDateTime("10-23-00", vbLongDate)	Monday, October 23, 2000

The value of Format(*expr*, "@@...@"), where "@@...@" is a string of *n* "@" symbols, is the string consisting of the value of *expr* right-justified in a field of *n* spaces. This function is used with fixed-width fonts, such as Courier, to display columns of numbers so that the decimal points and commas are lined up or to display right-justified lists of words. The following examples use a string of 10 "@" symbols.

FUNCTION	STRING VALUE
Format(1234567890, "@@@@@@@@@@")	1234567890
Format(FormatNumber(1234.5), "@@@@@@@@@@")	1,234.50
Format(FormatNumber(12345.67), "@@@@@@@@@@")	12,345.67
Format(FormatCurrency(13580.17), "@@@@@@@@@@")	$13,580.17

2.4.11 Comments

1. The string "", which contains no characters, is different from " ", the string consisting of a single space.
2. The statement picBox.Print, with no string or number, simply skips a line in the picture box.
3. Good programming practice dictates that only string values be assigned to string variables and only numeric values be assigned to numeric variables. Although Visual Basic allows this convention to be violated, so doing sometimes results in the error message "Type mismatch."
4. The quotation-mark character (") can be placed into a string constant by using Chr(34). For example, after the statement

   ```
   txtBox.Text="George " & Chr(34)&"Babe"&Chr(34)&" Ruth"
   ```

   is executed, the text box contains

   ```
   George "Babe" Ruth
   ```

5. Most major programming languages require that all variables be declared before they can be used. Although declaring variables with Dim statements is optional in Visual Basic, you can tell Visual Basic to make declaration mandatory by typing:

```
Option Explicit
```

as the first line in the code window.

Then, if you use a variable without first declaring it in a Dim statement, the message "Variable not defined" will appear as soon as you attempt to run the program. One big advantage of using Option Explicit is that mistyping of variable names will be detected. Otherwise, malfunctions due to typing errors are often difficult to detect.

You can have Visual Basic automatically place Option Explicit at the top of every program you write. The steps are as follows:

a. Press Alt/T/O and click on the Editor tab to invoke the editor options.

b. If the square to the left of "Require Variable Declaration" does not contain a check mark, click on the square and press the OK button.

6. If Val is omitted from the statement

```
numVar = Val(txtBox.Text)
```

or Str is omitted from the statement

```
txtBox.Text = Str(numVar)
```

Visual Basic does not complain, but simply makes the conversion for you. However, errors can arise from omitting Val and Str. For instance, if the contents of txtBox1.Text is 34 and the contents of txtBox2.Text is 56, then the statement

```
numVar = txtBox1.Text + txtBox2.Text
```

assigns the number 3456 rather than 90 to *numVar*. (This is because Visual Basic does not perform the conversion until just before the assignment.) If txtBox1 is empty, then the statement

```
numVar = 3 * txtBox1.Text
```

will stop the program and produce the error message "Type mismatch." We follow the standards of good programming practice by always using Val and Str to convert values between text boxes and numeric variables. Similar considerations apply to conversions involving label captions.

7. Variable names should describe the role of the variable. Also, some programmers use a prefix, such as sng or str, to identify the type of a variable. For example, they would use names like sngInterestRate and strFirstName.

8. Trim is useful when reading data from a text box. Sometimes users type spaces at the end of input. Unless the spaces are removed, they can cause havoc elsewhere in the program. Also, Trim is useful in trimming the leading spaces from numbers that have been converted to strings with Str.

9. Several exercises involve a percentage change, which is calculated as 100* (newValue − oldValue) / oldValue. This amount is often coded as

```
perChange = (newValue - oldValue) / oldValue
picOutput.Print "The change is "; FormatPercent(perChange)
```

The variable perChange holds the decimal form of the percentage change. The FormatPercent function multiplies the decimal form by 100 and appends a percent symbol.

10. FormatCurrency(*n*, *r*) indicates negative numbers with parentheses instead of minus signs. If you prefer minus signs, use FormatCurrency(*n*, *r*, vbFalse). For instance, the value of FormatCurrency(−1234, 2, vbFalse) is "−$1,234.00".
11. As we saw in Comment 9 of the previous section, numbers ending in 5 are sometimes rounded down. Such is never the case with FormatNumber, FormatCurrency, and FormatPercent. For instance, FormatNumber(2.5) is "3.00" and FormatCurrency(8.945) is "$8.95".
12. The value of FormatDateTime(Now, vbLongDate) is today's date. For any positive number *n*, FormatDateTime(Now+n, vbLongDate) is the date *n* days from today and FormatDateTime(Now−n, vbLongDate) is the date *n* days ago.
13. The functions FormatNumber, FormatCurrency, FormatPercent, and FormatDateTime were added to Visual Basic in VB6.0. The same results can be obtained with the Format function alone. However, these new functions execute faster than Format and are easier to use. In addition, they can be placed in VBScript programs that are used to make Web pages interactive.

PRACTICE!

1. Compare the following two statements, where *phrase* is a string variable and *balance* is a numeric variable.

```
picBox.Print "It's whether I "; phrase
picBox.Print "The balance is"; balance
```

Why is the space preceding the second quotation mark necessary for the firstpicBox.Print statement but not for the second picBox.Print statement?

2. A label's caption is a string and can be assigned a value with a statement of the form

```
lblOne.Caption = strVar
```

What is one advantage to using a label for output as opposed to a text box?

3. Write code to add the numbers in txtBox1 and txtBox2, and place the sum in lblThree.

Solutions

1. In the second picBox.Print statement, the item following the second quotation mark is a positive number, which is displayed with a leading space. Because the corresponding item in the first picBox.Print statement is a string, which is *not* displayed with a leading space, a space had to be inserted before the quotation mark.
2. The user cannot enter data into a label from the keyboard. Therefore, if a control is to be used for output only, a label is preferred. *Note:* When using a label for output, you might want to set its BorderStyle property to "1-Fixed Single," so it will be discernable.
3.

```
lblThree.Caption = Str(Val(txtBox1.Text) +
    Val(txtBox2.Text))
```

2.5 INPUT AND OUTPUT

So far we have relied on assignment statements to assign values to variables. Data also can be stored in files and accessed through Input# statements, or data can be supplied by the user in a text box or input box. The Print method, with a little help from commas and the Tab function, can spread out and align the display of data in a picture box or on a printer. Message boxes grab the user's attention and display temporary messages. Comment statements allow the programmer to document all aspects of a program, including a description of the input used and the output to be produced.

2.5.1 Reading Data from Files

You can create data files using Windows' Notepad application. To invoke Notepad from Windows, click the Start button, point to Programs, point to Accessories, and click Notepad. As its name suggests, Notepad is an elementary word processor. You can use it to type and edit data used for Visual Basic files. What you type appears in the Notepad work area, which is the main part of the Notepad window. You can alter what you have typed, and save it as a file for use by Visual Basic.

A file can have either one item per line or many items (separated by commas) can be listed on the same line. Usually, related items are grouped together on a line. For instance, if a file consisted of payroll information, each line would contain the name of a person, that person's hourly wage, and the number of hours that person worked during the week (Figure 2.24). (In this book, strings are enclosed in quotation marks, to distinguish them from numbers, which are written without quotation marks.)

```
"Mike Jones",   7.35, 35
"John Smith",   6.75, 33
```

Figure 2.24. Contents of Staff.txt.

The items of data will be assigned to variables one at a time in the order they appear in the file. That is, "Mike Jones" will be the first value assigned to a variable. After all the items from the first line have been assigned to variables, subsequent requests for values will be read from the next line.

Data stored in a file can be read in order (that is, sequentially) and assigned to variables with the following steps.

1. Choose a number from 1 to 255 to be the reference number for the file.
2. Execute the statement

   ```
   Open "filespec" For Input As #n
   ```

   where *n* is the reference number. This procedure is referred to as *Opening a file for input*. It establishes a communications link between the computer and the disk drive for reading data *from* the disk. Data then can be input from the specified file and assigned to variables in the program.
3. Read items of data in order, one at a time, from the file with Input# statements. The statement

   ```
   Input #n, var
   ```

   causes the program to look in the file for the next available item of data and assign it to the variable *var*. In the file, individual items are separated by commas or line breaks. The variable in the Input# statement should be the same type (that is, string or numeric) as the data to be assigned to it from the file.

4. After the desired items have been read from the file, close the file with the statement

```
Close #n
```

EXAMPLE 2.4:

1. Write a program that uses a file for input and produces the same output as the following code. (The form design for all examples in this section consists of a command button and a picture box.)

```
Private Sub cmdDisplay_Click()
    Dim houseNumber As Single, street As String
    picAddress.Cls
    houseNumber = 1600
    street = "Pennsylvania Ave."
    picAddress.Print "The White House is located at";
    picAddress.Print houseNumber; street
End Sub
```

[Run, and then click the command button. The following is displayed in the picture box.]

```
The White House is located at 1600 Pennsylvania Ave.
```

SOLUTION

1. Use Windows' Notepad to create the file Data.txt containing the following two lines:

```
1600
"Pennsylvania Ave."
```

In the following code, the fifth line looks for the first item of data, 1600, and assigns it to the numeric variable *houseNumber*. (Visual Basic records that this piece of data has been used.) The sixth line looks for the next available item of data, "Pennsylvania Ave.", and assigns it to the string variable *street*. *Note:* You will have to alter the Open statement in the fourth line to tell it where the file Data.txt is located. For instance, if the file is in the root directory (that is, folder) of a diskette in drive A, then the line should read Open "A:\Data.txt" For Input As#1. If the file is located in the subdirectory (that is, folder) Vb6 of the C drive, then the statement should be changed to Open "C:\Vb6\Data.txt" For Input As#1. See Comment 1 for another option.

```
Private Sub cmdDisplay_Click()
    Dim houseNumber As Single, street As String
    picAddress.Cls
    Open "Data.txt" For Input As #1
    Input #1, houseNumber
    Input #1, street
    picAddress.Print "The White House is located at";
    picAddress.Print houseNumber; street
    Close #1
End Sub
```

A single Input# statement can assign values to several different variables. For instance, the two Input# statements in the solution of Example 2.2 can be replaced by the single statement

```
Input #1, houseNumber, street
```

In general, a statement of the form

```
Input #n, var1, var2, ..., varj
```

has the same effect as the sequence of statements

```
Input #n, var1
Input #n, var2
:
Input #n, varj
```

The next program uses the file Staff.txt in Figure 2.24 to compute weekly pay. Notice that the variables in the Input # statement are the same types (String, Single, Single) as the constants in each line of the file.

```
Private Sub cmdCompute_Click()
    Dim nom As String, wage As Single, hrs As Single
    picPay.Cls
    Open "Staff.txt" For Input As #1
    Input #1, nom, wage, hrs
    picPay.Print nom; hrs * wage
    Input #1, nom, wage, hrs
    picPay.Print nom; hrs * wage
    Close #1
End Sub
```

[Run, and then click the command button. The following will be displayed in the picture box.]

```
Mike Jones 257.25
John Smith 222.75
```

In certain situations, we must read the data in a file more than once. This is accomplished by closing the file and reopening it. After a file is closed and then reopened, subsequent Input # statements begin reading from the first entry of the file.

Here is a program that takes the average annual amounts of money spent by single-person households for several categories and converts these amounts to percentages. The data are read once to compute the total amount of money spent and then read again to calculate the percentage for each category. *Note:* These figures were compiled for the year 1995 by the Bureau of Labor Statistics.

Costs.txt consists of the following four lines:

"Transportation", 3887
"Housing", 7643
"Food", 3017
"Other", 7804

```
Private Sub cmdCompute_Click()
    Dim total As Single, category As String, amount As Single
    Open "Costs.txt" For Input As #1
    picPercent.Cls
    total = 0
    Input #1, category, amount
    total = total + amount
    Input #1, category, amount
```

```
        total = total + amount
        Input #1, category, amount
        total = total + amount
        Input #1, category, amount
        total = total + amount
        Close #1
        Open "Costs.txt" For Input As #1
        Input #1, category, amount
        picPercent.Print category, FormatPercent(amount / total)
        Input #1, category, amount
        picPercent.Print category, FormatPercent(amount / total)
        Input #1, category, amount
        picPercent.Print category, FormatPercent(amount / total)
        Input #1, category, amount
        picPercent.Print category, FormatPercent(amount / total)
        Close #1
    End Sub
```

[Run, and then click the command button. The following is displayed in the picture box.]

```
Transportation 17.39%
Housing 34.20%
Food 13.50%
Other 34.92%
```

2.5.2 Input from an Input Box

Normally, a text box is used to obtain input described by a label. Sometimes, we want just one piece of input and would rather not have a text box and label stay on the screen forever. The problem can be solved with an *input box*. When a statement of the form

```
stringVar = InputBox(prompt, title)
```

is executed, an input box similar to the one shown in Figure 2.25 pops up on the screen. After the user types a response into the text box at the bottom of the screen and presses Enter (or clicks OK), the response is assigned to the string variable. The *title* argument is optional and gives the caption to appear in the Title bar. The *prompt* argument is a string that tells the user what information to type into the text box.

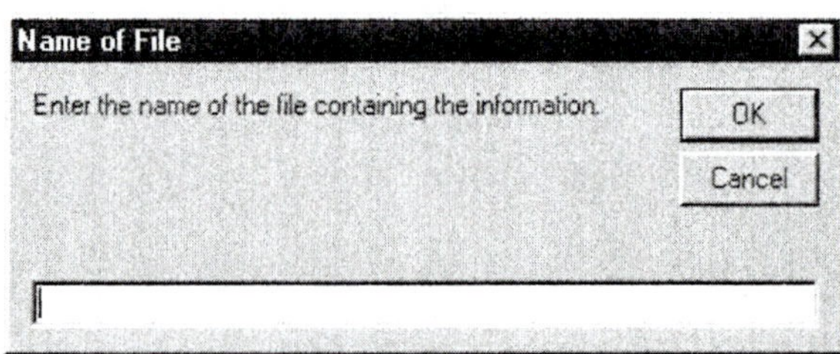

Figure 2.25. Sample input box.

When you type the parenthesis following the word InputBox, the editor displays a line containing the general form of the InputBox statement (Figure 2.26). This feature, which was added in Visual Basic 5.0, is called *Quick Info*. Optional parameters are surrounded by brackets. All the parameters in the general form of the InputBox statement are optional except for *prompt*.

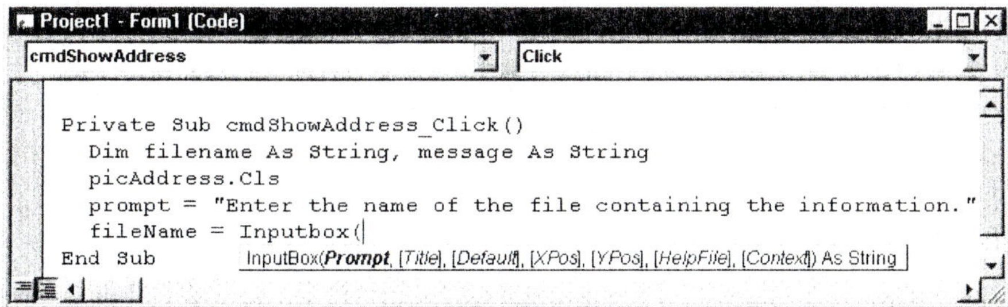

Figure 2.26. Quick Info feature.

In the following solution to Example 1, the file name is provided by the user in an input box.

```
Private Sub cmdDisplay_Click()
    Dim fileName As String, prompt As String, title As String
    Dim houseNumber As Single, street As String
    picAddress.Cls
    prompt = "Enter the name of the file."
    title = "Name of File"
    fileName = InputBox(prompt, title)
    Open fileName For Input As #1
    Input #1, houseNumber
    Input #1, street
    picAddress.Print "The White House is located at";
    picAddress.Print houseNumber; street
    Close #1
End Sub
```

[Run, and then click the command button. The input box of Figure 2.25 appears on the screen. Type Data.txt (possibly preceded with a path) into the input box and click on OK. The input box disappears and the following appears in the picture box.]

```
The White House is located at 1600 Pennsylvania Ave.
```

The response typed into an input box is treated as a single string value, no matter what is typed. (Quotation marks are not needed and, if included, are considered as part of the string.) Numeric data typed into an input box should be converted to a number with Val before it is assigned to a numeric variable or used in a calculation.

2.5.3 Formatting Output with Print Zones

Each line in a picture box can be thought of as being subdivided into zones, as shown in Figure 2.27 Each zone contains 14 positions, where the width of a position is the average width of the characters in the font.

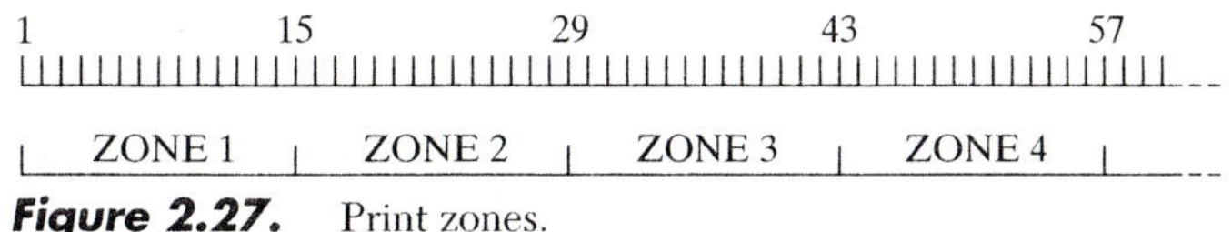

Figure 2.27. Print zones.

We have seen that when the Print method is followed by several items separated by semicolons, the items are displayed one after another. When commas are used instead of semicolons, the items are displayed in consecutive zones. For instance, if the

Font property of picBox is set to Courier, when the motto of the state of Alaska is displayed with the statements

```
picBox.Print "North", "to", "the", "future."
picBox.Print"123456789012345678901234567890123456789012345678900"
```

the resulting picture box is

```
North           to              the             future.
12345678901234567890123456789012345678901234567890
```

where each word is in a separate print zone. This same output can be achieved with the code

```
Dim a As String, b As String, c As String, d As String
a = "North"
b = "to"
c = "the"
d = "future."
picBox.Print a, b, c, d
picBox.Print"12345678901234567890123456789012345678901234567890"
```

The following program uses Print zones to organize expenses for public and private schools into columns of a table. The data represent the average expenses for 1999–2000. (The Font setting for picTable is the default font MS Sans Serif.)

```
Private Sub cmdDisplay_Click()
    picTable.Cls
    picTable.Print " ", "Pb 2-yr", "Pr 2-yr", "Pb 4-yr",
    picTable.Print "Pr 4-yr"
    picTable.Print
    picTable.Print "Tuit & Fees", 1627, 7182, 3356, 15380
    picTable.Print "Bks & Suppl", 645, 681, 681, 700
    picTable.Print "Board", 2128, 4583, 4730, 5959
    picTable.Print " ", "-----", "-----", "-----", "-----"
    picTable.Print "Total", 4400, 12446, 8767, 22039
End Sub
```

[Run, and then click the command button. The following is displayed in the picture box.]

	PB 2-YR	PR 2-YR	PB 4-YR	PR 4-YR
Tuit & Fees	1627	7182	3356	15380
Bks & Suppl	645	681	681	700
Room & Board	2128	4583	4730	5959
	———	———	———	———
Total	4400	12446	8767	22039

2.5.4 Tab Function

If an item appearing in a Print statement is preceded by

```
Tab(n);
```

where *n* is a positive integer, that item will be displayed (if possible) beginning at the *n*th position of the line. (Exceptions are discussed in Comment 10.)

Here is a program that uses the Tab function to organize data into columns of a table. The data represent the number of bachelor's degrees conferred (in units of 1000). (*Source:* National Center of Educational Statistics.)

```
Private Sub cmdDisplay_Click()
    picTable.Cls
    picTable.Print Tab(10); "1970-71"; Tab(20); "1980-81";
    picTable.Print Tab(30); "1990-91"
    picTable.Print
    picTable.Print "Male"; Tab(10); 476; Tab(20); 470;
    picTable.Print Tab(30); 490
    picTable.Print "Female"; Tab(10); 364; Tab(20); 465;
    picTable.Print Tab(30); 560
    picTable.Print "Total"; Tab(10); 840; Tab(20); 935;
    picTable.Print Tab(30); 1050
End Sub
```

[Run, and then click the command button. The resulting picture box is shown.]

	1970-71	1980-81	1990-91
Male	476	470	490
Female	364	465	560
Total	840	935	1050

2.5.5 Using a Message Box for Output

Sometimes you want to grab the user's attention with a brief message such as "Correct" or "Nice try, but no cigar." You want this message only to appear on the screen until the user has read it. This mission is easily accomplished with a *message box* such as the one shown in Figure 2.28 When a statement of the form

```
MsgBox prompt, , title
```

is executed, where *prompt* and *title* are strings, a message box with *prompt* displayed and the title bar caption *title* appears, and stays on the screen until the user presses Enter or clicks OK. For instance, the statement MsgBox "Nice try, but no cigar.", "Consolation" produces Figure 2.28 If you use double quotation marks ("") for *title*, the title bar will be blank.

Figure 2.28. Sample message box.

2.5.6 Line Continuation Character

Up to 1023 characters can be typed in a line of code. If you use a line with more characters than can fit in the window, Visual Basic scrolls the window toward the right as needed. However, most programmers prefer having lines that are no longer than the width of the code window. This can be achieved with the underscore character (_)

preceded by a space. Make sure the underscore doesn't appear inside quotation marks, though. For instance, the line

```
msg ="640K ought to be enough for anybody. (Bill Gates, 1981)"
```

can be written as

```
msg ="640K ought to be enough for" & _
"anybody. (Bill Gates, 1981)"
```

2.5.7 Output to the Printer

You print text on a sheet of paper in the printer in much the same way you display text in a picture box. Visual Basic treats the printer as an object named Printer. If *expr* is a string or numeric expression, then the statement

```
Printer.Print expr
```

sends *expr* to the printer in exactly the same way picBox.Print sends output to a picture box. You can use semicolons, commas for print zones, and Tab.

Font properties can be set with statements like

```
Printer.Font.Name = "Script"
Printer.Font.Bold = True
Printer.Font.Size = 12
```

Another useful printer command is

```
Printer.NewPage
```

which starts a new page.

Windows' print manager usually waits until an entire page has been completed before starting to print. To avoid losing information, execute the statement

```
Printer.EndDoc
```

when you are finished printing.

The statement

```
PrintForm
```

prints the content of the form.

2.5.8 Internal Documentation

Now that we have the capability to write more complicated programs, we must concern ourselves with program documentation. *Program documentation* is the inclusion of comments that specify the intent of the program, the purpose of the variables, the nature of the data in the files, and the tasks performed by individual portions of the program. To create a comment line, just begin the line with an apostrophe. Such a line is completely ignored when the program is executed. (The keyword Rem can be used instead of the apostrophe. Rem is an abbreviation for Remark.) Program documentation appears whenever the program is displayed or printed. Also, a line of code can be documented by adding an apostrophe followed by the desired information to the end of the line. Comments (also known as Rem statements) appear green on the screen.

EXAMPLE 2.5:

1. Document the first program on page 59.

SOLUTION

1. In the following program, the first comment describes the entire program, the next three comments give the meanings of the variables, and the final comment describes the items in each line of the file.

```
Private Sub cmdCompute_Click()
    'Compute weekly pay
    Dim nom As String 'Employee name
    Dim wage As Single 'Hourly pay
    Dim hrs As Single 'Number of hours worked during week
    picPay.Cls
    Open "Staff.txt" For Input As #1
    'person's name, person's wage, person's hours worked
    Input #1, nom, wage, hrs
    picPay.Print nom; hrs * wage
    Input #1, nom, wage, hrs
    picPay.Print nom; hrs * wage
    Close #1
End Sub
```

Some of the benefits of documentation are as follows:

1. Other people can easily comprehend the program.
2. The program can be understood when read later.
3. Long programs are easier to read because the purposes of individual pieces can be determined at a glance.

2.5.9 Comments

1. Visual Basic provides a convenient device for accessing a file that resides in the same folder as the (saved) program. After a program has been saved in a folder, the value of App.Path is the string consisting of the name of the folder. Therefore, if a program contains a line such as

   ```
   Open App.Path & "\Data.txt" For Input As #1
   ```

   Visual Basic will look for the file Data.txt in the folder containing the program.
2. The text box and input box provide a whole new dimension to the capabilities of a program. The user, rather than the programmer, can provide the data to be processed.
3. A string used in a file does not have to be enclosed by quotation marks. The only exceptions are strings containing commas or leading and trailing spaces.
4. If an Input # statement looks for a string and finds a number, it will treat the number as a string. Suppose the first two entries in the file Data.txt are the numbers 2 and 3.

```
Private Sub cmdButton_Click()
    Dim a As String, b As String
    picBox.Cls
    Open "Data.txt" For Input As #1
    Input #1, a, b
    picBox.Print a + b
    Close #1
End Sub
```

```
[Run and then click the command button. The following is
displayed in the picture box.]

23
```

5. If an Input # statement looks for a number and finds a string, the Input # statement will assign the value 0 to the numeric variable. For instance, suppose the first two entries in the file Data.txt are "ten" and 10. Then after the statement

   ```
   Input #1, num1, num2
   ```

   is executed, where *num1* and *num2* are numeric variables, the values of these variables will be 0 and 10.

6. If all the data in a file have been read by Input # statements and another item is requested by an Input # statement, a box will appear displaying the message "Input past end of file."

7. Numeric data in a text box, input box, or file must be a constant. It *cannot* be a variable or an expression. For instance, num, 1 / 2, and 2 + 3 are not acceptable.

8. To skip a Print zone, just include two consecutive commas.

9. Print zones are usually employed to align information into columns. Because most fonts have proportionally-spaced characters, wide characters occupy more than one fixed-width column and narrow characters occupy less. The best and most predictable results are obtained when a fixed-pitch font (such as Courier) is used with print zones.

10. The Tab function cannot be used to move the cursor to the left. If the position specified in a Tab function is to the left of the current cursor position, the cursor will move to that position on the next line. For instance, the line

    ```
    picBox.Print "hello"; Tab(3); "good-bye"
    ```

    results in the output

    ```
    hello
      good-bye
    ```

11. The statement Close, without any reference number, closes all open files.

PRACTICE!

1. What is the difference in the outcomes of the following two sets of lines of code?

```
Input #1, num1, num2
picOutput.Print num1 + num2
```

```
Input #1, num1
Input #1, num2
picOutput.Print num1 + num2
```

2. What is the difference in the outcomes of the following two sets of lines of code?

```
strVar = InputBox("How old are you?", "Age")
numVar = Val(strVar)
picOutput.Print numVar
```

```
numVar = Val(InputBox("How old are you?", "Age"))
picOutput.Print numVar
```

Solutions

1. The outputs are identical. This book tends to use a single Input # statement for each line of the file.
2. The outcomes are identical. This book uses the second style.

2.6 BUILT-IN FUNCTIONS

2.6.1 Algebraic Functions

Table 2-5 shows four well-known algebraic functions that are part of the Visual Basic language. Abs strips the minus signs from negative numbers while leaving other numbers unchanged. Exp raises the number e (approximately 2.71828) to a power. Log gives the power to which e must be raised to obtain the input value. Sqr returns the nonnegative number whose square is the input value.

TABLE 2-5 Visual Basic built-in algebraic functions

VISUAL BASIC FUNCTION	NAME	CORRESPONDING MATHEMATICAL FUNCTION
Abs	Absolute value function	$\|x\|$
Exp	Exponential function	e^x
Log	Natural logarithmic function	$\ln x$
Sqr	Square root function	$\sqrt{x}$

EXAMPLE 2.6: The following program evaluates these four functions.

```
Private Sub cmdEvaluate_Click()
    Dim x As Single, y As Single
    'Illustrate the use of the built-in algebraic functions
    picOutput.Cls
```

```
    x = 3
    y = -5
    picOutput.Print Abs(1.2); Abs(y); Abs(5 * x + 3 * y)
    picOutput.Print Exp(1); Exp(0); Exp(x + y)
    picOutput.Print Log(1); Log(2); Log(Exp(x))
    picOutput.Print Sqr(4); Sqr(x + 1)
End Sub
```

[Run, and press the command button. The following is displayed in the picture box.]

```
1.2  5  0
2.71828182845905  1  0.135335283236613
0  0.693147180559945  3
2  2
```

EXAMPLE 2.7: The program in this example applies in this example the absolute value function.

```
Private Sub cmdDisplay_Click()
    'Apply the Abs function
    picoutput.Cls
    picOutput.Print "The difference between your age and the"
    picOutput.Print "median age in the United States is";
    picOutput.Print Abs(35 - Val(txtAge.Text)); "years."
End Sub
```

[Run, type your age into the text box, and press the command button. If you typed 21, the following is displayed in the picture box.]

```
The difference between your age and the
median age in the United States is 14 years.
```

EXAMPLE 2.8: The following program applies the functions Exp and Log.

```
Private Sub cmdDisplay-Click()
    Dim amount As Single, interestRate As Single
    amount = txtAmount.Text
    interestRate = txtRate.Text
    picOutput.Print "With interest compounded continuously,"
    picOutput.Print "in two years"
    picOutput.Print "the money will grow to";
    picOutput.Print FormatCurrency(amount * Exp(interestRate * 2));
    picOutput.Print " dollars."
    picOutput.Print
    picOutput.Print "The money will double in ";
    picOutput.Print FormatNumber(Log(2) / interestRate);
    picOutput.Print " years."
End Sub
```

```
[Run, type numbers into the text boxes, and then click the
command button.]
```

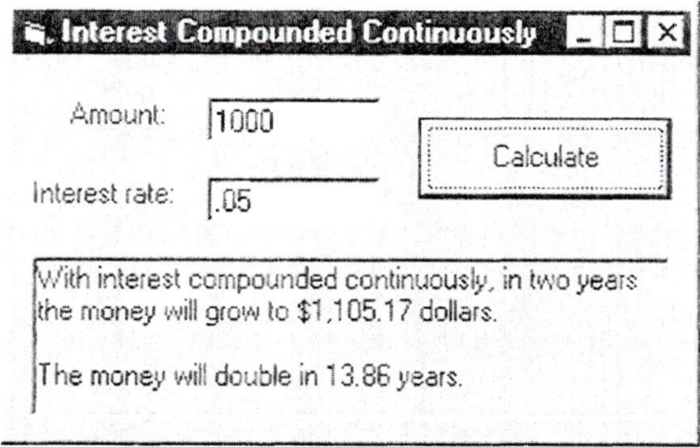

2.6.2 Trigonometric Functions

Table 2-6 shows the four trigonometric functions that are part of the Visual Basic language. The angles for these functions are measured in radians. Atn(x) is the angle between $-\pi/2$ and $\pi/2$ whose tangent is x. Since an angle of $\pi/4$ radians has tangent 1, Atn(1) has value $\pi/4$ and 4*Atn(1) has value π. Therefore, the statement π = 4*Atn(1) provides an accurate way to assign π its value. The first three functions are determined by the point of intersection of the circle of radius 1 and the angle (with fixed side on the positive x-axix) having the input value. Cos is the x-coordinate of the point, Sin is the y-coordinate of the point, and Tan is the y-coordinate divided by the x-coordinate. For an angle x between 0 and $\pi/2$ degrees, the three functions are also defined in terms of the lengths of the sides of a right triangle having an angle of x radians by

$$\text{Cos(x)} = \frac{\text{length of side adjacent to the angle}}{\text{length of hypotenuse}}$$

$$\text{Sin(x)} = \frac{\text{length of side opposite the angle}}{\text{length of hypotenuse}}$$

$$\text{Tan(x)} = \frac{\text{length of side opposite the angle}}{\text{length of side adjacent to the angle}}$$

TABLE 2-6 Visual Basic's built-in trigonometric functions.

VISUAL BASIC FUNCTION	NAME	CORRESPONDING MATHEMATICAL FUNCTION
Cos	Cosine function	$\cos x$
Sin	Sine function	$\sin x$
Tan	Tangent function	$\tan x$
Atn	Inverse tangent function	$\arctan x$ or $\tan^{-1}x$

EXAMPLE 2.9: Here is a program that illustrates these four trigonometric functions.

```
Private Sub cmdDisplay_Click()
    Dim pi As Single, angleInDegrees As Single,
        angleInRadians As Single
    'Illustrate the use of the built-in trigonometric
        functions
    picOutput.Cls
    pi = 4 * Atn(1)
    picOutput.Print Cos(pi); Sin(pi); Tan(pi)
    angleInDegrees = 45
        'Angle measured in degrees
    angleInRadians = angleInDegrees * (pi / 180)
        'Angle measured in radians
    picOutput.Print Cos(angleInRadians); Sin(angleInRadians);
        Tan(angleInRadians)
End Sub
```

```
[Run, and press the command button. The following is displayed
in the picture box.]

-1  -3.258414E-07  3.258414E-07
.7071067  .7071068  1
```

EXAMPLE 2.10: This program applies the Sin and Cos functions to analyze projectile motion. (Air resistance is neglected.)

```
Private Sub cmdCalculate_Click()
    Dim pi As Single, angleInRadians As Single
    Dim timeInAir As Single, distance As Single
    'Apply the built-in trigonometric functions
    'Suppose a projectile is fired from ground level at a
        specified
    'angle of elevation (in degrees) and initial velocity (in
        feet per second)
    picOutput.Cls
    pi = 4 * Atn(1)
    angleInRadians = txtAngle * (pi / 180) 'Angle measured in
        radians
    timeInAir = txtVel * Sin(angleInRadians) / 16
    picOutput.Print "The projectile is in the air for";
        timeInAir; "seconds."
    distance = txtVel * Cos(angleInRadians) * timeInAir
    picOutput.Print "The projectile lands"; distance; "feet
        away."
End Sub
```

```
[Run, type 40 into the first text box, type 137 into the
second text box, and press the command button.]
```

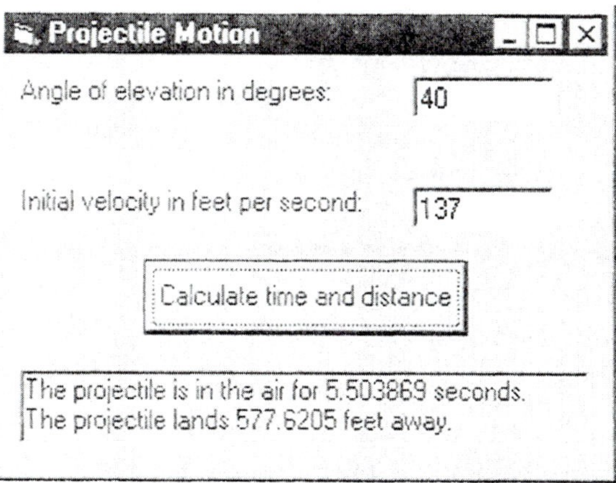

EXAMPLE 2.11: The following program uses the Tan function to obtain the height of a building given the distance of the building from an observer and angle of elevation from the ground to the top of the building. The function Atn is used to obtain the value of π, which is needed to convert from degrees to radians.

```
Private Sub cmdCalculate_Click()
    Dim pi As Single, angleInRadians As Single, height As
        Single
    'Compute the height of a building
    picOutput.cls
    pi = 4 * Atn(1)
    angleInRadians = (pi/180) * txtAngle 'Convert from
        degrees to radians
    height = txtDistance Tan(angleInRadians)
    picOutput.Print "The height of the building is"; height;
        "feet."
End Sub
```

```
[Run, type numbers into the text boxes, and press the command
button.]
```

Determine Height of a Building

Distance from building (in feet): 100

Angle of elevation (in degrees) to top of building: 50

Calculate Height of Building

The height of the building is 119.1754 feet.

2.6.3 Miscellaneous Functions

Table 2-7 shows three well-known algebraic functions that are part of the Visual Basic language. *Fix* throws away the decimal part of a number. *Int* returns the greatest whole number less than or equal to the input value. Fix and Int have the same effect on positive numbers. Noninteger negative numbers are increased by Fix and are decreased by Int. For example, Fix(5.7) = Int(5.7) = 5, Fix(–5.7) = –5, and Int(–5.7) = –6.

Sgn tells whether a number is positive, negative, or zero. (Sgn(x) is 1, –1, or 0 if x is positive, negative, or zero, respectively.)

TABLE 2-7 Miscellaneous Visual Basic built-in functions.

VISUAL BASIC FUNCTION	NAME
Fix	Truncate function
Int	Greatest integer function
Sgn	Sign function

EXAMPLE 2.12: The program in this example illustrates the Fix, Int, and Sgn functions.

```
Private Sub cmdDisplay_Click()
    'Illustrate the use of several built-in functions
    picOutput.Cls
    picOutput.Print Fix(1.2); Fix(-3.7)
    picOutput.Print Int(1.2); Int(-3.7)
    picOutput.Print Sgn(2); Sgn(-2); Sgn(0)
End Sub
```

```
[Run and press the command button. The following is displayed
in the picture box.]
```

```
1 -3
1 -4
1 -1   0
```

2.6.4 Types of Numeric Variables

Visual Basic can work with five types of numeric variables, referred to as integer, long integer, single-precision, double-precision, and currency. So far, all numeric variables have been integer or single-precision. Table 2-8 describes the five sets of numbers. Integers are used to save time and memory space. Long integers give perfect accuracy in certain whole number calculations. Double-precision numbers should be used when values must be especially precise. Currency numbers are useful for calculations involving money.

Currency variables are stored as 64-bit (8-byte) numbers in an integer format scaled by 10,000 to give a fixed-point number with 15 digits to the left of the decimal point and 4 digits to the right. This representation provides a range of -922,337,203,685,477.5808 to 922,337,203,685,477.5807. A variable is declared in a Dim statement to have type long integer, double-precisior, or currency by using the keywords Long, Double, or Currency.

If a value of one type is assigned to a variable of another type, the value is converted to the type of the variable if possible. For instance, if a number with a decimal part is assigned to an integer variable, the number is rounded to the nearest integer. If the rounded value is too large, then an error message is generated.

TABLE 2-8 Visual Basic numeric variable types.

TYPE	DESCRIPTION
Integer	Whole numbers from −32,768 to 32,767
Long integer	Whole numbers from −2,147,483,648 to 2,147,483,647
Single-precision	0 and numbers with 7 significant digits and magnitude between about $1.4°10^{-45}$ and $3.4°10^{38}$
Double-precision	0 and numbers with 15 significant digits and magnitude between about $4.9°10^{-324}$ and $1.8°10^{308}$
Currency	Numbers from −922,337,203,685,477.5808 to 922,337,203,685,477.5807, with four digits to the right of the decimal point and up to fifteen to the left of the decimal point. Arithmetic is exact within this range.

2.6.5 Comments

1. When Visual Basic rounds to the nearest integer, numbers such as 3.5 or 4.5 are rounded to the nearest even number. That is, both of these numbers would be rounded to 4.

2. The built-in trigonometric functions return double-precision values, no matter what the type of the argument.

3. The remaining trigonometric functions can be defined in terms of the functions Cos, Sin, Tan, and Atn as follows:

```
secant (x) = 1 / Cos (x)
cosecant(x) = 1 / Sin(x)
cotangent(x) = 1 / Tan(x)
arcsin (x) = Atn(x / Sqr (1 - x * x)); x ≠ -1, 1
```

$$\text{arccos}(x) = \frac{\pi}{2} - \text{Atn}(x / \text{Sqr}(1 - x * x));\ x \neq -1, 1$$

$$\text{arccot}(x) = \frac{\pi}{2} - \text{Atn}(x)$$

$$\text{arcsec}(x) = \frac{\pi}{2} - \text{Sgn}(x) * (\frac{\pi}{2} - \text{Atn}(\text{Sqr}(x * x - 1)))$$

$$\text{arccsc}(x) = \text{Sgn}(x) * (\frac{\pi}{2} - \text{Atn}(\text{Sqr}(x * x - 1)))$$

4. The common logarithmic function can be defined in terms of the natural logarithmic function as follows:

$$\log_{10}x = \text{Log}(x)/\text{Log}(10)$$

In general, $\log_b x = \text{Log}(x)/\text{Log}(b)$

PRACTICE!

1. Write lines of code that request a number of inches and convert it to feet and inches.

Solutions

1. The solution requires long division. When m is divided into n, the quotient is $q = \text{Int}(n/m)$ and the remainder is $r = n - qm$.

```
Dim length As Single, feet As Single, remainder As Single
'Convert inches to feet and inches
length = InputBox("Enter length in inches:",
    "Length to Convert")
feet = Int(length / 12)
remainder = length - feet * 12
picOutput.Print feet; "feet"; remainder; "inches"
```

2.7 PROGRAMMING PROJECTS

1. Write a program that allows the user to specify two numbers and then adds, subtracts, or multiplies them when the user clicks on the appropriate command button. The output should give the type of arithmetic performed and the result.
2. The resistance of a conductor made from a homogeneous material is given by

$$R = \rho \cdot L/A$$

where ρ is the resistivity of the material (in ohm · meters), L is the length of the conductor (in meters), and A is the area of a cross section (in square meters). For a bar of annealed copper, $\rho = 1.724 \cdot 10^{-8}$ ohm·meters. $L = 200$ cm, and $A = .25\text{cm}^2$. Write a program to convert the length and the area to meters and square meters, respectively, and calculate the resistance of the bar. The material, the resistivity, the length, and the area should be entered into text boxes. The computer should display the material and the resistance as shown in the sample run below.

```
[Run, enter the information into the text boxes, and press the
command button.]
```

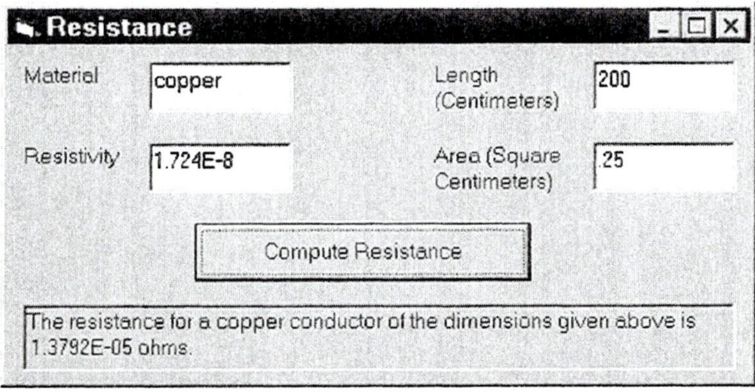

3. Write a program to produce three fines of a trigonometry table. The program should request a number of degrees, n, as input and display the values of the sine,

cosine, tangent, and cotangent functions for angles of $n - 1$, n, and $n + 1$ degrees. The values should be displayed with five decimal places neatly in labeled columns. A sample output is as follows.

```
[Run and respond with 120 for the degree of the angle. The
output in the picture box is shown below.]

  Degrees     Sin         Cos         Tan          Cot
  119         0.87462     -.48481     -1.80405     -.55431
  120         0.86602     -.50000     -1.73205     -.57735
  121         0.85717     -.51504     -1.66428     -.60086
```

4. The general law of perfect gases states that

$$PV/T = nR = \text{constant}$$

where P is the gas pressure (in atmospheres), V is the volume (in liters), T is the temperature (in degrees Kelvin), n is the number of moles, and R is the constant of perfect gases (.082 liter-atm/Kelvin-mole). Write a program to produce Table 2-9 for the case $n = 1$, $V = RT/P$. The temperatures and pressures should be stored in a text file.

TABLE 2-9 Relationships between temperatures, pressures, and volumes in a perfect gas.

Temperature (Celsius)	Pressure (atm)	Temperature (Kelvin)	Volume (liter)
150	2.280	423	15.213
200	17.287	473	2.244
250	74.375	523	0.577

5. Table 2.14 gives the distribution of the U.S. population (in thousands) by age group and sex. Write a program to produce the table shown in Figure 2.29 For each age group, the column labeled %Males gives the percentage of the people in that age group that are male and similarly for the column labeled %Females. The last column gives the percentage of the total population in each age group. (*Note:* Store the information in Figure 2.10 in a data file. For instance, the first line in the file should be "Under 20", 39168, 37202. Read and add up the data once to obtain the total population, and then read the data again to produce the table.)

TABLE 2-10 U.S. resident population (1996) in thousands.

AGE GROUP	MALES	FEMALES
Under 20	39,168	37,202
20–64	76,761	78,291
Over 64	13,881	19,980

```
                 U.S. Population (in thousands)

Age group    Males     Females    %Males    %Females    %Total

Under 20    39,168    37,202    51.29%    48.71%    28.79%
20-64       76,761    78,291    49.51%    50.49%    58.45%
Over 64     13,881    19,980    40.99%    59.01%    12.76%
```

Figure 2.29. Output of Programming Project 5.

KEY TERMS

Assignment statement
Condition
Control
Event procedure
Form window
Function
Input box
Message box
Method
Numeric data type
Object
Operator
Property
Scope
String data type
Variable

Problems

PROBLEMS FOR SECTION 2.1

1. Why are command buttons sometimes called "push buttons?"
2. How can you tell if a program is running by looking at the screen?
3. Create a form with two command buttons, run the program, and click on each button. Do you notice anything different about a button after it has been clicked?
4. Place a text box on a form and select the text box. What is the effect of pressing the various arrow keys while holding down the Ctrl key? The Shift key?
5. Place three text boxes vertically on a form with Text3 above Text2, and Text2 above Text1. Then run the program and successively press Tab. Notice that the text boxes receive the focus from bottom to top. Experiment with various configurations of command buttons and text boxes to convince yourself that objects get the focus in the order in which they were created.
6. While a program is running, an object is said to *lose focus* when the focus moves from that object to another object. In what three ways can the user cause an object to lose focus?

In Problems 7 to 24, carry out the task. Use a new form for each exercise.

7. Place CHECKING ACCOUNT in the title bar of a form.
8. Create a text box containing the words PLAY IT, SAM in blue letters.
9. Create an empty text box with a yellow background.
10. Create a text box containing the word HELLO in large italic letters.
11. Create a text box containing the sentence "After all is said and done, more is said than done." The sentence should occupy three lines and each line should be centered in the text box.
12. Create a borderless text box containing the words VISUAL BASIC in bold white letters on a red background.
13. Create a text box containing the words VISUAL BASIC in Courier font.
14. Create a command button containing the word PUSH.
15. Create a label containing the word ALIAS.
16. Create a label containing the word ALIAS in white on a blue background.
17. Create a label with a border containing the centered italicized word ALIAS.
18. Create a label containing VISUAL on the first line and BASIC on the second line. Each word should be right justified. (*Note:* An extra space will appear after "VISUAL.")
19. Create a label containing a picture of a diskette. (*Hint:* Use the Wingdings character < .) Make the diskette large.

20. Create a label with a border and containing the bold word ALIAS in the Terminal font.
21. Create a picture box with a yellow background.
22. Create a picture box with no border and a red background.
23. Create a picture box containing two command buttons.
24. Create a picture box with a blue background containing a picture box with a white background.

In Problems 25 to 30, create the interface shown in the figure. (These exercises give you practice creating objects and assigning properties. The interfaces do not necessarily correspond to actual programs.)

25.

Dynamic Duo

Batman

Robin

26.

Enter Names

Name

Enter

27.

Fill in the Blank

Toto, I don't think we're in

A Quote from the Wizard of Oz

28.

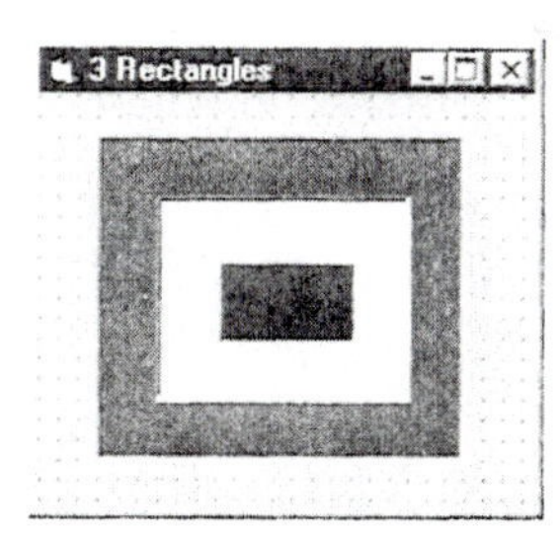

29.

An Uncle's Advice

The three most important things in life are

1 Be kind.

2 Be kind.

3 Be kind.

Henry James' advice to his nephew

30.

3 Rectangles

PROBLEMS FOR SECTION 2.2

In Problems 1 to 4, describe the contents of the text box after the command button is clicked.

1.

```
Private Sub cmdButton_Click()
     txtBox.Text = "Hello"
End Sub
```

2.

```
Private Sub cmdButton_Click()
     txtBox.ForeColor = vbRed
     txtBox.Text = "Hello"
End Sub
```

3.
```
Private Sub cmdButton_Click()
     txtBox.Font.Italic = True
     txtBox.Text = "Hello"
End Sub
```

4.
```
Private Sub cmdButton_Click()
     txtBox.Font.Size = 24
     txtBox.Text = "Hello"
End Sub
```

In Problems 5 to 8, assume the three objects on the form were created in the order txtOne, txtTwo, and lblOne. Also assume that txtOne has the focus. Determine the output displayed in lblOne when Tab is pressed.

5.
```
Private Sub txtOne_LostFocus()
     lblOne.ForeColor = vbGreen
     lblOne.Caption = "Hello"
End Sub
```

6.
```
Private Sub txtOne_LostFocus()
     lblOne.Caption = "Hello"
End Sub
```

7.
```
Private Sub txtTwo_GotFocus()
     lblOne.Font.Name = "Courier"
     lblOne.Font.Size = 24
     lblOne.Caption = "Hello"
End Sub
```

8.
```
Private Sub txtTwo_GotFocus()
     lblOne.Font.Italic = True
     lblOne.Caption = "Hello"
End Sub
```

In Problems 9 to 12, determine the errors.

9.
```
Private Sub cmdButton_Click()
     frmHi = "Hello"
End Sub
```

10.
```
Private Sub cmdButton_Click()
     txtOne.ForeColor = "red"
End Sub
```

11.
```
Private Sub cmdButton_Click()
     txtBox.Caption = "Hello"
End Sub
```

12.
```
Private Sub cmdButton_Click()
     lblTwo.Text = "Hello"
End Sub
```

In Problems 13 to 28, write a line (or lines) of code to carry out the task.

13. Display "E.T. phone home." in lblTwo.
14. Display "Play it, Sam." in lblTwo.
15. Display "The stuff that dreams are made of." in red letters in txtBox.

16. Display "Life is like a box of chocolates." in Courier font in txtBox.
17. Delete the contents of txtBox.
18. Delete the contents of lblTwo.
19. Make lblTwo disappear.
20. Remove the border from lblTwo.
21. Give picBox a blue background.
22. Place a bold red "Hello" in lblTwo.
23. Place a bold italic "Hello" in txtBox.
24. Make picBox disappear.
25. Give the focus to cmdButton.
26. Remove the border from picBox.
27. Place a border around lblTwo and center its contents.
28. Give the focus to txtBoxTwo.

In Problems 29 to 32, the interface and initial properties are specified. Write the code to carry out the stated task.

29. When one of the three command buttons is pressed, the words on the command button are displayed in the label with the stated alignment.

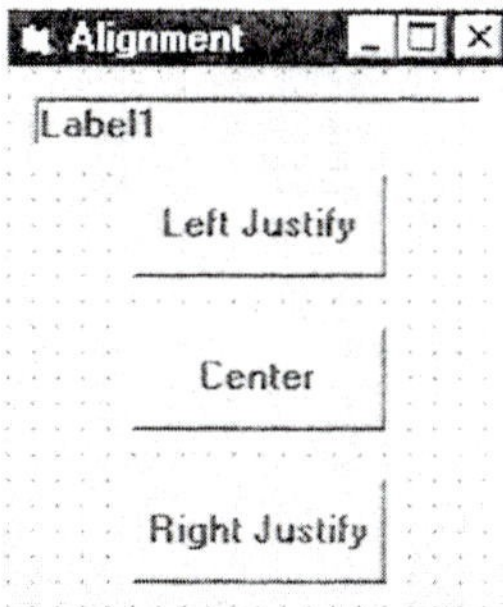

OBJECT	PROPERTY	SETTING
frmEx29	Caption	Alignment
lblShow	BorderStyle	1-Fixed Single
cmdLeft	Caption	Left Justify
cmdCenter	Caption	Center
cmdRight	Caption	Right Justify

30. When one of the command buttons is pressed, the face changes to a smiling face (Wingdings character "J") or a frowning face (Wingdings character "L").

OBJECT	PROPERTY	SETTING
frmEx30	Caption	Face
lblFace	Font	Wingdings
	Caption	K
	Font Size	24
cmdSmile	Caption	Smile
cmdFrown	Caption	Frown

31. Pressing the command buttons alters the background and foreground colors in the text box.

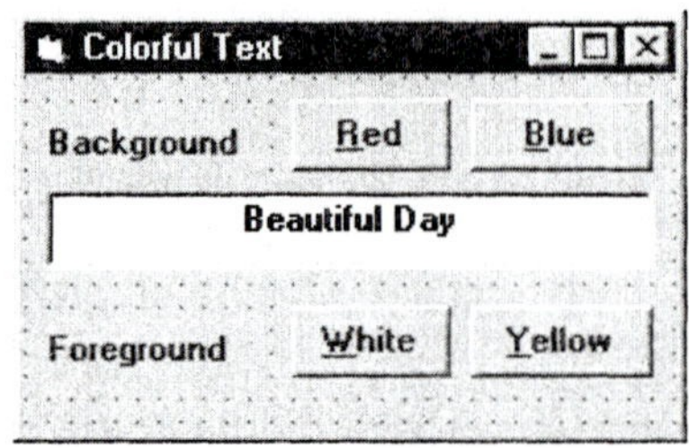

OBJECT	PROPERTY	SETTING
frmEx31	Caption	Colorful Text
lblBack	Caption	Background
cmdRed	Caption	&Red
cmdBlue	Caption	&Blue
txtShow	Text	Beautiful Day
	Alignment	2—Center
lblFore	Caption	Foreground
cmdWhite	Caption	&White
cmdYellow	Caption	&Yellow

32. While one of the three text boxes has the focus, its text is bold. When it loses the focus, it ceases to be bold. The command buttons enlarge text (Font.Size = 12) or return text to normal size (Font.Size = 8).

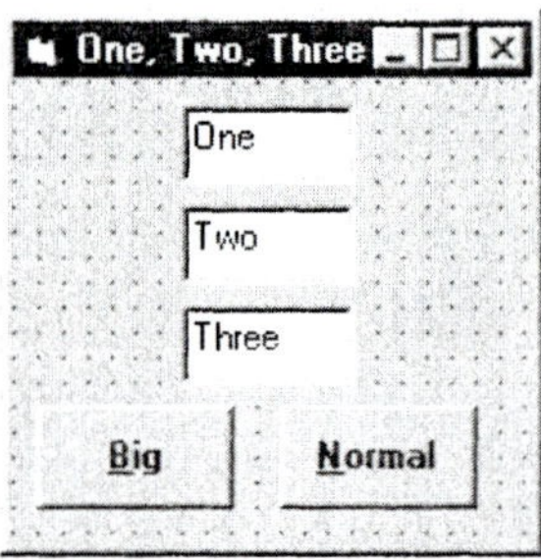

OBJECT	PROPERTY	SETTING
frmEx32	Caption	One, Two, Three
txtOne	Text	One
txtTwo	Text	Two
txtThree	Text	Three
cmdBig	Caption	&Big
cmdNormal	Caption	&Normal

In Problems 33 to 36, write a program with a Windows-style interface to carry out the task.

33. Allow the user to click on command buttons to change the size of the text in a text box and alter its appearance between bold and italics.
34. A form contains two text boxes and one large label between them with no preset caption. When the focus is on the first text box, the label reads "Enter your full name." When the focus is on the second text box, the label reads "Enter your phone number, including area code."
35. Use the same form and properties as in Exercise 30, with the captions for the command buttons replaced with Vanish and Reappear. Clicking a button should produce the stated result.
36. Simulate a traffic light with three small square picture boxes placed vertically on a form. Initially, the bottom picture box is solid green and the other picture boxes are white. When the Tab key is pressed, the middle picture box turns yellow and the bottom picture box turns white. The next time Tab is pressed, the top picture box turns red and the middle picture box turns white. Subsequent pressing of the Tab key cycles through the three colors. *Hint:* First, place the bottom picture box on the form, then the middle picture box, and finally the top picture box.

PROBLEMS FOR SECTION 2.3

In Problems 1 to 4, evaluate the numeric expression without the computer, and then use Visual Basic to check your answer.

1. 1 / (2 ^ 5)
2. 3 + (4 * 5)
3. (5 − 3) * 4
4. 3 * ((−2) ^ 5)

In Problems 5 to 8, write the number in scientific notation as it might be displayed by the computer.

5. 3 billion
6. 12,300,000
7. 4 / (10 ^ 8)
8. 32 * (10 ^ 20)

In Problems 9 to 12, determine whether or not the name is a valid variable name.

9. balance
10. room&Board
11. fOrM_1040
12. 1040B

In Problems 13 to 16, evaluate the numeric expression where a = 2, b = 3, and c = 4.

13. (a * b) + c
14. a * (b + c)
15. b ^ (c − a)
16. (c − a) ^ b

In Problems 17 to 22, write an event procedure to calculate and display the value of the expression.

17. $7 \cdot 8 + 5$
18. $(1 + 2 \cdot 9)^3$
19. $\dfrac{1}{2 + 3}$
20. $\dfrac{1 + 2}{\frac{1}{3} + \frac{1}{4}}$
21. $\dfrac{5 + \dfrac{2\frac{1}{2}}{9 - 3\frac{1}{4}}}{2^{7/8} + \dfrac{3}{4^{.7}}}$
22. $\dfrac{\dfrac{11 - .3^2}{19^{\frac{1}{4}}}}{1 - \dfrac{2^{1.6}}{7\frac{1}{2}}}$

In Problems 23 to 26, determine whether the condition is true or false. Assume a = 2 and b = 3.

23. 3 * a = 2 * b

24. (5 – a) * b < 7

25. b <= 3

26. 3E–02 < .01 * a

In Problems 27 to 30, find the value of the given function. Assume a = 5.

27. Sqr(64)

28. Int(10.75)

29. Round(3.1279, 3)

30. Round(–2.6)

In Problems 31 to 36, determine the output displayed in the picture box by the lines of code.

31.
```
amount = 10
picOutput.Print amount - 4
```

32.
```
a = 4
b = 5 * a
picOutput.Print a + b; b - a
```

33.
```
mass1 = 4
acceleration = 5
force1 = mass1 * acceleration
mass2 = 10
force2 = mass2 * acceleration
picOutput.Print force1 + force2; force 2 - force1
```

34.
```
electronCharge = 1.6E-19
voltage = 1
electronVolt = electronCharge * voltage
picOutput.Print electronVolt
```

35.
```
current = 200
current = 25 + current
picOutput.Print current
```

36.
```
density = 1
volume = 4
mass = density * volume
picOutput.Print mass
volume = 5
mass = mass + density * volume
picOutput.Print mass
```

In Problems 37 to 40, identify the errors.

37.
```
a = 2
b = 3
a + b = c
picOutput.Print c
```

38.
```
a = 2
b = 3
c = d = 4
picOutput.Print 5((a + b) / (c + d)
```

39.
```
balance = 1,234
deposit = $100
picOutput.Print balance + deposit
```

40.
```
.05 = interest
balance = 800
picOutput.Print interest * balance
```

In Problems 41 to 44, write code starting with Private Sub cmdCompute_ Click() and picOutput.Cls statements, ending with an End Sub statement, and having one line for each step. Lines that display data should use the given variable names.

41. The following steps calculate the amount of work done by a force moving a body a certain distance in the direction of the force.

    a. Assign the value 160 to the variable *force.*
    b. Assign the value 14 to the variable *distance.*
    c. Assign the product of force and *distance* to the variable *work.*
    d. Display the value of the variable *work.*

42. The following steps calculate the kinetic energy of a body in motion.

    a. Assign the value 2000 to the variable *mass.*
    b. Assign the value 20 to the variable *velocity.*
    c. Assign the value 1/2 times the value of *mass* times the square of the value of *velocity* to the variable *kineticEnergy.*
    d. Display the value of the variable kineticEnergy.

43. Beginning with 10 grams of radioactive cobalt, the following steps calculate the amount remaining after 3 years.

    a. Assign the value 10 to the variable *radioCobalt.*
    b. Decrease the variable *radioCobalt* by 12% of its value.
    c. Decrease the variable *radioCobalt* by 12% of its value.
    d. Decrease the variable *radioCobalt* by 12% of its value.
    e. Display the value of the variable *radioCobalt.*

44. The following steps calculate the percentage reduction in area of a material in tension. This value is a measure of the ductility of the material, the ability to be of being easily molded or shaped.

    a. Assign the value .6 to the variable *originalArea.*
    b. Assign the value .501 to the variable *finalArea.*
    c. Assign to the variable *ductility,* 100 times the value of the difference between *originalArea* and *finalArea* divided by *originalArea.*
    d. Display the value of the variable *ductility.*

In Problems 45 to 50, write an event procedure to solve the problem and display the answer in a picture box. The program should use variables for each of the quantities.

45. Suppose each acre of farmland produces 18 tons of corn. How many tons of corn can be produced on a 30-acre farm?

46. Suppose a ball is thrown straight up in the air with an initial velocity of 50 feet per second and an initial height of 5 feet. How high will the ball be after 3 seconds? *Note:* The height after *t* seconds is given by the expression −16*t*2 + *vot* + *ho*, where *vo* is the initial velocity and *ho* is the initial height.
47. If a light-year is 5,878,000,000,000 miles and the distance of the star Sirius from Earth is 8.6 light-years, how many miles is Sirius from Earth?
48. If a baseball is pitched at 90 feet per second and home plate is 60.5 feet from the pitcher's mound, how long will it take for the ball to reach the batter?
49. A U.S. Geological Survey showed that Americans use an average of 1600 gallons of water per person per day, including industrial use. How many gallons of water are used each year in the United States? *Note:* The current population of the United States is about 270 million people.
50. According to FHA specifications, each room in a house should have a window area equal to at least 10% of the floor area of the room. What is the minimum window area for a 14- by 16-ft room?

PROBLEMS FOR SECTION 2.4

In Problems 1 to 8, determine the output displayed in the picture box by the lines of code.

1.
```
picOutput.Print "Hello"
picOutput.Print "12" & "34"
```

2.
```
picOutput.Print "Welcome; my friend."
picOutput.Print "Welcome"; "my friend."
```

3.
```
picOutput.Print "12"; 12; "TWELVE"
```

4.
```
picOutput.Print Chr(104) & Chr(105)
```

5.
```
Dim r As String, b As String
r = "A ROSE"
b = " IS "
picOutput.Print r; b; r; b; r
```

6.
```
Dim massOfElectron As Single, mass As String
massOfElectron = 9.1E-31
mass = "9.1E-31"
picOut.Print massOfElectron
picOutput.Print mass
```

7.
```
Dim houseNumber As Single
Dim street As String
houseNumber = 1234
street = "Main Street"
picOutput.Print houseNumber; street
```

8.
```
Dim word1 As String, word2 As String
word1 = "NUCLEAR "
word2 = "PLANT"
picOutput.Print word1 & word2
```

In Problems 9 to 11, identify any errors.

9.
```
Dim phone As Single
phone = "234-5678"
picOutput.Print "My phone number is "; phone
```

10.
```
Dim quote As String
quote = I came to Casablanca for the waters.
picOutput.Print quote; " "; "Bogart"
```

11.
```
Dim end As String
end = "happily ever after."
PicOutput.Print "They lived "; end
```

In Problems 12 to 15, determine whether the condition is true or false.

12. `"9W" <>"9w"`

13. `"Inspector" <"gadget"`

14. `"Car" <"Train"`

15. `"99" <"ninety-nine"`

In Problems 16 to 21, determine the output of the given function.

16. `UCase("McD's")`

17. `Left("harp", 2)`

18. `Mid("ABCDE", 2, 3)`

19. `Instr("shoe", "h")`

20. `Left("ABCD", 2)`

21. `UCase("$2 bill")`

In Problems 22 to 36, determine what will be displayed in the picture box by the given lines of code.

22. `picBox.Print FormatNumber(-12.3456, 3)`

23. `picBox.Print FormatNumber(12345)`

24.
```
numVar = Round(12345.9)
picBox.Print FormatNumber(numVar, 3)
```

25. `picBox.Print FormatCurrency(12345.67, 0)`

26. `picBox.Print FormatPercent(3 / 4, 1)`

27. `picBox.Print FormatDateTime(Now + 1, vbLongDate)`

28. `picBox.Print FormatDateTime("7-4-1776", vbLongDate)`

(*Note*: The Declaration of Independence was signed on a Thursday.)

29.
```
strVar = FormatDateTime(Now, vbLongDate)
picBox.Print Right(strVar, 4)
```

30. `picBox.Print "Pay to France "; FormatCurrency(27267622)`

31. `picBox.Print "The interest rate is "; FormatPercent(0.045)`

32.
```
picBox.Print "On 1/1/98, the US pop. was ";
     FormatNumber(268924000, 0)
```

33. `picBox.Print "The minimum wage is "; FormatCurrency(5.15)`

34.
```
picBox.Print FormatPercent(.893); " of new computers use
     Windows."
```

35.
```
picBox.Font.Name = "Courier"
picBox.Print "12345678"
strVar = FormatNumber(1999.958, 0)
picBox.Print Format(strVar, "@@@@@@@@")
```

36. In the program that follows, determine the output displayed in the picture box when the command buttons are pressed in the following order: First, Second, First.

```
Dim word As String

Private Sub cmdFirst_Click()
    word = word & "Yada "
    picOutput.Print word
End Sub

Private Sub cmdSecond_Click()
    picOutput.Print word
End Sub
```

In Problems 37 to 40, write code starting with Private Sub cmdDisplay_ Click() and picOutput.Cls statements, ending with an End Sub statement, and having one line for each step. Lines that display data should use the given variable names.

37. The following steps give the name and birth year of a famous inventor.

    a. Declare all variables used in the steps below.
    b. Assign "Thomas" to the variable *firstName*.
    c. Assign "Alva" to the variable *middleName*.
    d. Assign "Edison" to the variable *lastName*.
    e. Assign 1847 to the variable *yearOfBirth*.
    f. Display the inventor's full name followed by a comma and his year of birth.

38. The following steps compute the price of ketchup.

    a. Declare all variables used in the steps below.
    b. Assign "ketchup" to the variable *item*.
    c. Assign 1.80 to the variable *regularPrice*.
    d. Assign .27 to the variable *discount*.
    e. Display the phrase "1.53 is the sale price of ketchup."

39. The following steps display a copyright statement.

    a. Declare all variables used in the steps below.
    b. Assign "Prentice Hall, Inc." to the variable *publisher*.
    c. Display the phrase "© Prentice Hall, Inc."

40. The following steps give advice.

    a. Declare all variables used in the steps below.
    b. Assign "Fore" to the variable *prefix*.
    c. Display the phrase "Forewarned is Forearmed."

In Problems 41 to 50, the interface and initial properties are specified. Write the code to carry out the stated task.

41. After values are placed in the x and y text boxes, pressing Compute Sum places x + y in the sum picture box.

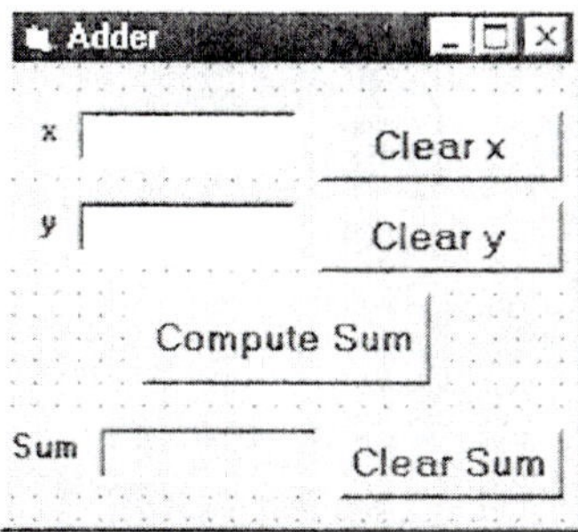

OBJECT	PROPERTY	SETTING
frmEx41	Caption	Adder
lblX	Caption	x
txtNum1	Text	(blank)
cmdClearX	Caption	Clear x
lblY	Caption	y
txtNum2	Text	(blank)
cmdClearY	Caption	Clear y
cmdCompute	Caption	Compute Sum
lblSum	Caption	Sum
picSum		
cmdClearSum	Caption	Clear Sum

42. When cmdCelsius is pressed, the temperature is converted from Fahrenheit to Celsius, the title bar changes to Celsius, cmdCelsius is hidden, and cmdFahr becomes visible. If cmdFahr is now pressed, the temperature is converted from Celsius to Fahrenheit, the title bar reverts to Fahrenheit, cmdFahr is hidden, and cmdCelsius becomes visible. Of course, the user can change the temperature in the text box at any time. (*Note:* The conversion formulas are C = (5/9) * (F − 32) and F = (9/5) * C + 32.)

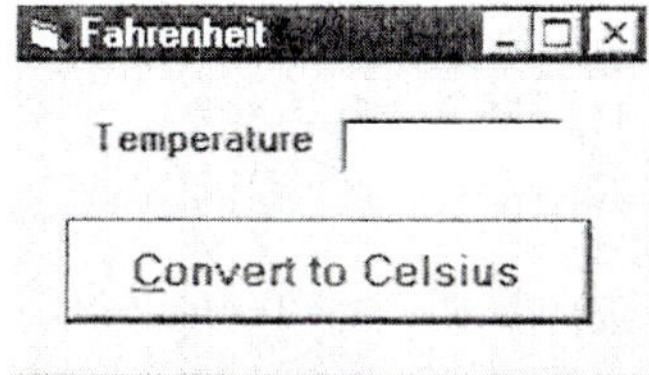

OBJECT	PROPERTY	SETTING
frmEx42	Caption	Fahrenheit
lblTemp	Caption	Temperature
txtTemp	Text	(blank)
cmdCelsius	Caption	Convert to Celsius
cmdFahr	Caption	Convert to Fahrenheit
	Visible	False

43. If n is the number of seconds between lightning and thunder, the storm is $n/5$ miles away. Write a program that requests the number of seconds between lightning and thunder and reports the distance of the storm.

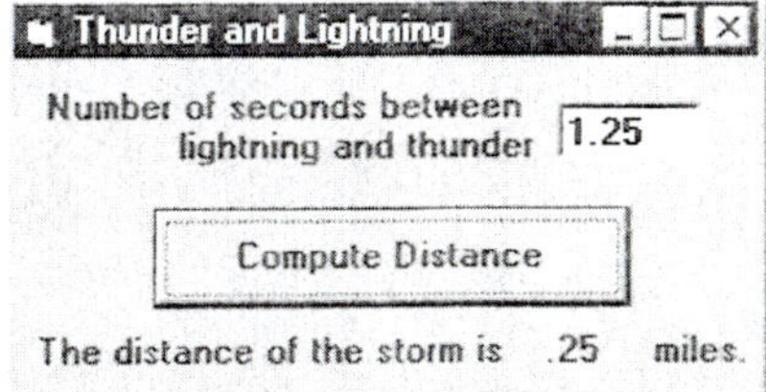

OBJECT	PROPERTY	SETTING
frmStorm	Caption	Thunder and Lightning
lblNumSec	Caption	Number of seconds between lightning and thunder
txtNumSec	Text	(blank)
cmdCompute	Caption	Compute Distance
lblDistance	Caption	The distance of the storm is
lblNumMiles	Caption	(blank)
lblMiles	Caption	miles

44. Write a program to request as input the name of a baseball team, the number of games won, and the number of games lost, and then display the percentage of games won.

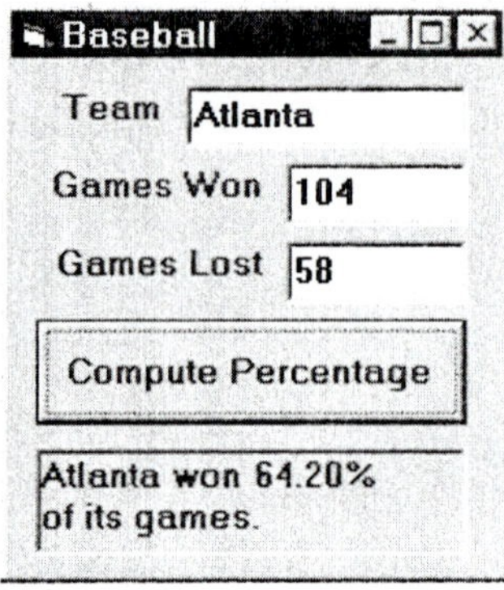

OBJECT	PROPERTY	SETTING
frmBaseball	Caption	Baseball
lblTeam	Caption	Team
txtTeam	Text	(blank)
lblWon	Caption	Games Won
txtWon	Text	(blank)
lblLost	Caption	Games Lost
txtLost	Text	(blank)
cmdCompute	Caption	Compute Percentage
picPercent		

45. The numbers of calories burned per hour by bicycling, jogging, and swimming are 200, 475, and 275, respectively. A person loses 1 pound of weight for each 3500 calories burned. Write a program that allows the user to input the number of hours spent at each activity and then calculates the number of pounds worked off.

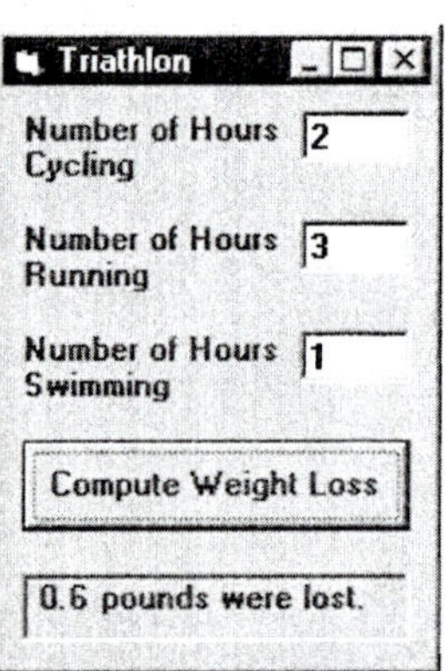

OBJECT	PROPERTY	SETTING
frmTriathlon	Caption	Triathlon
lblCycle	Caption	Number of Hours Cycling
txtCycle	Text	(blank)
lblRun	Caption	Number of Hours Running
txtRun	Text	(blank)
lblSwim	Caption	Number of Hours Swimming
txtSwim	Text	(blank)
cmdCompute	Caption	Compute Weight Loss
picWtLoss		

46. The American College of Sports Medicine recommends that you maintain your *training heart rate* during an aerobic workout. Your training heart rate is computed as .7*(220 − *a*) + .3 * *r*, where *a* is your age, and *r* is your resting heart rate (your pulse when you first awaken). Write a program to request a person's age and resting heart rate and then calculate the training heart rate. (Determine *your* training heart rate.)

In Problems 47 to 50, write a program with a Windows-style interface to carry out the task. The program should use variables for each of the quantities and display the outcome with a complete explanation, as in Example 5.

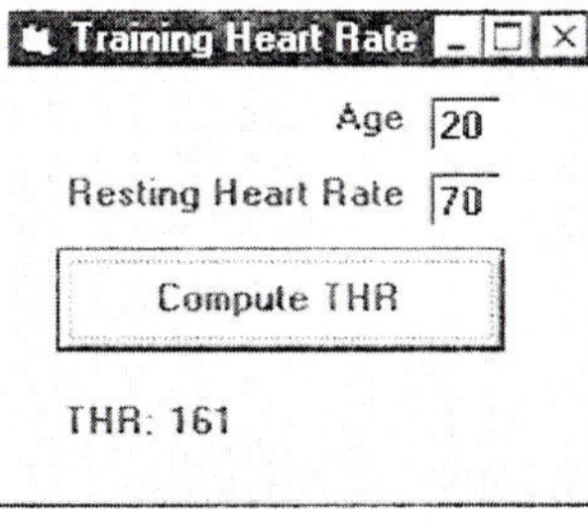

OBJECT	PROPERTY	SETTING
frmWorkout	Caption	Training Heart Rate
lblAge	Caption	Age
txtAge	Text	(blank)
lblRestHR	Caption	Resting Heart Rate
txtRestHR	Text	(blank)
cmdCompute	Caption	Compute THR
lblTHR	Caption	THR:
lblTrainHR	Caption	(blank)

47. If a company's annual revenue is $550,000 and its expenses are $410,000, what is its net income (revenue minus expenses)?
48. Write a program that requests a letter, converts it to uppercase, and gives its first position in the sentence "THE QUICK BROWN FOX JUMPS OVER A LAZY DOG." For example, if the user responds by typing *b* into the text box, then the message *B first occurs in position 11 is displayed.*
49. Calculate the amount of a waiter's tip, given the amount of the bill and the percentage tip. (Test the program with $20 and 15 percent.)
50. Write a program that requests a sentence, a word in the sentence, and another word, and then displays the sentence with the first word replaced by the second. For example, if the user responds by typing "What you don't know won't hurt you" into the first text box and *know* and *owe* into the second and third text boxes, then the message "What you don't owe won't hurt you" is displayed.

PROBLEMS FOR SECTION 2.5

In Problems 1 to 10, assume that the file Data.txt (shown to the right of the code) has been opened for input with reference number 1. Determine the output displayed in the picture box by the lines of code.

1.
```
Dim num As Single
Input #1, num
picOutput.Print num * num
```

Data.txt

```
4
```

2.
```
Dim word As String
Input #1, word
picOutput.Print "un" & word
```

Data.txt

```
"speakable"
```

3.
```
Dim str1 As String, str2 As String
Input #1, str1, str2
picOutput.Print str1; str2
```

Data.txt

```
"base"
"ball"
```

4.

```
Dim num1 As Single, num2 As Single
Dim num3 As Single
Input #1, num1, num2, num3
picOutput.Print (num1 + num2) * num3
```

Data.txt

```
3
4
5
```

5.

```
Dim yrOfBirth As Single, curYr As Single
Input #1, yrOfBirth
Input #1, curYr 'Current year
picOutput.Print "Age:"; curYr - yrOfBirth
```

Data.txt

```
1979
1999
```

6.

```
Dim str1 As String, str2 As String
Input #1, str1
Input #1, str2
picOutput.Print str1 & str2
```

Data.txt

```
"A, my name is "
"Alice"
```

7.

```
Dim word1 As String, word2 As String
Input #1, word1
Input #1, word2
picOutput.Print word1 & word2
```

8. The pressure at any depth beneath the surface of a liquid is given by

$$P = 0.433 \cdot S_g \cdot h$$

where P is the pressure expressed in pounds per square inch, S_g is a characteristic of the liquid called specific gravity, and h is the depth expressed in feet.

```
Dim h As Single, sg As Single, k As Single, p As Single
Open "Data.txt" For Input As #1
Input #1, h, sg, k
p = k * sg * h
picOutput.Print p
Close #1
```

(Assume the file Data.txt contains the following: 150, 1.08, .433)

9. The potential energy (in joules) of a body of mass m elevated to a height h is given by

$$PE = m \cdot g \cdot h$$

where g is the acceleration of gravity expressed in meters per second squared. The mass and the height are expressed in kilograms and meters, respectively.

The energy (in joules) required to accelerate an object of mass m from rest to a velocity v (meters per second) is called kinetic energy and is given by

$$KE = mv^2 / 2$$

```
Dim p As String, m As Single, g As Single, h As Single,
   pe As Single
'potential energy, mass, gravity, height, potential energy
Dim k As String, v As Single, ke As Single
'kinetic energy, velocity, kinetic energy
Open "Data.txt" For Input As #1
Input #1, p, m, g, h
pe = m * g * h
picOutput.Print p; "=" pe; "joules"
Input #1, k, v
ke = m * v ^ 2 / 2
picOutput.Print k; " =" ke; "joules"
Close #1
```

(Assume the file Data.txt contains the following:
`"Potential Energy", 10, 9.8, 2, "Kinetic Energy", 25)`

10.
```
Dim h As Single, a As String, p As String, c As Single
Open "Data.txt" For Input As #1
Input #1, h, a
Input #1, p, c
picOutput.Print a; " ="; h
picOutput.Print p; " ="; c
Close #1
Open "Data.txt" For Input As #1
Input #1, c
picOutput.Print c
Close #1
```

(Assume the file Data.txt contains the following:
`600, "altitude", "Pollution concentration", 4)`

In Problems 11 to 20, determine the output displayed in the picture box by the following lines of code.

11.
```
Dim bet As Single 'Amount bet at roulette
bet = Val(InputBox("How much do you want to bet?", "Wager"))
picOutput.Print "You might win"; 36 * bet; "dollars."
```

(Assume that the response is 5.)

12.
```
Dim word As String
word = InputBox("Word to negate:")
picOutput.Print "un"; word
```

(Assume that the response is *tied*.)

13.
```
Dim lastName As String, message As String, firstName As String
lastName = "Jones"
message = "What is your first name Mr. " & lastName
firstName = InputBox(message)
picOutput.Print "Hello "; firstName; " "; lastName
```
(Assume that the response is *John*.)

14.
```
Dim intRate As Single 'Current interest rate
intRate = Val(InputBox("Current interest rate?"))
picOutput.Print "At the current interest rate, ";
picOutput.Print "your money will double in";
picOutput.Print 72 / intRate; "years."
```

(Assume that the response is 6.)

15.
```
picOutput.Print 1; "one", "won"
```

16.
```
picOutput.Print 1, 2; 3
```

17.
```
picOutput.Print "one",
picOutput.Print "two"
```

18.
```
picOutput.Print "one", , "two"
```

19.
```
picOutput.Font.Name = "Courier" 'Fixed-width font
picOutput.Print "1234567890"
picOutput.Print Tab(4); 5
```

20.
```
picOutput.Font.Name = "Courier" 'Fixed-width font
picOutput.Print "1234567890"
picOutput.Print "Hello"; Tab(3); "Good-bye"
```

In Problems 21 to 32, assume that the file Data.txt (shown below the code) has been opened for input with reference number 1. Identify any errors.

21.
```
Dim str1 As String, str2 As String
Input #1, str1, str2
picOutput.Print "Hello "; str1
```

Data.txt
```
"John Smith"
```

22.
```
Dim num As Single
Input #1, num
picOutput.Print 3 * num
```

Data.txt
```
1 + 2
```

23.
```
'Each line of Data.txt contains
'building, height, # of stories
Dim building As String
Dim ht As Single
Input #1, building, ht
picOutput.Print building, ht
Input #1, building, ht
picOutput.Print building, ht
```

Data.txt
```
"World Trade Center", 1350, 110
"Sears Tower", 1454, 110
```

24.
```
Dim num As Single
num = InputBox(Pick a number from 1 to 10.)
picOutput.Print "Your number is"; num
```

25.
```
Dim statePop As Single
statePop = Val(InputBox("State Population?"))
picOutput.Print "The population should grow to";
picOutput.Print 1.01 * statePop; "by next year."
```

(Assume that the response is *8,900,000*)

26.
```
info = InputBox()
```

27.
```
Printer.Name = Courier
```

28.
```
txtBox.Text = "one", "two"
```

29.
```
lblTwo.Caption = 1, 2
```

30.
```
Printer.Print "Hello"; Tab(200); "Good-bye"
```

31.
```
Form.Caption = "one"; Tab(10); "two"
```

32.
```
Dim rem As Single 'Number to remember
Input #1, rem
picOutput.Print "Don't forget to ";
picOutput.Print "remember the number"; rem
```

Data.txt

4

In Problems 33 to 36, write code starting with Private Sub cmdDisplay_ Click() and picOutput.Cls statements, ending with an End Sub statement, and having one or two lines for each step. Lines that display data should use the given variable names.

33. The following steps display the changes in political activities for first-year college students from 1996 to 1997. Assume the file Politics.txt consists of the two lines

"frequently discuss politics", 16.2, 13.7
"worked on a political campaign", 6.6, 8.2

a. Declare all variables used in the steps below.

b. Use an Input # statement to assign values to the variables *activity*, *percent96*, and *percent97*.

c. Display a sentence giving the change in the percentage of students engaged in the activity.

d. Repeat steps (b) and (c).

34. The following steps display information about Americans' eating habits. Assume the file Data.txt consists of the single line

"soft drinks", "million gallons", 23

a. Declare all variables used in the steps below.
b. Open the file Data.txt for input.
c. Use an Input # statement to assign values to the variables *food, units,* and *quantityPerDay*.
d. Display a sentence giving the quantity of a food item consumed by Americans in one day.

35. The following steps calculate the percent increase in a typical grocery basket of goods:

a. Declare all variables used in the steps below.
b. Assign 200 to the variable *begOfYearPrice*.
c. Request the price at the end of the year with an input box and assign it to the variable *endOfYearPrice*.
d. Assign 100 * (*endOfYearPrice* – *begOfYearPrice*) / *begOfYearPrice* to the variable *percentIncrease*.
e. Display a sentence giving the percent increase for the year.

(Test the program with a $215 end-of-year price.)

36. The following steps calculate the amount of money earned in a walk-a-thon.

a. Declare all variables used in the steps below.
b. Request the amount pledged per mile from an input box and assign it to the variable *pledge*.
c. Request the number of miles walked from an input box and assign it to the variable *miles*.
d. Display a sentence giving the amount to be paid.

(Test the program with a pledge of $2.00 and a 15-mile walk.)

In Problems 37 and 38, write a line of code to carry out the task.

37. Pop up a message box stating "The future isn't what it used to be."
38. Pop up a message box with "Taking Risks Proverb" in the title bar and the message "You can't steal second base and keep one foot on first."
39. Table 2-11 summarizes the month's activity of three checking accounts. Write a program that displays the account number and the end-of-month balance for each account and then displays the total amount of money in the three accounts. Assume the data are stored in a data file.

TABLE 2-11 Checking-account activity.

ACCOUNT NUMBER	BEGINNING-OF-MONTH BALANCE	DEPOSITS	WITHDRAWALS
AB4057	1234.56	345.67	100.00
XY4321	789.00	120.00	350.00
GH2222	321.45	143.65	0.00

40. The ductility of a material in tension is characterized by its elongation. The percent of elongation is defined as

$$\text{Percent elongation} = (L_f - L_i) \cdot 100/L_i$$

where L_i and L_f are the initial and final lengths, respectively. Write a program that requests initial and final lengths of a steel bar as input, and displays the percent elongation. (Test the program with $L_i = 2.0\ m$ and $L_f = 2.8$ m.)

41. Write a program to compute semester averages. Each line in a data file should contain a student's Social Security number and the grades for three hourly exams and the final exam. (The final exam counts as two hourly exams.) The program should display each student's Social Security number and semester average, and then the class average. Use the data in Table 2-12.

TABLE 2-12 Student grades.

SOC. SEC. NO.	EXAM 1	EXAM 2	EXAM 3	FINAL EXAM
123-45-6789	67	85	90	88
111-11-1111	93	76	82	80
123-32-1234	85	82	89	84

42. The variation of the acceleration of gravity g with elevation is defined as

$$g = M_e \cdot G/R^2$$

where $M_g = 5.96 \cdot 10^{24}$ kilograms is the mass of the earth, $R = R_e + H$ where $R_e = 637 \cdot 10^6$ meters is the radius of the earth, H is the elevation in meters, and $G = 6.671 \cdot 10^{-11}\ \text{N} \cdot \text{m}^2/\text{kg}^2$ is the gravitational constant. The expression for g can be written in a simplified form:

$$g = 39.75 \cdot 10^{13}/(637 \cdot 10^6 + H^2)$$

Table 2-13 gives the locations of some measurement stations and their respective elevations. Write a program with this information in a data file that displays the location, elevation, and value of g for each location in the table.

TABLE 2-13 Station locations and elevations.

LOCATION	ELEVATION H (METERS)
Denver	1638
Himalaya	3000

43. Isotopes are elements that have the same number of electrons and protons, but differ in the number of neutrons. The atom density N_i of an isotope is the number of atoms per cubic centimeter and is given by

$$N_i = A_i \cdot d \cdot N_g/(100 \cdot M)$$

where

d is the density (g/cm^3),

N_g is Avogadro's number $= 6.023 \cdot 10^{23}\ \text{mole}^{-1}$,

M is the atomic weight (g/mole), and

A_i is the percent abundance of the isotope.

Write a program to display the name and atom density N_i of each element in Table 2-14. The information from the table should be stored in a text file.

TABLE 2-14 Isotope data.

ISOTOPE	DENSITY (g/cm^3)	ABUNDANCE (g)	ATOMIC WEIGHT (g/mole)
Uranium 235	18.46	.72	235.0439
Uranium 238	18.70	99.27	238.0508

PROBLEMS FOR SECTION 2.6

In Problems 1 through 16, find the value of the given function.

1. Abs(– 4.5)
2. Abs(– 2.3E– 05)
3. Exp(0)
4. Exp(1)
5. Log(2.71829)
6. Log(Exp(6))
7. Sqr(64)
8. Sqr(3 * 12)
9. Fix(3.75)
10. Fix(– 4.9)
11. Int(– 10.75)
12. Int(9 – 2)
13. Sin(0)
14. Sgn(Sqr(8) – Sqr(10))
15. Sgn(3.14159)
16. Atn(Sqr(3))

In Problems 17 through 24, find the value of the given function where *a* = 5 and *b* = 3.

17. Atn(2 * b – a)
18. Sqr(a – 5)
19. Int(– a/2)
20. Log(3 * a – 5 * b)
21. Sqr(4 + a)
22. Abs(b – a)
23. Int(b * .5)
24. Cos(3.14159/(b + 1))
25.

In Problems 25 and 26, write a Visual Basic statement to evaluate the given expression.

26. $3.2\tan\left[\dfrac{\sqrt{3/8}}{11 + 1/8}\right]$

27. $\dfrac{\log_e(10 + \tan(2 - 1/7))}{1 + e^{(2.5 + .66^4)}}$

In Problems 27 and 28, determine the output displayed in the picture box by the lines of code.

28.
```
Dim num as Single
num = 3
picOutput.Print Tan(Atn(num))
```

29.
```
Dim m As Single, n As Single, max as Single
m = InputBox("Enter a number:", "First Number")
n = InputBox("Enter a number:", "Second Number")
max-(m + n + Sgn(m - n) * (m - n)) / 2
picOutput.Print "The larger number is"; max
```

(Assume the user responds with 5, 6)

In Problems 29 and 30, determine the errors.

30.
```
Dim a As Integer, b As Integer
a = 20000
b = a + a
picOutput.Print b
```

31.
```
Dim m As Single, n As Single
picOutput.Print Sqr(m - 2 * n)
```

3

Controlling Program Flow

SECTIONS

- 3.1 General Procedures
- 3.2 Decision Structures
- 3.3 Do Loops
- 3.4 For...Next Loops
- 3.5 Case Study: Numerical Integration
- 3.6 Programming Projects

OBJECTIVES

After reading this chapter, you should be able to:

- Understand the use of the two types of general procedures: Sub procedures and function procedures.
- Incorporate the If block and Select Case block decision structures in your programs.
- Use the Do loop control structure.
- Use the For...Next loop control structure.

3.1 GENERAL PROCEDURES

An event procedure contains a block of code (enclosed by Private Sub and End Sub statements) that is executed when the associated event occurs. A *general procedure* is similar to an event procedure. The primary difference is that an event procedure is executed as the result of an event occurring (usually determined by the user), whereas a general procedure is executed whenever the programmer decides to execute it. There are two types of general procedures—*Sub procedures* and *function procedures*.

3.1.1 Sub procedures

The simplest type of Sub procedure has the form

```
Private Sub ProcedureName()
    block of code
End Sub
```

A Sub procedure is invoked with a statement of the form

```
Call ProcedureName
```

General procedures allow a problem to be broken into small problems to be solved one at a time. Also, they eliminate repetitive code, can be reused in other programs, and allow a team of programmers to work on a single program.

The rules for naming general procedures are identical to the rules for naming variables. The name chosen for a Sub procedure should describe the task it performs. Sub procedures can be either typed (in entirety) directly into the code window, or into a template created with the following steps:

1. Press Alt/T/P to select Add Procedure from the Tools menu.
2. Type in the name of the procedure. (Omit parentheses.)
3. Select Sub from the Type box and Private from the Scope box.
4. Press the Enter key or click on OK.

Consider the next program, which calculates the sum of two numbers. This program will be revised to incorporate Sub procedures.

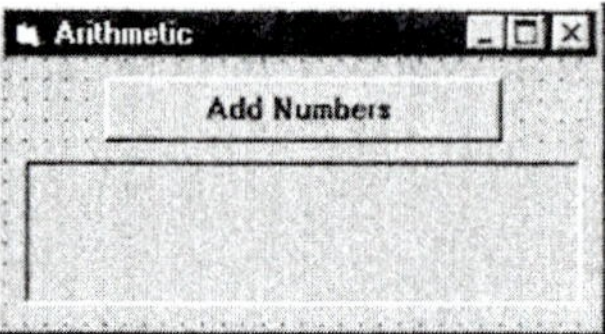

OBJECT	PROPERTY	SETTING
frmArithmetic	Caption	Arithmetic
cmdAdd	Caption	Add Numbers
picResult		

```
Private Sub cmdAdd_Click()
    Dim num1 As Single, num2 As Single
    'Display the sum of two numbers
    picResult.Cls
    picResult.Print "This program displays a sentence "
    picResult.Print "identifying two numbers and their sum."
    picResult.Print
    num1 = 2
    num2 = 3
    picResult.Print "The sum of"; num1; "and"; num2; "is";
    picResult.Print num1 + num2
End Sub
```

```
[Run, and then click the command button. The following is
displayed in the picture box.]
```

```
This program displays a sentence
identifying two numbers and their sum.

The sum of 2 and 3 is 5
```

The tasks performed by this program can be summarized as follows:

1. Explain purpose of program.
2. Display numbers and their sum.

Sub procedures allow us to write and read the program in such a way that we first focus on the tasks and later on how to accomplish each task.

The following program uses a Sub procedure to accomplish the first task of the preceding program. When the statement Call ExplainPurpose is reached, execution jumps to the Private Sub ExplainPurpose statement. The lines between Private Sub ExplainPurpose and End Sub are executed, and then execution continues with the line following the Call statement.

```
Private Sub cmdAdd_Click()
     Dim num1 As Single, num2 As Single
     'Display the sum of two numbers
     picResult.Cls
     Call ExplainPurpose
     picResult.Print
     num1 = 2
     num2 = 3
     picResult.Print "The sum of"; num1; "and"; num2; "is";
     picResult.Print num1 + num2
End Sub

Private Sub ExplainPurpose()
     'Explain the task performed by the program
     picResult.Print "This program displays a sentence"
     picResult.Print "identifying two numbers and their sum."
End Sub
```

In Example 1, the cmdAdd_Click event procedure is referred to as the *calling procedure* and the ExplainPurpose Sub procedure is referred to as the *called procedure*. The second task performed by the program in Example 1 also can be handled by a Sub procedure. The values of the two numbers, however, must be transmitted to the Sub procedure. This transmission is called *passing*.

The following revision of the program in Example 1 uses a Sub procedure to accomplish the second task. The statement Call Add(2, 3) causes execution to jump to the Private Sub Add(num1 As Single, num2 As Single) statement, which assigns the number 2 to *num1* and the number 3 to *num2*.

```
Call Add(2, 3)

Private Sub Add(num1 As Single, num2 As Single)
```

After the lines between Private Sub Add (num1 As Single, num2 As Single) and End Sub are executed, execution continues with the line following Call Add(2, 3); namely, the End Sub statement in the event procedure. *Note:* If you use Add Procedure to create a template for the Sub procedure, you must type in "num1 As Single, num2 As Single" after leaving the Add Procedure dialog box.

```
Private Sub cmdAdd_Click()
     'Display the sum of two numbers
     picResult.Cls
     Call ExplainPurpose
     picResult.Print
     Call Add(2, 3)
End Sub

Private Sub Add(num1 As Single, num2 As Single)
     'Display numbers and their sum
     picResult.Print "The sum of"; num1; "and"; num2; "is";
         num1 + num2
     End Sub

Private Sub ExplainPurpose()
     'Explain the task performed by the program
     picResult.Print "This program displays a sentence"
     picResult.Print "identifying two numbers and their sum."
End Sub
```

Sub procedures make a program easy to read, modify, and debug. The event procedure gives an unencumbered description of what the program does, and the Sub procedures fill in the details. Another benefit of Sub procedures is that they can be called several times during the execution of the program. This feature is especially useful when there are many statements in the Sub procedure.

Here is an extension of the program in Example 2 that displays several sums.

```
Private Sub cmdAdd_Click()
    'Display the sums of several pairs of numbers
    picResult.Cls
    Call ExplainPurpose
    picResult.Print
    Call Add(2, 3)
    Call Add(4, 6)
    Call Add(7, 8)
End Sub

Private Sub Add(num1 As Single, num2 As Single)
    'Display numbers and their sum
    picResult.Print "The sum of"; num1; "and"; num2; "is";
    picResult.Print num1 + num2
End Sub

Private Sub ExplainPurpose()
    'Explain the task performed by the program
    picResult.Print "This program displays sentences"
    picResult.Print "identifying pairs of numbers and their
      sums."
End Sub

[Run, and then click the command button. The following is
displayed in the picture box.]

This program displays sentences
identifying pairs of numbers and their sums.
The sum of 2 and 3 is 5
The sum of 4 and 6 is 10
The sum of 7 and 8 is 15
```

The variables *num1* and *num2* appearing in the Sub procedure Add are called *parameters*. They are merely temporary place holders for the numbers passed to the Sub procedure; their names are not important. The only essentials are their type, quantity, and order. In this Add Sub procedure, the parameters must be numeric variables, and there must be two of them. For instance, the Sub procedure could have been written

```
Private Sub Add(this As Single, that As Single)
    'Display numbers and their sum
    picResult.Print "The sum of"; this; "and"; that; "is";
    picResult.Print this + that
End Sub
```

A string also can be passed to a Sub procedure. In this case, the receiving parameter in the Sub procedure must be followed by the declaration As String.

The following program passes a string and two numbers to a Sub procedure. When the Sub procedure is first called, the string parameter *state* is assigned the string constant "Hawaii", and the numeric parameters *pop* and *area* are assigned the numeric constants 1134750 and 6471, respectively. The Sub procedure then uses these parameters to carry out the task of calculating the population density of Hawaii. The second Call statement assigns different values to the parameters.

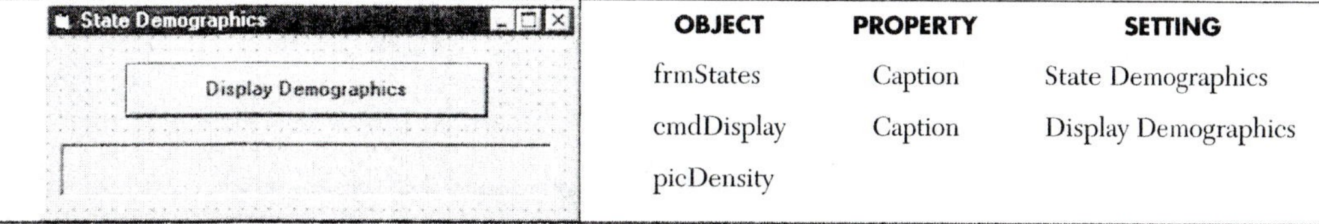

OBJECT	PROPERTY	SETTING
frmStates	Caption	State Demographics
cmdDisplay	Caption	Display Demographics
picDensity		

```
Private Sub cmdDisplay_Click()
    'Calculate the population densities of states
    picDensity.Cls
    Call CalculateDensity("Hawaii", 1134750, 6471)
    Call CalculateDensity("Alaska", 570345, 591000)
End Sub

Private Sub CalculateDensity(state As String, pop As Single,
   area As Single)
    Dim rawDensity As Single, density As Single
    'The density (number of people per square mile)
    'will be displayed rounded to a whole number
    rawDensity = pop / area
    density = Round(rawDensity) 'round to whole number
    picDensity.Print "The density of "; state; " is";
    picDensity.Print density;
    picDensity.Print "people per square mile."
End Sub
```

[Run, and then click the command button. The following is displayed in the picture box.]

```
The density of Hawaii is 175 people per square mile.
The density of Alaska is 1 people per square mile.
```

The parameters in the density program can have any names, as with the parameters in the addition program of Example 3. The only restriction is that the first parameter be a string variable and that the last two parameters be numeric variables of type Single. For instance, the Sub procedure could have been written

```
Private Sub CalculateDensity(x As String, y As Single, z As
   Single)
    Dim rawDensity As Single, density As Single
    'The density (number of people per square mile)
    'will be rounded to a whole number
    rawDensity = y / z
    density = Round(rawDensity)
    picDensity.Print "The density of "; x; " is"; density;
    picDensity.Print "people per square mile."
End Sub
```

When nondescriptive names are used for parameters, the Sub procedure should contain comment statements giving the meanings of the variables. Possible comment statements for the preceding program are

```
'x name of the state
'y population of the state
'z area of the state
```

3.1.2 Variables and Expressions as Arguments

The items appearing in the parentheses of a Call statement are called *arguments*. These should not be confused with parameters, which appear in the heading of a Sub procedure. In Example 3, the arguments of the Call Add statements were constants. These arguments also could have been variables or expressions. For instance, the event procedure could have been written as follows (Figure 3.1).

```
Private Sub cmdAdd_Click()
    Dim x As Single, y As Single, z As Single
    'Display the sum of two numbers
    picResult.Cls
    Call ExplainPurpose
    picResult.Print
    x = 2
    y = 3
    Call Add(x, y)
    Call Add(x + 2, 2 * y)
    z = 7
    Call Add(z, z + 1)
End Sub
```

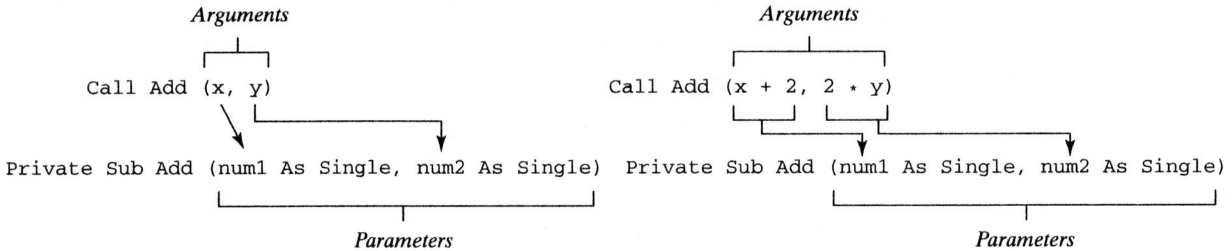

Figure 3.1. Passing arguments to parameters.

This feature allows values obtained as input from the user to be passed to a Sub procedure.

The following variation of the addition program requests the two numbers as input from the user. Notice that the names of the arguments, *x* and *y*, are different than the names of the parameters. The names of the arguments and parameters may be the same or different; what matters is that the order, number, and types of the arguments and parameters match.

```
Private Sub cmdCompute_Click()
    Dim x As Single, y As Single
    'This program requests two numbers and
    'displays the two numbers and their sum.
    x = Val(InputBox("FirstNumber:", "Add Two Numbers"))
    y = Val(InputBox("Second Number:", "Add Two Numbers"))
    Call Add(x, y)
End Sub
```

```
Private Sub Add(num1 As Single, num2 As Single)
    'Display numbers and their sum
    picResult.Cls
    picResult.Print "The sum of"; num1; "and"; num2; "is";
    picResult.Print num1 + num2
End Sub
```

[Run, click the command button, and respond to the requests for numbers with 23 and 67. The following is displayed in the picture box.]

```
The sum of 23 and 67 is 90
```

Here is a variation of Example 4 that obtains its input from the file Demograp.txt. The second Call statement uses different variable names for the arguments to show that using the same argument names is not necessary (Figure 3.2).

Demograp.txt contains the following two lines:

"Hawaii", 1134750, 6471

"Alaska", 570345, 591000

```
Private Sub cmdDisplay_Click()
    Dim state As String, pop As Single, area As Single
    Dim s As String, p As Single, a As Single
    'Calculate the population densities of states
    picDensity.Cls
    Open "Demograp.txt" For Input As #1
    Input #1, state, pop, area
    Call CalculateDensity(state, pop, area)
    Input #1, s, p, a
    Call CalculateDensity(s, p, a)
    Close #1
End Sub

Private Sub CalculateDensity(state As String, pop As Single,
   area As Single)
    Dim rawDensity As Single, density As Single
    'The density (number of people per square mile)
    'will be rounded to a whole number
    rawDensity = pop / area
    density = Round(rawDensity)
    picDensity.Print "The density of "; state; " is";
    picDensity.Print density;
    picDensity.Print "people per square mile."
End Sub
```

[Run, and then click the command button. The following is displayed in the picture box.]

```
The density of Hawaii is 175 people per square mile.
The density of Alaska is 1 people per square mile.
```

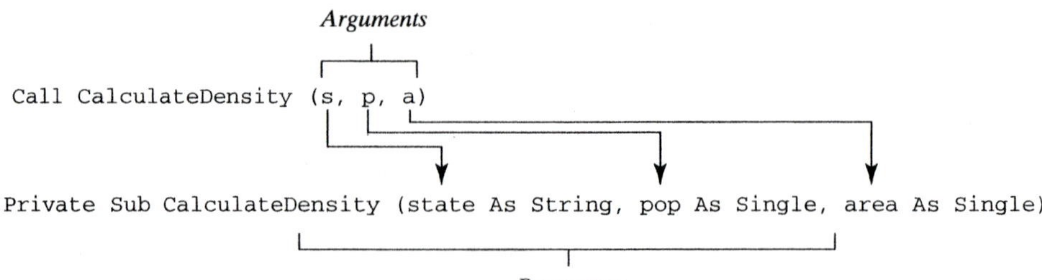

Figure 3.2. Passing arguments to parameters in Example 6.

3.1.3 Passing Values Back from Sub procedures

Suppose a variable, call it *arg*, appears as an argument in a Call statement, and its corresponding parameter in the Sub statement is *par*. After the Sub procedure is executed, *arg* will have whatever value *par* had in the Sub procedure. Hence, not only is the value of *arg* passed to *par*, but the value of *par* is passed back to *arg*.

This program illustrates the transfer of the value of a parameter to its calling argument.

```
Private Sub cmdDisplay_Click()
    Dim amt As Single
    'Illustrate effect of value of parameter on value of
      argument
    picResults.Cls
    amt = 2
    picResults.Print amt;
    Call Triple(amt)
    picResults.Print amt
End Sub

Private Sub Triple(num As Single)
    'Triple a number
    picResults.Print num;
    num = 3 * num
    picResults.Print num;
End Sub

[Run, and then click the command button. The following is
displayed in the picture box.]

2  2  6  6
```

Although this feature may be surprising at first glance, it provides a vehicle for passing values from a Sub procedure back to the place from which the Sub procedure was called. Different names may be used for an argument and its corresponding parameter, but only one memory location is involved. Initially, the cmdDisplay_Click( ) event procedure allocates a memory location to hold the value of *amt* (Figure 3.3 a). When the Sub procedure is called, the parameter *num* becomes the Sub procedure's name for this memory location (Figure 3.3 b). When the value of *num* is tripled, the value in the memory location becomes 6 (Figure 3.3 c). After the completion of the procedure, the parameter name *num* is forgotten; however, its value lives on in *amt* (Figure 3.3 d). The variable *amt* is said to be passed by reference.

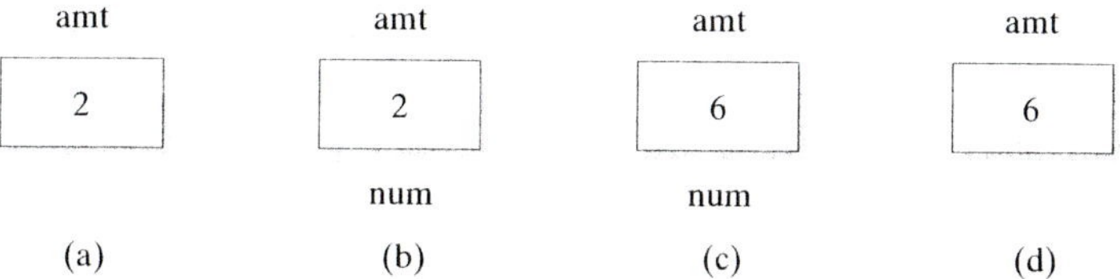

Figure 3.3. Passing a variable by reference to a Sub procedure.

Passing by reference has a wide variety of uses. In the next example, it is used as a vehicle to transport a value from a Sub procedure back to an event procedure.

The following variation of Example 5 uses a Sub procedure to acquire the input. The variables *x* and *y* are not assigned values prior to the execution of the first Call statement. Therefore, before the Call statement is executed, they have the value 0. After the Call statement is executed, however, they have the values 2 and 3. These values then are passed by the second Call statement to the Sub procedure Add.

```
Private Sub cmdCompute_Click()
    Dim x As Single, y As Single
    'Display the sum of the two numbers
    Call GetNumbers(x, y)
    Call Add(x, y)
End Sub

Private Sub Add(num1 As Single, num2 As Single)
    Dim sum As Single
    'Display numbers and their sum
    picResult.Cls
    sum = num1 + num2
    picResult.Print "The sum of"; num1; "and"; num2; "is";
    picResult.Print sum
End Sub

Private Sub GetNumbers(num1 As Single, num2 As Single)
    'Get the two numbers
    num1 = Val(InputBox("First number:", "Add Two Numbers"))
    num2 = Val(InputBox("Second number:", "Add Two Numbers"))
End Sub
```

In most situations, a variable with no preassigned value is used as an argument of a Call statement for the sole purpose of carrying back a value from the Sub procedure.

The following variation of Example 8 allows the cmdCompute_Click event procedure to be written in the input–process–output style:

```
Private Sub cmdCompute_Click()
    Dim x As Single, y As Single, s As Single
    'Display the sum of two numbers
    Call GetNumbers(x, y)
    Call CalculateSum(x, y, s)
    Call DisplayResult(x, y, s)
End Sub
```

```
Private Sub CalculateSum(num1 As Single, num2 As Single, _
                         sum As Single)
     'Add the values of num1 and num2
     'and assign the value to sum
     sum = num1 + num2
End Sub

Private Sub DisplayResult(num1 As Single, num2 As Single, _
                          sum As Single)
     'Display a sentence giving the two numbers and their sum.
     picResult.Cls
     picResult.Print "The sum of"; num1; "and"; num2; "is";sum
End Sub

Private Sub GetNumbers(num1 As Single, num2 As Single)
     'Get the two numbers
     num1 = Val(InputBox("First number:", "Add Two Numbers"))
     num2 = Val(InputBox("Second number:", "Add Two Numbers"))
End Sub
```

3.1.4 Function Procedures

A *Function procedure* (also known as a *user-defined function*) is a function created by the programmer in the same manner as a Sub procedure. A Function procedure is used in the same way as a built-in function. Like a built-in function, a user-defined function has a single output that is usually either a string or a number. A Function procedure is defined in a function block of the form

```
Private Function FunctionName(var1 As Type1, var2 As Type2, ...)
        As dataType
   statement(s)
   FunctionName = expression
End Function
```

Function names should be suggestive of the role performed and must conform to the rules for naming variables. The type *dataType*, which specifies the type of the output, will be one of String, Integer, Single, and so on. In the preceding general code, the next-to-last line assigns the output, which must be of type *dataType*, to the function name. Two examples of functions are as follows:

```
Private Function FtoC(t As Single) As Single
     'Convert Fahrenheit temperature to Celsius
     FtoC = (5 / 9) * (t - 32)
End Function

Private Function FirstName(nom As String) As String
     Dim firstSpace As Integer
     'Extract the first name from the full name nom
     firstSpace = InStr(nom, " ")
     FirstName = Left(nom, firstSpace - 1)
End Function
```

In each of the preceding functions, the value of the function is assigned by a statement of the form *FunctionName* = *expression*. The variables *t* and *nom* appearing in the preceding functions are parameters. They can be replaced with any variable of the same type without affecting the function definition. For instance, the function FtoC could have been defined as

```
Private Function FtoC(temp As Single) As Single
    'Convert Fahrenheit temperature to Celsius
    FtoC = (5 / 9) * (temp - 32)
End Function
```

Like Sub procedures, functions can be created from a code window with Alt/T/P. The only difference is that the circle next to the word Function should be selected.

This program uses the function FtoC.

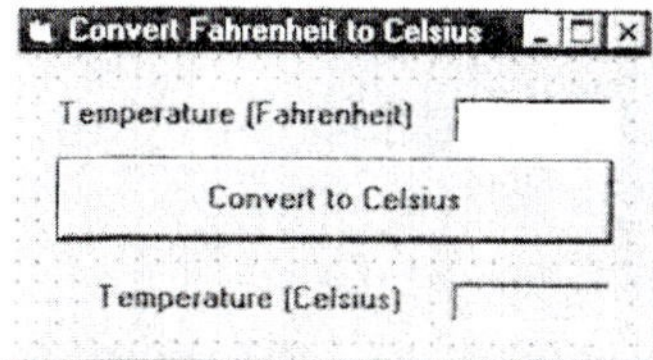

OBJECT	PROPERTY	SETTING
frmConvert	Caption	Convert Fahrenheit to Celsius
lblTempF	Caption	Temperature (Fahrenheit)
txtTempF	Text	(blank)
cmdConvert	Caption	Convert to Celsius
lblTempC	Caption	Temperature (Celsius)
picTempC		

```
Private Sub cmdConvert_Click()
    picTempC.Cls
    picTempC.Print FtoC(Val(txtTempF.Text))
End Sub

Private Function FtoC(t As Single) As Single
    'Convert Fahrenheit temperature to Celsius
    FtoC = (5 / 9) * (t - 32)
End Function

[Run, type 212 into the text box, and then click the command
button.]
```

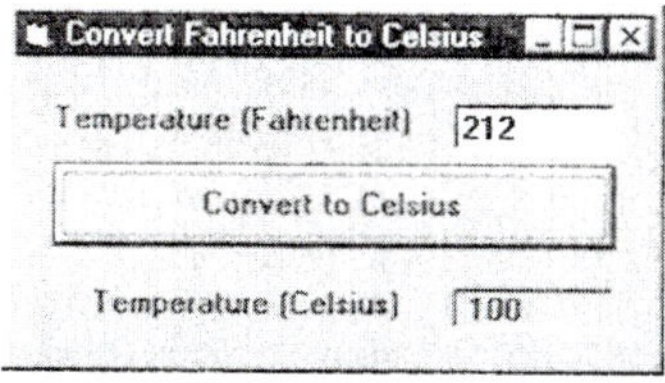

The following program uses the function FirstName.

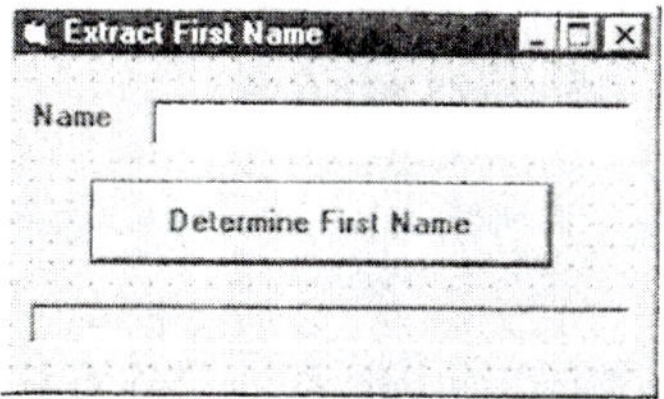

OBJECT	PROPERTY	SETTING
frmName	Caption	Extract First Name
lblName	Caption	Name
txtFullName	Text	(blank)
cmdDetermine	Caption	Determine First Name
picFirstName		

```
Private Sub cmdDetermine_Click()
    Dim nom As String
    'Determine a person's first name
    nom = txtFullName.Text
    picFirstName.Cls
    picFirstName.Print "The first name is "; FirstName(nom)
End Sub

Private Function FirstName(nom As String) As String
    Dim firstSpace As Integer
    'Extract the first name from a full name
    firstSpace = InStr(nom, " ")
    FirstName = Left(nom, firstSpace - 1)
End Function
```

[Run, type Thomas Woodrow Wilson into the text box, and then click the command button.]

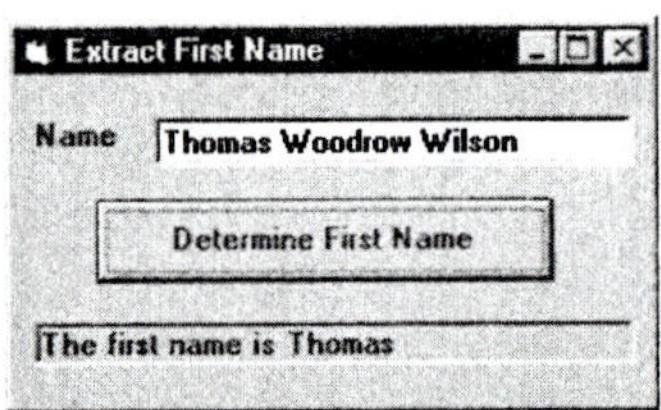

The input to a user-defined function can consist of one or more values. The function in the next example has four parameters. One-letter parameter and variable names have been used so the mathematical formulas will look familiar and be readable. Because the names are not descriptive, the meanings of these variables are carefully stated in comment statements.

3.1.5 Comments

1. Variables dimensioned inside general procedures have local scope, just as they do with event procedures. Variables declared in the (Declarations) section of (General) are recognized by every procedure—event and general.
2. After a general procedure has been defined, Visual Basic automatically reminds you of the procedure's parameters when you type in a statement that calls the procedure. As soon as you type in the left parenthesis following the procedure name, a banner appears giving the names and types of the parameters. The help feature is called *Parameter Info* (Figure 3.4).
3. A Sub procedure can call another Sub procedure. If so, after the End Sub of the called Sub procedure is reached, execution continues with the line in the calling Sub procedure that follows the Call statement.
4. When you create a general procedure without parameters, Visual Basic automatically adds a pair of empty parentheses at the end of the procedure name. Call statements should not use the empty parentheses. The use of parentheses is optional for function calls.
5. When a variable argument is passed by reference to a general procedure, any changes to the corresponding parameter inside the procedure will

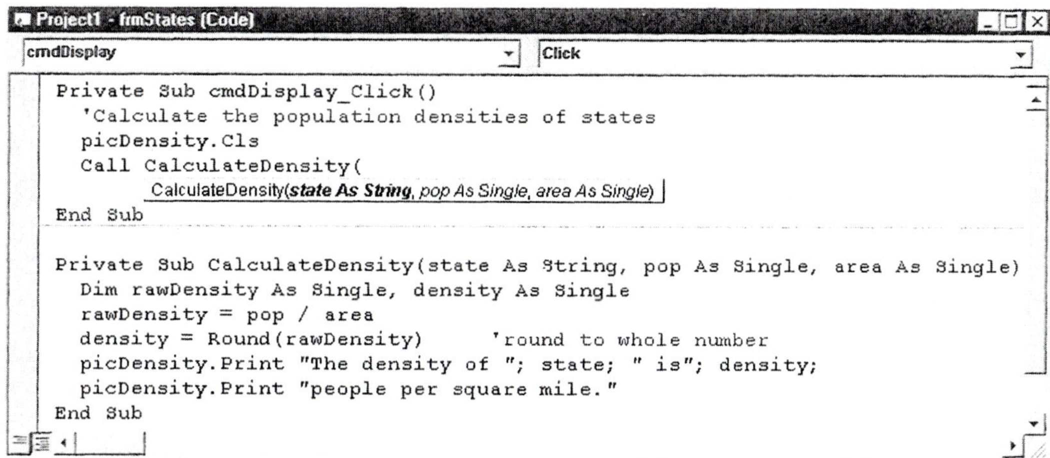

Figure 3.4. The Parameter Info help feature.

change the value of the original argument when the procedure finishes. This change can be prevented by surrounding the argument by an extra pair of parentheses or by preceding the parameter in the top line of the procedure definition with ByVal. In this case, the argument is said to be *passed by value*.

6. Sub procedures are easily distinguished from event procedures. The names of event procedures always begin with the name of control, followed by an underscore character and the name of an event.
7. Functions can perform the same tasks as Sub procedures. They can request input and display text; however, they are primarily used to calculate a single value. Normally, Sub procedures are used to carry out other tasks.
8. Functions differ from Sub procedures in the way they are accessed. Sub procedures are invoked with Call statements, whereas functions are invoked by placing them where you would otherwise expect to find a constant, variable, or expression.
9. To obtain a list of all the general procedures in a program, select (General) from the Code window's Object box, and then click on the down-arrow button to the right of the Procedure box. If you click on one of the procedures in the list, the cursor will move to that procedure.

PRACTICE!

1. What is wrong with the following code?

```
Private Sub cmdDisplay_Click()
    Dim phone As String
    phone = txtPhoneNum.Text
    Call AreaCode(phone)
End Sub

Private Sub AreaCode()
    picOutput.Print "Your area code is "; Left(phone, 3)
End Sub
```

2. What is displayed in the picture box when cmdCompute is clicked?

```
Private Sub cmdCompute_Click()
     Dim gallonsPerBushel As Single, apples As Single
     'How many gallons of apple cider can we make?
     Call GetData(gallonsPerBushel, apples)
     Call DisplayNumOfGallons(gallonsPerBushel, apples)
End Sub

Private Function Cider(g As Single, x As Single) As Single
     Cider = g * x
End Function

Private Sub DisplayNumOfGallons(galPerBu As Single,
     apples As Single)
     picOutput.Cls
     picOutput.Print "You can make";
         Cider(galPerBu,apples);
     picOutput.Print "gallons of cider."
End Sub

Private Sub GetData(gallonsPerBushel As Single,
     apples As Single)
     'gallonsPerBushel Number of gallons of cider one
         'bushel of apples makes apples Number
         'of bushels of apples available
     gallonsPerBushel = 3
     apples = 9
End Sub
```

Solutions

1. The statement Private Sub AreaCode() must be replaced by Private Sub AreaCode(phone As String). Whenever a value is passed to a Sub procedure, the Sub statement must provide a parameter to receive the value.
2. You can make 27 gallons of cider. In this program, the function was used by a Sub procedure rather than by an event procedure.

3.2 DECISION STRUCTURES

An *If block* allows a program to decide on a course of action based on whether a certain condition is true or false. A block of the form

```
If condition Then
     action1
     Else
     action2
End If
```

causes the program to take *action1* if *condition* is true and *action2* if *condition* is false. Each action consists of one or more Visual Basic statements. After an action is taken, execution continues with the line after the If block. Figure 3.5 contains the pseudocode and flowchart for an If block.

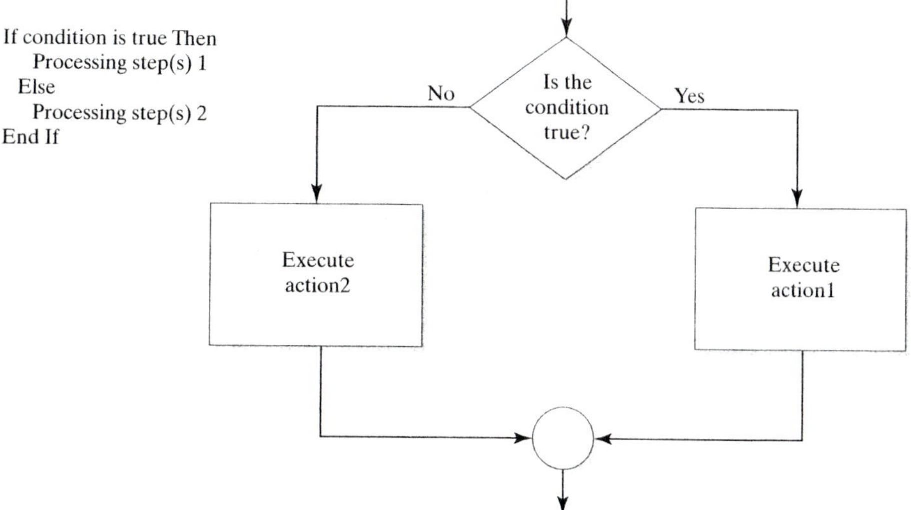

Figure 3.5. Pseudocode and flowchart for an If block.

Problem

1. Write a program to find the larger of two numbers input by the user.

Solution

1. In the following program, the condition is Val(txtFirstNum.Text) > Val(txtSecondNum.Text), and each action consists of a single assignment statement. With the input 3 and 7, the condition is false, and so the second action is taken.

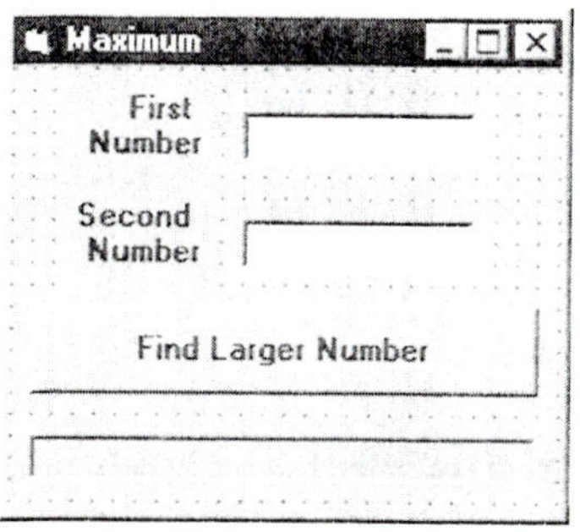

OBJECT	PROPERTY	SETTING
frmMaximum	Caption	Maximum
lblFirstNum	Caption	First Number
txtFirstNum	Text	(blank)
lblSecondNum	Caption	Second Number
txtSecondNum	Text	(blank)
cmdFindLarger	Caption	Find Larger Number
picResult.Cls		

```
Private Sub cmdFindLarger_Click()
     Dim largerNum As Single
     picResult.Cls
     If Val(txtFirstNum.Text) > Val(txtSecondNum.Text) Then
         largerNum = Val(txtFirstNum.Text)
       Else
         largerNum = Val(txtSecondNum.Text)
     End If
     picResult.Print "The larger number is"; largerNum
End Sub
```

[Run, type 3 and 7 into the text boxes, and press the command button.]

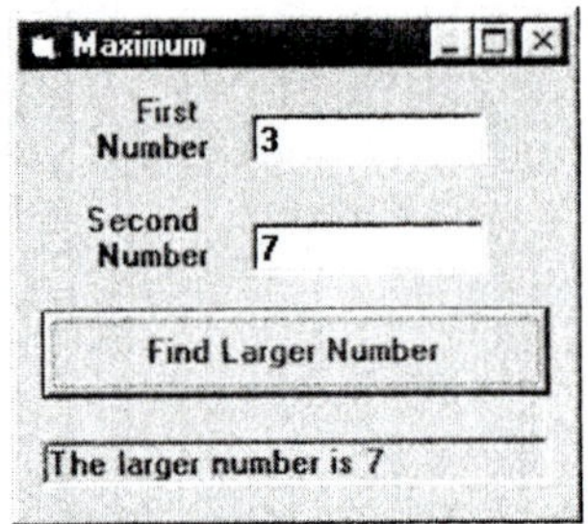

Problem

1. Write a program that requests the costs and revenue for a company and displays the message "Break even" if the costs and revenue are equal or otherwise displays the profit or loss.

Solution

1. In the following program, the action following Else is another If block. We say that the program uses *nested If blocks*.

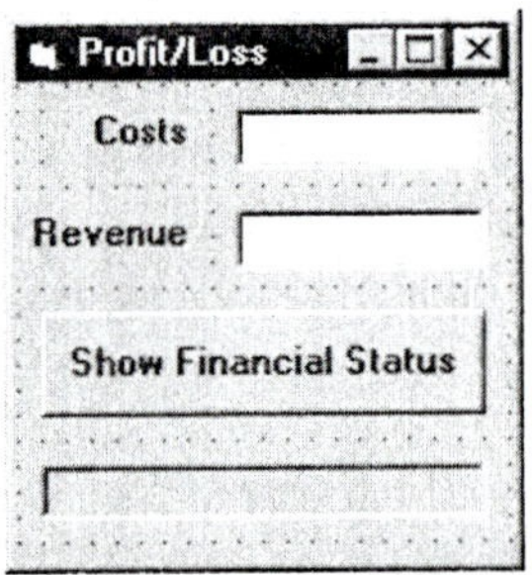

OBJECT	PROPERTY	SETTING
frmP/L	Caption	Profit/Loss
lblCosts	Caption	Costs
txtCosts	Text	(blank)
lblRev	Caption	Revenue
txtRev	Text	(blank)
cmdShow	Caption	Show Financial Status
picResult		

```
Private Sub cmdShow_Click()
    Dim costs As Single, revenue As Single, profit As Single,
        loss As Single
    costs = Val(txtCosts.Text)
    revenue = Val(txtRev.Text)
    picResult.Cls
    If costs = revenue Then
        picResult.Print "Break even"
    Else
        If costs << revenue Then
            profit = revenue - costs
            picResult.Print "Profit is ";
                FormatCurrency(profit)
          Else
            loss = costs - revenue
            picResult.Print "Loss is "; FormatCurrency(loss)
        End If
    End If
End Sub
```

[Run, type 9500 and 8000 into the text boxes, and press the command button.]

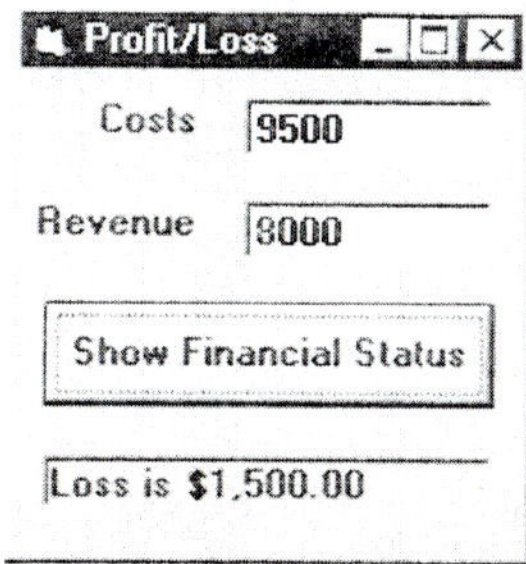

The Else part of an If block can be omitted. This important type of If block appears in the next example.

This program offers assistance to the user before presenting a quotation.

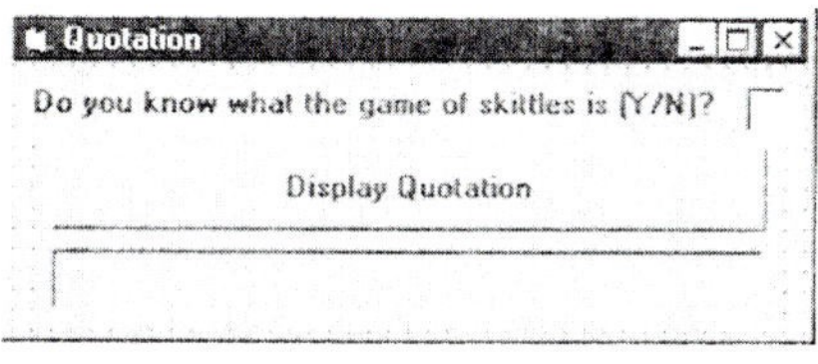

OBJECT	PROPERTY	SETTING
frmQuote	Caption	Quotation
lblQuestion	Caption	Do you know what the game of skittles is (Y/N)?
txtAnswer	Text	(blank)
cmdDisplay	Caption	Display Quotation
picQuotation		

```
Private Sub cmdDisplay_Click()
  Dim message As String
  message = "Skittles is an old form of bowling in which a" _
          & " wooden disk is used to knock down nine pins" _
          & " in a square."
  If UCase(txtAnswer.Text) = "N" Then
      MsgBox message, , ""
  End If
  picQuote.Cls
  picQuote.Print "Life ain't all beer and skittles.";
  picQuote.Print "- Du Maurier (1894)"
End Sub
```

[Run, type N into the text box, and press the command button.]

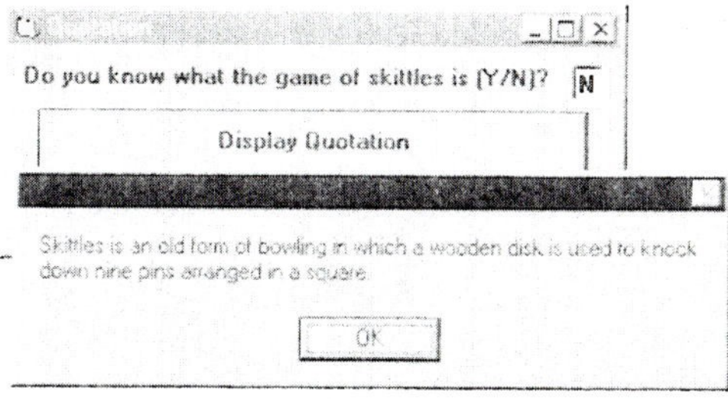

[Press OK.]

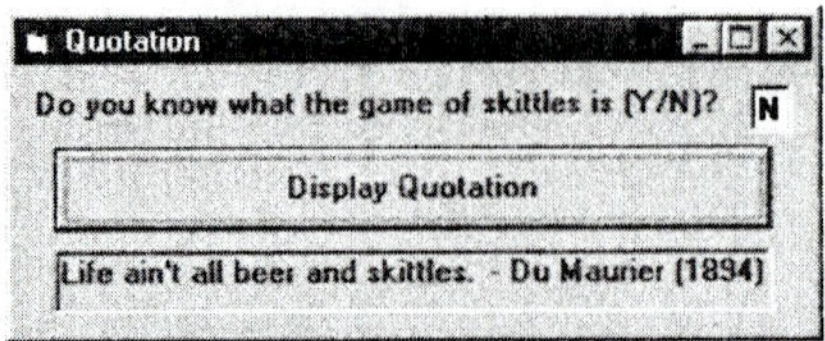

Note: Rerun the program, type Y into the text box, press the command button, and observe that the description of the game is bypassed.

3.2.1 Select Case Blocks

A Select Case block is an efficient decision-making structure that simplifies choosing among several actions. It avoids complex nested If constructs. If blocks make decisions based on the truth value of a condition; Select Case choices are determined by the value of an expression called a *selector.* Each of the possible actions is preceded by a clause of the form

Case valueList,

where *valueList* itemizes the values of the selector for which the action should be taken.

The following program converts the finishing position in a horse race into a descriptive phrase. After the variable *position* is assigned a value from txtPosition, the computer searches for the first Case clause whose value list contains that value and executes the succeeding statement. If the value of *position* is greater than 5, then the statement following Case Else is executed.

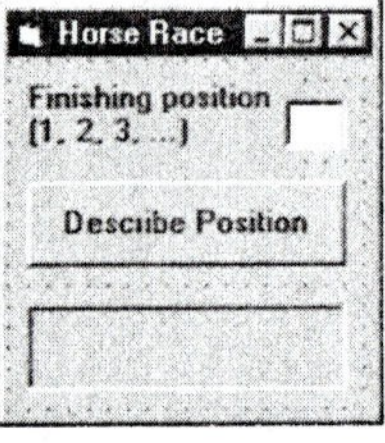

OBJECT	PROPERTY	SETTING
frmRace	Caption	Horse Race
lblPosition	Caption	Finishing position (1, 2, 3, ...)
txtPosition	Text	(blank)
cmdDescribe	Caption	Describe Position
picOutcome		

```
Private Sub cmdDescribe_Click()
    Dim position As Integer 'Selector
    position = Val(txtPosition.Text)
    picOutcome.Cls
    Select Case position
      Case 1
         picOutcome.Print "Win"
      Case 2
         picOutcome.Print "Place"
      Case 3
         picOutcome.Print "Show"
      Case 4, 5
         picOutcome.Print "You almost placed"
         picOutcome.Print "in the money."
      Case Else
         picOutcome.Print "Out of the money."
    End Select
End Sub
```

```
[Run, type 2 into the text box, and press the command button.]
```

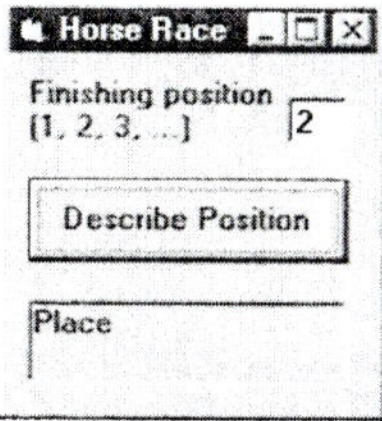

Here is a variation of Example 4, in which the value lists specify ranges of values. The first value list provides another way to specify the numbers 1 to 3. The second value list covers all numbers from 4 on.

```
Private Sub cmdDescribe_Click()
    Dim position As Integer
    'Describe finishing positions in a horse race
    picOutcome.Cls
    position = Val(txtPosition.Text)
    Select Case position
      Case 1 To 3
          picOutcome.Print "In the money."
          picOutcome.Print "Congratulations"
      Case Is > 3
          picOutcome.Print "Not in the money."
    End Select
End Sub
```

```
[Run, type 2 into the text box, and press the command button.]
```

The general form of the Select Case block is

```
Select Case selector
    Case valueList1
        action1
    Case valueList2
        action2
          ⋮
    Case Else
        action of last resort
End Select
```

where Case Else (and its action) is optional, and each value list contains one or more of the following types of items separated by commas:

1. A constant;
2. A variable;
3. An expression;
4. An inequality sign preceded by Is and followed by a constant, variable, or expression; and/or
5. A range expressed in the form *a* To *b*, where *a* and *b* are constants, variables, or expressions.

Different items appearing in the same list must be separated by commas. Each action consists of one or more statements. After the selector is evaluated, the computer looks for the first value-list item containing the value of the selector and carries out its associated action.

The following program uses several different types of value lists. With the response shown, the first action was selected because the value of y – x is 1.

OBJECT	PROPERTY	SETTING
frmRhyme	Caption	One, Two, Buckle My Shoe
lblEnterNum	Caption	Enter a number from 1 to 10
txtNumber	Text	(blank)
cmdInterpret	Caption	Interpret Number
picPhrase		

```
Private Sub cmdInterpret_Click()
    Dim x As Integer, y As Integer, num As Integer
    'One, Two, Buckle My Shoe
    picPhrase.Cls
    x = 2
    y = 3
    num = Val(txtNumber.Text)
    Select Case num
      Case y - x, x
        picPhrase.Print "Buckle my shoe."
      Case Is <= 4
        picPhrase.Print "Shut the door."
      Case x + y To x * y
        picPhrase.Print "Pick up sticks."
      Case 7, 8
        picPhrase.Print "Lay them straight."
      Case Else
        picPhrase.Print "Start all over again."
    End Select
End Sub
```

[Run, type 4 into the text box, and press the command button.]

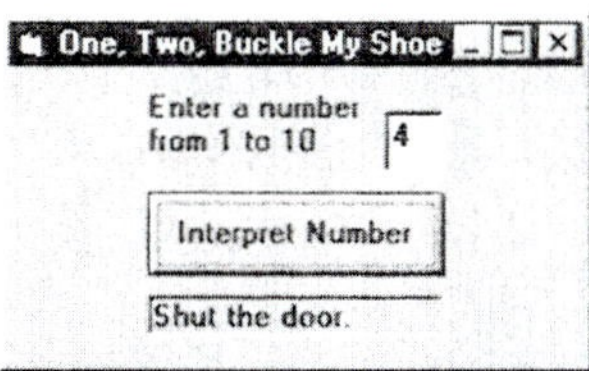

In each of the three preceding examples the selector was a numeric variable; however, the selector also can be a string variable or an expression.

This program has the string variable *firstName* as a selector.

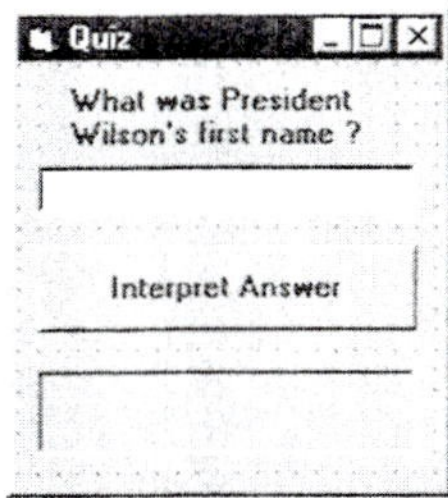

OBJECT	PROPERTY	SETTING
frmQuiz	Caption	Quiz
lblQuestion	Caption	"What was President Wilson's first name?"
txtName Text	(blank)	
cmdInterpret	Caption	Interpret Answer
picAnswer		

```
Private Sub cmdInterpret_Click()
      Dim firstName As String
      'Quiz
      picAnswer.Cls
      firstName = txtName.Text
      Select Case firstName
        Case "Thomas"
          picAnswer.Print "Correct."
        Case "Woodrow"
          picAnswer.Print "Sorry, his full name was"
          picAnswer.Print "Thomas Woodrow Wilson."
        Case "President"
          picAnswer.Print "Are you for real?"
        Case Else
          picAnswer.Print "Nice try, but no cigar."
      End Select
End Sub
```

[Run, type Woodrow into the text box, and press the command button.]

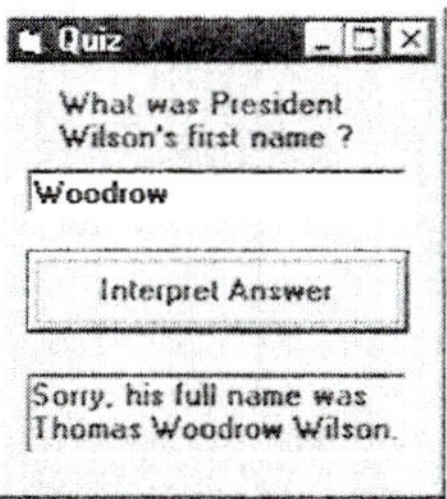

3.2.2 Logical Operators

Programming situations often require more complex conditions than those considered so far. For instance, suppose we would like to state that the value of a numeric variable, *n*, is strictly between 2 and 5. The proper Visual Basic condition is

```
(2 < n) And (n < 5)
```

The condition (2 < n) And (n < 5) is a combination of the two conditions 2 < n and n < 5 with the logical operator And.

The three main logical operators are And, Or, and Not. If *cond1* and *cond2* are conditions, then the condition

cond1 And *cond2*

is true if both *cond1* and *cond2* are true. Otherwise, it is false. The condition

cond1 Or *cond2*

is true if either *cond1* or *cond2* (or both) is true. Otherwise, it is false. The condition

Not *cond1*

is true if *cond1* is false, and is false if *cond1* is true.

The If block in the following program has a logical operator in its condition.

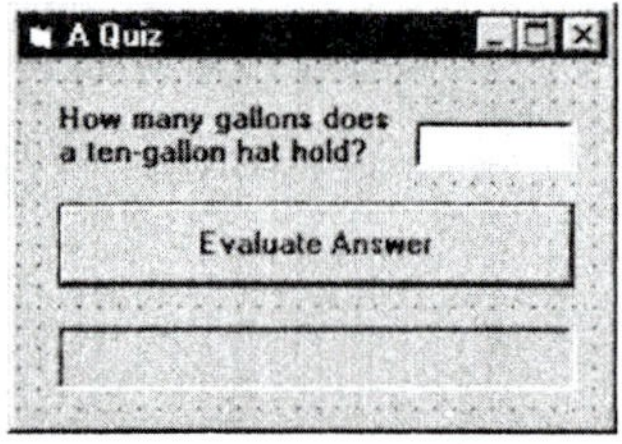

OBJECT	PROPERTY	SETTING
frmQuiz	Caption	A Quiz
lblQuestion	Caption	How many gallons does a ten-gallon hat hold?
txtAnswer	Text	(blank)
cmdEvaluate	Caption	Evaluate Answer
picSolution		

```
Private Sub cmdEvaluate_Click()
    Dim answer As Single
    'Evaluate answer
    picSolution.Cls
    answer = Val(txtAnswer.Text)
    If (answer >= .5) And (answer <= 1) Then
        picSolution.Print "Good, ";
      Else
        picSolution.Print "No, ";
    End If
        picSolution.Print "it holds about 3/4 of a gallon."
End Sub
```

```
[Run, type 10 into the text box, and press the command
button.]
```

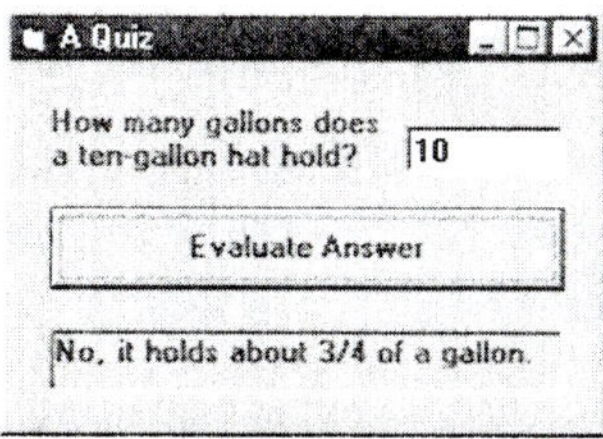

3.2.3 Comments

1. Conditions evaluate to either True or False. These two values are called the *truth values* of the condition.

2. The actions of an If block and the word Else do not have to be indented. For instance, the If block of Example 1 can be written

```
If Val(txtFirstNum.Text) > Val(txtSecondNum.Text) Then
     largerNum = Val(txtFirstNum.Text)
   Else
     largerNum = Val(txtSecondNum.Text)
End If
```

However, because indenting improves the readability of the block, it is regarded as good programming style. As soon as you see the word If, your eyes can easily scan down the program to find the matching End If and the enclosed Else clause. You then immediately have a good idea of the size and complexity of the block.

3. Care should be taken to make If blocks easy to understand. For instance, in Figure 3.6. the block on the left is difficult to follow and should be replaced by the clearer block on the right.

```
If cond1 Then
   If cond2 Then
     action
   End If
End If
```

```
If cond1 And cond2 Then
  action
End If
```

Figure 3.6. A confusing If block and an improvement.

4. Visual Basic also has a single-line If statement of the form

   ```
   If condition Then action1 Else action2,
   ```

   which is a holdover from earlier, unstructured versions of BASIC; it is seldom used in this text.

5. Some programming languages do not allow a value to appear in two different value lists; Visual Basic does. If a value appears in two different value lists, the action associated with the first value list will be carried out.

6. In Visual Basic, if the value of the selector does not appear in any of the value lists and there is no Case Else clause, execution of the program will continue with the statement following the Select Case block.

7. If the word Is, which should precede an inequality sign in a value list, is accidentally omitted, the smart editor will automatically insert it when checking the line.

8. A Case clause of the form Case b To c selects values from *b* to *c* inclusive. However, the extreme values can be excluded by placing the action inside an If block beginning with If (*selector* <> b) And (*selector* <> c) Then the value of *b* must be less than or equal to the value of *c* in a Case clause of the form Case b To c.

9. A condition such as 2 < n < 5 should never be used, because Visual Basic will not evaluate it as intended. The correct condition is (2 < n) And (n < 5).

10. A common error is to replace the condition Not (*n* < 3) by condition (3 > *n*). The correct replacement is (3 >= *n*).

PRACTICE!

1. Suppose the user is asked to input a number into txtNumber for which the square root is to be taken. Fill in the If block so that the lines of code below either will display the message "Number can't be negative" or will display the square root of the number.

```
Private Sub cmdTakeSquareRoot_Click()
  Dim num As Single
  'Check reasonableness of data
  num = Val(txtNumber.Text)
  If



  End If
End Sub
```

2. The selector of a Select Case block is the numeric variable *num*. Determine whether each of the following Case clauses is valid.

   a. Case 1, 4, Is < 10
   b. Case Is < 5, Is >= 5
   c. Case num = 2

3. Complete Table 3-1

TABLE 3-1 Truth values of logical operators.

COND1	COND2	COND1 AND COND2	COND1 OR COND2	NOT COND2
True	True	True		
True	False		True	
False	True			False
False	False			

Solutions

1.
```
If num < 0 Then
        MsgBox "Number can't be negative.", , "Input Error"
        txtNumber.Text = ""
        txtNumber.SetFocus
        Else
        picSquareRoot.Print Sqr(num)
End If
```

2. a. Valid. These items are redundant because 1 and 4 are just special cases of Is < 10. However, this makes no difference in Visual Basic.

   b. Valid. These items are contradictory. However, Visual Basic looks at them one at a time until it finds an item containing the value of the selector. The action following this Case clause will always be carried out.

   c. Not valid. It should be Case 2.

3.

COND1	COND2	COND1 AND COND2	COND1 OR COND2	NOT COND2
True	True	True	True	False
True	False	False	True	True
False	True	False	True	False
False	False	False	False	True

3.3 DO LOOPS

A *loop*, one of the most important structures in Visual Basic, repeats a sequence of statements a number of times. At each repetition, or *pass*, the statements act upon variables whose values are changing.

The *Do loop* repeats a sequence of statements either as long as, or until, a certain condition is true. A Do statement precedes the sequence of statements, and a Loop statement follows the sequence of statements. The condition, along with either the word While or Until, follows the word Do or the word Loop. When Visual Basic executes a Do loop of the form

```
Do While condition
statement(s)
Loop,
```

it first checks the truth value of *condition*. If *condition* is false, then the statements inside the loop are not executed, and the program continues with the line after the Loop statement. If *condition* is true, then the statements inside the loop are executed. When the statement Loop is encountered, the entire process is repeated, beginning with the testing of *condition* in the Do While statement. In other words, the statements inside the loop are repeatedly executed only as long as (that is, while) the condition is true. Figure 3.7 contains the pseudocode and flowchart for this loop.

Do While condition is true
    Processing step(s)
Loop

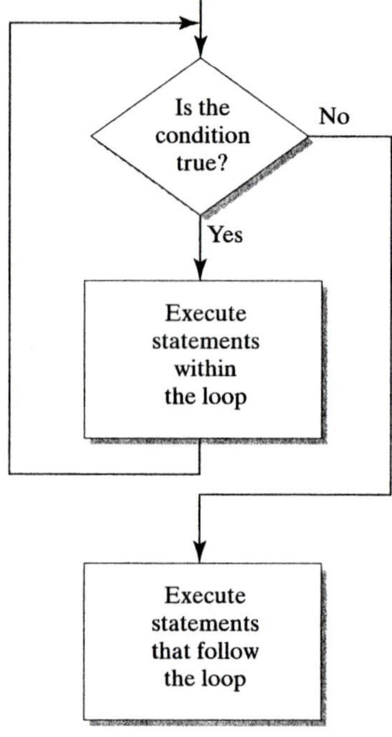

Figure 3.7. Pseudocode and flowchart for a Do While loop.

Problem

Write a program that displays the numbers from 1 to 10.

Solution

The condition in the Do loop is "num <= 10".

```
Private Sub cmdDisplay_Click()
     Dim num As Integer
     'Display the numbers from 1 to 10
     num = 1
     Do While num <= 10
        picNumbers.Print num;
        num = num + 1
     Loop
End Sub
```

```
[Run, and click the command button. The following is displayed
in the picture box.]

1   2   3   4   5   6   7   8   9   10
```

Do loops are commonly used to ensure that a proper response is received from the InputBox function.

This program requires the user to give a password before a secret file can be accessed.

```
Private Sub cmdDisplay_Click()
     Dim passWord As String, info As String
     If UCase(txtName.Text) = "SECRET.TXT" Then
        passWord = ""
```

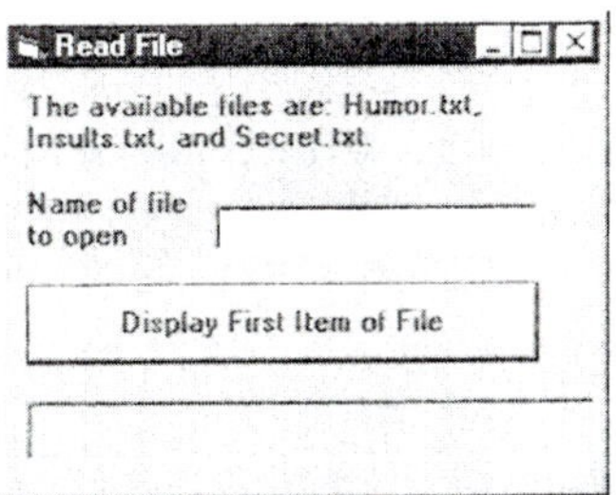

OBJECT	PROPERTY	SETTING
frmFile	Caption	Read File
lblFiles	Caption	The available files are: Humor.txt, Insults.txt, and Secret.txt.
lblName	Caption	Name of file to open
txtName	Text	(blank)
cmdDisplay	Caption	Display First Item of File
picItem		

```
            Do While passWord <> "SHAZAM"
                passWord = InputBox("What is the password?")
                passWord = UCase(passWord)
            Loop
        End If
        Open txtName.Text For Input As #1
        Input #1, info
        picItem.Cls
        picItem.Print info
        Close #1
End Sub
```

```
[Run, type Secret.txt into the text box, and click the command
button.]
```

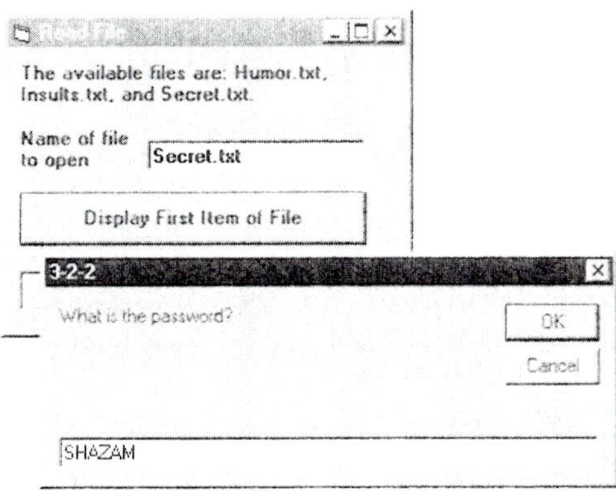

Note: If a file other than Secret.txt is requested, the statements inside the loop are not executed.

In Examples 1 and 2 the condition was checked at the top of the loop (that is, before the statements were executed). Alternatively, the condition can be checked at the bottom of the loop when the statement Loop is reached. When Visual Basic encounters a Do loop of the form

Do
    statement(s)
Loop Until *condition*

it executes the statements inside the loop and then checks the truth value of *condition*. If *condition* is true, then the program continues with the line after the Loop statement. If *condition* is false, then the entire process is repeated beginning with the Do statement. In other words, the statements inside the loop are executed at least once and then are repeatedly executed *until* the condition is true. Figure 3.8 shows the pseudocode and flowchart for this type of Do loop.

The following program is equivalent to Example 2, except that the condition is tested at the bottom of the loop.

Do
  statement(s)
Loop Until condition is true

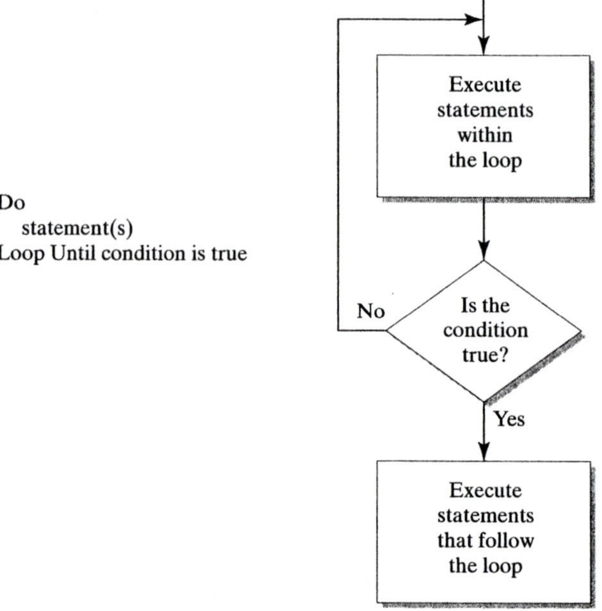

Figure 3.8. Pseudocode and flowchart for a Do loop with condition tested at the bottom.

```
Private Sub cmdDisplay_Click()
      Dim passWord As String, info As String
      If UCase(txtName.Text) = "SECRET.TXT" Then
        Do
          passWord = InputBox("What is the password?")
          passWord = UCase(passWord)
        Loop Until passWord = "SHAZAM"
      End If
      Open txtName.Text For Input As #1
      Input #1, info
      picItem.Cls
      picItem.Print info
      Close #1
End Sub
```

3.3.1 Bisection Method for Finding a Zero of a Function

Suppose the mathematical function $f(x)$ is defined and continuous on the interval $[a, b]$, and $f(a)$ has a different sign than $f(b)$. (See Figure 3.9) Then the equation $f(x) = 0$ must have a solution between a and b. That is, there must exist a number c between a and b with $f(c) = 0$. Such a number c is called a *zero* of the function. The flowchart in Figure 3.10 describes an algorithm, known as the *bisection method*, for finding c. At each iteration, the length of the subinterval containing c is halved. Halving continues until the subinterval reaches a certain tolerance length (such as .00001) or until c is found exactly (an unlikely event). Because single-precision numbers are only accurate to 7 significant figures, the choice of an appropriate tolerance level depends on the magnitude of the zero. For instance, .1 is an appropriate tolerance level if c is near 100,000,000, and 10^{-31} is appropriate if c is very close to 0. In general, .00001 is a good tolerance level for medium-sized values of c

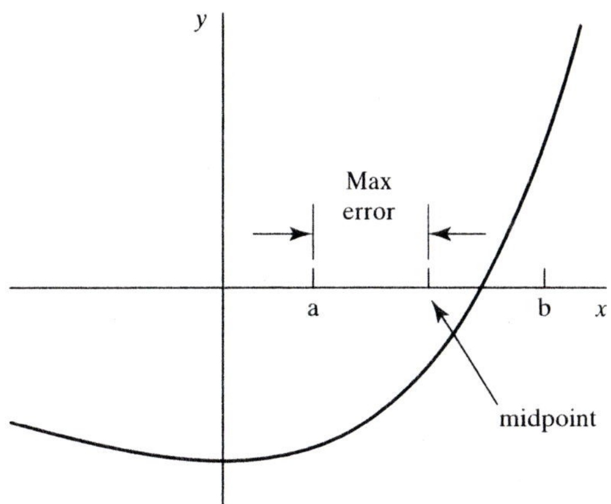

Figure 3.9. A function with a zero in the interval [a, b].

EXAMPLE 3.1: The following program finds a zero of the function $e^x - x - 4$. This function is graphed in Figure 3.9.

```
Private Sub cmdFindZero_Click()
    Dim tolerance As Single, a As Single, b As Single,
        message As String
    'The Bisection Method
    'Approximate a zero of a function f(x) between the user
        supplied
    'values a and b, where f(a) and f(b) have different signs
    tolerance = Val(txtTolerance)
    a = Val(txtA.Text)
    b = Val(txtB.Text)
    If Sgn(f(a)) = Sgn(f(b)) Then
        message = "f(a) and f(b) must have different signs. " & _
            "Enter new values for a and/or b."
        MsgBox message
        txtA.SetFocus
      Else
        'Find the zero between a and b
        lblZero = BisectionMethod(tolerance, a, b)
    End If
End Sub

Private Function f(x As Single) As Single
    f = Exp(x) - x - 4
End Function
```

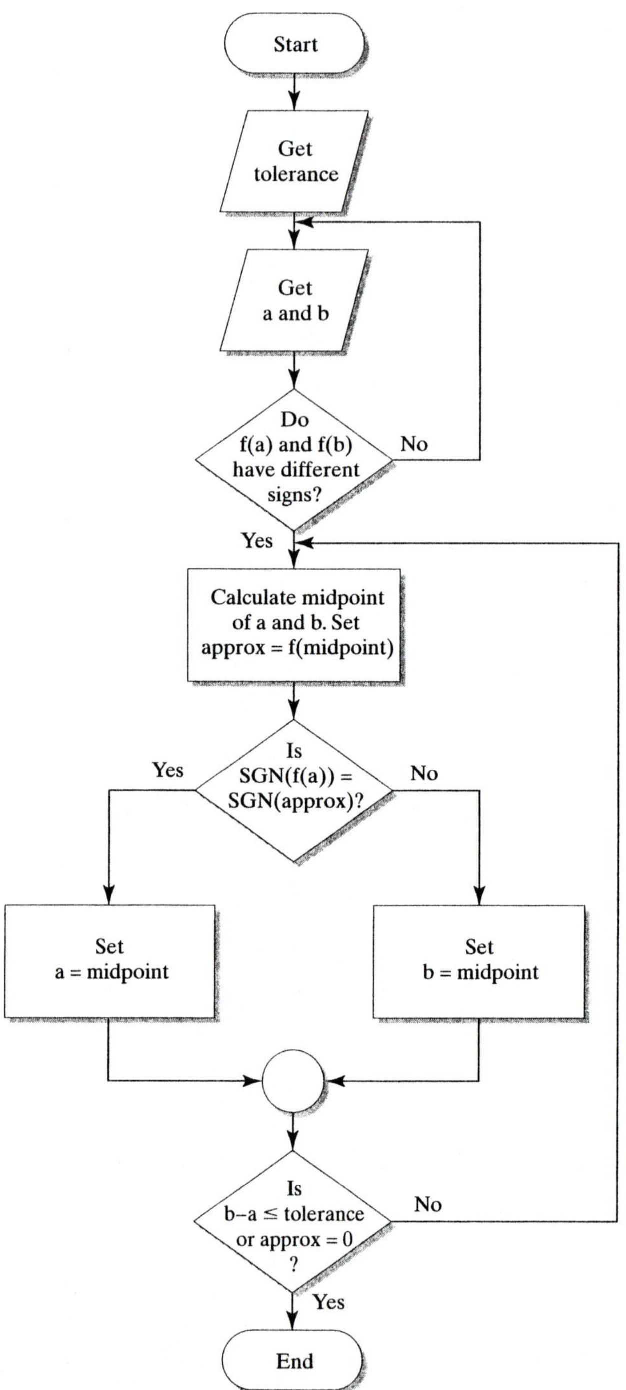

Figure 3.10. Flowchart for the bisection method.

```
Private Function BisectionMethod(tol As Single, a As Single, _
                  b As Single) As Single 'Find the zero
                  'between a and b
   Do
      midpoint = (a + b) / 2
      approx = f(midpoint)
```

```
      If Sgn(f(a)) = Sgn(approx) Then
         a = midpoint
         Else
         b = midpoint
      End If
      Loop Until ((b - a) <= tol) Or (approx = 0)
      BisectionMethod = midpoint
   End Function
```

[Run, enter values into the three text boxes, and press the command button.]

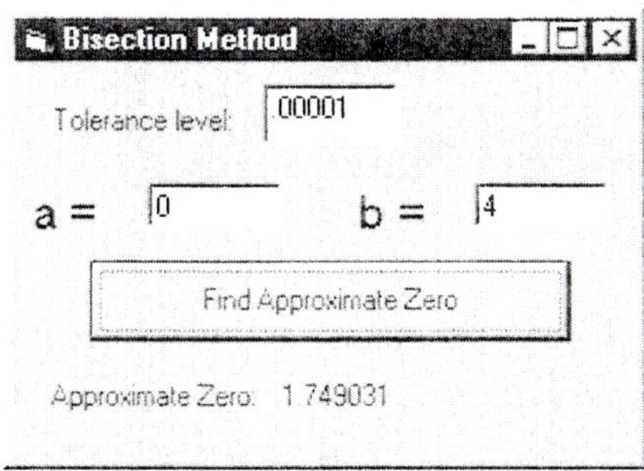

3.3.2 Derivatives

The derivative of the function $f(x)$ at $x = a$ is defined as

$$f'(a) = \lim_{h \to 0} \frac{f(a+h) - f(a)}{h}.$$

One way to attempt an estimation of $f'(a)$ is to choose a positive value of h that is as close to zero as Visual Basic allows, and then to evaluate the quotient. Unfortunately, round-off errors can easily invalidate the result obtained in this manner. A better method, which usually avoids problems with round-off errors, evaluates the formula $(f(a + h) - f(a))/h$ for smaller and smaller values of h, until the difference between successive approximations falls below a predetermined level.

EXAMPLE 3.2: Write a program to calculate the derivative of $f(x) = 3x^3 - 2x^2$ at $x = c$, where the value of c is input by the user.

SOLUTION

The following program starts with h equal to 1 and then successively halves h to generate approximations to the slope of the function. When the difference between successive approximations is less than .0001, the most recent approximation is reported as the slope of the function.

```
Private Sub cmdCalculateDer_Click()
    Dim x As Double, h As Double 'Double-precision
       improves accuracy
    'Determine the slope of a function at a point
    Dim current As Double, past As Double
    x = txtC             'Value where derivative is desired
    h = 1
    current = (f(x + h) - f(x)) / h
```

```
    Do
        past = current
        h = h / 2
        current = (f(x + h) - f(x)) / h
    Loop Until Abs(past - current) < 0.0001
    lblDerivative = FormatNumber(current, 4)
End Sub

Private Function f(x As Double) As Double
    f = 3 * x ^ 3 - 2 * x ^ 2
End Function
```

[Run, enter a value for c into the text box, and press the command button.]

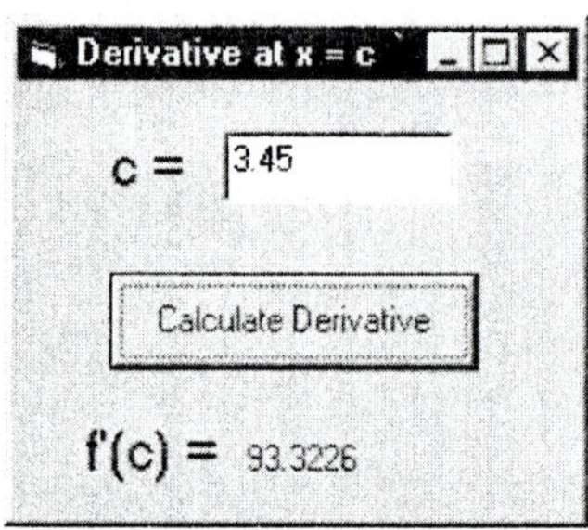

The following program uses the counter *numPeople*, the accumulator *total*, and the flag *perfectFlag*. The first Do loop reads the entire contents of the file. The second Do loop stops reading the file when the person whose name is specified in the text box is located. The first three lines of the file Grades.txt are

"Michael", 85
"Brittany", 82
"Christopher", 100

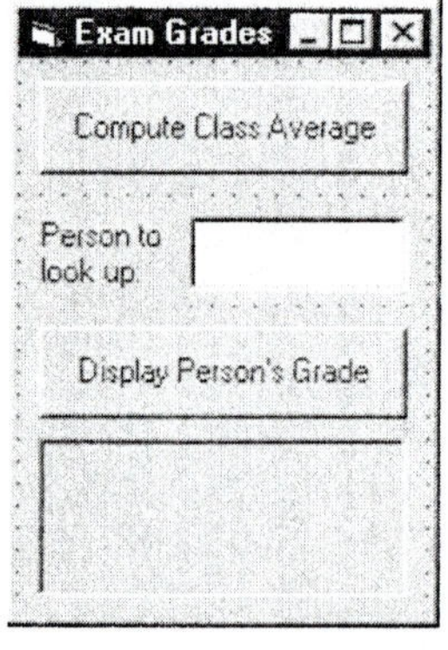

OBJECT	PROPERTY	SETTING
frmGRADES	Caption	Exam Grades
cmdAverage	Caption	Compute Class Average
lblPerson	Caption	Person to look up:
txtPerson	Text	(blank)
cmdGrade	Caption	Display Person's Grade
picOutput		

```
Private Sub cmdAverage_Click()
    Dim numPeople As Integer, total As Integer
    Dim perfectFlag As Boolean
    Dim nom As String, grade As Integer
    Open "Grades.txt" For Input As #1
    numPeople = 0
    total = 0
```

```
    perfectFlag = False
    Do While Not EOF(1)
       Input #1, nom, grade
       numPeople = numPeople + 1
       total = total + grade
       If grade = 100 Then
          perfectFlag = True
       End If
    Loop
    Close #1
    picOutput.Cls
    picOutput.Print "Class average is"; total / numPeople
    If perfectFlag = True Then
       picOutput.Print "Someone had 100."
    End If
End Sub

Private Sub cmdGrade_Click()
    Dim nom As String, grade As Integer
    Open "Grades.txt" For Input As #1
    Do While (nom <> txtPerson.Text) And (Not EOF(1))
       Input #1, nom, grade
    Loop
    Close #1
    If nom = txtPerson.Text Then
       picOutput.Print nom; grade
       Else
       picOutput.Print "Person not found."
    End If
End Sub

[Run, press the first command button, type Brittany into the
text box, and press the second command button.]
```

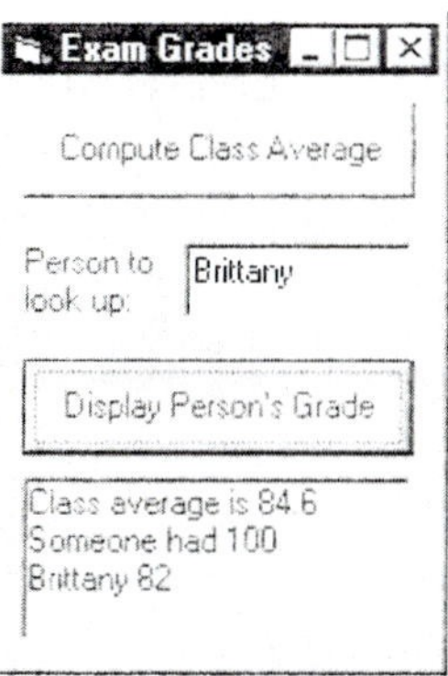

The first Do loop in Example 5 illustrates the proper way to process a list of data contained in a file. The Do loop should be tested at the top with an end-of-file condition. (If the file is empty, no attempt is made to input data from the file.) The first set of data should be input *after* the Do statement, and then the data should be processed. Figure 3.11 contains the pseudocode and flowchart for this technique.

Do While there are still data in the file
Get an item of data
Process the item
Loop

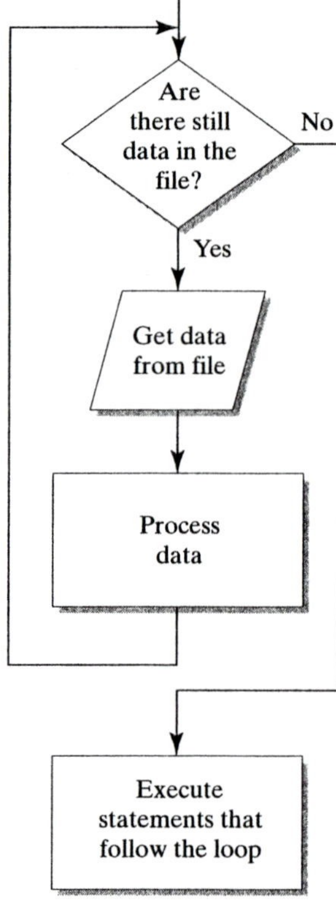

Figure 3.11. Pseudocode and flowchart for processing data from a file.

3.3.3 Comments

1. Be careful to avoid infinite loops—that is, loops that are never exited. The following loop is infinite because the condition "num <> 0" will always be true. *Note:* The loop can be terminated by pressing Ctrl+Break.

```
Private Sub cmdButton_Click()
    Dim num As Single
    'An infinite loop
    num = 7
    Do While num <> 0
        num = num - 2
    Loop
End Sub
```

Notice that this slip-up can be avoided by changing the condition to "num>= 0".

2. Visual Basic allows the use of the words While and Until either at the top or bottom of a Do loop. In this text, the usage of these words is restricted for these reasons.

   a. Restricting the use simplifies reading the program. The word While proclaims testing at the top, and the word Until proclaims testing at the bottom.

   b. Standard pseudocode uses the word While to denote testing a loop at the top and the word Until to denote testing at the bottom.

3. Good programming practice requires that all variables appearing in a Do loop be assigned values before the loop is entered rather than relying on default values. For instance, the code at the left in what follows should be replaced with the code at the right.

```
'Add 1 through 10                 'Add 1 through 10
Do While num < 10                     num = 0
    num = num + 1                     sum = 0
    sum = sum + num                   Do While num < 10
Loop                                      num = num + 1
                                          sum = sum + num
                                      Loop
```

4. When flagVar is a variable of Boolean type, the statements

`If flagVar = True Then` and `If flagVar = False Then`

can be replaced by

`If flagVar Then` and `If Not flagVar Then`

Similarly, the statements

`Do While flagVar = True` and `Do While flagVar = False`

can be replaced by

`Do While flagVar` and `Do While Not flagVar`

PRACTICE!

1. How do you decide whether a condition should be checked at the top of a loop or at the bottom?
2. Change the following loop so it will be executed at least once.

```
Do While continue = "Yes"
    answer = InputBox("Do you want to continue? (Y or N)")
    If UCase(answer) = "Y" Then
        continue = "Yes"
      Else
        continue = "No"
    End If
Loop
```

Solutions

1. As a rule of thumb, the condition is checked at the bottom if the loop should be executed at least once.
2. Either precede the loop with the statement continue = "Yes" or change the first line to Do and replace the Loop statement with Loop Until continue <> "Yes".

3.4 FOR...NEXT LOOPS

When we know exactly how many times a loop should be executed, we can use a special type of loop, called a For...Next loop. For...Next loops are easy to read and write, and have features that make them ideal for certain common tasks. The following code uses a For...Next loop to display a table.

```
Private Sub cmdDisplayTable_Click()
    Dim i As Integer
    'Display a table of the first 5 numbers and their squares
    picTable.Cls
    For i = 1 To 5
       picTable.Print i; i ^ 2
    Next i
End Sub
```

```
[Run and click on cmdDisplayTable. The following is displayed
in the picture box.]
```

```
1  1
2  4
3  9
4  16
5  25
```

Here is an equivalent program written with a Do loop.

```
Private Sub cmdDisplayTable_Click()
   Dim i As Integer
   'Display a table of the first 5 numbers and their squares
   picTable.Cls
   i = 1
   Do While i <<= 5
      picTable.Print i; i ^ 2
      i = i + 1
   Loop
End Sub
```

In general, a portion of a program of the form

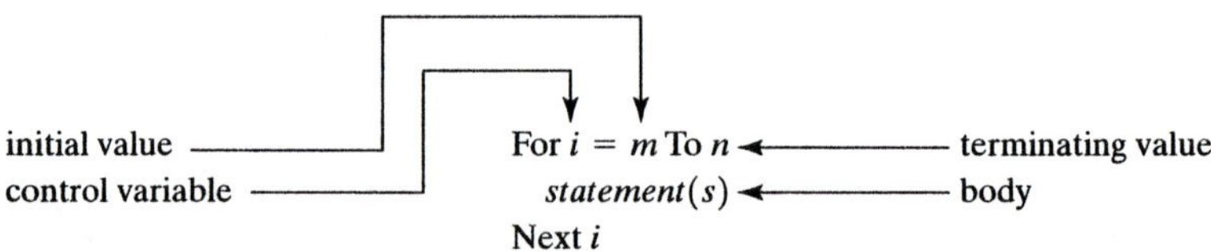

constitutes a For...Next loop. The pair of statements For and Next cause the statements between them to be repeated a specified number of times. The For statement designates a numeric variable, called the *control variable*, that is initialized and then automatically changes after each execution of the loop. Also, the For statement gives the range of values this variable will assume. The Next statement increments the control variable. If $m \leq n$, then i is assigned the values $m, m + 1, \ldots, n$ in order, and the body is executed once for each of these values. If $m > n$, then the statements in the body are not executed, and execution continues with the statement after the For...Next loop.

When program execution reaches a For...Next loop, such as the one shown previously, the For statement assigns to the control variable i the initial value m and checks to see whether i is greater than the terminating value n. If so, then execution jumps to the line following the Next statement. If $i <= n$, the statements inside the loop are executed. Then, the Next statement increases the value of i by 1 and checks this new value to see if it exceeds n. If not, the entire process is repeated until the value of i exceeds n. When this happens, the program moves to the line following the loop. Figure 3.12 contains the pseudocode and flowchart of a For...Next loop.

```
For i = m to n
Processing step(s)
Next i
```

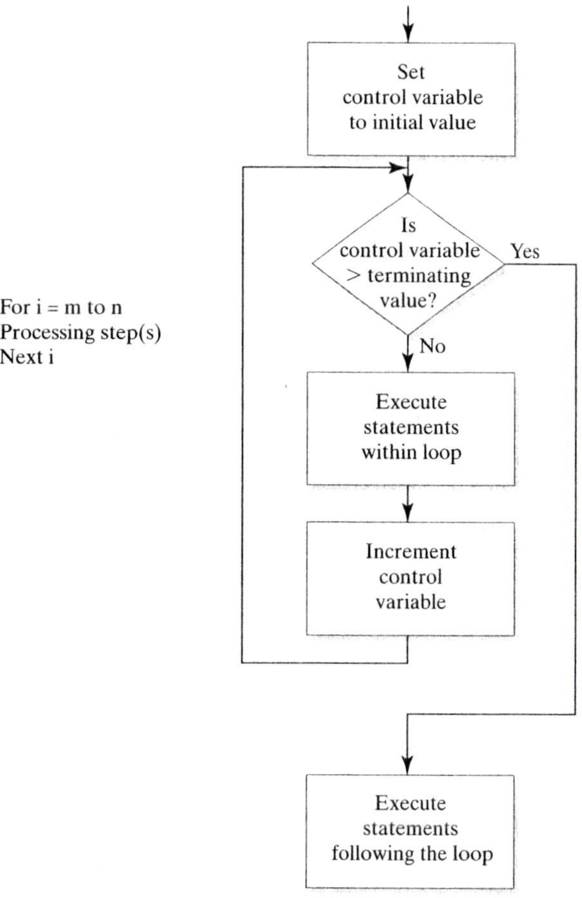

Figure 3.12. Pseudocode and flowchart of a For...Next loop.

The control variable can be *any* numeric variable. The most common single letter names are i, j, and k; however, if appropriate, the name should suggest the purpose of the control variable.

Suppose the population of a city is 300,000 in the year 1998 and is growing at the rate of 3 percent per year. The following program displays a table showing the population each year until 2002.

OBJECT	PROPERTY	SETTING
frmPOP	Caption	POPULATION GROWTH
cmdDisplay	Caption	Display Population
picTable		

```
Private Sub cmdDisplay_Click()
    Dim pop As Single, yr As Integer
    'Display population from 1998 to 2002
    picTable.Cls
    pop = 300000
    For yr = 1998 To 2002
      picTable.Print yr, FormatNumber(pop, 0)
      pop = pop + .03 * pop
    Next yr
End Sub
```

[Run, and click the command button.]

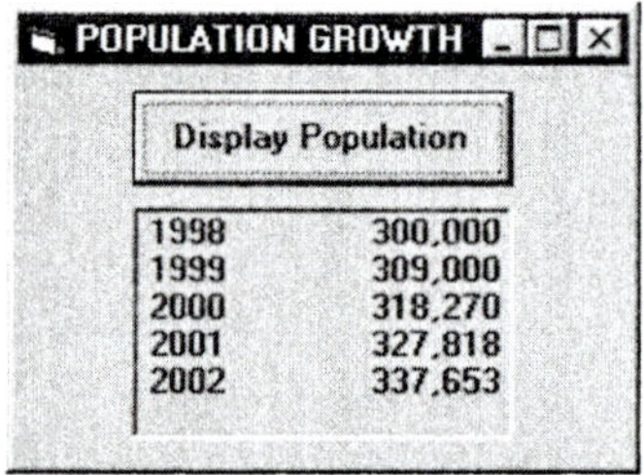

The initial and terminating values can be constants, variables, or expressions. For instance, the For statement in the preceding program can be replaced by

```
firstYr = 1998
lastYr = 2002
For yr = firstYr To lastYr
```

In the program above, the control variable was increased by 1 after each pass through the loop. A variation of the For statement allows any number to be used as the increment. The statement

For $i = m$ To n Step s

instructs the Next statement to add s to the control variable instead of 1. The numbers m, n, and s do not have to be whole numbers. The number s is called the *step value* of the loop.

The following program displays the values of the index of a For...Next loop for terminating and step values input by the user.

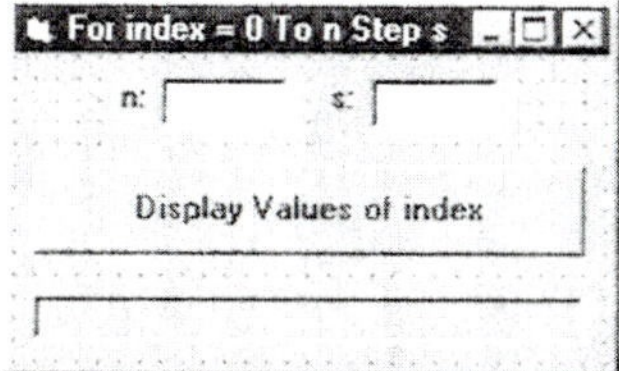

OBJECT	PROPERTY	SETTING
frmIndex	Caption	For index = 0 To n Step s
lblN	Caption	n:
txtEnd	Text	(blank)
lblS	Caption	s:
txtStep	Text	(blank)
cmdDisplay	Caption	Display Values of index
picValues		

```
Private Sub cmdDisplay_Click()
    Dim n As Single, s As Single, index As Single
    'Display values of index ranging from 0 to n Step s
    picValues.Cls
    n = Val(txtEnd.Text)
    s = Val(txtStep.Text)
    For index = 0 To n Step s
      picValues.Print index;
    Next index
End Sub

[Run, type 3.2 and .5 into the text boxes, and click the
command button.]
```

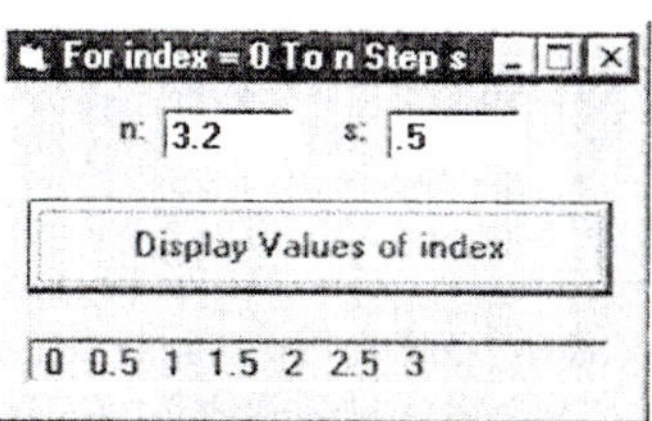

In the examples considered so far, the control variable was successively increased until it reached the terminating value. However, if a negative step value is used and the initial value is greater than the terminating value, then the control value is decreased until reaching the terminating value. In other words, the loop counts backward or downward.

This program accepts a word as input and displays it backwards:

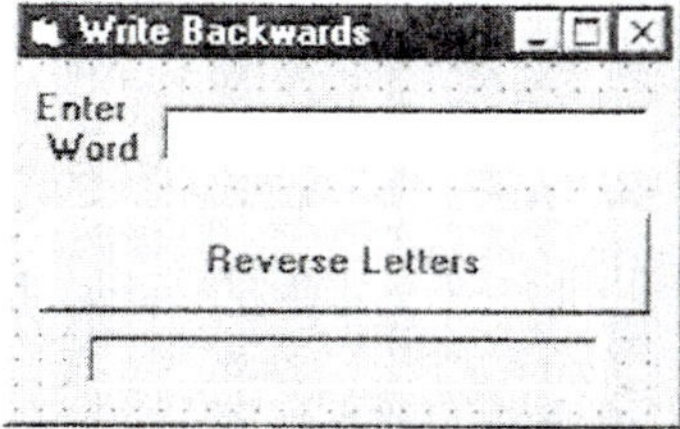

OBJECT	PROPERTY	SETTING
frmReverse	Caption	Write Backwards
lblWord	Caption	Enter Word
txtWord	Text	(blank)
cmdReverse	Caption	Reverse Letters
picTranspose		

```
Private Sub cmdReverse_Click()
    Dim m As Integer, j As Integer
    Dim word As String, reverse As String
    'Write a word backwards
    picTranspose.Cls
    word = txtWord.Text
    m = Len(word)
    reverse = ""
    For j = m To 1 Step -1
       reverse = reverse + Mid(word, j, 1)
    Next j
    picTranspose.Print reverse
End Sub
```

[Run, type SUEZ into the text box, and click the command button.]

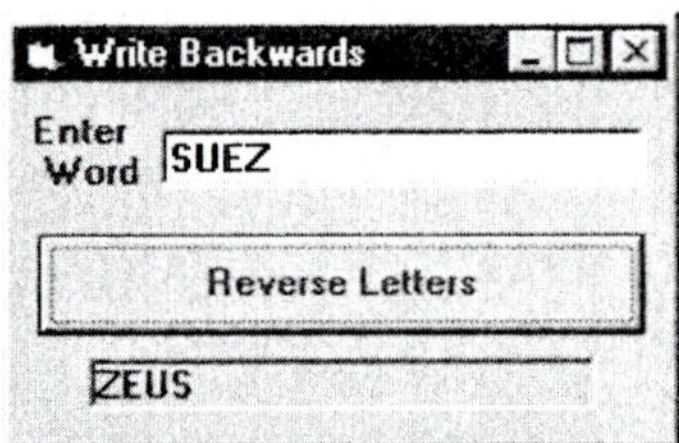

Note: The initial and terminating values of a For...Next loop can be expressions. For instance, the seventh and ninth lines of the event procedure in Example 3 can be consolidated to

```
For j = Len(word) To 1 Step -1
```

The body of a For...Next loop can contain *any* sequence of Visual Basic statements. In particular, it can contain another For...Next loop. However, the second loop must be completely contained inside the first loop and must have a different control variable. Such a configuration is called *nested loops*. Figure 3.13 shows several examples of valid nested loops.

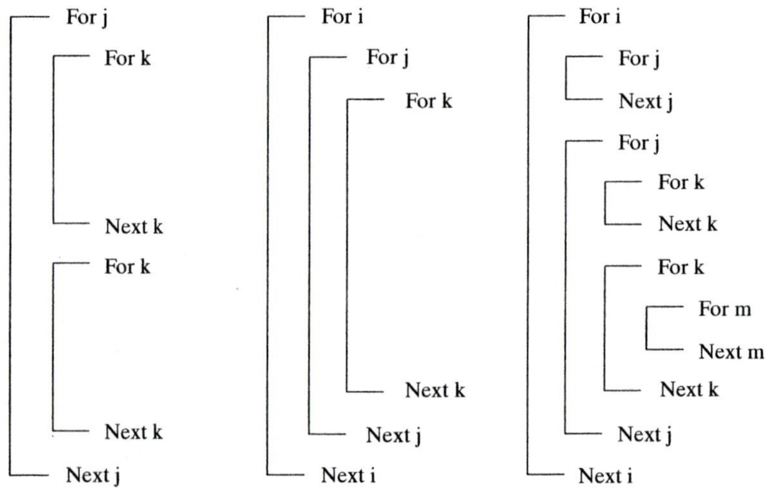

Figure 3.13. Nested loops.

Problem

Write a program to display the products of the integers from 1 to 4.

Solution

In the following program, *j* denotes the left factors of the products, and *k* denotes the right factors. Each factor takes on a value from 1 to 4. The values are assigned to *j* in the outer loop and to *k* in the inner loop. Initially, *j* is assigned the value 1 and then the inner loop is traversed four times to produce the first row of products. At the end of these four passes, the value of *j* will still be 1, and the value of *k* will have been incremented to 5. The picTable.Print statement just before Next j guarantees that no more products will be displayed in that row. The first execution of the outer loop is then complete. Following this, the statement Next j increments the value of *j* to 2. The statement beginning For k is then executed. It resets the value of *k* to 1. The second row of products is displayed during the next four executions of the inner loop and so on.

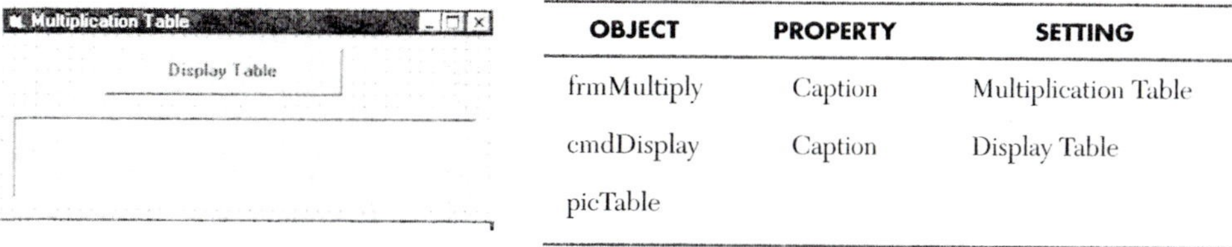

OBJECT	PROPERTY	SETTING
frmMultiply	Caption	Multiplication Table
cmdDisplay	Caption	Display Table
picTable		

```
Private Sub cmdDisplay_Click()
    Dim j As Integer, k As Integer
    picTable.Cls
    For j = 1 To 4
       For k = 1 To 4
          picTable.Print j; "x"; k; "="; j * k,
       Next k
       picTable.Print
    Next j
End Sub
```

[Run and press the command button.]

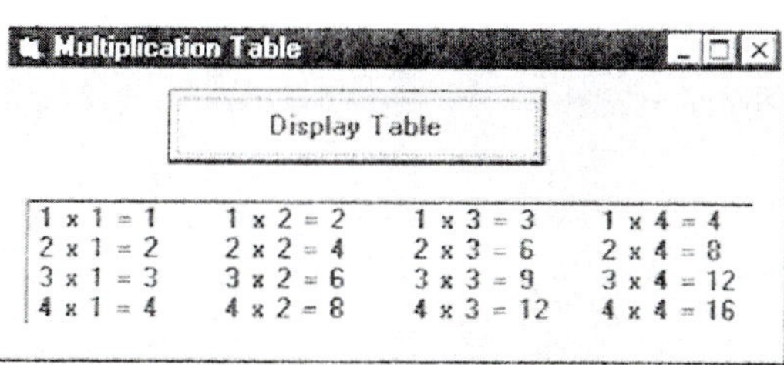

EXAMPLE 3.3: The coefficient of the rth term in the binomial expansion of $(x + y)^n$ is the binomial coefficient

$$C(n, r) = \frac{n!}{r!(n - r)!} \tag{3-1}$$

It is also the number of ways of selecting a subset of r elements from a set of n elements. The definition of $C(n, r)$ above will not produce a proper result for large values of n and r due to roundoff error and/or overflow. A method more likely to succeed uses the fact that

$$C(n, r + 1) = \frac{n - r}{r + 1} \cdot C(n, r) \tag{3-2}$$

```
Private Sub cmdCompute_click()
    'Compute binomial coefficient
    Dim n As Integer, r As Integer
    n = txtN
    r = txtR
    lblBinCoef.Caption = FormatNumber(BinaryCo(n, r), 0)
End Sub

Private Function BinaryCo(n As Integer, r As Integer)
                              As Single
    'Calculate the binary coefficient C(n, r)
    Dim b As Single, i As Integer
    b = 1
    For i = 0 To r - 1
        b = ((n -i) / (i + 1)) * b
    Next i
    BinaryCo = b
End Function
```

[Run, enter values for n and r, and press the command button.]

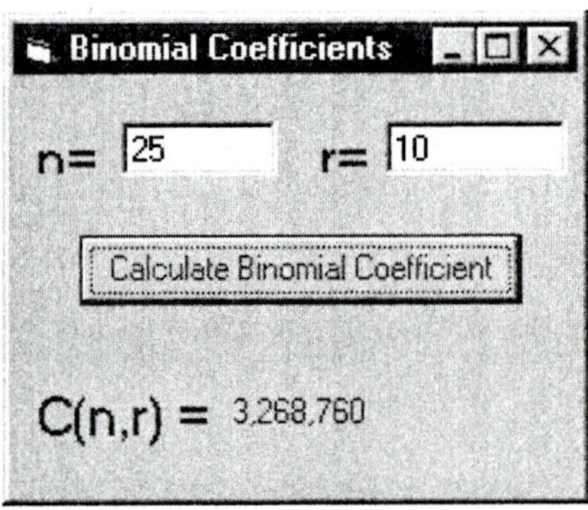

3.4.1 Comments

1. The body of a For...Next loop need not be indented. However, because indenting improves the readability of the program, it is good programming style. As soon as you see the word For, your eyes can easily scan down the program to find the matching Next statement. You then know two facts

immediately: the number of statements in the body of the loop and the number of passes that will be made through the loop.

2. For and Next statements must be paired. If one is missing, the program will generate the error message "For without Next" or"Next without For."

3. Consider a loop beginning with For $i = m$ To n Step s. The loop will be executed exactly once if m equals n no matter what value s has. The loop will not be executed at all if m is greater than n and s is positive, or if m is less than n and s is negative.

4. The value of the control variable should not be altered within the body of the loop; doing so might cause the loop to repeat indefinitely or have an unpredictable number of repetitions.

5. Noninteger step values can lead to roundoff errors with the result that the loop is not executed the intended number of times. For instance, a loop beginning with For $i = 1$ To 2 Step .1 will be executed only 10 times instead of the intended 11 times. It should be replaced with For $i = 1$ To 2.01 Step.1.

PRACTICE!

1. Why won't the following lines of code work as intended?

```
For i = 15 To 1
    picBox.Print i;
Next i
```

2. When is a For...Next loop more appropriate than a Do loop?

Solutions

1. The loop will never be entered, since 15 is greater than 1. The intended first line might have been

```
For i = 15 To 1 Step -1
```

or

```
For i = 1 To 15
```

2. If the exact number of times the loop will be executed is known before entering the loop, then a For...Next loop should be used. Otherwise, a Do loop is more appropriate.

3.5 CASE STUDY: NUMERICAL INTEGRATION

This case study develops a sophisticated numerical method for approximating the area under a curve Figure 3.14 shows the area under the graph of a function defined on the interval $[a, b]$. In Figure 3.15 the interval is subdivided into n subintervals, each of length $h = (b - a)/n$, where $a_0 = a$, $a_1 = a + h$, $a_2 = a + 2h$, ..., $a_{n-1} = a + (n - 1)h$, $a_n = b$. Vertical lines drawn from these points to the curve divide the region under the curve into n strips.

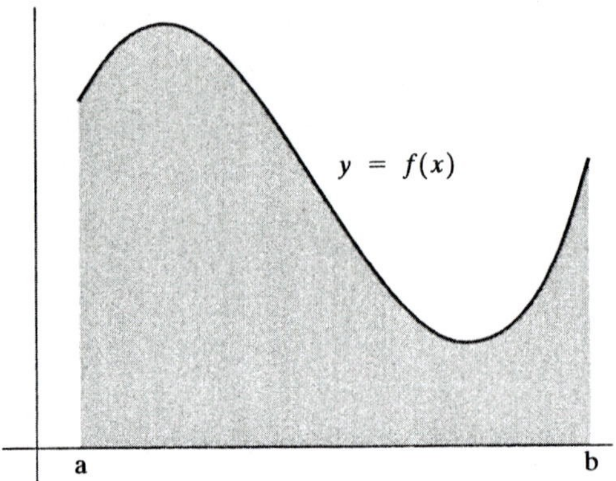

Figure 3.14. Area under a curve.

The area under the curve is approximated by estimating the area of each strip and adding the results. Three well-known approximation methods are the midpoint rule, trapezoidal rule, and Simpson's rule, which approximate the area of each strip with the area of a rectangle, trapezoid, and parabola, respectively. We will focus on the trapezoidal rule. The technique developed, however, also yields the Simpson's rule approximation as a byproduct.

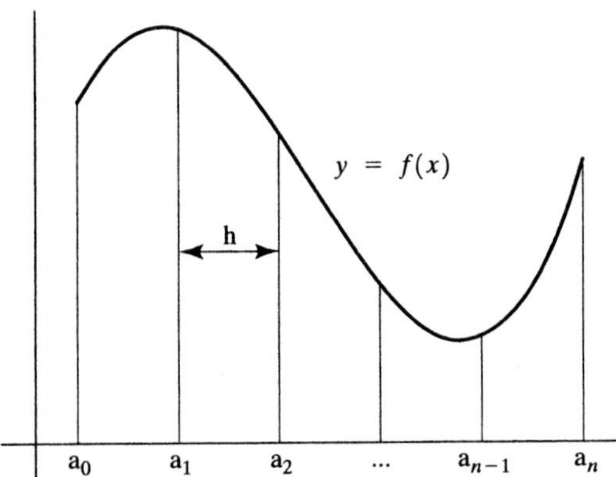

Figure 3.15. Area subdivided into strips.

Figure 3.16 shows the approximation of the area under the curve by trapezoids and Figure 3.17 gives the formula for the area of a trapezoid. The sum of the areas of the trapezoids in Figure 3.16 is

$$\frac{f(a_0) + f(a_1)}{2} \cdot h + \frac{f(a_1) + f(a_2)}{2} \cdot h + \frac{f(a_2) + f(a_3)}{2} \cdot h + \cdots + \frac{f(a_{n-1}) + f(a_n)}{2} \cdot h$$

$$= \left[\frac{1}{2}f(a_0) + f(a_1) + f(a_2) + f(a_3) + \cdots + f(a_{n-1}) + \frac{1}{2}f(a_n)\right] \cdot h$$

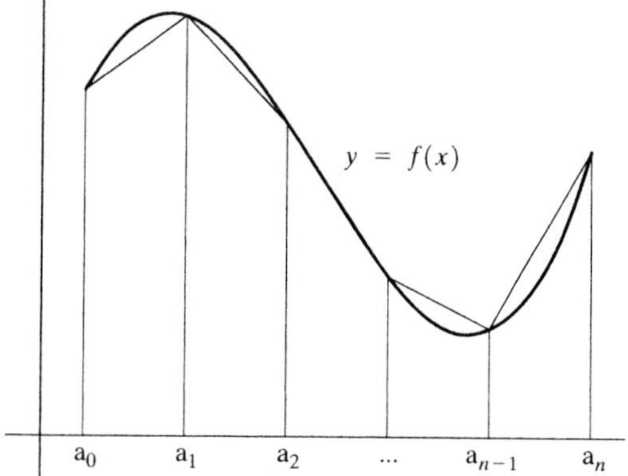

Figure 3.16. Area approximated by trapezoids.

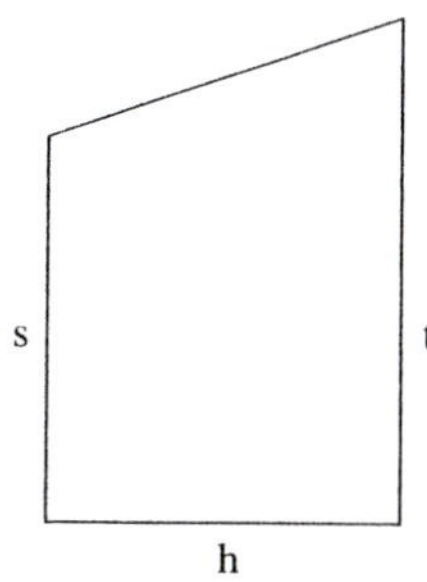

$$\text{Area} = \left(\frac{s}{2} + \frac{t}{2}\right)\cdot h$$

Figure 3.17. Area of a trapezoid.

Trapezoidal Rule: if $n \geq 2$ and $h = \dfrac{b-a}{n}$, then

$$\int_a^b f(x)\,dx = \left[\frac{1}{2}f(a_0) + f(a_1) + f(a_2) + \cdots + f(a_{n-1}) + \frac{1}{2}f(a_n)\right]\cdot h,$$

where $a_0 = a,\ a_1 = a + h,\ a_2 = a + 2h,\ \cdots,\ a_n = b$.

Theoretically, the trapezoidal rule gives better approximations as n gets larger. In general, when n is doubled, the difference between the actual value of the definite integral and the value given by the trapezoidal rule is divided by 4. Practically, however, if n is too large, roundoff errors will invalidate the trapezoidal rule. Our algorithm for determining a good value for n is as follows.

1. Apply the trapezoidal rule for $n = 1$, that is, with a single trapezoid.
2. Double the value of n and apply the trapezoidal rule.
3. Repeat Step 2 until two successive approximations differ by a predetermined tolerance level or until the value of n is greater than another predetermined level.

This method has two compelling features. First, the $n + 1$ function values calculated in the n subinterval approximation are reused in the $2n$ subinterval approximation, making the method very efficient. Second, the value for Simpson's rule can be obtained from two successive approximations. Let's consider these features one at a time.

The trapezoidal rule can be written in the form

$$[\text{trapezoidal rule value for } n] = [\text{sum}] \cdot h,$$

where

$$\text{sum} = \left[\frac{1}{2}f(a_0) + f(a_1) + f(a_2) + \cdots + f(a_{n-1}) + \frac{1}{2}f(a_n)\right].$$

When n is an even number,

$$\text{sum} = \text{evenSum} + \text{oddSum}$$

where

$$\text{evenSum} = \frac{1}{2}f(a_0) + f(a_2) + f(a_4) + \cdots + f(a_{n-2}) + \frac{1}{2}f(a_n)$$

$$\text{oddSum} = f(a_1) + f(a_3) + f(a_5) + \cdots + f(a_{n-1}).$$

Now, the total sum for the trapezoidal rule with n subintervals is the even sum for the trapezoidal rule with $2n$ subintervals. This fact can be best illustrated with a concrete example.

Consider the interval [1, 3] and let n = 1, 2, 4, and 8 successively. When the total sums are spread out as shown below, each total sum is seen to be the even sum for the next higher approximation.

$$\frac{1}{2}f(1) \qquad\qquad\qquad\qquad\qquad\qquad\qquad\qquad + \frac{1}{2}f(3)$$

$$\frac{1}{2}f(1) \qquad\qquad\qquad + f(2) \qquad\qquad\qquad + \frac{1}{2}f(3)$$

$$\frac{1}{2}f(1) \qquad + f(1.5) \qquad + f(2) \qquad + f(2.5) \qquad + \frac{1}{2}f(3)$$

$$\frac{1}{2}f(1) + f(1.25) + f(1.5) + f(1.75) + f(2) + f(2.25) + f(2.5) + f(2.75) + \frac{1}{2}f(3)$$

Because of this feature of the trapezoidal rule, each approximation requires that only the odd sum be calculated.

$$\begin{aligned}[\text{trapezoidal rule value for } 2n] &= [\text{total sum for } 2n] \cdot h \\ &= ([\text{even sum for } 2n] + [\text{odd sum for } 2n]) \cdot h \\ &= ([\text{total sum for } n] + [\text{odd sum for } 2n]) \cdot h\end{aligned}$$

As mentioned earlier, Simpson's rule uses parabolas to estimate the area of each strip in Figure 3.16. Simpson's rule is more powerful than the trapezoidal rule in that, in general, when n is doubled the difference between the actual value of the definite integral and the value given by Simpson's rule is divided by 16. The Simpson's rule value with n parabolas can be obtained as

$$(4\,[\text{trapezoidal rule value for } 2n] - [\text{trapezoidal rule value for } n])/3.$$

3.5.1 Designing the Numerical Integration Program

The program can be divided into the following tasks:

1. Initialize special values.
2. Compute the approximations of the area.
3. Display the results.

Each of these tasks can be divided into smaller subtasks.

1. *Initialize special values.* The interval of integration must be specified along with the tolerance levels. The iterative algorithm terminates when successive approximations are close together or when the number of intervals becomes very large. Closeness should be decided in a relative, rather than an absolute sense. Here's why. If the.values of the approximations are large, say 1,000,000, then requiring that two successive approximations differ by a small value, say .0001, is unrealistic. A better method is to require that two successive approximations differ by .0001 times the second approximation. As a safety valve, the iterations should terminate if the number of subintervals becomes too large. Thus, Task 1 is divided into the following subtasks:

   1.1 Record the endpoints; of the interval.

   1.2 Set the level of accuracy desired for the relative error between successive approximations (say, .0001).

   1.3 Set the maximum number of subintervals allowed (say, 2^{19} or 524,288).

2. *Compute the approximations of the area.* The algorithm first approximates the area with a single trapezoid and then repeatedly doubles the number of trapezoids until successive approximations are close. Each approximation need only compute every other function value since the sum of the other half of the function values is obtained from the previous approximation. Finally, a simple formula computes the Simpson's rule approximation from the last and next-to-last trapezoidal approximations to the area. The subtasks for this task are then:

   2.1 Approximate area with a single trapezoid.

   2.2 Approximate area with twice as many subintervals.

      2.2.1 Compute the sum of function values of odd-numbered subdivision points.

   2.3 Compute the Simpson's rule approximation to the area.

3. *Display the results.* For completeness, the accuracy level and number of subintervals should be displayed along with the values for the trapezoidal and Simpson's rules. Task 3 is therefore divided into the following subtasks.

   3.1 Display the accuracy level.

   3.2 Display the number of subintervals.

   3.3 Display the trapezoidal rule area.

   3.4 Display the Simpson's rule area.

The top-down chart in Figure 3.18 shows the stepwise refinement of the problem.

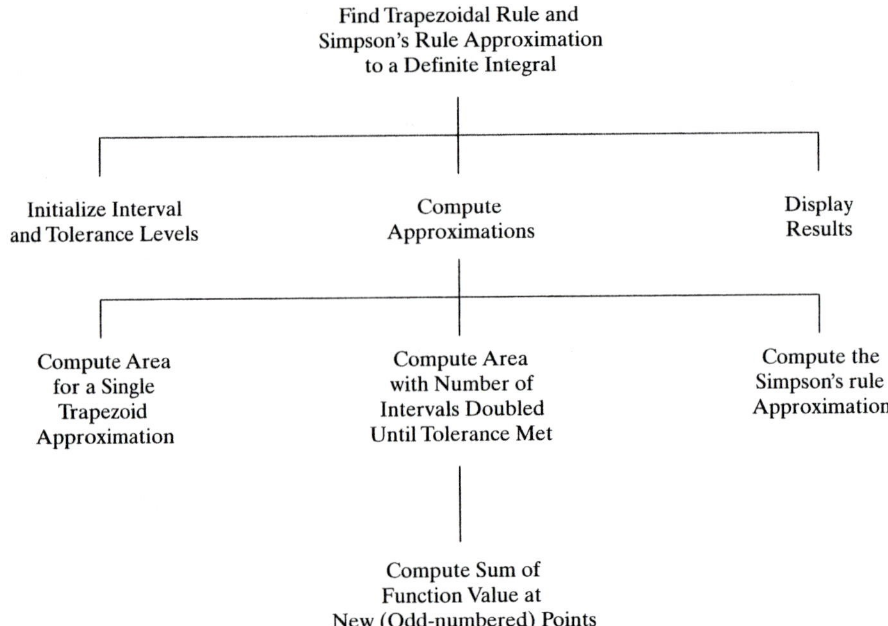

Figure 3.18. Top-down chart for the numerical integration program.

3.5.2 Pseudocode for the Numerical Integration Program

```
INITIALIZE PERTINENT VALUES (Text boxes and Form_Load)
  Specify left endpoint of interval (txtA)
  Specify right endpoint of interval (txtB)
  Specify level of accuracy desired for relative error (txtAccuracy)
  Specify maximum number of subintervals allowed (in Form_Load)

COMPUTE APPROXIMATIONS OF AREA (Sub procedure ApproximateArea)
  Initialize the number of subintervals to 1
  APPROXIMATE AREA USING A SINGLE TRAPEZOID (Sub procedure SingleTrap)
    Determine the length of the interval
    Compute the sum of one half the values of the function at each endpoint
    Compute the area of the single trapezoid (sum * length of interval)
  Do
    Record the previously computed area
    Double the number of subintervals (trapezoids) used to compute the area
    Determine the length of each subinterval
    APPROXIMATE AREA USING TWICE AS MANY SUBINTERVALS
        (Sub procedure SumTrapezoids)
      Determine the sum of the function values at the new set of subdividing points by
      using the previous sum plus the
      SUM OF THE Private Function VALUES AT THE NEW ODD NUMBERED
          POINTS (Function OddSum)
        Initialize the sum accumulator to zero
        For odd-numbered subdividing points from 1 To
            [number of subintervals -1]
          Increase the sum accumulator by the value of the function at the odd
              numbered subdividing point
        Next
```

Assign the sum accumulator to the function name
Compute the new approximation to the area using the sum of the function values times the subinterval length
Loop Until the relative error falls to the given level of accuracy or the number of subintervals reaches the maximum number
Calculate the SIMPSON'S RULE APPROXIMATION (Function SimpsonsRule) of the area using the final and next-to-last trapezoidal approximations

DISPLAY RESULTS OF TRAPEZOIDAL AND SIMPSON'S RULE
(Sub procedure DisplayResults)
Display the number of subintervals
Display the area obtained by the trapezoidal rule
Display the area obtained by applying Simpson's rule

3.5.3 Writing the Numerical Integration Program

Table 3-2 shows each of the tasks discussed above and the procedure that carries out the task.

TABLE 3-2 Tasks and their procedures.

TASK	PROCEDURE
1. Specify maximum number of subintervals.	Form_Load
2. Compute Approximations of area.	ApproximateArea
2.1 Approximate area using a single trapezoid.	SingleTrap
2.2 Approximate area using twice as many subintervals.	SumTrapezoids
2.2.1 Compute sum of function values of odd-numbered subdivision points.	OddSum
2.3 Compute the Simpson's rule approximation.	SimpsonsRule
3. Display results.	DisplayResults

The following program finds the area under the graph of the function $f(x) = xe^x$ over the interval [1, 3]. This function is given the name Func(x). Integration by parts can be used to show that the exact value of the area is 163.7944 to four decimal places.

```
Dim maxN As Single
'The approximating process will terminate when either the
'relative error between successive approximations
'is reduced to the accuracy value or the number of
'subintervals reaches or exceeds maxN.

Private Sub Form_Load()
    maxN = 2 ^ 19
End Sub

Private Sub cmdCompute_Click()
    Dim n As Single                  'Number of subintervals
    Dim trapArea As Single           'Trapezoidal rule
                                     'approximation to the area
    Dim simpArea As Single           'Simpson's rule
                                     'approximation to the area
    Call ApproximateArea(n, trapArea, simpArea)
    Call DisplayResults(n, trapArea, simpArea)
End Sub
```

```
Private Sub ApproximateArea(n As Single, trapArea As Single,
                            simpArea As Single)
   Dim sum As Single
   Dim previousArea As Single
   Dim h As Single
   'Use trapezoids to approximate the area under a curve over
   'the interval from a to b. Stop the approximating process
   'when either the relative error between successive
   'approximations to the area is reduced to at most the value
   'of accuracy, or n, the number of subintervals, reaches
   'maxN. Use previousArea, the previous approximation to the
   'area, along with the final approximation to compute
   'simpArea, the Simpson's rule approximation to the area.
   n = 1                           'Number of subintervals
   Call SingleTrap(sum, trapAxea)
   Do
      previousArea = trapArea      'Record previously computed
                                   'area
      n = 2 * n                    'Double the number of
                                   'subintervals
      h = (Val(txtB.Text) - Val(txtA.T)) / n
      'Compute width of subintervals
      Call SumTrapezoids(n, h, sum, trapArea)
   Loop Until (Abs(trapArea - previousArea) <=
      Val(txtAccuracy.Text)* Abs(trapArea)) Or n >= maxN)
   simpArea = SimpsonsRule(previousArea, trapArea)
End Sub

Private Sub DisplayResults(n, trapArea, simpArea)
   'Display the number of subintervals,
   'and area approximations
   lblNumSubIntervals.Caption = n
   lblTrap.Caption = trapArea
   lblSimp.Caption = simpArea
End Sub

Private Function Func(x) As Single
   'Integrand
   Func = x * Exp(x)
End Function

Private Function OddSum n, h) As Single
   Dim sum As Single
   'Determine the sum c the function values at the
   'n/2 points which lie odd multiples of h to the
   'right of a.
   sum = 0                         'Sum of function values
   For i = 1 To n - 1 Step 2
      sum = sum + Func(Val(txtA.Text) + i * h)
   Next i
   OddSum = sum
End Function

Private Function SimpsonsRule(nIntervalTrapArea,_
                  twoNIntervalTrapArea) As Single
   'Calculate the Simpson's rule approximation
```

```
    SimpsonsRule = (4 * twoNIntervalTrapArea -
                    nIntervalTrapArea) / 3
End Function

Private Sub SingleTrap(sum As Single, area As Single)
    'Estimate the area under a curve for the interval
    'from a tob by using a single trapezoid. The sum
    'of the function values is also returned for use in
    'the trapezoidal approximation with 2 subintervals.
    sum = (Func(Val(txtA.Text)) / 2 + _
           Func(Val(txtB.Text)) / 2)
    area = sum * (Val(txtB.Text) - Val(txtA.Text))
End Sub

Private Sub SumTrapezoids(n As Single, h As Single,_
                    sum As Single, area As Single)
    'Estimate the area under a curve by dividing the interval
    'from a to b into n subintervals of width h and using
    'trapezoids to approximate the area for each subinterval.
    'The sum of function values for the case of n 2
    'subintervals is known and used to compute a new sum of
    'function values for n subintervals, which may in turn
    'be used when approximating the area with 2n subintervals.
    sum = sum + OddSum(n, h)
    area sum * h
End Sub

[Run, enter values for a, b, and accuracy, and press the
command button.]
```

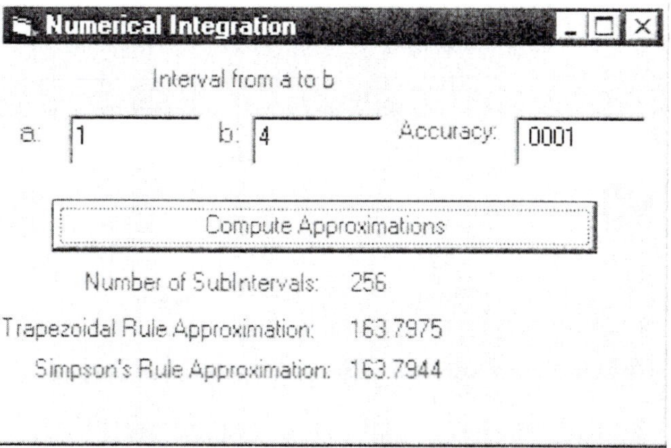

3.6 PROGRAMMING PROJECTS

1. One of the most important engineering tools is the technique known as modeling. Models are used to predict the behavior of systems that are too complex to be amenable to exact analysis. Consider a city whose rectangular boundary forms the base of a box-shaped air shed. The model for the air

shed over the city is called the *box model*. The problem is to relate air pollutant emissions to the resulting air quality. We assume pollutants are being emitted from the city, and also that the wind blows fresh air into one side of the box and causes polluted air to be blown out the opposite side. If the initial pollution concentration in the box is zero, then the steady state or the final concentration (in grams per cubic meter) is

$$C_{final} = P/(vLh),$$

where v is the speed of the wind (in meters per second), L and h are the base and the height of the box (in meters) respectively, and P is the pollutant emission rate (in grams per hour). Write a program that

a. Requests the parameters L (in miles), h (in feet), and P (in milligrams per hour).

b. Converts the parameters to the appropriate units and displays the pollution concentration for different values of v as shown below.

A possible output with 20 as length of city in miles, 600 as height of box in feet, and 19E + 10 as pollution emission rate in mg/hr is:

```
L = 32180 meters
h = 182.8 meters
P = 1.9E+08 grams per hour

Wind speed                Pollution concentration
(miles per hour)          (grams per cubic meter)
 10                        .0020
 20                        .0010
 30                        .0007
```

2. Write a program to solve equations of the form $ax + b = c$, where the numbers a, b, and c are supplied via text boxes. Allow for the case where a is 0. If so, there will either be no solution or every number will be a solution.

3. Write a program to determine the real roots of the quadratic equation $ax^2 + bx + c = 0$ (where $a \neq 0$) after requesting the values of a, b, and c. Use a Sub procedure to ensure that a is nonzero. *Note:* The equation has 2, 1, or 0 solutions depending upon whether the value of $b^2 - 4ac$ is positive, zero, or negative. In the first two cases the solutions are given by the quadratic formula

$$\frac{-b \pm \sqrt{b^2 - 4ac}}{2a}.$$

4. An electric circuit can be:

a. Resistive (composed of resistors only) with impedance Z given by $Z = R$, where R is the equivalent resistance.

b. Capacitive (composed of capacitors only) with impedance given by $Z = 1/(C \cdot w)$, where w is the angular frequency and C is the equivalent capacitance.

c. Inductive (composed of inductors only) with impedance given by $Z = L \cdot w$, where L is the equivalent inductance.

d. *R–L* series (composed of a resistor and an inductor in series) with impedance given by

$$Z = \sqrt{R^2 + (L \cdot w)^2}$$

e. *R–C* series (composed of a resistor and a capacitor in series) with impedance given by

$$Z = \sqrt{R^2 + 1/(C \cdot w)^2}$$

f. *R–L–C* series (consists of a resistor, a capacitor, and an inductor in series) with impedance given by

$$Z = \sqrt{R^2 + (Lw - 1/(C \cdot w))^2}$$

Write a program to calculate the impedance of a circuit. The program should request the type of circuit (from the list above), then the values of the components of the circuit, calculate the corresponding impedance, and display the result. Some sample outputs of the program are:

```
[Run, give "inductive" for the type of the circuit, enter .02
for the inductance, and enter 100 for the angular frequency.
The following sentence is displayed in the picture box.]

The impedance Z of the inductive circuit is 2 Ohms.

[Run, give "resistive" for the type of the circuit and enter
100 for the resistance. The following sentence is displayed in
the picture box.]

The impedance Z of the resistive circuit is 100 Ohms.
```

KEY TERMS

Accumulator
Argument
Boolean data type
Control variable
Counter
Do loop
EOF function
Flag
Function procedure (user-defined function)
General procedure
If block
Nested loops
Parameter
Repetition
Selector
Sub procedure

Problems

PROBLEMS 3.1

In Problems 1 to 20, determine the output displayed in the picture box when the command button is clicked.

1.
```
Private Sub cmdDisplay_Click()
    Call Question
    Call Answer
End Sub
```

```
Private Sub Answer()
    picOutput.Print "Because they were invented in the
       northern"
    picOutput.Print "hemisphere where sundials move
       clockwise."
End Sub

Private Sub Question()
    picOutput.Print "Why do clocks run clockwise?"
End Sub
```

2.
```
Private Sub cmdDisplay_Click()
    'The fates of Henry the Eighth's six wives
    Call CommonFates
    picOutput.Print "died;"
    Call CommonFates
    picOutput.Print "survived."
End Sub

Private Sub CommonFates()
    'The most common fates
    picOutput.Print "Divorced, beheaded, ";
End Sub
```

3.
```
Private Sub cmdDisplay_Click()
    'Good advice to follow
    Call Advice
End Sub

Private Sub Advice()
    picOutput.Print "Keep cool, but don't freeze."
    Call Source
End Sub

Private Sub Source()
    picOutput.Print "Source: A jar of mayonnaise."
End Sub
```

4.
```
Private Sub cmdDisplay_Click()
    'Opening lines of Tale of Two Cities
    Call Times("best")
    Call Times("worst")
End Sub

Private Sub Times(word As String)
    'Display line
    picOutput.Print "It was the "; word; " of times."
End Sub
```

5.
```
Private Sub cmdDisplay_Click()
    'Sentence using number, thing, and place
    Call Sentence(168, "hour", "a week")
    Call Sentence(76, "trombone", "the big parade")
End Sub

Private Sub Sentence(num As Single, thing As String,
    where As String)
    picOutput.Print num; thing; "s in "; where
```

```
End Sub
```

6.
```
Private Sub cmdDisplay_Click()
    Dim a As String, b As String
    a = "Thermodynamics"
    b = "The temperatures"
    Call Display(Left(a, 13)+ Chr(32) + & Mid(b, 5, 11))
    picOutput.Print " is expressed in degrees Kelvin."
End Sub

Private Sub Display(sentence As String)
    picOutput.Print sentence;
End Sub
```

7.
```
Private Sub cmdDisplay_Click()
    Call HowMany(24)
    picOutput.Print "a pie."
End Sub

Private Sub HowMany(num As Integer)
    Call What(num)
    picOutput.Print " baked in ";
End Sub

Private Sub What(num As Integer)
    picOutput.Print num; "blackbirds";
End Sub
```

8.
```
Private Sub cmdDisplay_Click()
    picOutput.Print "The mass of an object is";
    Call Constant
    Call Weight("is not")
    picOutput.Print "It varies with the acceleration of
       gravity."
End Sub

Private Sub Constant()
    picOutput.Print " constant."
End Sub

Private Sub Weight(statement As String)
    picOutput.Print "The weight of a body "; statement;
End Sub
```

9.
```
Private Sub cmdDisplay_Click()
    Dim num As Single
    num = 7
    Call AddTwo(num)
    picOutput.Print num
End Sub

Private Sub AddTwo(num As Single)
    num = num + 2
End Sub
```

10.
```
Private Sub cmdDisplay_Click()
    Dim term As String
    term = "Fall"
```

```
    Call Plural(term)
    picOutput.Print term
End Sub

Private Sub Plural(term As String)
    term = term & "s"
End Sub
```

11.
```
Private Sub cmdDisplay_Click()
    Dim a As Single
    a = 5
    Call Square(a)
    picOutput.Print a
End Sub

Private Sub Square(num As Single)
    num = num * num
End Sub
```

12.
```
Private Sub cmdDisplay_Click()
    Dim radioactiveRays As String
    radioactiveRays = "alpha rays"
    Call Another
    picOutput.Print radioactiveRays
    Call Another
End Sub

Private Sub Another()
    picOutput.Print radioactiveRays
    radioactiveRays = "beta rays"
End Sub
```

13.
```
Private Sub cmdConvert_Click()
    Dim temp As Single
    'Convert Celsius to Fahrenheit
    temp = 95
    picOutput.Print CtoF(temp)
End Sub

Private Function CtoF(t As Single) As Single
    CtoF = (9 / 5) * t + 32
End Function
```

14.
```
Private Sub cmdDisplay_Click()
    Dim nmoles As Single
    'Determine the number of atoms in a substance given
       the number of moles
    nmoles = 3.4
    picOutput.Print "Number of atoms is"; NumberOfAtoms
       (nmoles)
End Sub

Private Function NumberOfAtoms (x As Single) As Single
    na = 6.023E+23
    NumberOfAtoms = na * x
End Function
```

15.
```
Private Sub cmdDisplay_Click()
    Dim p As Single
    'Rule of 72
```

```
        p = Val(txtPopGr.Text) 'Population growth as a
            percent
        picOutput.Print "The population will double in";
        picOutput.Print DoublingTime(p); "years."
    End Sub

    Private Function DoublingTime(x As Single) As Single
        'Estimate time required for a population to double
        'at a growth rate of x percent
        DoublingTime = 72 / x
    End Function
```

(Assume that the text box contains the number 3.)

16.
```
    Private Sub cmdDisplay_Click()
        Dim days As String, num As Integer
        'Determine the day of the week from its number
        days = "SunMonTueWedThuFriSat"
        num = Val(InputBox("Enter the number of the day"))
        picOutput.Print "The day is "; DayOfWeek(days, num)
    End Sub

    Private Function DayOfWeek(x As String, n As Integer) As
      String
        Dim position As Integer
        'x string containing 3-letter abbreviations of days
            of the week
        'n the number of the day
        position = 3 * n - 2
        DayOfWeek = Mid(x, position, 3)
    End Function
```

(Assume that the response is 4.)

17.
```
    Private Sub cmdDisplay_Click()
        Dim a As String
        'Demonstrate local variables
        a = "Choo "
        picOutput.Print TypeOfTrain()
    End Sub

    Private Function TypeOfTrain() As String
        Dim a As String
        a = a & a
        TypeOfTrain = a & "train"
    End Function
```

18.
```
    Private Sub cmdDisplay_Click()
        Dim num As Single
        'Triple a number
        num = 5
        picOutput.Print Triple(num);
        picOutput.Print num
    End Sub

    Private Function Triple(x As Single) As Single
        Dim num As Single
        num = 3
        Triple = num * x
    End Function
```

19.
```
Private Sub cmdDisplay_Click()
    Dim word As String
    word = "moral"
    Call Negative(word)
    word = "political"
    Call Negative(word)
End Sub

Private Function AddA(word As String) As String
    AddA = "a" & word
End Function

Private Sub Negative(word As String)
    picOutput.Print word; " has the negative "; AddA(word)
End Sub
```

20. If the annual consumption of oil grows from an initial value A_0 at a rate r, then after n years the annual consumption is $A_n = A_0 (1 + r)^n$.

```
Private Sub cmdDisplay_Click()
    Dim y As Integer, r As Single, ao As Single, n As
       Integer
    'Predict the consumption of oil.
    y = 1998      'year
    r = .05
    ao = 9
    n = 10
    Call Display(y, r, ao, n)
End Sub

Private Sub Display (year As Integer, r As Single, ao As
                     Single, n As Integer)
   picOutput.Print "In"; year + n; "the consumption of
      oil will be";
   picOutput.Print Consumption(r, ao, n); "billion
      barrels."
End Sub

Private Function Consumption(r As Single, ao As Single, n
As Integer) As Single
    Consumption = ao * (1 + r) A n
End Function
```

In Problems 21 to 24, find the errors.

21.
```
Private Sub cmdDisplay_Click()
    Dim n As Integer
    n = 5
    Call Alphabet
End Sub

Private Sub Alphabet(n As Integer)
    picOutput.Print Left("abcdefghijklmnopqrstuvwxyz", n)
End Sub
```

22.
```
Private Sub cmdDisplay_Click()
    Dim value As Single, unit As String
    value = 2
```

```
     unit = "amperes"
     Call Current (value, unit)
End Sub

Private Sub Current (value as Single)
     picOutput.Print "The current in the resistor is";
     picOutput.Print value; " "; unit
End Sub
```

23.
```
Private Sub cmdDisplay_Click()
     Dim answer As Single
     'Select a greeting
     answer = Val(InputBox("Enter 1 or 2."))
     picOutput.Print Greeting(answer)
End Sub

Private Function Greeting(x As Single) As Single
     Greeting = Mid("hellohi ya", 5 * x - 4, 5)
End Function
```

24.
```
Private Sub cmdDisplay_Click()
     Dim am As Integer, m As Single, substance As String
     'Determine the number of moles of atoms in a given mass
        of substance
     am = Val(InputBox("Enter atomic mass:"))
     m  = Val(InputBox("Enter mass of substance:"))
     substance = InputBox("Enter name of substance:")
     picOutput.Print "The number of moles in"; m; "grams of";
     picOutput.Print substance; " is"; NumberOfMoles(am, m);"."
End Sub

Private Function NumberOfMoles(am As Integer, m As
     Single) As Single
     NumberOfMoles(am, m) = m / am
End Function
```

In Problem 25, rewrite the program so input, processing, and output are each performed by Calls to Sub procedures.

25.
```
Private Sub cmdDisplay_Click()
     Dim equation As String, n As Integer, f As String, a
        As String
     equation = InputBox("What is Newton's Second Law of
        Motion?")
     n = Instr(equation, " ")
     f = Left(equation, n - 1)
     a = Mid(equation, n + 19, 12)
     picOutput.Print "The resultant "; f; " acting on a
        body"
     picOutput.Print "is proportional to its "; a; "."
End Sub
```

(NOTE: Newton's Second Law of Motion is "Force equals mass times acceleration.")

26. The velocity v and the acceleration a of a body revolving in a circle of radius r are

$$v = 2\pi r/t \qquad a = v^2/r \qquad (3\text{-}3)$$

where r is expressed in meters and t is the period or the duration, of a complete revolution (in seconds).

The moon revolves about the earth in a circle of radius r = 239,000 miles and requires 27.3 days to make a complete revolution. Write a program to calculate its velocity and acceleration. The program should request the radius and convert it to meters (1 mile = 1609 meters) with a function, request t (in days) and convert it to seconds with another function, calculate velocity and acceleration with functions, and display the results with a Sub procedure. A sample output is shown below.

```
[Run, enter the data into the text boxes, and press the
command button.]
```

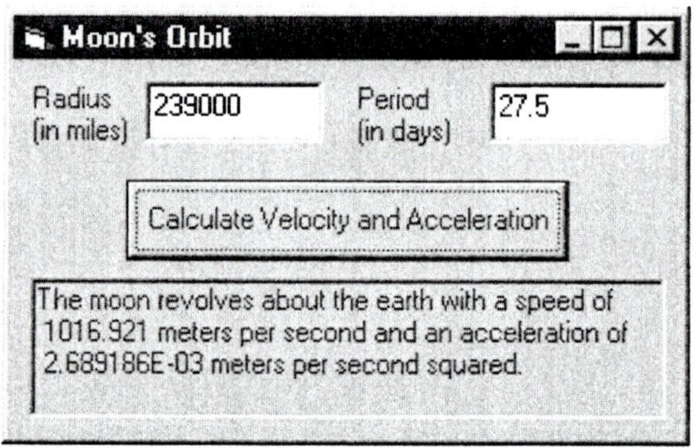

27. The period P of a pendulum of length L and maximum displacement angle α is given by the formula

$$P = \sqrt{L/g}\left(1 + \frac{1}{4}\sin^2\left(\frac{\alpha}{2}\right)\right),$$

where g is the acceleration due to gravity. Write a program that requests as input the length of the pendulum in centimeters and the maximum angle of displacement in radians, and displays as output the period of the pendulum in seconds. *Note:* g = 980 cm/sec^2.

28. Some metals are easier to heat than others. The *specific heat capacity* of a metal can be used to calculate the amount of heat needed to raise the temperature of a metal object by a certain amount. If m is the mass of an object, c is the specific capacity of the metal (in Joules/grams × Kelvin) of the metal, and the initial and final temperatures are t_1 and t_2 respectively, then the heat, Q (in Joules), required to raise the object from t_1 to t_2 is given by

$$Q = mc(t_2 - t_1).$$

Write a program that requests the values of m, t_1, and t_2 and calculates the amount of heat required to raise an aluminum object (c = 0.897 J/g · K) of mass m from t_1 to t_2. Use a Sub procedure to obtain the input and a function to compute Q.

29. In 1998, the federal government developed the body mass index (BMI) to determine ideal weights. Body mass index is calculated as 703 times the weight in pounds, divided by the square of the height in inches, and then

rounded to the nearest whole number. Write a program that accepts a person's weight and height as input and gives the person's body mass index. (*Note:* A BMI of 19 to 25 corresponds to a healthy weight.)

30. Kepler's Third Law states that for objects with an elliptical orbit (such as satellites orbiting Earth or planets orbiting the sun), the square of the Period is proportional to a^3, where a is half the length of the major axis of the ellipse. For a nearly circular satellite orbit above Earth, $a \approx$ [radius of Earth (6378 kilometers)] + [altitude of satellite] and if Period is expressed in minutes and the length of the major axis is expressed in kilometers, then $\text{Period}^2 = 2.7513 \times 10^{-8}a^3$. Write a program to produce Table 3-3. The information should be stored in a text file and the period should be computed with a user-defined function. *Note:* Earth-imaging satellites must get above the atmospheric drag, low-altitude communications satellites must stay below the inner Van Allen Belt, and geosynchronous communications satellites must have a period of about one day.

TABLE 3-3 Orbiting Satellites.

TYPE OF SATELLITE	ALTITUDE (in km)	PERIOD (in mm)
Earth imaging	400	92
Low-altitude communications	1500	115
Geosynchronous communication	35789	1436

PROBLEMS 3.2

1.
```
Private Sub cmdDisplay_Click()
    Dim lf As Single 'Lower flammability limit of Propane
    Dim uf As Single 'Upper flammability limit of Propane
    Dim c As Single  'Concentration of Propane in air
    lf = 2.2
    uf = 7.7
    c = Val(InputBox("Enter the concentration of propane
        in the air:"))
    picOutput.Print "The propagation of flame does";
    If (c > uf) Or (c < lf) Then
        picOutput.Print " not";
    End If
    picOutput.Print " occur on contact with a source of
        ignition."
End Sub
```

(Assume the response is 4.7.)

2. A collection of n resistors $R_1, R_2, \ldots, R_n$, may be connected in series or parallel in a circuit. If they are connected in series, the equivalent resistance is

$$R_{eq} = R_1 + R_2 + \ldots + R_n.$$

If they are connected in parallel, the equivalent resistance can be calculated from the equation

$$\frac{1}{R_{eq}} = \frac{1}{R_1} + \frac{1}{R_2} + \cdots + \frac{1}{R_n}.$$

```
Private Sub cmdDisplay_Click()
     Dim r1 As Single, r2 As Single, r3 As Single, circuit As
        String
     Dim geq As Single
     'Determine the equivalent resistor for a circuit
     Open "Data.txt" For Input As #1
     Input #1, r1, r2, r3, circuit
     Close #1
     If circuit = "series" Then
          picOutput.Print "Req ="; r1 + r2 + r3
          Else
          geq = (1 / r1) + (1 / r2) + (1 / r3)
          picOutput.Print "Req ="; 1 / geq
     End If
End Sub
```

(Assume the file Data.txt contains the following; 4, 8, 12, "parallel")

3.
```
Private Sub cmdDisplay_Click()
  Dim pi As Single, obj As String, dimension As Single
  'Calculate a volume
  pi = 4 * Atn(1)
  obj = InputBox("Enter type of object:")
  dimension = Val(InputBox("Enter dimension:"))
  If obj = "cube" Then
      picOutput.Print "Volume of the cube ="; dimension ^ 3
    Else
      If obj = "sphere" Then
           picOutput.Print "Volume of the sphere =";
           picOutput.Print (4 / 3) * pi * dimension ^ 3
         Else
           picOutput.Print "Not a valid object."
        End If
     End If
   End Sub
```

(Assume the responses are "sphere" and 1.8.)

4.
```
Private Sub cmdDisplay_Click()
     Dim num As Single
     num = Val(InputBox("Enter a number from -1 to 1:"))
     picOutput.Print "The function value is"; F(num)
End Sub

Private Function F(x As Single) As Single
     If x < 0 Then
         F = x + 1
         Else
         F = Sqr(x)
     End If
End Function
```

5.
```
Private Sub cmdDisplay_Click()
  Dim nom As String
  nom = InputBox("Who developed the stored program
    concept?")
  Select Case UCase(nom)
    Case "JOHN VON NEUMANN", "VON NEUMANN"
      picOutput.Print "Correct"
```

```
    Case "JOHN MAUCHLY", "MAUCHLY", "J. PRESPER ECKERT",
      "ECKERT"
      picOutput.Print "He worked with the developer, von
        Neumann, on the ENIAC."
    Case Else
      picOutput.Print "Nope"
  End Select
End Sub
```

(Determine the output for each of the following responses: Grace Hopper, Eckert, John von Neumann)

6.

```
Private Sub cmdDisplay_Click()
  Dim n As Integer
  'List of environmental factors that affect
  'flammability limits of a gas or vapor.
  n = Val(InputBox("Enter 1, 2, or 3:"))
  Select Case n
    Case 1
      picOutput.Print "Temperature:"
      picoutput.Print "Lower flammability limits
        decrease as";
      picOutput.Print "temperature increases."
    Case 2
      picOutput.Print "Pressure:"
      picOutput.Print "Upper flammability limits
        increase as";
      picOutput.Print "pressure increases."
    Case 3
      picOutput.Print "Oxygen:"
      picOutput.Print "Upper flammability limits
        increase as";
      picOutput.Print "oxygen concentration increases."
  End Select
End Sub
```

(Determine the output for each of the following responses: 1, 2, 3)

7.

```
Private Sub cmdDisplay_Click()
  Dim a As Single, b As Single, c As Single
  'Type of nondegenerate conic section that is the graph
    of Ax^2 + Bxy + Cy^2 + Dx + Ey + F = 0
  a = Val(InputBox("Enter coefficient of x ^ 2:"))
  b = Val(InputBox("Enter coefficient of x * y:"))
  c = Val(InputBox("Enter coefficient of y ^ 2:"))
  Select Case b ^ 2 - 4 * a * c
    Case Is < 0
      picOutput.Print "circle or ellipse"
    Case 0
      picOutput.Print "parabola"
    Case Else
      picOutput.Print "hyperbola"
  End Select
End Sub
```

(Determine the output for each of the following responses: 2, 0, −1)

8. The rotation of a body with a constant angular acceleration is described by

$$theta(t) = alpha \cdot t^2/2 + w_0 \cdot t + theta_0,$$

where *theta*(t) is the rotation angle at time t, $theta_0$ is the rotation angle at time t = 0, w_0 is the initial angular velocity, and *alpha* is the angular acceleration.

```
Private Sub cmdDisplay_Click()
  Dim alpha As Single, wO As Single, thetaO As Single
  Dim theta As Single, t As Single
  'Determine whether the equation can be solved for time
  'given the other values.
  alpha = Val(InputBox("Enter the value of the
    coefficient alpha:"))
  w0 = Val(InputBox("Enter the value of the coefficient
    w0:"))
  theta0 Val(InputBox("Enter the value of the
    coefficient thetaO:"))
  theta Val(InputBox("Enter the value for theta(t):"))
  Select Case w0 ^ 2 - 2 * alpha * (theta0 - theta)
    Case Is < 0
      picOutput.Print "The equation has no real
        solutions."
    Case 0
      picOutput.Print "The equation has exactly one
        solution."
    Case Is > 0
      picOutput.Print "The equation has two real
        solutions."
  End Select
End Sub
```

(Determine the output for each of the following responses: 1, 2, 4, 3; 1, 5, 2, 1; 1, 2, 1, 1)

In Problems 9 to 14, identify the errors.

9.
```
Private Sub cmdDisplay_Click()
  Dim major As String
  If major = "Math" Or "EE" Then
    picOutput.Print "yes"
  End If
End Sub
```

10.
```
Private Sub cmdDisplay_Click()
  If 2 <> 3
    picOutput.Print "Numbers are not equal"
  End If
End Sub
```

11.
```
Private Sub cmdDisplay_Click()
  Dim switch As String
  'Change switch from "on" to "off", or from "off" to
    "on"
  switch = InputBox("Enter status of switch (on or
    off):")
  If switch = "off" Then
      switch = "on"
  End If
  If switch = "on" Then
      switch = "off"
  End If
End Sub
```

12.
```
Private Sub cmdDisplay_Click()
  Dim h As Single
  'H: Concentration of hydrogen ions in a solution
  h = Val(InputBox("Enter hydrogen ion concentration:"))
  picOutput.Print "The solution is ";
    If h > 1.1E-07 Then
        picOutput.Print "acidic."
      Else
        If h < 9E-08 Then
            picOutput.Print "basic."
          Else
            picOutput.Print "neutral."
    End If
End Sub
```

13.
```
Private Sub cmdDisplay_Click()
  Dim word As String
  word = "Semiconductors"
  Select Case Left(word)
    Case S
      picOutput.Print "Semiconductors form a class
        intermediate";
      picOutput.Print " between metal and insulators."
  End Select
End Sub
```

14.
```
Private Sub cmdDisplay_Click()
  Select Case
    Case Is < .1
      picOutput.Print "The electric field is greater than
        100."
    Case .1 TO .2
      picOutput.Print "The electric field is approximately
        equal to 100."
    Case Is > .2
      picOutput.Print "The electric field is less than
        100."
  End Select
End Sub
```

In Problems 15 to 18, simplify the code.

15.
```
If a = 2 Then
      a = 3 + a
```

```
    Else
      a = 5
End If
```

16.
```
Dim source As String
source = InputBox("Enter the status of the source:")
If Not (source <> "ON") Then
    picOutput.Print "The source is ON and the current
      flows in the circuit."
  Else
    If (source = "OFF") Or (source = "disconnected") Then
        picOutput.Print "No current flows in the circuit."
    End If
End If
```

17.
```
If j = 7 Then
    b = 1
  Else
    If j <> 7 Then
      b = 2
    End If
End If
```

18.
```
Dim sigma As Single
sigma = Val(InputBox("Enter the stress produced in the
    bar by a force:"))
If sigma < 26000 Then
    If sigma > 20000 Then
        picOutput.Print "A stress of 20,000 to 26,000
            causes";
        picOutput.Print " an elongation of 1.4 mm"
    End If
End If
```

19.
```
Dim a As Integer, unit As String
a = Val(InputBox("Enter a positive integer:"))
If a = 3 Then
  unit = "Celsius"
  picOutput.Print "Express the temperature in "; unit; "."
End If
If a = 2 Then
  unit = "Fahrenheit"
  picOutput.Print "Use "; unit; " for temperature."
End If
If a = 1 Then
  unit = "kelvin"
  picOutput.Print "Convert the temperature to "; unit; "."
End If
```

20.
```
Dim a As Single
a = Val(InputBox("Enter a positive number:"))
If a = 1 Then
    picOutput.Print "The process is isothermal."
    'Process takes place at a constant temperature.
End If
If (a >= 2) And (a < 3) Then
    picOutput.Print "The process is adiabatic."
    'No heat is transferred in or out.
```

```
End If
If (a = 3) Or (3 < a And a <= 4) Then
    picOutput.Print "The process is isochoric."
    'The volume remains unchanged.
End If
If (a = 5) Or (a >= 6) Then
    picOutput.Print "The process is isobaric."
    'Process takes place at a constant pressure.
End If
```

21. Write a quiz program to ask "What is the unit of power?" The program should display "Correct" if the answer is "watt" or should display "Try again" otherwise.

22. A particle, originally at rest, is subjected to a force F whose direction is constant but whose magnitude varies with time according to the relation

$$F = F_0(1 - ((t - T)/T^2)) \quad (3\text{-}4)$$

for t between 0 and T (F_0 and T are constants). For $t > T$, $F = F_0$ and for $t < 0$, $F = 0$. Write a program that requests the values of F_0, T, and t as input and displays the value of F. Test the program with the responses $F_0 = 5$ newtons, $T = 100$ seconds, and $t = 89$ seconds.

23. Write a program that requests the names of three chemical elements and their proton and neutron numbers as input, and calculates their mass numbers. (Mass number = proton number + neutron number.) The program then should display the elements and their mass numbers in order from the highest to the lowest mass number. (Test the program with the responses Hydrogen, 1, 0; Sodium, 11, 12; and Oxygen, 8, 8.)

24. The work done by a force F in changing the elongation of a spring, of stiffhess K, from χ_1 to χ_2 is

$$W = K(\chi_2^2 - \chi_1^2)^2, \quad (3\text{-}5)$$

where χ_1 and χ_2 are the initial and final lengths of the spring, respectively. The work done by a load P to elongate a bar by an amount delta is

$$W = EA \cdot delta^2/(2L) \quad (3\text{-}6)$$

where E is the elasticity, A is the area of a cross section, *delta* is the elongation, and L is the length of the bar. Write a program that requests the body type (Spring or Bar) as input. If the body is a spring, the program should request the values of K, χ_1, and χ_2; if it is a bar, the program should request the values of E, A, *delta*, and L. Then the program should calculate the work and display the result. (Try the program with the responses "Spring", $K = 8$ N/m, $\chi_1 = .1$ m, $\chi_2 = .115$ m, and the responses Bar, E = $2 \cdot 10^{11}$ (*Pa*, $L = 2.0$ m, A = $12 \cdot 10^{-4}$ m^2, *delta* = $1.4 \cdot 10^{-3}$ m).

25. Table 3-4 shows significant inventions made each year from 1962 through 1966. Write a program that requests the year BASIC was invented and responds with either the message "Correct," a significant invention made that year (if the answer is 1962, 1963, 1965, or 1966), or the message "You are off by more than 3 years." In the first two cases, the program should also give the name of the inventor.

TABLE 3-4 Significant Inventions.

YEAR	INVENTION	INVENTOR
1962	Minicomputer	Digital Equipment Corporation
1963	Cassette tapes	Phillips Corporation
1964	BASIC	Kemeny and Kurtz
1965	Word processor	IBM
1966	Noise reduction system	Ray M. Dolby

26. Write a program to request a positive number n, and the real and imaginary parts of a complex number as input, and display the real and imaginary parts of the nth power of the complex number.
27. Write a program that requests the coefficients a, b, and c of the quadratic equation $ax^2 + bx + c = 0$ as input and displays the number of real roots of the equation.
28. The programming language FORTRAN has a built-in function named ATAN2(y, x) that accepts the Cartesian coordinates of a point in the plane with the vertical coordinate first, and returns the value of the standard position angle in radians from $-\pi$ to π. The angle will be positive if the first coordinate is positive. Write a Visual Basic equivalent to ATAN2(y, x).

PROBLEMS 3.3

In Problems 1 to 6, determine the output displayed in the picture box when the command button is clicked.

1.
```
Private Sub cmdDisplay_Click()
    Dim q As Single
    q = 3
    Do While q < 15
       q = 2 * q - 1
    Loop
    picOutput.Print q
End Sub
```

2.
```
Private Sub cmdDisplay_Click()
    Dim info As String, counter As Integer, letter As
      String
    'Simulate InStr; search for the letter t
    info = "Potato"
    counter = 0
    letter = ""
    Do While (letter <> "t") And (counter < Len(info))
       counter = counter + 1
       letter = Mid(info, counter, 1)
       If letter = "t" Then
          picOutput.Print counter
       End If
    Loop
    If letter <> "t" Then
       picOutput.Print 0
    End If
End Sub
```

3.
```
Private Sub cmdDisplay_Click()
  Dim counter As Integer, resultant As Single, n As
    Integer, force As Single
  'Determine the resultant of all forces
  'acting on a body along the same axis
  counter = 0
  resultant = 0
  n = Val(InputBox("Enter the number of forces:"))
  Do
    force = Val(InputBox("Enter the value of the force:"))
    resultant = resultant + force
    counter = counter + 1
  Loop Until counter = n
  picOutput.Print "Resultant ="; resultant
End Sub
```

(Assume the response for the number of forces is 5 and the values of the forces are 2, −11, 3, −1, 5)

4.
```
Private Sub cmdDisplay_Click()
    'Display list of noble gases
    Dim gas As Single
    Open "Data.txt" For Input As #1
    Do While Not EOF(1)
        Input #1, gas
        picOutput.Print gas
    Loop
End Sub
```

(Assume the file Data.txt contains the following noble gases:
Helium, Neon, Argon, Krypton, Xenon, Radon)

5.
```
Private Sub cmdDisplay_Click()
    'Display some numerical constants
    Dim constantName As String, value As Single, unit As
      String
    Open "Data.txt" For Input As #1
    Do While Not EOF(1)
        Input #1, constantName, value, unit
        picOutput.Print constantName; " ="; value; unit
    Loop
    Close #1
End Sub
```

(Assume the file Data.txt contains the following constant names, values, and units)

```
"Speed of light", 2.9979E8, "meters per second"
"Planck's constant", 6.626E-34, "joule-seconds"
"Avogadro's number", 6.022E23, "molecules per mole")
```

6.
```
Private Sub cmdDisplay_Click()

    'Determine the maximum of a set of values
    'representing experimental values of surface tension
    'of certain liquids at 20 degrees Celsius.
    Dim max As Single, value As Single, rowMax As Single
    max = 0
    Open "Data.txt" For Input as #1
    Do While Not EOF(1)
       Input #1, value
       rowMax = 0
       Do While value <> -2
       If value > rowMax Then
          rowMax = value
       End If
       Input #1, value
       Loop
       picOutput.Print rowMax
       If rowMax > max Then
          max = rowMax
       End If
    Loop
    Close #1
    picOutput.Print max

End Sub
```

(Assume the file Data.txt contains the following surface tensions of ethyl alcohol, carbon tetrachloride, benzene, glycerine, mercury, olive oil, soap solution, and water: `22.3, 26.8, 28.9, -2, 63.1, 465, 32, -2, 25, 72.9`)

In Problems 7 to 10, identify the errors.

7.
```
Private Sub cmdDisplay_Click()

    Dim q As Single
    q = 1
    Do While q > 0
       q = 3 * q - 1
       picOutput.Print q;
    Loop

End Sub
```

8.
```
Dim g As Single, rho As Single, h As single

'Determine the atmospheric pressure Pa = rho * g * h
'for different values of h, where rho is the density of
'Mercury, g is the acceleration of gravity, and h is
'the height of the Mercury column.
g = 9.8
rho = 13.6
Do While h <= 3
   h = 1
   picOutput.Print "Height ="; h; " Pa ="; rho * g * h
   h = h + 1
Loop
```

9.
```
Dim answer As String, nmoles As Single, mass As Single
'Determine the molality of a solution.
'Molality is the moles of solute per kg of solvent.
answer = InputBox("Do you want to continue? (Y/N)")
Do
    nmoles = Val(InputBox("Enter number of moles:"))
    mass = Val(InputBox("Enter mass of solvent:"))
    picOutput.Print "Molality ="; nmoles / mass
    answer = InputBox("Do you want to continue? (Y/N)")
Until answer = "Y"
```

10.
```
Dim flag As Boolean, radius As Single
flag = False
Do While Not flag
    radius = Val(InputBox("Enter radius:"))
    If radius * radius < 0 Then
        flag = True
    End If
Loop
```

In Problems 11 to 14, replace each phrase containing Until with an equivalent phrase containing While and vice versa. For instance, the phrase Until sum = 100 would be replaced by While sum <> 100.

11. `Until num < 7`

12. `Until nom = "Bob"`

13. `While response = "Y"`

14. `While total = 10`

15. The change, δ, in the dimensions of a block of material of length L is given by

$$\delta = \alpha T L, \qquad (3\text{-}7)$$

where T is the change in temperature (in degrees Celsius) and α is the coefficient of thermal expansion which is a property of the material. For a block of aluminum of length 3.0 m and $\alpha = 23 \cdot 10^{-6}/°\text{C}$, calculate δ for different values of T ($T = 10, 15, 20, \ldots$). Stop when δ exceeds $4 \cdot 10^{-3}$ meters and display the corresponding temperature.

16. After the engine of a moving motor boat is turned off, the speed of the boat decreases as it continues to move across the water. If the boat's speed in miles/hour when the motor is turned off is initSpeed, then its speed after moving *distance* feet is given by

$$\text{speed} = \text{initSpeed} * \text{Exp}(-2 * (\text{distance} / 5280)). \qquad (3\text{-}8)$$

a. Write a function that accepts a boat's initial speed and the distance it has traveled since the motor was turned off as input, and computes its speed at that distance.

b. Suppose to safely ground a boat on the beach, it should be moving between 2 and 5 miles/hour. Use the function in (a) to write a program that requests the initial speed of a boat and outputs the distance from the beach the motor should be turned off in order to drift safely to the beach. (*Hint:* Use a loop to increase the distance until the function yields a value in the desired range.)

17. Write a program to accept a positive integer as input and display the binary representation of the number. *Note:* The binary representation of *n* should be returned as a string, *strNum*. The rightmost character of *strNum* is "0" if *n* Mod 2 is 0 and 1 otherwise. The next character of *strNum* is the rightmost character of the binary representation of *n*\2. [Note: \ is called *integer division*. *m**n* is the same as Int(*m*/*n*).]

18. Write a program that requests an integer greater than 1 as input and factors it into a product of prime numbers. The corresponding flowchart appears in Figure 3.19.

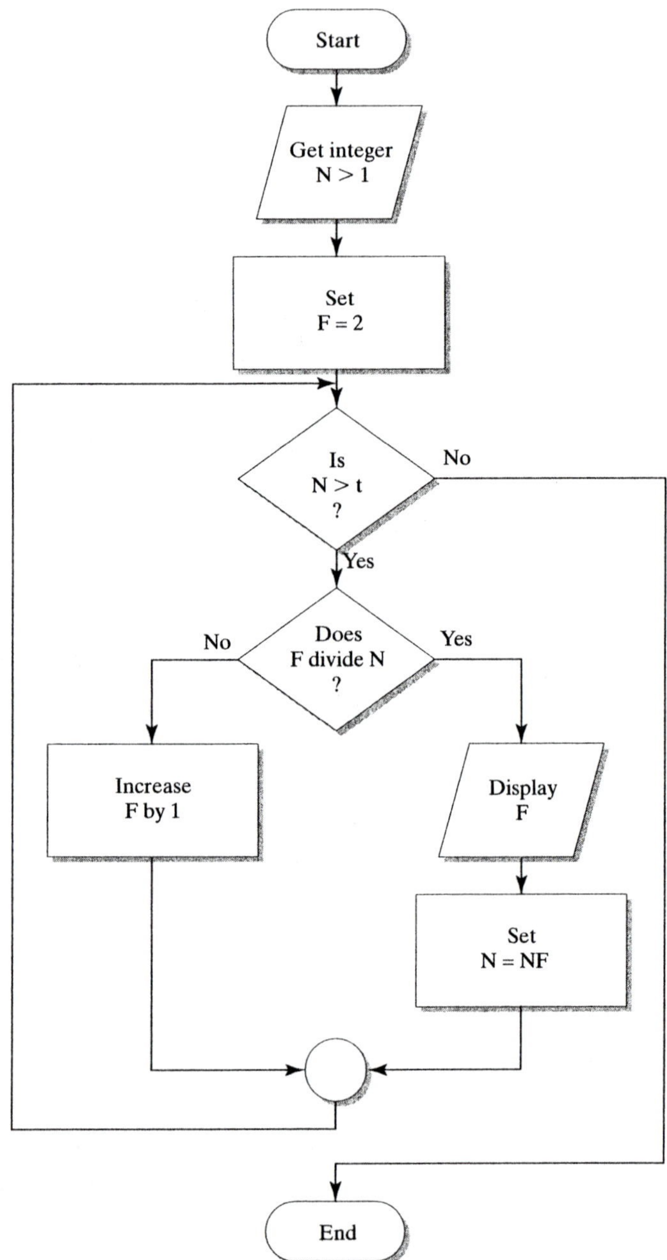

Figure 3.19. Prime factors.

19. Write a program that requests two positive integers as input and displays their greatest common divisor. The corresponding flowchart appears in Figure 3.20.

20. Table 3-5 contains some SI derived quantities and their units and symbols. Write a program that requests a symbol and gives the corresponding quantity and its unit. The user should be informed if the unit is not in the table.

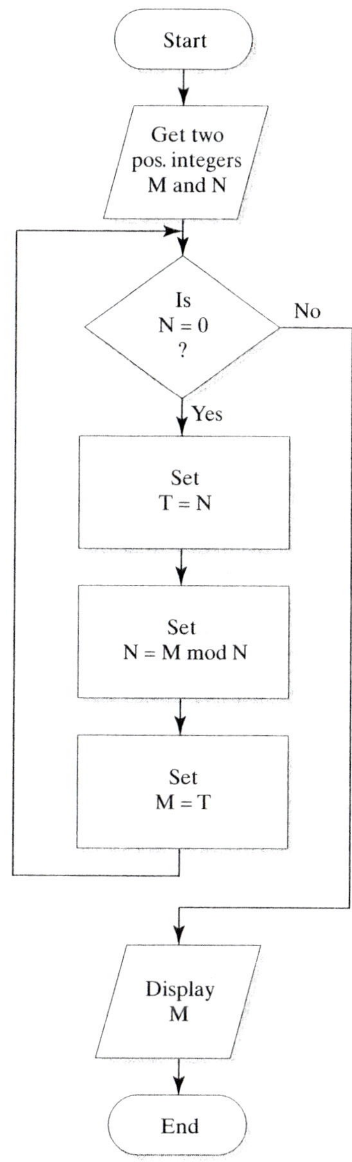

Figure 3.20. Greatest common divisor.

TABLE 3-5 SI units.

QUANTITY	UNIT	SYMBOL
frequency	hertz	Hz
force	newton	N
pressure	pascal	Pa
power	watt	W
inductance	henry	H
energy	joule	J
capacitance	farad	F

21. Suppose a program accesses a text file of positive numbers. Write a function that accepts a number as input, returns True if the number is in the list, and returns False if the number is not in the list.

PROBLEMS 3.4

In Problems 1 to 8, determine the output displayed in the picture box when the command button is clicked.

1.
```
Private Sub cmdDisplay_Click()
     Dim i As Integer
     For i = 1 To 4
         picOutput.Print "Pass #"; i
     Next i
End Sub
```

2.
```
Private Sub cmdDisplay_Click()
     Dim i As Integer
     For i = 3 To 6
         picOutput.Print 2 * i;
     Next i
End Sub
```

3.
```
Private Sub cmdDisplay_Click()
     'The voltage in the secondary of a transformer is
     'es = ep * ns / np. The variable ep is the voltage
     'in the primary, ns and np are the number of turns in
     'the secondary and primary windings, respectively.
     Dim np As Single, ep As Single, ns As Integer
     np = 100
     ep = 125   'volts
     For ns = 100 To 400 Step 100
         picOutput.Print "Es ="; ep * ns / np; "volts."
     Next ns
End Sub
```

4.
```
Private Sub cmdDisplay_Click()
     Dim countdown As Integer
     For countdown = 10 To 1 Step -1
         picOutput.Print countdown;
     Next countdown
     picOutput.Print "blastoff"
End Sub
```

5.
```
Private Sub cmdDisplay_Click()
    Dim num As Integer, i As Integer
    num = 5
    For i = num To 2 * num + 3
        picOutput.Print i;
    Next i
End Sub
```

6.
```
Private Sub cmdDisplay_Click()
    Dim i As Single
    For i = 3 To 5 Step .25
        picOutput.Print i;
    Next i
    picOutput.Print i
End Sub
```

7.
```
Private Sub cmdDisplay_Click()
    Dim i As Integer, j As Integer
    For i = 0 To 2
        For j = 0 To 3
            picOutput.Print i + 3 * j + 1; "";
        Next j
        picOutput.Print
    Next i
End Sub
```

8.
```
Pivate Sub cmdDisplay_Click()
    'Generate a table with For Next…loops
    Dim k As Integer, i As Integer, powerOfTen As Single,
      prefix As String
    Open "Data.txt" For Input As #1
    For k = 1 To 2
        For i = 1 To 3
            Input #1, powerOfTen
            picOutput.Print powerOfTen;""
        Next i
        picOutput.Print
        For j = 1 To 3
            Input #1, prefix
            picOutput.Print prefix; "  "
        Next j
        picOutput.Print
    Next k
    Close #1
End Sub
```

(Assume the file Data.txt contains the following factors and prefixes:

```
1E-15, 1E-12, IE-9, "femto", "pico", "nano"
1E-6, 1E-3, 1E-2, "micro", "milli", "centi")
```

In Problems 9 and 10, identify the errors.

9.
```
Private Sub cmdDisplay_Click()
    Dim j As Single
    For j = 1 To 25.5 Step -1
        picOutput.Print j
    Next j
End Sub
```

10.
```
Private Sub cmdDisplay_Click()
    Dim i As Integer
    For i = 1 To 3
        picOutput.Print i; 2 ^ i
End Sub
```

In Problems 11 and 12, rewrite the program using a For...Next loop.

11.
```
Private Sub cmdDisplay_Click()
    Dim num As Integer
    num = 1
    Do While num <<= 10
        picOutput.Print num
        num = num + 2
    Loop
End Sub
```

12.
```
Private Sub cmdDisplay_Click()
    picOutput.Print "hello"
    picOutput.Print "hello"
    picOutput.Print "hello"
    picOutput.Print "hello"
End Sub
```

In Problems 13 to 26, write a program to complete the stated task.

13. Display a row of 10 stars (asterisks).
14. Request a number from 1 to 20 and display a row of that many stars (asterisks).
15. Find the sum 1 + 1/2 + 1/3 + 1/4 + ... + 1/100.
16. Find the sum of the odd numbers from 1 to 99.
17. The resistance of a resistor is measured 10 times, and the values determined are given in Table 3-6. Calculate the mean (average) value. Recall that, given a set of readings $x_1, x_2, \ldots, x_n$, the mean value x_m is defined as

$$x_m = (x_1 + x_2 + \ldots + x_n)/n. \tag{3-9}$$

TABLE 3-6 Measured resistances.

100.0	100.2	99.3	100.1	100.1
100.9	99.9	99.9	100.0	100.5

18. In an R–C series circuit, the voltage and the current flowing through the capacitor after t seconds during the charging phase are

$$v(t)=V_0[1 - e^{-t/(RC)}] \tag{3-10}$$

$$I(t)=I_0e^{-t/(RC)} \tag{3-11}$$

Request a number n from 1 to 30 and one of the letters V (for voltage) or C (for current) and calculate the voltage or the current for integer values of t microseconds from 1 to n, depending on whether V or C was selected. Assume V_0 = 10 volts, I_0 = 3.33 amperes, R = ohms, and $C = 10^{-6}$ farads.

19. The magnetic field B produced by a straight wire carrying an electric current I at a distance is given by

$$B = 2 \cdot 10^{-7} \cdot I/r \tag{3-12}$$

where B is expressed in tesla (T), I is in amperes (A), and r is in meters (m). Display the value of B for each value of I. Assume that $r = .01\ m$ and I varies from 1 to 10 A in increments of .5A.

20. Sequences of numbers can be generated by recursive formulas where each number in the sequence (except the first) is calculated from previous ones. For example, 1, 3, 7, 15, 31, ... can be generated from the formulas

$$y_1 = 1, y_{n+1} = 2y_n + 1,$$

where y_{n+1}, is the term in the sequence to be calculated and y_n, is the previous term.

  a. Write a program to display the first 10 terms in the above sequence.

  b. Change the program in part (a) to let the user input the number of the term to be found.

  c. Repeat parts (a) and (b) with the recursion formula for the Fibonacci sequence (1, 1, 2, 3, 5, 8, 13,...): $y_1 = 1, y_2 = 1, y_{n+2} = y_{n+1} + y_n$.

21. The proper divisors of the positive integer n are the positive integers less than n that divide n. Write a program that requests a positive integer as input and displays its proper divisors.

22. A beam that is freely supported at both ends is called a simple beam. Figure 3.21 shows a simple beam and the deflection caused when a force P is applied. If x is the shortest distance from the point of application of the force and one of the ends, then the maximum deflection M of the beam is

$$M = \frac{Px\sqrt{3}}{27LEI}(L^2 - x^2)^{3/2}.$$

where L is the length of the beam with no force applied, E is Young's modulus (the ratio of the unit stress to the unit strain) which depends on the material of which the beam is made, and I is the moment of inertia which is determined by a cross-section of the beam. Consider a 72-inch simple steel beam with rectangular cross-section having $E = 30 \cdot 10^6$ lb/in^2, $I = 10.7$ in^4, and $P = 4000$ lb. Write a program that produces a table of maximum deflections as the position of the load is moved from the left end of the beam to the right end in increments of 6 inches.

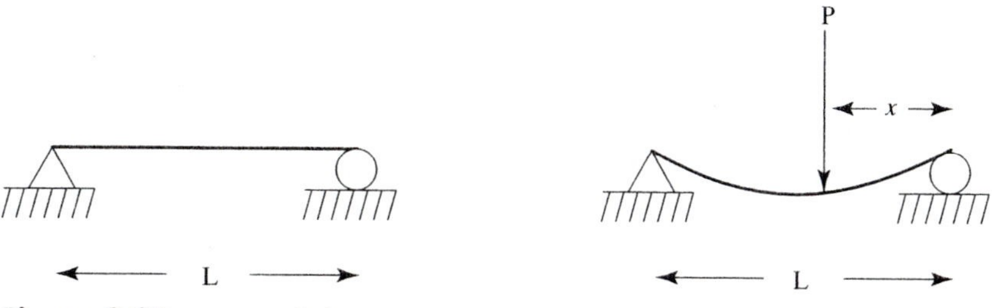

Figure 3.21. A simple beam.

23. The midpoint rule provides a method of approximating the value of a definite integral. Suppose the interval $[a, b]$ is subdivided into n subintervals of length $\Delta x = (b - a)/n$, and $x_1, x_2, \ldots, x_n$ are the midpoints of these subintervals. The midpoint rule states that

$$\int_a^b f(x)\,dx \approx [f(x_1) + f(x_2) + \cdots + f(x_n)]\,\Delta x. \tag{3-13}$$

Write a program to approximate the definite integral of the function $f(x) = e^{-x^2}$ on the interval [0, 2]. Try $n = 5$, $n = 10$, $n = 20$, $n = 40$, and $n = 80$. *Note:* The exact value of the integral to five decimal places is .88208.

24. *Snell's Law.* Where two materials meet, a light ray will be refracted as it passes between them. Snell's Law states that for light passing from one material to another, $n_1 \sin(\theta_1) = n_2 \sin(\theta_2)$, where n is the index of refraction and θ is the angle from the line perpendicular to the plane of intersection (Figure 3.22). Write a program that requests values for n_1 and n_2, and then computes and prints on the printer a listing of θ_2 as a function of θ_1 in increments of 1 degree. Typical values for n are 1.00 for air, 1.33 for water, and 1.52 for glass. *Note:* If $n_2 < n_1$, it will not be possible to go all the way out to $\theta_1 = 90°$; your program must test for the condition that wants to have $\sin(\theta_2) > 1$. The function arcsin can be defined as arcsin(x) = Atn(x/Sqr(1 − x^2)).

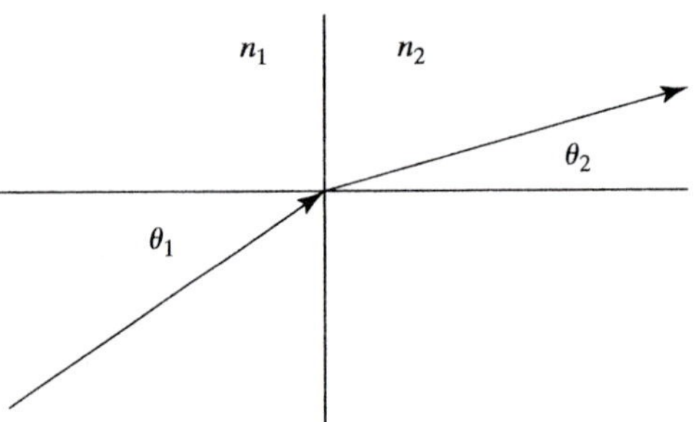

Figure 3.22. Refraction of a ray of light.

25. Write a program with a user-defined function that requests an interval $[a, b]$ and a positive integer n and examines the function values at $n + 1$ evenly spaced points from a through b. Letting $h = (b - a)/n$, the points are a, $a + h$, $a + 2h$, … , b. The program should use the Sub procedure Signs (a, b, n, pos, neg, zero) and display the numbers of function values that are positive, negative, and zero. (Try the program with the function (x − 2)sin(x/20) on the interval [1, 3].)

26. Write a program to accept an integer n as input and display the factorial of n, $n!$.

4

Arrays

SECTIONS

- 4.1 Creating and Accessing Arrays
- 4.2 Sorting and Searching
- 4.3 Arrays and Sequential Files
- 4.4 Programming Projects

OBJECTIVES

After reading this chapter, you should be able to:

- Understand when the use of arrays is preferable to the use of simple variables.
- Create and access arrays in your programs.
- Sort the contents of an array.
- Search for a particular item in an array.
- Use arrays to help create and work with sequential files in Visual Basic.

4.1 CREATING AND ACCESSING ARRAYS

A *variable* (or simple variable) is a name to which Visual Basic can assign a single value. An *array variable* is a collection of simple variables of the same type to which Visual Basic can efficiently assign a list of values.

Suppose you want to evaluate the exam grades for 30 students. Not only do you want to compute the average score, but you also want to display the names of the students whose scores are above average. You might place the 30 pairs of student names and scores in a data file and run the program outlined.

```
Private Sub cmdButton_Click()
    Dim student1 As String, score1 As Single
    Dim student2 As String, score2 As Single
    Dim student3 As String, score3 As Single
    Dim student30 As String, score30 As Single
    'Analyze exam grades
    Open "Scores.txt" For Input As #1
    Input #1, student1, score1
    Input #1, student2, score2
    Input #1, student3, score3
    .
    .
    Input #1, student30, score30
    'Compute the average grade
    .
    .
    'Display names of above average students
    .
    .
End Sub
```

This program is going to be uncomfortably long. What's most frustrating is that the 30 Dim statements and 30 Input# statements are very similar and look as if they should be condensed into a short loop. A shorthand notation for the many related variables would be welcome. It would be nice if we could just write

```
For i = 1 To 30
    Input #1, studenti, scorei
Next i
```

Of course, this will not work. Visual Basic will treat *studenti* and *scorei* as two variables and keep reassigning new values to them. At the end of the loop, they will have the values of the 30th student.

Visual Basic provides a data structure called an *array* that lets us do what we tried to accomplish in the loop. The variable names will be similar to those in the Input# statement. They will be

```
student(1), student(2), student(3), …, student(30)
```

and

```
score(1), score(2), score(3), …, score(30).
```

We refer to these collections of variables as the array variables *student*() and *score*(). The numbers inside the parentheses of the individual variables are called *subscripts*, and each individual variable is called a *subscripted variable* or *element*. For instance, *student*(3) is the third subscripted variable of the array *student*(), and *score*(20) is the 20th subscripted variable of the array *score*(). The elements of an array are assigned successive memory locations. Figure 4.1 shows the memory locations for the array *score*().

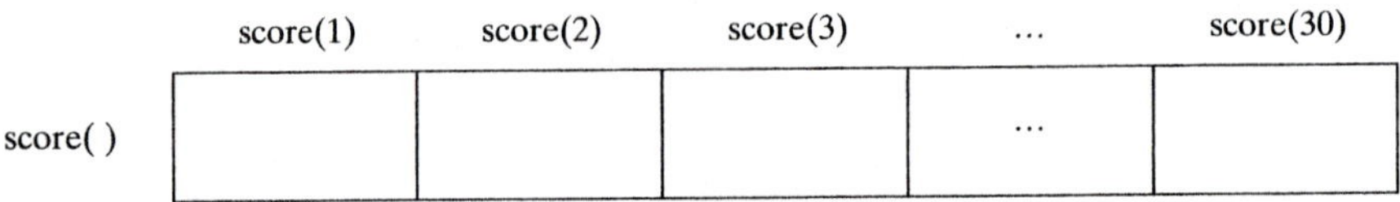

Figure 4.1. The array *score*().

Array variables have the same kinds of names as simple variables. If *arrayName* is the name of an array variable and *n* is a positive whole number, then the statement

```
Dim arrayName(1 To n) As varType
```

reserves space in memory to hold the values of the subscripted variables *arrayName*(1), *arrayName*(2), *arrayName*(3), …, *arrayName*(*n*). The spread of the subscripts specified by the Dim statement is called the *range* of the array, and the Dim statement is said to *dimension* the array. The subscripted variables will all have the same data type; namely, the type specified by varType. For instance, they could be all String variables or all Integer variables. In particular, the statements

```
Dim student(1 To 30) As String
Dim score(1 To 30) As Integer
```

dimension the arrays needed for the preceding program.

Frequently, arrays are dimensioned at the top of the code window; that is, in the (Declarations) section of (General). As discussed in Section 2.4, such arrays have *form-level scope*. That is, they are recognized by all procedures and retain their value when the procedures are exited.

Values can be assigned to subscripted variables with assignment statements and displayed with Print methods. The statement

```
Dim score(1 To 30) As Integer
```

sets aside a portion of memory for the numeric array *score*() and places the default value 0 in each element.

	score(1)	score(2)	score(3)	...	score(30)
score( )	0	0	0	...	0

The statements

```
score(1) = 87
score(3) = 92
```

assign values to the first and third elements.

	score(1)	score(2)	score(3)	...	score(30)
score( )	87	0	92	...	0

The statements

```
For i = 1 To 4
    picBox.Print score(i);
Next i
```

then produce the output 87 0 92 0 in picBox.

The following program creates a string array consisting of the names of the first five World Series winners. Figure 4.2 shows the array created by the program.

```
'Create array for five strings

Dim teamName(1 To 5) As String 'in (Declarations) section of
  (General)
Private Sub cmdWhoWon_Click()
     Dim n As Integer
     'Fill array with World Series Winners
     teamName(1) = "Red Sox"
     teamName(2) = "Giants"
     teamName(3) = "White Sox"
     teamName(4) = "Cubs"
     teamName(5) = "Cubs"
     'Access array of five strings
     n = Val(txtNumber.Text)
     picWinner.Cls
     picWinner.Print "The "; teamName(n); " won World Series
       number"; n
End Sub
```

```
[Run, type 2 into the text box, and click the command button.]
```

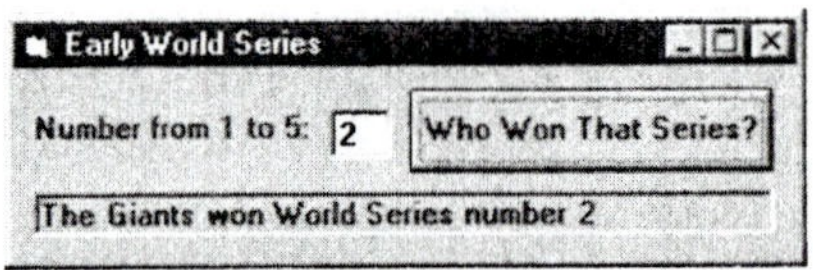

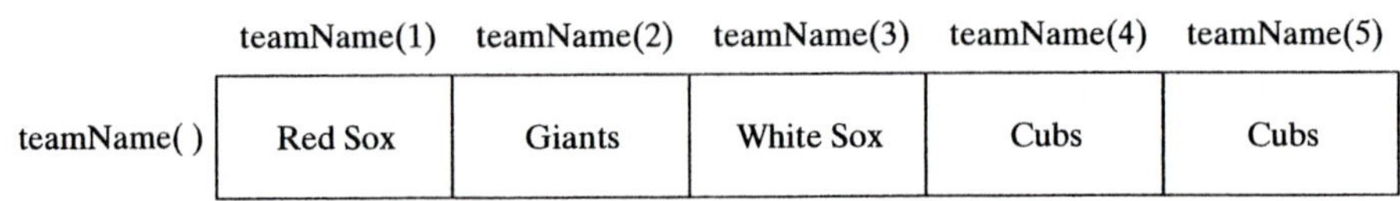

Figure 4.2. The array *teamName*()

In the program above, the array *teamName* was assigned values within the cmdWhoWon_Click event procedure. Every time the command button is clicked, the values are reassigned to the array. This manner of assigning values to an array can be very inefficient, especially in programs with large arrays where the task of the program may be repeated numerous times for different user input. When the data to be placed in an array are known at the time the program first begins to run, a more efficient location for the statements that fill the array is in Visual Basic's *Form_Load* event procedure. The Form_Load event procedure is executed by Visual Basic once as soon as the program is run, and this execution is guaranteed to occur before the execution of any other event or general procedure in the program. The next program uses the Form_Load procedure to improve on the previous program.

Modify the above to request the name of a baseball team as input and search the array to determine whether or not the team name appears in the array. Load the array values only once.

```
'Create array for five strings
Dim teamName(1 To 5) As String 'in (Declarations) section of
  (General)
Private Sub cmdDidTheyWin_Click()
    Dim team As String, foundFlag As Boolean, n As Integer
    'Search for an entry in a list of strings
    team = txtName.Text
    foundFlag = False
    n = 0
    Do
        n = n + 1
        If UCase(teamName(n)) = UCase(team) Then
            foundFlag = True
        End If
    Loop Until (foundFlag = True) Or (n = 5)
    'Above line can be replaced with Loop Until (foundFlag) Or
      (n = 5)
    picWinner.Cls
    If foundFlag = False Then 'Can be replaced by If Not
          foundFlag
        picWinner.Print "The "; team; " did not win any";
        picWinner.Print " of the first five World Series."
      Else
        picWinner.Print "The "; teamName(n); " won World Series
```

```
            number"; n
    End If
End Sub

Private Sub Form_Load()
    'Fill array with World Series winners
    teamName(1) = "Red Sox"
    teamName(2) = "Giants"
    teamName(3) = "White Sox"
    teamName(4) = "Cubs"
    teamName(5) = "Cubs"
End Sub
```

[Run, type White Sox into the text box, and click the command button.]

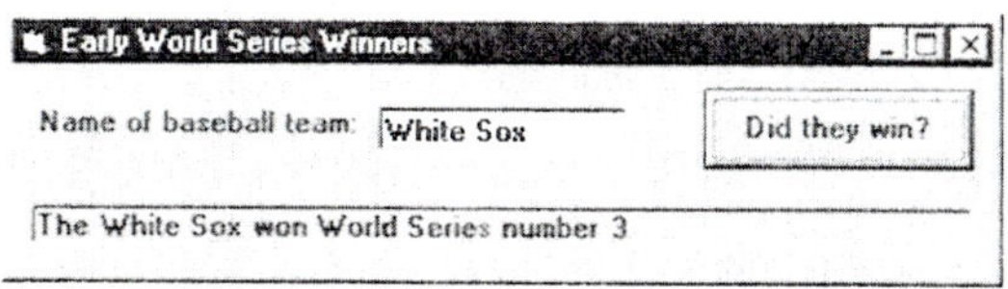

We could have written the program in Example 2 with a For...Next loop beginning For n= 1 To 5. However, such a loop would unnecessarily search the entire list when the sought-after item was found early. The wasted time could be significant for a large array.

In some applications, arrays are needed only temporarily to help a procedure complete a task. Visual Basic also allows us to create array variables that are local to a specific procedure and that exist temporarily while the procedure is executing. If the statement

```
Dim arrayName(1 To n) As varType
```

is placed inside an event procedure, then space for n subscripted variables is set aside in memory each time the procedure is invoked and released when the procedure is exited.

In the program above, values were assigned to the elements of the array with assignment statements. However, data for large arrays are more often stored in a data file and read with Input# statements. Example 3 uses this technique. Also, because the task of the program is likely to be performed only once during a run of the program, a local array is used.

Problem

1. Table 4-1 gives names and test scores from a mathematics contest given in 1953. Write a program to display the names of the students scoring above the average for these eight students.

TABLE 4-1 The top scores on the Fourth Annual Mathematics Contest Sponsored by the Metropolitan NY section of the MAA. *Source: The Mathematics Teacher*, February 1953

NAME	SCORE	NAME	SCORE
Richard Dolen	135	Paul H. Monsky	150
Geraldine Ferraro	114	Max A. Plager	114
James B. Fraser	92	Robert A. Schade	91
John H. Maltby	91	Barbara M. White	124

Solution

1. The following program creates a string array to hold the names of the contestants and a numeric array to hold the scores. The first element of each array holds data for the first contestant, the second element of each array holds data for the second contestant, and so on (Figure 4.3). Note that the two arrays can be dimensioned in a single Dim statement by placing a comma between the array declarations.

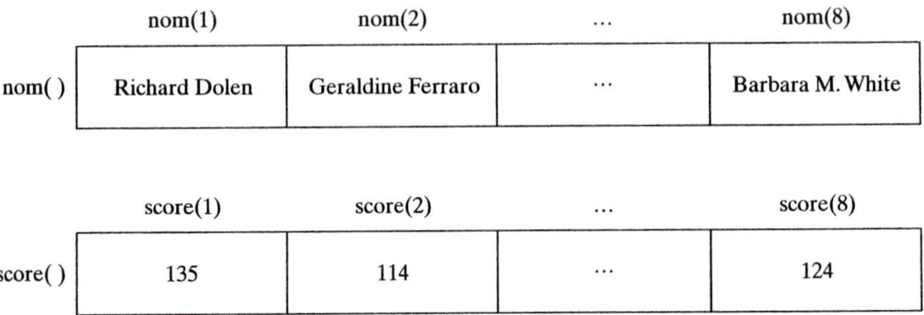

Figure 4.3. Arrays created by Example 1.

```
Private Sub cmdShow_Click()
   Dim total As Integer, student As Integer, average As Single
   'Create arrays for names and scores
   Dim nom(1 To 8) As String, score(1 To 8) As Integer
   'Assume the data has been placed in the file "Scores.txt"
   '(The first line of the file is "Richard Dolen", 135)
   Open "Scores.txt" For Input As #1
   For student = 1 To 8
      Input #1, nom(student), score(student)
   Next student
   Close #1
   'Analyze exam scores
   total = 0
   For student = 1 To 8
      total = total + score(student)
   Next student
   average = total / 8
   'Display all names with above-average grades
   picTopStudents.Cls
   For student = 1 To 8
      If score(student) > average Then
         picTopStudents.Print nom(student)
      End If
   Next student
End Sub
```

[Run, and click the command button.]

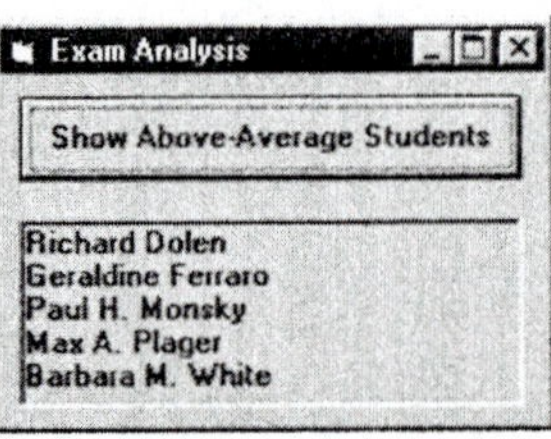

In Example 3, the number of students to be processed had to be known at the time the program was written. In actual practice, the amount of data that a program will be processing is not known in advance. Programs should be flexible and incorporate a method for handling varying amounts of data. Visual Basic makes this possible with the statement

```
ReDim arrayName (1 to n) As varType
```

which can use variables or expressions when indicating the subscript range. However, ReDim statements can only be used inside procedures.

This program reworks Example 3 for the case when the amount of data is not known in advance.

```
Private Sub cmdShow_Click()
    Dim numStudents As Integer, nTemp As String, sTemp As
      Integer
    Dim student As Integer, total As Integer, average As Single
    'Determine amount of data to be processed
    numStudents = 0
    Open "Scores.txt" For Input As #1
    Do While Not EOF(1)
        Input #1, nTemp, sTemp
        numStudents = numStudents + 1
    Loop
    Close #1
    'Create arrays for names and scores
    ReDim nom(1 To numStudents) As String, score(1 To
      numStudents) As Integer
    Open "Scores.txt" For Input As #1
    For student = 1 To numStudents
        Input #1, nom(student), score(student)
    Next student
    Close #1
    'Analyze exam scores
    total = 0
    For student = 1 To numStudents
        total = total + score(student)
    Next student
    average = total / numStudents
    'Display all names with above-average grades
    picTopStudents.Cls
    For student = 1 To numStudents
        If score(student) >> average Then
            picTopStudents.Print nom(student)
        End If
    Next student
End Sub
```

[Run, and click the command button.]

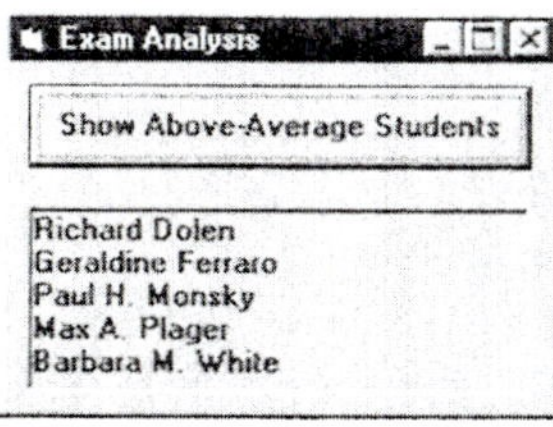

An alternative approach to program flexibility that does not require reading the data file twice is to require that the data file begin with a line that holds the number of records to be processed. If Scores.txt is modified by adding a new first line that gives the number of students, then the 4th through 18th lines of Example 4 can be replaced with

```
'Create arrays for names and scores
Open "Scores.txt" For Input As #1
Input #1, numStudents
ReDim nom(1 To numStudents) As String, score(1 To numStudents)
  As Integer
For student = 1 To numStudents
    Input #1, nom(student), score(student)
Next student
Close #1
```

The range of an array need not just begin with 1. A statement of the form

```
Dim arrayName(m To n) As varType
```

where m is less than or equal to n, creates an array with elements *arrayName*(m), *arrayName*($m + 1$), *arrayName*($m + 2$), ... , *arrayName*(n). The same holds for ReDim.

In the previous program, the ReDim statement allowed us to create arrays whose size was not known before the program was run. On the other hand, the arrays that were created were local to the event procedure cmdShow_Click. Many applications require form-level arrays whose size is not known in advance. Unfortunately, Dim statements cannot use variables or expressions to specify the subscript range. The solution offered by Visual Basic is to allow the (Declarations) section of (General) to contain Dim statements of the form

```
Dim arrayName() As varType
```

where no range for the subscripts of the array is specified. An array created in this manner will be form-level but cannot be used until a ReDim statement is executed in a procedure to establish the range of subscripts. The"As *varType*" clause can be omitted from the ReDim statement.

The first World Series was held in 1903 and has been held in most subsequent years. Suppose the file Winners.txt contains the outcome for each year. The first four lines of the file are "Red Sox"; "(no series)"; "Giants"; "White Sox". Write a program to display the years, if any, of the World Series that were won by the team specified by the user.

```
'Create form-level array
Dim teamName() As String
Dim lastYear As Integer 'Last year recorded in Winners.txt

Private Sub cmdDidTheyWin_Click()
    Dim teamToFind As String, numWon As Integer, series As
      Integer
    'Search for World Series won by user's team
    teamToFind = UCase(txtName.Text)
    picSeriesWon.Cls
    For series = 1903 To lastYear
        If UCase(teamName(series)) = teamToFind Then
            numWon = numWon + 1
```

```
          If numWon = 1 Then
               picSeriesWon.Print "The "; teamName(series);
               picSeriesWon.Print " won the following World
                 Series: ";
            Else
               'Separate from previous
             picSeriesWon.Print ",";
             If (numWon = 5) Or (numWon = 16) Then
                'Start a new line at 5th and 16th win
                picSeriesWon.Print
             End If
          End If
          picSeriesWon.Print Str(series);
      End If
   Next series
   If numWon = 0 Then
      picSeriesWon.Print "The "; teamToFind;
      picSeriesWon.Print" did not win any World Series."
   End If
End Sub

Private Sub Form_Load()
   Dim series As Integer, team As String
   'Determine the last year recorded in the file Winners.txt
   lastYear = 1902
   Open "Winners.txt" For Input As #1
   Do While Not EOF(1)
      Input #1, team
      lastYear = lastYear + 1
   Loop
   Close #1
   'Fill array with World Series winners
   Open "Winners.txt" For Input As #1
   ReDim teamName(1903 To lastYear)
   For series = 1903 To lastYear
      Input #1, teamName(series)
   Next series
   Close #1
End Sub
```

[Run, type Yankees into the text box, and click the command button.]

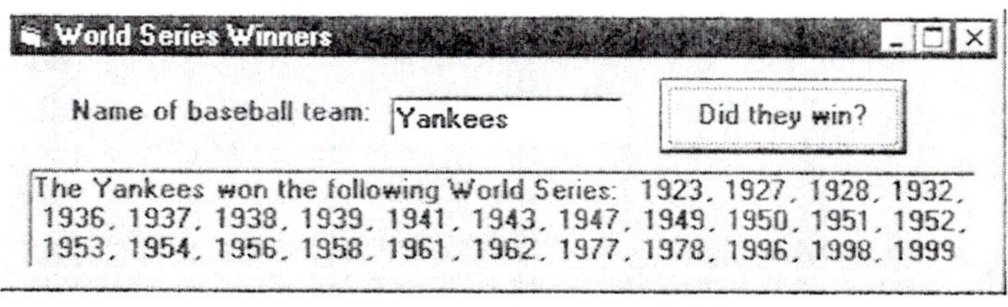

4.1.1 Two-Dimensional Arrays

Each array discussed so far held a single list of items. Such array variables are called *single-subscripted variables*. An array can also hold the contents of a table with several rows and columns. Such arrays are called *two-dimensional arrays* or *double-subscripted variables*. Table 4-2 gives the road mileages between several cities. It has four rows and four columns.

TABLE 4-2 Road mileages between selected U.S. cities

	CHICAGO	**LOS ANGELES**	**NEW YORK**	**PHILADELPHIA**
Chicago	0	2054	802	738
Los Angeles	2054	0	2786	2706
New York	802	2786	0	100
Philadelphia	738	2706	100	0

Two-dimensional array variables store the contents of tables. They have the same types of names as other array variables. The only difference is that they have two subscripts, each with its own range. The range of the first subscript is determined by the number of rows in the table, and the range of the second subscript is determined by the number of columns. The statement

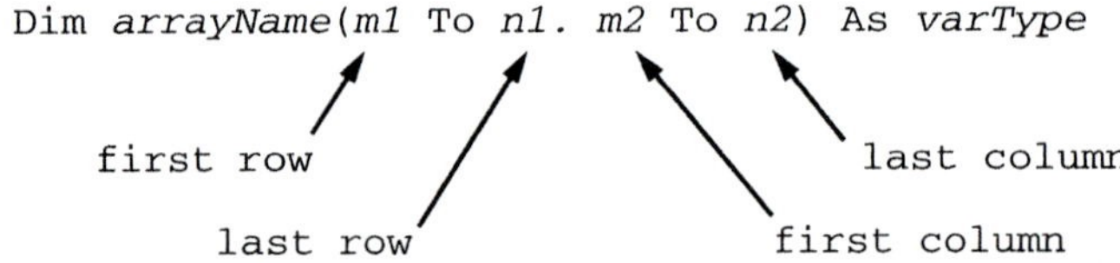

dimensions an array of type *varType* corresponding to a table with rows labeled from *m1* To *n1* and columns labeled from *m2* To *n2*. The entry in the *j*th row, *k*th column is *arrayName*(*j*, *k*). For instance, the data in Table 4-2 can be stored in an array named rm( ). The statement

```
Dim rm(1 To 4, 1 To 4) As Single
```

will dimension the array. Each element of the array has the form *rm*(*row, column*). The entries of the array are

rm(1,1) = 0   rm(1,2) = 2054   rm(1,3) = 802   rm(1,4) = 738
rm(2,1) = 2054   rm(2,2) = 0   rm(2,3) = 2786   rm(2,4) = 2706
rm(3,1) = 802   rm(3,2) = 2786   rm(3,3) = 0   rm(3,4) = 100
rm(4,1) = 738   rm(4,2) = 2706   rm(4,3) = 100   rm(4,4) = 0

As with one-dimensional arrays, when a two-dimensional array is created using Dim in the (Declarations) section of (General), the array becomes a form-level subscripted variable, and is therefore accessible in all event procedures and general procedures and retains whatever values are assigned until the program is terminated. Two-dimensional arrays also can be created with Dim that are local to a procedure and cease to exist once the procedure is exited. When the range of the subscripts is given by one or more variables, the proper statement to use is

```
ReDim arrayName(m1 To n1, m2 To n2) As varType
```

4.1.2 Vectors and Matrices

Vectors and matrices are represented as one- and two-dimensional numeric arrays, respectively. The statements

```
Dim vec (1 To n) As Single
Dim mat (1 To m, 1 To n) As Single
```

declare a vector having n entries and an $m \times n$ matrix; that is, a matrix of m rows and n columns.

Programs involving matrices commonly use procedures to carry out matrix operations. The UBound function can be used to obtain the size of a matrix. The values of UBound(mat, 1) and UBound(mat, 2) are the number of rows and columns of the matrix, respectively. Also, beginning with Version 6.0, Visual Basic user-defined functions can return arrays.

EXAMPLE 4.1: The following program multiplies a column vector on the left by a 3 * 5 matrix and displays the entries of the product. The sizes of the vector and the product are determined by the UBound function from the dimensions of the matrix. The program can be modified for a matrix of a different size.

```
Private Sub cmdMultiply_Click()
    'Multiply a vector by a matrix
    picOutput.Cls
    Dim matrix (1 To 3, 1 To 5) As Single
    ReDim vector (1 To UBound (matrix, 2)) As Single
    ReDim result (1 To UBound (matrix, 1)) As Single
    Call FillEntries (matrix(), vector())
    result = Product (matrix(), vector())
    Call ShowEntries (result())
End Sub

Private Sub FillEntries (matrix() As Single, vector() As
  Single)
    Open "Matrix1.txt" For Input As #1
    For row = 1 To UBound (matrix, 1)
        For col = 1 To UBound (matrix, 2)
            Input #1, matrix (row, col)
        Next col
    Next row
    Close #1
    Open "Matrix2.txt" For Input As #2
    For row = 1 To UBound (matrix, 2)
        Input #2, vector (row)
    Next row
End Sub

Private Function Product (matrix() As Single,
                    vector() As Single) As Single()
    Dim C(1 To 3) As Single
    For row = 1 To UBound (matrix, 1)
        C(row) = 0
        For col = 1 To UBound (matrix, 2)
            C(row) = C(row) + matrix (row, col) * vector(col)
        Next col
    Next row
    Product = C()
End Function
```

```
Private Sub ShowEntries(result() As Single)
    For row = 1 To UBound (result)
        picOutput.Print result (row)
    Next row
End Sub
```

(Assume the file Matrix1.txt contains

7, 2, 5, 2, 8
5, 2, 3, 3, 9
6, 8, 4, 1, 6

and the file Matrix2.txt contains 7, 2, 5, 2, 9. Run and click on the command button. The following will be displayed in the picture box.)

```
154
141
134
```

4.1.3 Comments

1. Arrays must be dimensioned in a Dim or ReDim statement before they are used. If a statement such as $a(6) = 3$ appears without a previous Dim or ReDim of the array $a()$, then the error message "Sub or Function not defined" will be displayed when an attempt is made to run the program.
2. Subscripts in ReDim statements can be numeric expressions. Subscripts whose values are not whole numbers are rounded to the nearest whole number. Subscripts outside the range of the array produce an error message as shown below when the last line inside the event procedure is reached.

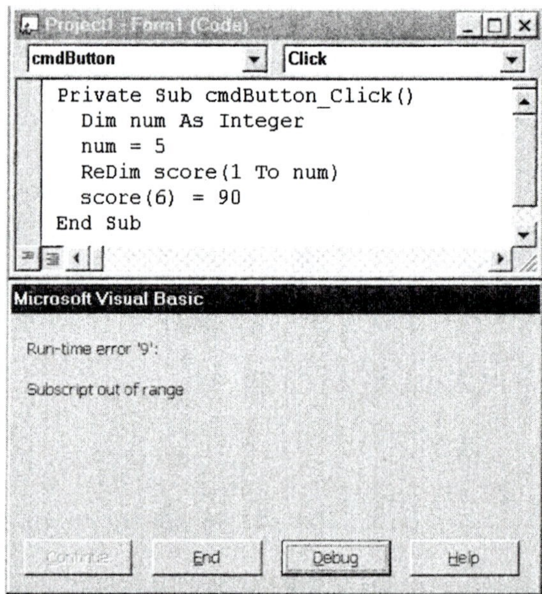

3. The two arrays in the math contest program are referred to as *parallel arrays* because subscripted variables having the same subscript are related.

4. The integers *m* and *n* in the statement Dim *arrayName*(*m* To *n*) As *varType* can be positive, negative, or zero. The only restriction is that *m* cannot be greater than *n*. The same holds true for ReDim statements.
5. Until a value is assigned to an element of an array, the element has its default value. Numeric variables have a default value of 0, and string variables have the default value " ", the empty string.
6. The statement Dim *arrayName*(0 To *n*) As *varType* can be replaced by the statement Dim *arrayName*(*n*) As *varType*. The same holds for the ReDim statement.
7. An array that is not dimensioned in the (Declarations) section of (General) but rather is declared in a procedure, is local to that procedure and unknown in all other procedures. However, an entire local array can be passed to another procedure. The name of the array, followed by an empty set of parentheses, must appear as an argument in the calling statement, and an array variable name of the same type must appear as a corresponding parameter in the procedure definition of the procedure that is to receive the array.

PRACTICE !

1. When should arrays be used to hold data?
2. a. Give an appropriate Dim statement to declare a string array to hold the names of the *Time* magazine "Man of the Year" awards for the years 1980 through 1989.
   b. Write a statement to assign to the array element for 1982 the name of that year's winner, "The Computer."

Solutions

1. Arrays should be used when
   a. Several pieces of data of the same type will be entered by the user.
   b. Computations must be made on the items in a data file *after* all of the items have been read.
   c. Lists of corresponding data are being analyzed.
2. a. Dim manOfTheYear(1980 To 1989) As String
   b. manOfTheYear(1982) = "The Computer"

4.2 SORTING AND SEARCHING

4.2.1 Ordered Arrays

An array is said to be *ordered* if its values are in either ascending or descending order. The following arrays illustrate the different types of ordered and unordered arrays. In an ascending ordered array, the value of each element is less than or equal to the value of the next element. That is,

```
[each element]≤[next element]
```

For string arrays, the ANSI table is used to evaluate the "less than or equal to" condition.

Ordered Ascending Numeric Array

dates()	1492	1776	1812	1929	1969

Ordered Descending Numeric Array

discov()	1610	1541	1513	1513	1492

Ordered Ascending String Array

king()	Edward	Henry	James	John	Kong

Ordered Descending String Array

lake()	Superior	Ontario	Michigan	Huron	Erie

Unordered Numeric Array

rates()	8.25	5.00	7.85	8.00	6.50

Unordered String Array

char()	G	R	E	A	T

A *sort* is an algorithm for ordering an array. Of the many different techniques for sorting an array, we discuss the *bubble sort*. It requires swapping the values stored in a pair of variables. If *var1*, *var2*, and *temp* are all variables of the same type (that is, all numeric or all string), then the statements

```
temp = var1
var1 = var2
var2 = temp
```

assign *var1*'s value to *var2*, and *var2*'s value to *var1*.

Problem

1. Write a program to alphabetize two words supplied in text boxes.

Solution

1.
```
Private Sub cmdAlphabetize_Click()
    Dim firstWord As String, secondWord As String, temp As
      String
    'Alphabetize two words
    firstWord = txtFirstWord.Text
    secondWord = txtSecondWord.Text
    If firstWord >> secondWord Then
       temp = firstWord
       firstWord = secondWord
       secondWord = temp
    End If
    picResult.Cls
    picResult.Print firstWord; " before "; secondWord
End Sub
```

```
[Run, type the following text into the text boxes, and click
the command button.]
```

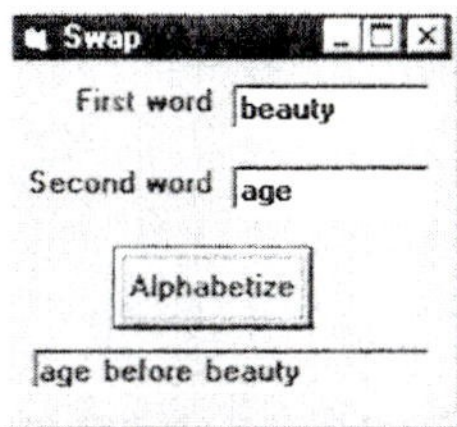

4.2.2 Bubble Sort

The bubble sort is an algorithm that compares adjacent items and swaps those that are out of order. If this process is repeated enough times, the list will be ordered. Let's carry out this process on the list Pebbles, Barney, Wilma, Fred, and Dino. These are the steps for each pass through the list:

1. Compare the first and second items. If they are out of order, swap them.
2. Compare the second and third items. If they are out of order, swap them.
3. Repeat this pattern for all remaining pairs. The final comparison and possible swap are between the next to last and last elements.

The first time through the list, this process is repeated to the end of the list. This is called the first pass. After the first pass, the last item (Wilma) will be in its proper position. Therefore, the second pass does not have to consider it, and so requires one less comparison. At the end of the second pass, the last two items will be in their proper position. (The items that must have reached their proper position have been underlined.) Each successive pass requires one less comparison. After four passes, the last four items will be in their proper positions, and, hence, the first will be also.

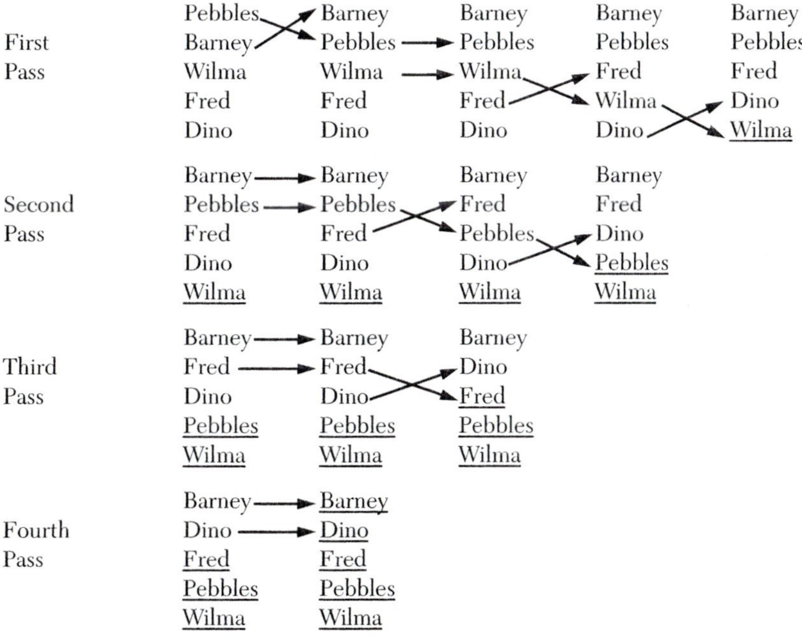

Problem

1. Write a program to alphabetize the names Pebbles, Barney, Wilma, Fred, Dino.

Solution

1. Sorting the list requires a pair of nested loops. The inner loop performs a single pass, and the outer loop controls the number of passes.

```
Dim nom(1 To 5) As String

Private Sub cmdSort_Click()
    Dim passNum As Integer, i As Integer, temp As String
    'Bubble sort names
    For passNum = 1 To 4 'Number of passes is 1 less than
        number of items
      For i = 1 To 5 - passNum 'Each pass needs 1 less
        comparison
        If nom(i) > nom(i + 1) Then
          temp = nom(i)
          nom(i) = nom(i + 1)
          nom(i + 1) = temp
        End If
      Next i
    Next passNum
    'Display alphabetized list
    picNames.Cls
    For i = 1 To 5
      picNames.Print nom(i),
    Next i
End Sub

Private Sub Form_Load()
    'Fill array with names
    nom(1) = "Pebbles"
    nom(2) = "Barney"
    nom(3) = "Wilma"
    nom(4) = "Fred"
    nom(5) = "Dino"
End Sub

[Run, and click the command button.]
```

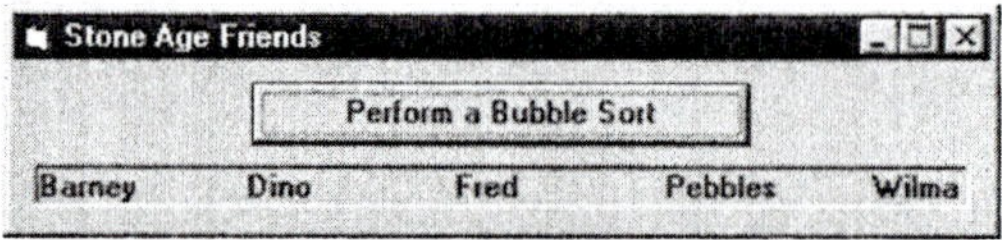

Problem

1. Table 4-3 contains facts about the 10 most populous metropolitan areas with listings in ascending order by city name. Sort the table in descending order by population.

TABLE 4-3 The 10 most populous metropolitan areas

METRO AREA	POPULATION IN MILLIONS	MEDIAN INCOME PER HOUSEHOLD	% NATIVE TO STATE	% ADVANCED DEGREE
Boston	4.2	$40,666	73	12
Chicago	8.1	$35,918	73	8
Dallas	3.9	$32,825	64	8
Detroit	4.7	$34,729	76	7
Houston	3.7	$31,488	67	8
Los Angeles	14.5	$36,711	59	8
New York	18.1	$38,445	73	11
Philadelphia	5.9	$35,797	70	8
San Francisco	6.3	$41,459	60	11
Washington	3.9	$47,254	32	17

Note: Column 4 gives the percentage of residents who were born in their current state of residence. Column 5 gives the percentage of residents age 25 or older with a graduate or professional degree. *Source:* The 1990 Census.

Solution

1. Data are read from a file into parallel arrays by the Form_Load event procedure. When cmdDisplayStats is clicked, the collection of parallel arrays is sorted based on the array *pop*(). Each time two items are interchanged in the array *pop*(), the corresponding items are interchanged in each of the other arrays. This way, for each city, the items of information remain linked by a common subscript.

```
Dim city(1 To 10) As String, pop(1 To 10) As Single
Dim income(1 To 10) As Single
Dim natives(1 To 10) As Single, advDeg(1 To 10) As Single

Private Sub cmdDisplayStats_Click()
    Call SortData
    Call ShowData
End Sub

Private Sub Form_Load()
    Dim j As Integer
    'Assume that the data for city name, population,
    'medium income, % native, and % advanced degree
    'have been placed in the file "Citystat.txt"
    '(First line of file is "Boston",4.2,40666,73,12)
    Open "Citystat.txt" For Input As #1
    For j = 1 To 10
       Input #1, city(j), pop(j), income(j), natives(j),_
                advDeg(j)
```

```
    Next j
    Close #1
End Sub

Private Sub ShowData()
    Dim j As Integer
    'Display ordered table
    picTable.Cls
    picTable.Print "Pop. in", "Med. income", "% Native", _
                   "% Advanced"
    picTable.Print "Metro Area", "millions", "per hsd", _
                   "to State", "Degree"
    picTable.Print
    For j = 1 To 10
      picTable.Print city(j); Tab(16); pop(j), _
                     income(j), natives(j), advDeg(j)
    Next j
End Sub

Private Sub SortData()
    Dim passNum As Integer, index As Integer
    'Bubble sort table in descending order by population
    For passNum = 1 To 9
      For index = 1 To 10 - passNum
        If pop(index) << pop(index + 1) Then
          Call SwapData(index)
        End If
      Next index
    Next passNum
End Sub

Private Sub SwapData(index As Integer)
    'Swap entries
    Call SwapStr(city(index), city(index + 1))
    Call SwapNum(pop(index), pop(index + 1))
    Call SwapNum(income(index), income(index + 1))
    Call SwapNum(natives(index), natives(index + 1))
    Call SwapNum(advDeg(index), advDeg(index + 1))
End Sub

Private Sub SwapNum(a As Single, b As Single)
    Dim temp As Single
    'Interchange values of a and b
    temp = a
    a = b
    b = temp
End Sub

Private Sub SwapStr(a As String, b As String)
    Dim temp As String
    'Interchange values of a and b
    temp = a
    a = b
    b = temp
End Sub
```

```
[Run, and click the command button.]
```

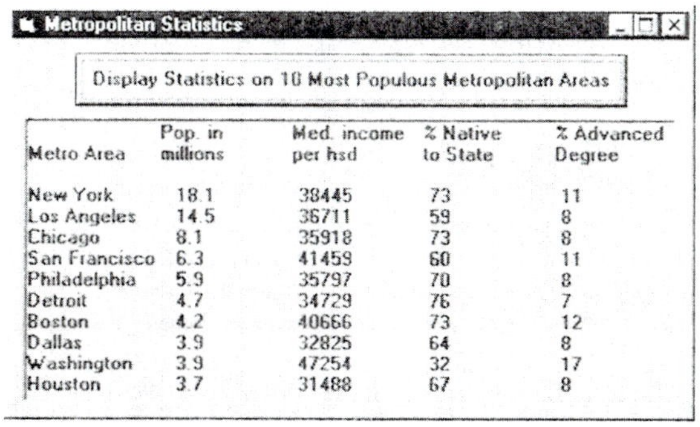

Metropolitan Statistics

Display Statistics on 10 Most Populous Metropolitan Areas

Metro Area	Pop. in millions	Med. income per hsd	% Native to State	% Advanced Degree
New York	18.1	38445	73	11
Los Angeles	14.5	36711	59	8
Chicago	8.1	35918	73	8
San Francisco	6.3	41459	60	11
Philadelphia	5.9	35797	70	8
Detroit	4.7	34729	76	7
Boston	4.2	40666	73	12
Dallas	3.9	32825	64	8
Washington	3.9	47254	32	17
Houston	3.7	31488	67	8

4.2.3 Searching

Suppose we had an array of 1000 names in alphabetical order and wanted to locate a specific person in the list. One approach would be to start with the first name and consider each name until a match was found. This process is called a *sequential search*. We would find a person whose name begins with "A" rather quickly, but 1000 comparisons might be necessary to find a person whose name begins with "Z." For much longer lists, searching could be a time-consuming matter. However, there is a method called a *binary search*, that shortens the task considerably.

Let 's call the sought item the *quarry*. The binary search looks for the *quarry* by determining in which half of the list it lies. The other half is then discarded, and the retained half is temporarily regarded as the entire list. The process is repeated until the item is found. A flag can indicate whether the *quarry* has been found.

The algorithm for a binary search of an ascending list is as follows (Figure 4.4 shows the flowchart for a binary search):

1. At each stage, denote the subscript of the first item in the retained list by *first* and the subscript of the last item by *last*. Initially, the value of *first* is 1, the value of *last* is the number of items in the list, and the value of *flag* is False.

2. Look at the middle item of the current list, the item having the subscript *middle* = Int((*first* + *last*) / 2).

3. If the middle item is the *quarry*, then *flag* is set to True and the search is over.

4. If the middle item is greater than the *quarry*, then the *quarry* should be in the first half of the list. So the subscript of the *quarry* must lie between *first* and *middle* − 1. That is, the new value of *last* is *middle* − 1.

5. If the middle item is less than the *quarry*, then the *quarry* should be in the second half of the list of possible items. So the subscript of the *quarry* must lie between *middle* + 1 and *last*. That is, the new value of *first* is *middle* + 1.

6. Repeat Steps 2 to 5 until the *quarry* is found or until the halving process uses up the entire list. (When the entire list has been used up, *first* > *last*.) In the second case, the *quarry* was not in the original list.

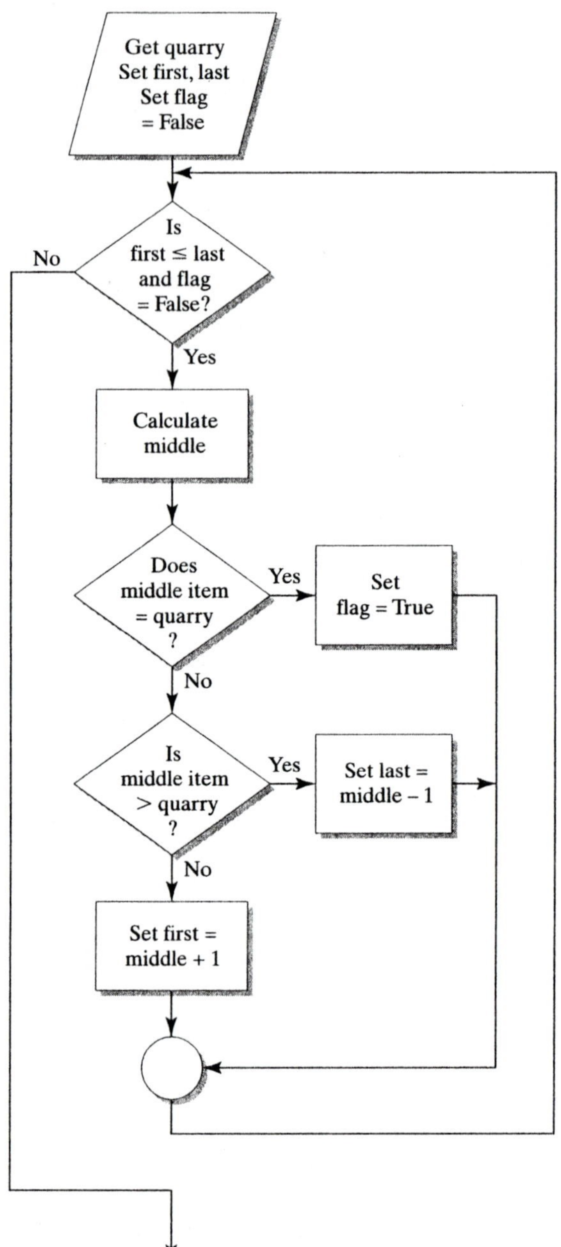

Figure 4.4. Flowchart for a binary search.

In the next program, the array *firm*() contains the alphabetized names of up to 100 corporations. The program requests the name of a corporation as input and uses a binary search to determine whether or not the corporation is in the array.

```
Dim firm(1 To 100) As String
Dim numFirms As Integer

Private Sub BinarySearch(corp As String, result As String)
    Dim foundFlag As Boolean
    Dim first As Integer, middle As Integer, last As Integer
    'Array firm() assumed already ordered alphabetically
    'Binary search of firm() for corp
```

```
    foundFlag = False
    first = 1
    last = numFirms
    Do While (first <= last) And (Not foundFlag)
       middle = Int((first + last) / 2)
       Select Case UCase(firm(middle))
          Case corp
             foundFlag = True
          Case Is > corp
             last = middle - 1
          Case Is < corp
             first = middle + 1
       End Select
    Loop
    If foundFlag Then
       result = "found"
     Else
       result = "not found"
    End If
End Sub

Private Sub cmdSearch_Click()
    Dim corp As String, result As String
    corp = UCase(Trim(txtCorporation.Text))
    Call BinarySearch(corp, result)
    'Display results of search
    picResult.Cls
    picResult.Print corp; " "; result
End Sub

Private Sub Form_Load()
    'Fill array with data from FIRMS.TXT
    Open "Firms.txt" For Input As #1
    numFirms = 0
    Do While (Not EOF(1)) And (numFirms < 100)
       numFirms = numFirms + 1
       Input #1, firm(numFirms)
    Loop
End Sub

[Run, type IBM into the text box, and click the command button.]
```

Suppose the array contains 100 corporations and the corporation input in Example 4 is in the second half of the array. On the first pass, *middle* would be assigned Int((1 + 100)/2) = Int(50.5) = 50, and then *first* would be altered to 50 + 1 = 51. On the second pass, *middle* would be assigned Int((51 + 100)/2) = Int(75.5) = 75. If the corporation is not the array element with subscript 75, then either *last* would be assigned 74 or *first* would be assigned 76, depending on whether the corporation appears before or after the 75th element. Each pass through the loop halves the range of subscripts containing the corporation until the corporation is located.

In Example 4, the binary search merely reported whether or not an array contained a certain item. After finding the item, its array subscript was not needed. However, if related data are stored in parallel arrays (as in Table 4-4), the subscript of the found item can be used to retrieve the related information in the other arrays. This process is called a *table lookup*.

4.2.4 Comments

1. In Example 3, parallel arrays already ordered by one field were sorted by another field. Usually, parallel arrays are sorted by the field to be searched when accessing the file. This field is called the *key field*.
2. Suppose an array of 2000 items is searched sequentially—that is, one item after another—in order to locate a specific item. The number of comparisons would vary from 1 to 2000, with an average of 1000. With a binary search, the number of comparisons would be at most 11 because $2^{11} > 2000$.
3. The built-in function UCase converts all the characters in a string to uppercase. UCase is useful in sorting and searching arrays of strings when the alphabetic case (upper or lower) is unimportant. For instance, Example 4 includes UCase in the Select Case comparisons, and so the binary search will locate "Mobil" in the array even if the user entered "MOBIL."

PRACTICE!

1. The pseudocode for a bubble sort of an array of n items follows. Why is the terminating value of the outer loop $n - 1$ and the terminating value of the inner loop $n - j$?

```
For j = 1 To n - 1
     For k = 1 To n - j
         If [kth and (k+1)st items are out of order]
     Then               [interchange them]
     Next k
Next j
```

2. Complete the table below by filling in the values of each variable after successive passes of a binary search of a list of 20 items, where the sought item is in the 13th position.

FIRST	LAST	MIDDLE
1	20	10
11	20	

Solutions

1. The outer loop controls the number of passes, one less than the number of items in the list. The inner loop performs a single pass, and the jth pass consists of $n - j$ comparisons.
2.

FIRST	LAST	MIDDLE
1	20	10
11	20	15
11	14	12
13	14	13

4.3 ARRAYS AND SEQUENTIAL FILES

Throughout this text we have processed data from files created with Windows' Notepad and saved on disk. Such files are stored on disk as a sequence of characters. (Two special characters, called the "carriage return" and "line feed" characters, are inserted at the end of each line to indicate where new lines should be started.) Such files are called *sequential files* or *text files*. Sequential files also can be created directly from Visual Basic.

Arrays and sequential files interact in several ways. For instance, the initial values of the elements of arrays are usually loaded from sequential files, and the final values are saved back into sequential files for later use. Also, arrays are used to sort the elements of sequential files. In this section, we first learn how to manage sequential files and then consider some ways that arrays and sequential files interact.

4.3.1 Creating a Sequential File from Visual Basic

The following steps create a new sequential file and write data to it.

1. Choose a file name. A file name can contain up to 255 characters consisting of letters, digits, and a few other assorted characters (including spaces and periods). In this book we use 8.3 format names where each name has a base name of at most 8 characters, and optionally a period followed by a three letter extension. (Such names are recognized by all utility programs.)
2. Choose a number from 1 to 511 to be the *reference number* of the file. While the file is in use, it will be identified by this number.
3. Execute the statement

   ```
   Open "filespec" For Output As #n
   ```

   where *n* is the reference number. This process is referred to as *opening a file for output*. It establishes a communications link between the computer and the disk drive for storing data *onto* the disk. It allows data to be output from the computer and recorded in the specified file.
4. Place data into the file with the Write # statement. If *a* is a string, then the statement

   ```
   Write #n, a
   ```

   writes the string *a* surrounded by quotation marks into the file. If *c* is a number, then the statement

   ```
   Write #n, c
   ```

   writes the number *c*, without any leading or trailing spaces, into file number *n*. The statement

   ```
   Write #n, a, c
   ```

   writes *a* and *c* as before, but with a comma separating them. Similarly, if the statement Write #*n* is followed by a list of several strings and/or numbers separated by commas, then all the strings and numbers appear as before, separated by commas. After each Write # statement is executed, the "carriage return" and "line feed" characters are placed into the file.
5. After all the data have been recorded in the file, execute

   ```
   Close #n
   ```

where n is the reference number. This statement breaks the communications link with the file and dissociates the number n from the file.

EXAMPLE 4.2: The following program uses Write # to store the contents of arrays containing names and dates of birth into a sequential file.

```
Dim nom(1 To 3) As String
Dim yr(1 To 3) As Integer

Private Sub cmdCreateFile_Click()
   Dim index As Integer
   Open "Yob.txt" For Output As #1
   For index = 1 To 3
      Write #1, nom(index), yr(index)
   Next index
   Close #1
End Sub

Private Sub Form_Load()
   nom(1) = "Elaine"
   yr(1) = 1961
   nom(2) = "George"
   yr(2) = 1959
   nom(3) = "Kramer"
   yr(3) = 1949
End Sub
```

```
(Run, click the command button, and then load the file Yob.txt
into Windows' Notepad. The following will appear on the
screen.]
"Elaine"1961
"George",1959
"Kramer",1949
```

Caution: If an existing sequential file is opened for output, the computer will erase the existing data and create a new empty file.

Write # statements allow us to create files just like the Notepad files that appear throughout this text. We already know how to read such files with Input # statements. The remaining major task is adding data to the end of sequential files.

4.3.2 Adding Items to a Sequential File

Data can be added to the end of an existing sequential file with the following steps.

1. Choose a number from 1 to 511 to be the reference number for the file. It need not be the number that was used when the file was created.
2. Execute the statement

   `Open "filespec" For Append As #n`

   where n is the reference number. This procedure is called *opening a file for append.* It allows data to be output and recorded at the end of the specified file.
3. Place data into the file with Write # statements.
4. After all the data have been recorded into the file, close the file with the statement Close #n.

The Append option for opening a file is intended to add data to an existing file. However, it also can be used to create a new file. If the file does not exist, then the Append option acts just like the Output option and creates the file.

The three options, Output, Input, and Append, are referred to as *modes*. A file should not be open in two modes at the same time. For instance, after a file has been opened for output and data have been written to the file, the file should be closed before being opened for input.

An attempt to open a nonexistent file for input terminates the program with the "File not found" error message. There is a function that tells us whether a certain file has already been created. If the value of

```
Dir("filespec")
```

is the empty string " ", then the specified file does not exist. (If the file exists, the value will be the file name.) Therefore, prudence often dictates that files be opened for input with code such as

```
If Dir("filespec") <> "" Then
    Open "filespec" For Input As #1
  Else
    message = "Either no file has yet been created or "
    message = message & "the file is not where expected."
    MsgBox message, , "File Not Found"
End If
```

There is one file-management operation that we have yet to discuss—deleting an item of information from a file. An individual item of a file cannot be changed or deleted directly. A new file must be created by reading each item from the original file and recording it, with the single item changed or deleted, into the new file. The old file is then erased and the new file renamed with the name of the original file. Regarding these last two tasks, the Visual Basic statement

```
Kill "filespec"
```

removes the specified file from the disk and the statement

```
Name "oldfilespec" As "newfilespec"
```

changes the filespec of a file. (*Note:* The Kill and Name statements cannot be used with open files. So doing generates a "File already open" message.)

EXAMPLE 4.3: The following program modifies the file created in Example 1.

OBJECT	PROPERTY	SETTING
frm4_3_2	Caption	Modify Yob.txt
lblName	Caption	Name
txtName	Text	(blank)
lb1YOB	Caption	Year of Birth
txtYOB	Text	(blank)
cmdAdd	Caption	Add Above Person to File
cmdDelete	Caption	Remove Above Person from File

```
Private Sub cmdAdd_Click()
   Dim message As String
   'Add a person's name and year of birth to file
   If (txtName.Text <> "") And (txtYOB.Text <> "") Then
      Open "Yob.txt" For Append As #1
      Write #1, txtName.Text, Val(txtYOB.Text)
      Close #1
      txtName.Text =""
      txtYOB.Text =""
      txtName.SetFocus
   Else
      message = "You must enter a name and year of birth."
      MsgBox message, , "Information Incomplete"
   End If
End Sub
Private Sub cmdDelete Click
   'Remove a person from the file if possible
   Dim message As String
   If txtName.Text <> "" Then
      If Dir("Yob.txt") <> "." Then
         Call DeletePerson
        Else
         message = "Either no file has yet been created or "
         message = message & "the file is not where expected."
         MsgBox message, , "File Not Found."
      End If
     Else
      MsgBox "You must enter a name.", , "Information
                 Incomplete"
   End If
   txtName.SetFocus
End Sub
Private Sub DeletePerson()
   Dim foundFlag As Boolean, nom As String, yr As Integer
   foundFlag = False
   Open "Yob.txt" For Input As #1
   Open "Temp" For Output As #2
   Do While Not EOF(1)
      Input #1, nom, yr
      If nom <> txtName.Text Then
         Write #2, nom, yr
        Else
         foundFlag = True
      End If
   Loop
   Close #1
   Close #2
   Kill "Yob.txt"
   Name "Temp" As "Yob.txt"
   If Not foundFlag Then
      MsgBox "The name was not found.", , ""
     Else
      txtName.Text = ""
      txtYOB.Text = ""
   End If
End Sub
```

The sequential file Yob.txt created in Example 1 is said to consist of three records of two fields each. A *record* holds all the data about a single individual. Each item of data is called a *field*. The two fields are "name" and "year of birth." Sequential files are commonly sorted on a specific field.

EXAMPLE 4.4: The following program sorts the sequential file Yob.txt by year of birth.

```
Private Sub cmdSort_Click()
    Dim numPeople As Integer
    'Sort data from Yob.txt file by year of birth
    numPeople = NumberOfRecords("Yob.txt")
    'Number of people in file
    ReDim nom(1 To numPeople) As String
    ReDim yearBorn(1 To numPeople) As Integer
    Call ReadData(nom(), yearBorn(), numPeople)
    Call SortData(nom(), yearBorn(), numPeople)
    Call WriteData(nom(), yearBorn(), numPeople)
End Sub

Private Function NumberOfRecords(filespec As String) As Integer
    Dim nom As String, yearBorn As Integer
    Dim n As Integer 'Used to count records
    Open filespec For Input As #1
    Do While Not EOF(1)
        Input #1, nom. yearBorn
        n = n + 1
    Loop
    Close #1
    NumberOfRecords = n
End Function

Private Sub ReadData(nom() As String, yearBorn() As Integer,
                     numPeople As Integer)
    Dim index As Integer
    'Read data from file into arrays
    Open "Yob.txt" For Input As #1
    For index = 1 To numPeople
        Input #1, nom(index), yearBorn(index)
    Next index
    Close #1
End Sub

Private Sub SortData(nom() As String, yearBorn() As Integer,
                     numPeople As Integer)
    Dim passNum As Integer, index As Integer
    'Bubble sort arrays by year of birth
    For passNum = 1 To numPeople - 1
        For index = 1 To numPeople - passNum
            If yearBorn(index) > yearBorn(index + 1) Then
                Call SwapData(nom(), yearBorn(), index)
            End If
        Next index
    Next passNum
End Sub
```

```
Private Sub SwapData(nom() As String, yearBorn() As Integer,
                    index As Integer)
    Dim stemp As String, ntemp As Integer
    'Swap names and years
    stemp = nom(index)
    nom(index) = nom(index + 1)
    nom(index + 1) = stemp
    ntemp = yearBorn(index)
    yearBorn(index) = yearBorn(index + 1)
    yearBorn(index + 1) = ntemp
End Sub

Private Sub WriteData(nom() As String, yearBorn () As Integer,
                      numPeople As Integer)
    Dim index As Integer
    'Write data back into file
    Open "Yob.txt" For Output As #1
    For index = 1 To numPeople
       Write #1, nom(index), yearBorn(index)
    Next index
    Close #1
End Sub
```

[Run, click the command button, and then load the file Yob.txt into Windows' Notepad. The following will appear on the screen.]

```
"Kramer",1949
"George",1959
"Elaine",1961
```

4.3.3 Comment

1. In the examples of this section, the files to be processed have been opened and closed within a single procedure. However, the solution to some programming problems requires that a file be opened just once the instant the program is run and stay open until the program is terminated. This is easily accomplished by placing the Open statement in the Form_Load event procedure and the Close and End statements in the click event procedure for a command button labeled "Quit."

PRACTICE!

1. Modify the event procedure cmdAdd_Click() of Example 2 to add a name and year of birth to the end of the file Yob.txt only if the name to be added is not already present in the file. (Assume that the existance of Yob.txt is checked prior to the execution of this event procedure.)

Solution

1. The file Yob.txt is first opened for Input and scanned for the new name. If the name is not found, Yob.tKt is reopened for Append and the name and year of birth are added to the end of the file.

```
Private Sub cmdAdd_Click()
   'Add a new person's name and year of birth to file
Dim foundFlag As Boolean, nom As String, yr As Integer
```

```
Dim message As String
    If (txtName.Text <> "") And (txtYOB.Text <> "" Then
        Open "Yob.txt" for Input as #1
        foundFlag = False
        Do While (Not(EOF(i)) And (Not foundFlag)
            Input #1, nom, yr
            If nom = txtName.Text Then
                foundFlag = True
            End If
        Loop
        Close #1
        If Not foundFlag Then
            Open "Yob.txt" For Append As 11
            Write #1, txtName.Text, Val(txtYOB.Text)
            Close #1
            txtName.Text = ""
            txtYOB.Text = ""
            txtName.SetFocus
        End If
    Else
        message = "You must enter a name and year of
                  birth."
        msgBox message, , "Information Incomplete"
    End If
End Sub
```

4.4 PROGRAMMING PROJECTS

1. Table 4-4 contains some lengths in terms of feet. Write a program that displays the nine different units of measure, requests the unit to convert from, the unit to convert to, and the quantity to be converted, and then displays the converted quantity. A typical outcome is shown in Figure 4.5

TABLE 4-4 Equivalent lengths

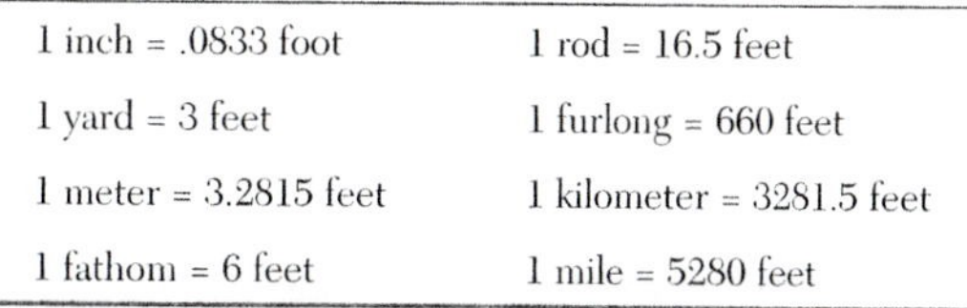

1 inch = .0833 foot	1 rod = 16.5 feet
1 yard = 3 feet	1 furlong = 660 feet
1 meter = 3.2815 feet	1 kilometer = 3281.5 feet
1 fathom = 6 feet	1 mile = 5280 feet

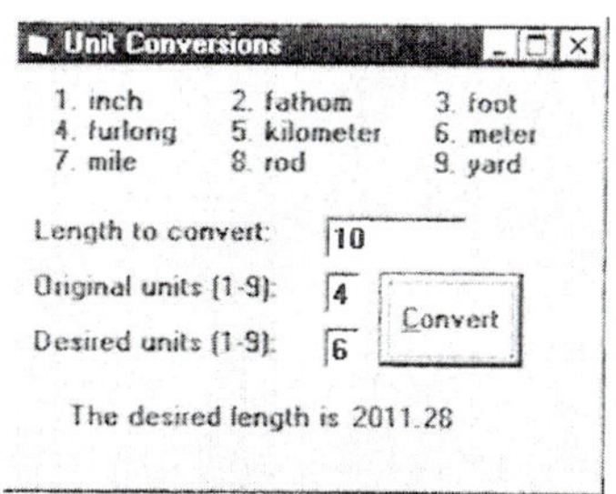

Figure 4.5. Possible outcome of Project 1.

2. *Elementary Row Operations*. The three elementary row operations for a matrix are:

1. Interchange two rows of the matrix.
2. Multiply a row of the matrix by a constant.
3. Add a constant multiple of one row of the matrix to another row.

Write a program that reads the dimensions and entries of a matrix from a data file and then repeatedly allows the user to select an elementary row operation to perform, display the current matrix, or quit. When an elementary row operation is selected, the program should request the information needed to carry out the operation. For instance, if row operation 2 is selected, the program should request the row number and the constant.

3. *Matrix Inversion by the Gauss Elimination Method.* The square $n \times n$ matrix B is the inverse of the square $n \times n$ matrix A if $A \cdot B = I_n$, the $n \times n$ identity matrix. The following algorithm finds the inverse of the matrix A.

   a. Construct the $n \times 2n$ matrix C with left half A and right half I_n.

   b. Successively perform elementary row operations on C until the left half is an $n \times n$ identity matrix. (See Programming Project 2.)

   c. After step (b) is complete, the right half of C will be the inverse of A.

Write a program to read the size of the matrix A and the entries of the matrix from a data file. The program should find and display the inverse of the matrix A. Try the program with the 4×4 matrix

$$\begin{bmatrix} 1 & 0 & -2 & 0 \\ 0 & 1 & 0 & -5 \\ -4 & 0 & 9 & 0 \\ 0 & 2 & 1 & -9 \end{bmatrix} \text{ which has inverse } \begin{bmatrix} 9 & 0 & 2 & 0 \\ -20 & -9 & -5 & 5 \\ 4 & 0 & 1 & 0 \\ -4 & -2 & -1 & 1 \end{bmatrix}$$

4. *Solving an Electric Circuit.* Kirchhoff s rules are used for handling a variety of network problems. Kirchhoff s voltage law (KVL) states that the sum of the voltage rises around a loop is equal to the sum of the voltage drops around the loop. Consider the circuit in Figure 4.6. The KVL equations for each loop can be written in an array form:

$$\begin{bmatrix} v_a \\ v_b \\ v_c \end{bmatrix} = \begin{bmatrix} (R_1 + R_2) & -R_1 & -R_2 \\ R_1 & -(R_1 + R_2) & R_3 \\ -R_2 & -R_3 & (R_2 + R_3 + R_4) \end{bmatrix} \begin{bmatrix} i_1 \\ i_2 \\ i_3 \end{bmatrix}.$$

   Write a program to

   a. Read the values of i_1, i_2, and i_3 and place them in a one-dimensional array.

   b. Read the values of the resistances and place them in a two-dimensional array.

   c. Calculate and display the voltages v_a, v_b, v_c.

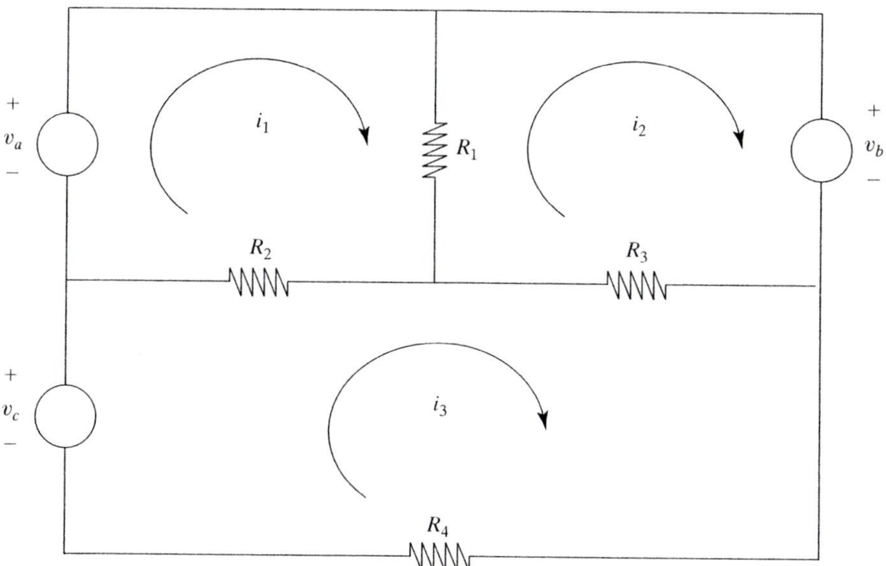

Figure 4.6. Electric circuit.

For example, for R_1, = 5, R_2 = 3, R_3 = 4, R_4 = 6, i_1 = 2.5, i_2 = 2, and i_3 = 1.5 you should get v_a = 5.5, v_b = 0.5, and v_c = 4.

5. Linear shift registers are used to generate sequences of zeros and ones, such as are needed for spread spectrum communications. Figure 4.7 shows an 8-bit shift register. Initially, each cell contains a zero or a one.

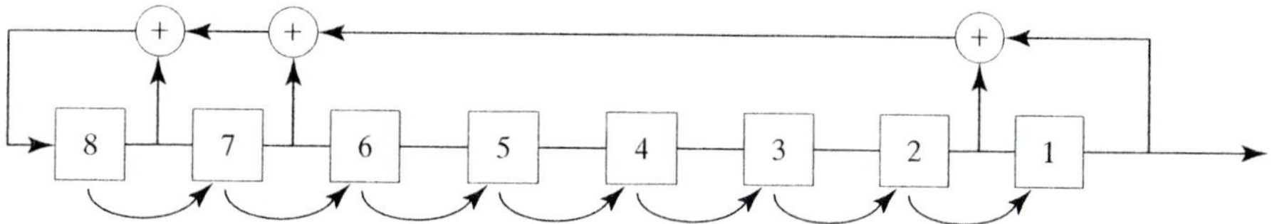

Figure 4.7. A linear shift register.

At the first pulse, the bit in cell 1 is transmitted, the bits in each of the other seven cells are shifted to the right, and cell 8 is filled with a modulo 2 sum (that is, 0 + 0 = 0, 1 + 0 = 1, 0 + 1 = 1, 1 + 1 = 0) of one or more of the initial bits in cells 1 through 8. For the shift register in Figure 4.7, New Bit 8 = Old Bit 8 + Old Bit 7 + Old Bit 2 + Old Bit 1 Mod 2. This process is repeated over and over again to transmit a sequence of zeros and ones. Table 4-4 shows the successive states of the shift register and the bits transmitted when the initial state is 0 0 0 0 0 0 0 1.

Eventually, the shift register of Figure 4.7 will return to its initial state and the sequence of bits transmitted will be repeated. This is always the case when Old Bit 1 is included in the formula for New Bit 8. The smallest value of p for which the sequence of bits repeats after p pulses is called the *period* of the sequence, and the sequence is called a *maximal length* sequence if it has period $2^n - 1$, where n is the number of cells in the shift register.

a. Write a program to determine the period of the sequence generated by the shift register in Figure 4.7 when the initial state is 0 0 0 0 0 0 0 1. Is this sequence a maximal length sequence?

b. Modify the program in (a) to determine the period of the sequence generated by a shift register for which New Bit 8 = Old Bit 7 + Old Bit 1 and having initial state 0 0 0 0 0 0 0 1. Is this sequence a maximal length sequence?

TABLE 4-5 Successive states and bits transmitted by the shif register in Figure 7.2

	STATES OF SHIFT REGISTER	BIT TRANSMITTED
Initial state	00000001	
After pulse 1	10000000	1
After pulse 2	11000000	0
After pulse 3	01100000	0
After pulse 4	10110000	0
After pulse 5	11011000	0
After pulse 6	01101100	0
After pulse 7	10110110	0
After pulse 8	01011011	0
After pulse 9	10101101	1
After pulse 10	01010110	1
After pulse 11	00101011	0

PROFESSIONAL SUCCESS

Evaluating Sort Algorithms

Many different algorithms have been devised for the purpose of ordering the elements of an array. Some of these, like the bubble sort algorithm discussed in the text, are extremely straightforward and easy to understand. The bubble sort algorithm, however, due to its inherent inefficiency, is rarely utilized in commercial software.

Algorithm efficiency is related to the number of comparison and swap operations required to order completely an N element array. The most efficient sort algorithms require $O(Nlog_2N)$ (on the order of $Nlog_2N$) operations to sort completely the array elements, while the least efficient routines, such as the bubble sort algorithm, requires $O(N_2)$ operations. The impact of this difference becomes apparent as the number of elements in the array increases. For instance, sorting a 10-element array requires on the order of 34 operations using an efficient routine such as the *heap* sort, and 100 operations using the bubble sort. These numbers increase to 665 and 10,000, respectively, for a 100-element array. Clearly, programs incorporating the bubble sort will require more time to complete their tasks than those using more efficient routines, such as the heap sort.

Programmers wishing to find efficient algorithms do not generally have to write them from scratch. There are many references available that contain algorithms in mathematical or pseudocode form; in addition, fully coded software modules in Visual Basic (or other languages), which can be incorporated into your program, may already exist in the public domain. Whichever source you use, it is important to test your completed program adequately to verify its accuracy and efficiency.

KEY TERMS

Array
Array variable
Binary search
Bubble sort
Dimension
Field
Form-level scope
Key field
Mode
Ordered array
Range
Record
Sequential search
Sequential (text) file
Sort
Subscript
Subscripted variable (element)
Table lookup
Two-dimensional array
Variable

Problems

PROBLEMS 4.1

In Problems 1 to 6, determine the output displayed in the picture box when the command button is clicked. All Dim statements for arrays are in the (Declarations) section of (General).

1.
```
Dim a(1 To 20) As Integer
Private Sub cmdDisplay_Click()
     a(5) = 1
     a(10) = 2
     a(15) = 7
     picOutput.Print a(5) + a(10);
     picOutput.Print a(5 + 10);
     picOutput.Print a(20)
End Sub
```

2.
```
Dim sq(1 To 5) As Integer
Private Sub cmdDisplay_Click()
     Dim i As Integer, t As Integer
     For i = 1 To 5
         sq(i) = i * i
     Next i
     picOutput.Print sq(3)
     t = 3
     picOutput.Print sq(5 - t)
End Sub
```

3.
```
Dim p(1 To 6) As Integer
Private Sub cmdDisplay_Click()
     Dim k As Integer
     Open "Data.txt" For Input As #1
     For k = 1 To 6
         Input #1, p(k)
     Next k
     Close #1
     For k = 6 To 1 Step -1
         picOutput.Print p(k);
     Next k
End Sub
```

(Assume that the file Data.txt contains the following entries:

4, 3, 11, 9, 2, 6)

4.
```
Open "Data.txt" For Input As #1
    Input #1, x, y
    ReDim power (1 To x, 1 To y)
    For j = 1 To x
        For k = 1 To y - j
            Input #1, power (j, k)
            picOutput.Print power (j, k) - k;
        Next k
        picOutput.Print
    Next j
Close #1
```

(Assume, the file Data.txt contains the following numbers:

2, 3, 28.5
33.8, 39.1, 43.2
48.0, 51.8, 60.0)

In Problems 5 and 6, identify the errors.

5.
```
Dim companies(1 To 100) As String
Private Sub Form_Load()
    Dim recCount As Integer, i As Integer
    Open "Complist.txt" For Input As #1
    Input #1, recCount
    ReDim companies(1 To recCount) As String
    For i = 1 To recCount
        Input #1, companies(i)
    Next i
    Close #1
End Sub
```

6.
```
Dim p(1 To 100) As Single
Private Sub cmdDisplay_Click()
    Dim i As Integer
    For i = 1 To 200
        p(i) = i / 2
    Next i
End Sub
```

In Problems 7 to 13, write a line of code or program segment to complete the stated task.

7. Dimension the string array *marx*() with subscripts ranging from 1 to 4 so that the array is visible to all parts of the program. Assign the four values Chico, Harpo, Groucho, and Zeppo to the array as soon as the program is run.
8. Dimension the string array *stooges*() with subscripts ranging from 1 to 3 so that the array is visible only to the event procedure cmdStooges_Click. Assign the three values Moe, Larry, and Curly to the array as soon as the command button is clicked.
9. Compare two arrays *a*() and *b*() of range 1 to 10 to see if they hold identical values; that is, if $a(i) = b(i)$ for all i.
10. Find the minimum and maximum values of a large array. Instead of comparing each number to the current minimum and maximum values, use the following algorithm, which requires 25 percent fewer comparisons.

a. Assign min = arrayVar(1), max = arrayVar(1), $n = 2$.

b. Assign the lesser of arrayVar(n) and arrayVar($n + 1$) to $k1$ and the other number to $k2$.

c. If $k1 <$ min then min = $k1$.

d. If $k2 >$ max then max = $k2$.

e. Increment n by 2 and repeat from step (b) if possible. Be sure to make provisions for handling the last array element if there are an even number of array indices.

11. Table 4-6 displays the approximate speed (in feet per second) of sound waves in various substances (at room temperature). Write a program to read the information into parallel arrays and print it out with the units miles per hour (1 ft/sec = 0.682 mph). The program should still work if more data is added to the data file.

TABLE 4-6 Speed of sound in various substances

SUBSTANCE	VELOCITY (FT/SEC)
Air	1,126
Hydrogen	4,315
Carbon dioxide	877
Water	4,820
Steel	16,800
Brass	11,500

12. Assume the matrices *matA*(), *matB*(), and *matC*() have the same size. Assign to *matC*() the sum of *matA*() and *matB*().

13. Assume the matrices *matA*(), *matB*(), and *matC*() have been dimensioned with the statements ReDim matA(1 To m, 1 To n), ReDim matB(1 To n, 1 To r), and ReDim matC(1 To m, 1 To r). Assign to *matC*() the product of *matA*() and *matB*.()

In Problems 14 to 20, write a program to perform the stated task.

14. Table 4-7 contains the names and number of units of the top 10 pizza chains in 1997. Write a program to place these data into a pair of parallel arrays, compute the total number of units for these 10 chains, and display a table giving the name and percentage of total units for each of the companies.

TABLE 4-7 Top 10 pizza chains for 1997 (and numbers of units). (*Source: Restaurants & Institutions*, July 1998.)

NAME	UNITS	NAME	UNITS
1. Pizza Hut	14,400	6. Godfather's	554
2. Domino's	5,950	7. Chuck E. Cheese	312
3. Little Caesar's	4,300	8. Picadilly Circus	680
4. Papa John's	1,517	9. Pizza Inn	514
5. Round Table	539	10. California Pizza Kitchen	80

15. A state highway department is interested in the variation of two-lane highways. By measuring the width of all two-lane concrete roads, the data contained in Table 4-8 were collected. The first array represents the data and the second represents the frequency of each measurement. Note that the frequency of each number in a row of array 1 is entered in the corresponding column in array 2. Place the measurements and the frequencies in two arrays and compute the mean value of the width of a two-lane highway.

TABLE 4-8 Width of two-lane state highways

MEASUREMENTS (METERS)					FREQUENCY		
56	57	60	61	63	2	5	4
64	65	66	67	68	1	4	1
69	70	71	72	73	1	2	2
					3	4	1
					1	6	1

16. The numbers in Table 4-9 (20 integers between I and 10) represent measurements of the velocity flow of a fluid. Write a program to display the number of times each integer appears.

TABLE 4-9 Fluid velocity data

2	3	2	2	1	5	10	8	9	8	9	7	5	3	1	5	10	6	6	4

17. A series of 20 measurements representing missile velocities resulted in the data of Table 4-10.

TABLE 4-10 Missile velocity measurements

980	660	850	1010	930	880	870	960	750	1020
970	890	970	900	1030	950	1000	940	970	600

These measurements are to be grouped into a frequency distribution table having six intervals that range from 500 to 1099. Write a program to create the following histogram. The velocities should be stored in a data file.

```
 500 — 599   0
 600 — 699   **2
 700 — 799   *1
 800 — 899   ***3
 900 — 999   **********10
1000 — 1099  ****4
```

18. We define the inner product of two vectors (in this case, numeric arrays) $p()$ and $q()$ of length n as the sum of the products of corresponding array elements; that is

$$\text{inner product} = p(1)q(1) + p(2)q(2) + \ldots + p(n)q(n)$$

Write a function to compute the inner product when $p()$, $q()$, and n are passed as arguments.

19. The center of mass of a system of n particles of mass $m_1, m_2, \ldots, m_n$ is specified by its coordinates x and y in the plane:

$$x = (m_1x_1 + m_2x_2 + \cdots + m_nx_n)/(m_1+m_2 + \cdots m_n)$$

$$y = (m_1y_1 + m_2y_2 + \cdots + m_ny_n)/(m_1+m_2 + \cdots m_n)$$

where x_i and y_i are the coordinates of the position of mass m_i. Write a program to:

a. Input the masses and the x- and y-coordinates into parallel arrays $m()$, $x()$, and $y()$.
b. Calculate the sum $(m_1 + m_2 + \ldots + m_n)$ and store it in the variable *sum*.
c. Calculate the scalar products $m \cdot x$ and $m \cdot y$.
d. Calculate the coordinates x and y of the center of mass.

The value of n should be entered with an InputBox statement. Test the program with $n = 3$, $m_1 = 20$ g, $m_2 = 50$ g, $m_3 = 60$ g, $(x_1, y_1) = (0, 0)$, $(x_2, y_2) = (20, 0)$, and $(x_3, y_3) = (3, 15)$.

20. Given the elements in Table 4-11, write a program to load the information into four arrays of range 1 to 6, *element*(), *symbol*(), *atomicNum*(), and *massMum*(), and ask the user for an element. Have the computer find the element and display its symbol, atomic number, and mass number. Account for the case in which the

21. user requests an element that is not in the table.

TABLE 4-11 Atomic data

ELEMENT	SYMBOL	ATOMIC	MASS
Hydrogen	H	1	1
Helium	He	2	4
Lithium	Li	3	7
Carbon	C	6	12
Sodium	Na	11	23
Oxygen	O	8	16

PROBLEM 4.2

In Problems 1 and 2, decide if the array is ordered.

month( )	January	February	March	April	May

pres( )	Adams	Adams	Bush	Johnson	Johnson

In Problems 3 and 4, determine the output displayed in the picture box when the command button is clicked.

22.
```
Private Sub cmdDisplay_Click()
    Dim p As Integer, q As Integer, temp As Integer
    p = 100
    q = 200
    temp = p
    p = q
    q = temp
    picOutput.Print p; q
End Sub
```

23.
```
Dim gag(1 To 2) As String
Private Sub cmdDisplay_Click()
    If gag(2) < gag(1) Then
        Dim temp As String
        temp = gag(2)
          gag(2) = gag(1)
          gag(1) = temp
    End If
    picOutput.Print gag(1), gag(2)
End Sub

Private Sub Form_Load()
    Open "Data.txt" For Input As #1
    Input #1, gag(1), gag(2)
    Close #1
End Sub
```

(Assume that the file Data.txt contains the following entries.) "Stan", "Oliver"

24. Which type of search would be best for the following array?

1	2	3	4	5
Paul	Ringo	John	George	Pete

25. Which type of search would be best for the following array?

1	2	3	4	5
Beloit	Green Bay	Madison	Milwaukee	Oshkosh

26. Consider the items Tin Man, Dorothy, Scarecrow, and Lion in that order. After how many swaps in a bubble sort will the list be in alphabetical order?
27. How many comparisons will be made in a bubble sort of six items?
28. How many comparisons will be made in a bubble sort of n items?
29. Modify the program in Example 2 so that it will keep track of the number of swaps and comparisons and display these numbers before ending.
30. Suppose a list of 5000 numbers is to be sorted, but the numbers consist of only 1, 2, 3, and 4. Describe a method of sorting the list that would be much faster than the bubble sort.

In Problems 31 to 37, write a short program (or procedure) to complete the stated task.

31. Table 4-12 shows the boiling points of selected metals. Write a program to read the information into parallel arrays and display it in increasing order of boiling point temperature.

TABLE 4-12 Boiling points of metals

METAL	BOILING POINT (°C)	METAL	BOILING POINT (°C)
Aluminum	2330	Manganese	1126
Barium	1640	Potassium	779
Calcium	1487	Rubidium	679
Cesium	690	Sodium	892
Lithium	1367	Strontium	1384

32. Exchange the values of the variables *x*, *y*, and *z* so that *x* has *y*'s value, *y* has *z*'s value, and *z* has *x*'s value.

33. Allow a number *n* to be input by the user. Then accept as input a list of *n* numbers. Place the numbers into an array and apply a bubble sort.

34. Table 4-13 presents statistics on the five leading athletic footwear brands. Read the data into three parallel arrays and display a similar table with sales in descending order.

TABLE 4-13 1997 U.S. market share in athletic footwear.
Source: Morgan Stanley Dean Whitter Research

BRAND	PAIRS OF SHOES SOLD (IN MILLIONS)	PERCENTAGE SHAR OF U.S. MARKET
Adidas USA	21.0	6.0
Fila	23.1	6.6
New Balance	9.5	2.7
Nike	146.7	41.9
Reebok	52.9	15.1

35. Write a program that requests a sequence of numbers from the user and then reports whether the numbers are in increasing order, decreasing order, or neither.

36. Write a program that accepts a student's name and seven test scores as input and calculates the average score after dropping the two lowest grades.

37. The *median* of a set of *n* measurements is a number such that half the *n* measurements fall below the median, and half fall above. If the number of measurements *n* is odd, the median is the middle number when the measurements are arranged in ascending or descending order. If the number of measurements *n* is even, the median is the average of the two middle measurements when the measurements are arranged in ascending or descending order. Write a program that requests a number *n* and a set of *n* measurements as input and then displays the median.

PROBLEM 4.3

In Problems 1 to 3, to determine the output displayed in the picture box when the command button is clicked.

1.
```
Private Sub cmdDisplay_Click()
```

```
    Dim salutation As String
    Open "Greeting.txt" For Output As #1
    Write #1, "Hello"
    Write #1, "Aloha"
    Close #1
    Open "Greeting.txt" For Input As #1
    Input #1, salutation
    picOutput.Print salutation
    Close #1
End Sub
```

2.

```
Private Sub cmdDisplay_Click()
    Dim salutation As String, welcome As String
    Open "Greeting.txt" For Output As #2
    Write #2, "Hello", "Aloha"
    Close #2
    Open "Greeting.txt" For Input As #1
    Input #1, salutation, welcome
    picOutput.Print welcome
    Close #1
End Sub
```

3.

```
Private Sub cmdDisplay_Click()
    Dim salutation As String
    Open "Greeting.txt" For Output As #2
    Write #2, "Hello"
    Write #2, "Aloha"
    Write #2, "Bon Jour"
    Close #2
    Open "Greeting.txt" For Input As #1
    Do While Not EOF(1)
       Input #1, salutation
       picOutput.Print salutation
    Loop
    Close #1
End Sub
```

In Problem 4, identify any errors. Assume Yob.txt is the file created in Example 1.

4.

```
Private Sub cmdDisplay_Click()
    Open Yob.txt For Append As #1
    Write #1, "Jerry", 1958
    Close #1
End Sub
```

5. Thermal conductivity is a measure of the ability of a metal to conduct heat. Table 4-14 contains a list of metals and their thermal conductivities. Run a program to place this information in the sequential file Constant.txt with statements of the form `Write #1, element, thermCond.`

TABLE 4-14 Thermal conductivities of metals

METAL	T. C.	METAL	T.C.
Aluminum	200	Glass	.812
Brass	109	Lead	34.7
Copper	405	Silver	406

6. The rate of flow of heat H (in joules per second) through a material in the steady state is directly proportional to the area A (in square meters) and the temperature difference $(T_2 - T_1)$ (in degrees Celsius), and is inversely proportional to the length L (in meters).

$$H = kA(T_2 - T_1)/L, \tag{4-1}$$

where k is the thermal conductivity of the material.

   a. Create the sequential file Param.txt to hold the values of the parameters A, L, T_1, and T_2. Write the values $A = .8\ m^2$, $L = 2\ m$, $T_1 = 0°C$, and $T_2 = 30°C$ into the file.

   b. Use the files Constant.txt from Problem 1 and Param.txt to display a table with three columns giving the metal, its thermal conductivity, and the corresponding value of H.

7. Suppose that the temperature T_2 has been changed to $T_2 = 100°C$. Use the file Param.txt from Problem 2 to create a sequential file Param2.txt containing the new value of T_2.

8. Write a program to allow additional metals and thermal conductivities to be input by the user and added to the end of the file Constant.txt of Problem 5.

9. Suppose the file Yob.txt contains many names and years, and that the names are in alphabetical order. Write a program that requests a name as input and either gives the person's age or reports that the person is not in the file. *Note:* Because the names are in alphabetical order, usually there is no need to search to the end of the file.

10. Suppose the file Yob.txt contains many names and years. Write a program that creates two files, called Seniors.txt and Juniors.txt, and copies all the data on people born before 1940 into the file Seniors.txt and the data on the others into the file Juniors.txt.

Problems 11 to 14 are related. They create and maintain the sequential file Average.txt to hold batting averages of baseball players.

11. Suppose the season is about to begin. Compose a program to create the sequential file containing the name of each player, his times at bat, and his number of hits. The program should allow the user to type a name into a text box and then click a command button to add a record to the file. The times at bat and number of hits initially should be set to 0. (*Hint:* Open the file for Output in the Form_Load event procedure and Close the file when a "Quit" command button is clicked.)

12. Each day, the statistics from the previous day's games should be used to update the file. Write a program to read the records one at a time and allow the user to enter the number of times at bat and the number of hits in yesterday's game for each player in appropriate text boxes on a form. When a command button is clicked, the program should update the file by adding these numbers to the previous figures. (*Hint:* Open files in the Form_Load event procedure. Close the files and end the program when all data have been processed.)

13. Several players are added to the league. Compose a program to update the file.

14. Compose a program to sort the file Average.txt with respect to batting averages and display the players with the top 10 batting averages. *Hint:* The file must be read once to determine the number of players and again to load the players into an array.

5

Additional Features of Visual Basic

SECTIONS

- 5.1 Graphics
- 5.2 Four Additional Controls
- 5.3 Debugging Tools
- 5.4 Programming Projects

OBJECTIVES

After reading this chapter, you should be able to:

- Draw graphs using Visual Basic.
- Understand the frame, check box, option button, and list box controls.
- Use a variety of techniques to help debug your Visual Basic programs.

5.1 GRAPHICS

Visual Basic has impressive graphics capabilities. Figure 5.1 shows two types of graphs of functions that can be displayed in a picture box. Initially the formula for the function is given explicitly. Then the function is given as the solution to a differential equation of the form $y' = g(t, y)$, with an initial condition.

The construction of such graphs requires that a good viewing window be specified.

5.1.1 Specifying a Viewing Window

Graphics displayed in a picture box have many similarities with graphics displayed on a graphing calculator. Figure 5.2 shows the WINDOW (sometimes called RANGE) settings for a graphing calculator and the resulting coordinate system. After the settings Xmin = a, Xmax = b, Ymin = c, and Ymax = d have been specified, each point on the screen can be identified by an ordered pair of numbers (x, y) where x is between a and b, and y is between c and d. The point at the upper-left corner of the screen will have coordinates (a, d) and the point at the lower-right corner of the screen will have coordinates (b, c). For instance, in Figure 5.2 the coordinates of the upper-left and lower-right points are $(-4, 8)$ and $(4, -5)$. The Visual Basic equivalent of a viewing window setting for a picture box is the statement

```
picBox.Scale (a, d)-(b, c)
```

After the Scale statement has been executed, points can be plotted, and lines and circles can be drawn with statements of the form

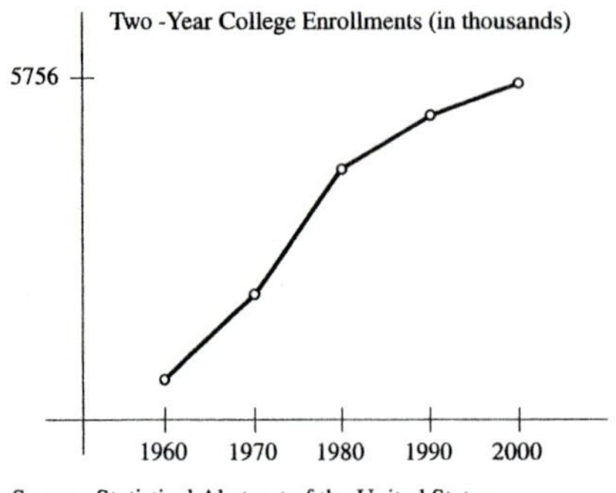

Line Chart

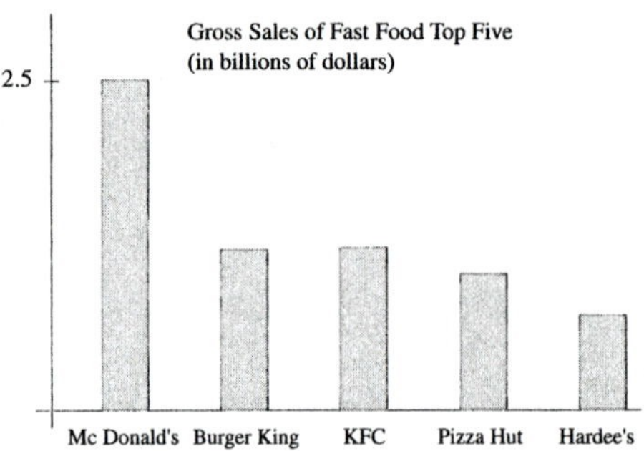

Bar Chart

Figure 5.1. Two types of graphs.

```
picBox.PSet (x,y)              'Draw point with coordinates (x,y)
picBox.Line (x1,y1)-(x2,y2)    'Draw line segment from (x1,y1)
                                to (x2,y2)
picBox.Circle (x,y),r          'Draw circle with center (x,y)
                                and radius r
```

For instance, the statement

```
picBox.Scale (-4, 8)-(4, -5)
```

is equivalent to the WINDOW settings of Figure 5.2.

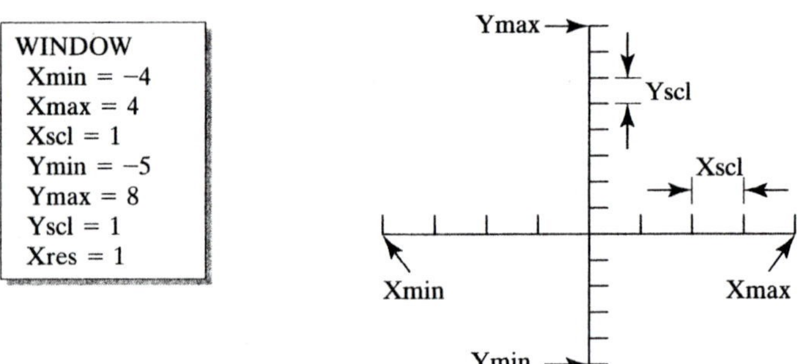

Figure 5.2. Graphing calculator setting for viewing rectangle.

This event procedure plots the point (7, 6) in a picture box and draws a circle of radius 3 about the point. The rightmost point to be drawn will have x coordinate 10; therefore the numbers on the x axis must range beyond 10. In this event procedure, we allow the numbers to range from −2 to 12.

```
Private Sub cmdDraw_Click()
  'Draw a circle with center (7, 6)and radius 3
  picOutput.Cls
  picOutput.Scale (-2, 12)-(12, -2)     'Specify viewing window
  picOutput.Line (-2, 0)-(12, 0)        'Draw x-axis
  picOutput.Line (0, -2)-(0, 12)        'Draw y-axis
  picOutput.PSet (7, 6)                 'Draw center of circle
  picOutput.Circle (7, 6), 3            'Draw the circle
End Sub
```

```
[Run, and then click the command button. The contents of the
picture box is shown in Figure 5.3.]
```

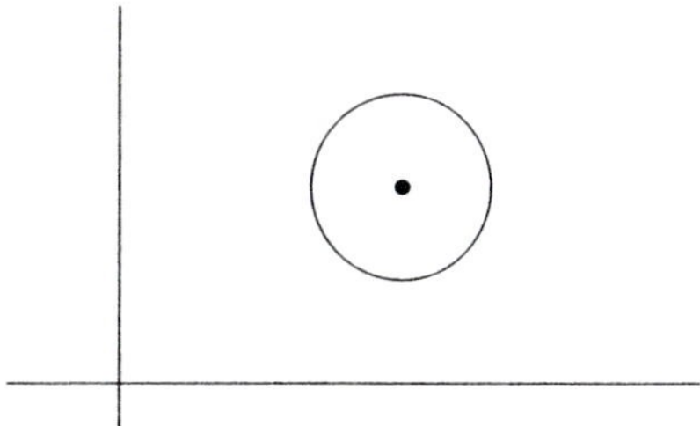

Figure 5.3. Graph for Example 1.

5.1.2 Drawing Graphs of Functions

This section creates graphs of functions. Initially, the formula for a function is given explicitly. Then the function is given as the solution to a differential equation of the form $y' = g(t, y)$ with an initial condition.

Design Concerns The graph of the function $f(x) = \sqrt{1 - x^2}$ will appear either as the top half of a circle or the top half of a nonround ellipse. The graphs of the pair of lines $f(x) = x$ and $f(x) = -x$ may or may not appear as perpendicular lines. The outcome depends on the dimensions of the picture box and the coordinates used in the Scale method. True aspect graphs result when the picture box is square and the coordinates for the Scale method satisfy $b - a = d - c$. (Graphing calculators refer to true aspect settings as square settings of the viewing window.) With true aspect settings, the graph of the function $f(x) = \sqrt{1 - x^2}$ is the top half of a circle, and the lines $f(x) = x$ and $f(x) = -x$ look perpendicular. We will use true aspect settings whenever practical.

Functions Given Explicitly

EXAMPLE 5.1: Write a program to draw the graph of the Log function (Figure 5.4).

SOLUTION

The Sub procedure Initialize specifies the ranges of values for the x-axis and the y-axis and draws the two axes. The Sub procedure Graph uses a For...Next loop to draw many points on the graph. The step size is set to 1/1000 of the length of the x-axis. Since the Log function is defined only for $x > 0$, plotting begins with a small positive value of x.

```
Private Sub cmdDrawGraph_Click()
    Dim a As Single, b As Single, c As Single, d As Single,
        s As Single
    'Graph the function Log(x)
    a = -1: b = 5                    'Extent of x-axis
    c = -3: d = 3                    'Extent of y-axis
    s = (b - a) / 1000               'Step size in For/Next loop
    Call Initialize (a, b, c, d)
    Call Graph (.01, b, s)
End Sub
```

```
Private Function f(x As Single) As Single
   f = Log(x)
End Function


Private Sub Graph (x1 As Single, x2 As Single, s As Single)
     Dim x As Single
     'Draw graph over interval [x1, x2] with step size s
     For x = x1 TO x2 Step s
        picOutput.PSet (x, f(x))
     Next x
End Sub


Private Sub Initialize (a As Single, b As Single,
                            c As Single, d As Single)
     'Set coordinate scales, draw axes
     picOutput.Scale (a, d)-(b, c)
     picOutput.Line (a, 0)-(b, 0)        'Draw x-axis
     picOutput.Line (0, c)-(0, d)        'Draw y-axis
End Sub


[Run and click on the command button.]
```

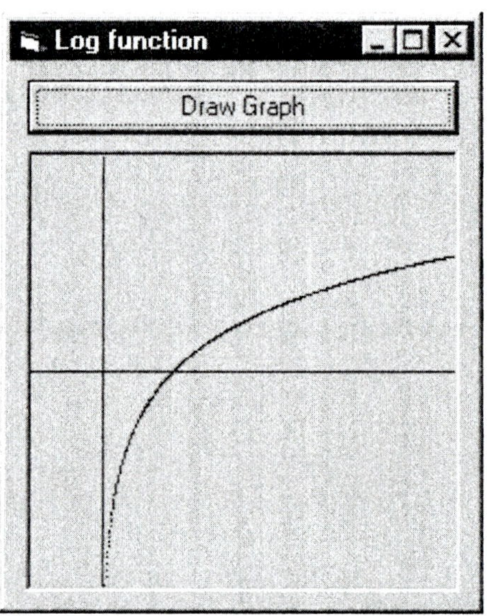

Figure 5.4. A graph of the function $f(x)$ = Log(x).

The program in Example 2 uses variables for the ranges of the x- and y-axes and passes the values of these variables to the Sub procedures. In practice, the programmer must experiment with different values of a, b, c, and d to obtain a good graph. The design of the program simplifies changing these values; only the fourth and fifth lines of the event procedure need to be altered.

The graph in Figure 5.4 looks choppy near the y-axis. The graph can be improved by using line segments instead of points. This is best accomplished by making use of the concept of the *last point referenced*. After each graphics statement is executed, a point mentioned in the statement is designated as the last point referenced. For the Circle or PSet statement, it is the point referred to. For Line statements, it is the second point listed. The statement

picOutput.Line −(a, b)

draws a line from the last point referenced to the point (a, b).

The revision of the Sub procedure shown next produces the graph shown in Figure 5.5. This figure contains all the points of Figure 5.4, but uses the last point referenced to connect these points with line segments.

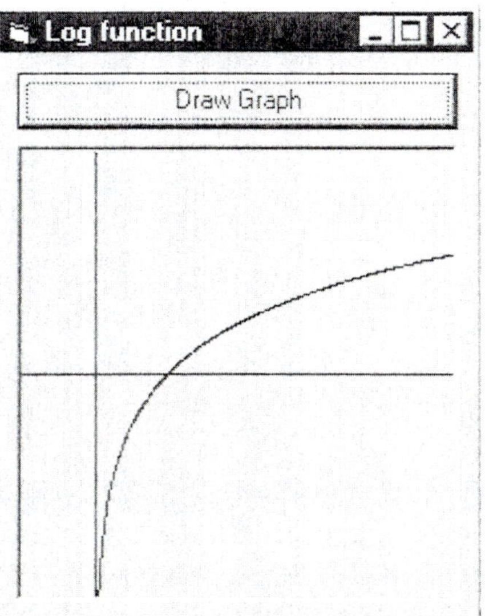

Figure 5.5. An improved graph of the function $f(x)$ = Log(x).

```
Private Sub Graph (x1, x2, s)
     Dim x As Single
     'Draw graph over interval [x1, x2] with step size s
     picOutput.PSet (x1, f(x1))
     For x = x1 TO x2 Step s
        picOutput.Line -(x, f(x))
     Next x
End Sub
```

Although the true aspect process produces an accurately scaled graph, the process is not appropriate for certain functions. For instance, a reasonable coordinate system for the graph of $f(x) = x^3$ from $x = -10$ to $x = 10$ is specified by the statement

picOutput.Scale (−10, −1000)−(10, 1000).

Since the graph of the Log function has a vertical asymptote at $x = 0$ and is not defined for negative values of x, the function was evaluated only to the right of its asymptote. Often there are points on both sides of a vertical asymptote. Also, vertical asymptotes are typically drawn as dashed fines. To draw a dashed line, precede the Line statement with the statement

```
picOutput.DrawStyle = 2.
```

EXAMPLE 5.2: Write a program to draw the graph of $f(x) = 5 + \frac{10x^2}{(x-1)(x-2)}$. See Figure 5.6.

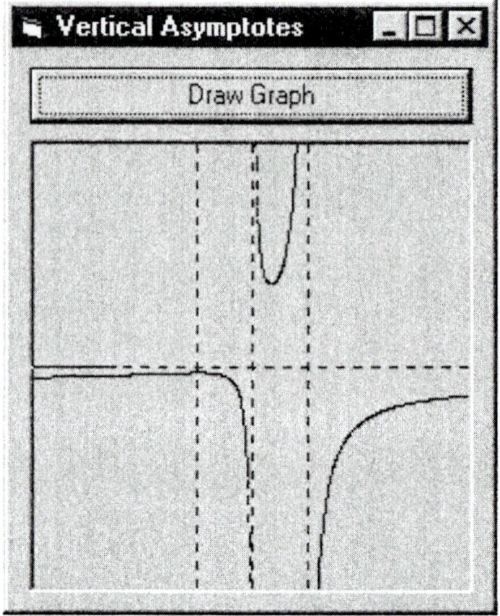

Figure 5.6. Graph of $f(x) = 5 + \frac{10x^2}{(x-1)(x-2)}$.

SOLUTION

The objective is to have the graph exhibit the key features of the function. Since the function has vertical asymptotes at $x = 1$ and $x = 2$, it has three pieces: the piece to the left of 1, the piece between 1 and 2, and the piece to the right of 2. These three pieces are each graphed by a separate call to the Sub procedure Graph. Evaluating the function at $x = 1$ and $x = 2$ produces a "Division by zero" error message. In addition, evaluating the function at a value of x very close to 1 or 2 might result in a number so large that an Overflow error message is generated. Therefore, the program stays s units from 1 and 2. (In extreme cases, a distance of $2*s$ or more may be required.) Experimentation was used to obtain the arguments for the Scale method.

```
Private Sub cmdDrawGraph,_Click()
  Dim a As Single, b As Single, c As Single, d As Single,
  Dim s As Single
  'Graph a function with asymptotes
  a = -3: b = 5                      'Extent of x-axis
  c = -200: d = 200                  'Extent of y-axis
  s = (b - a) / 1000                 'Step size in For/Next loop
  Call Initialize (a, b, c, d)
  Call Graph (a, 1 - s, s)           'Draw the piece from -3 to 1
  Call VerticalAsymptote (1,c,d)
  Call Graph (1 + s, 2 - s, s)       'Draw the piece from 1 to 2
  Call VerticalAsymptote (2, c, d)
  Call Graph (2 + s, b, s)           'Draw the piece from 2 to 5
End Sub

Private Function f(x As Single) As Single
    f = 5 + 10 * x ^ 2 / ((x - 1) * (x - 2))
End Function
```

```
Private Sub Graph (x1 As Single, x2 As Single, s As Single)
    Dim x As Single
    'Draw graph over interval [x1, x2] with Step s
    picOutput.PSet (x1, f(x1))
    For x = x1 TO x2 Step s
       picOutput.Line -(x, f(x))
    Next x
End Sub

Private Sub Initialize (a As Single, b As Single,
                        c As Single, d As Single)
    'Set coordinate scales, draw axes
    picOutput.Scale (a, c)-(b, d)
    picOutput.Line (a, 0)-(b, 0)      'Draw x-axis
    picOutput.Line (0, c)-(0, d)      'Draw y-axis
End Sub

Private Sub VerticalAsymptote (r As Single, c As Single,
                               d As Single)
    'Draw the vertical dashed line x = r
    picOutput.DrawStyle = 2
    picOutput.Line (r, c)-(r, d)
End Sub
```

Euler's Method for Graphing the Solution to a Differential Equation Consider a differential equation of the form

$$y' = g(t, y), t_0 \leq t \leq t_1, \text{ initial condition } y(t_0) = y_0$$

where $g(t, y)$ is a function of two variables. A function $f(t)$ is a solution of the differential equation if the equation holds when y is replaced by $f(t)$.

$$f'(t) = g(t, f(t)), \text{ and } f(t_0) = y_0$$

Some examples of such differential equations and their solutions are

DIFFERENTIAL EQUATION			SOLUTION
$y' = 3t^2/y^2$,	$0 \leq t \leq 5$,	$y(0) = 2$	$y = \sqrt[3]{3t^3 + 8}$
$y' = (t^3 + 1)y^2$,	$1 \leq t \leq 5$,	$y(1) = 4$	$y = -1/(.25t^4 + t - 1.5)$
$y' = .01y$,	$0 \leq t \leq 10$,	$y(0) = 5$	$y = 5e^{.01t}$

Solving a differential equation is not always practical, or possible. Euler's method generates a graph of the solution of the differential equation without requiring that the solution be found explicitly.

The initial point (t_0, y_0) is known to be on the graph of the solution. Suppose h is a small number and the point (t, y) is on the graph. Then the argument presented below shows $(t + h, y + g(t, y)*h)$ is a good approximation to a point on the graph. Euler's method begins with (t_0, y_0) and successively finds points with t coordinates $t_0 + h, t_0 + 2*h, t_0 + 3*h, \ldots$. The process is continued until the point with t coordinate t_1 is found.

Suppose (t, y) is a point on the graph of $f(t)$. Then, by the definition of the derivative,

$$\frac{f(t + h) - f(t)}{h} \approx f'(t)$$

and this is a good approximation if h is small. Therefore,

$$f(t + h) - f(t) \approx f'(t)^{*}h$$

or

$$f(t + h) \approx f(t) + f'(t)^{*}h$$

Since (t, y) is a point on the graph of the function, y is $f(t)$; that is, $f(t)$ can be replaced by y. Since $f(t)$ is a solution of the differential equation, $f'(t)$ can be replaced by $g(t, f(t))$. With the replacements, (1) becomes

$$f(t + h) \approx y + g(t, y)^{*}h$$

Equation (2) says that the y coordinate of the next point is $y + g(t, y)^{*}h$.

EXAMPLE 5.3: Use Euler's method to draw a graph of the solution to the differential equation $y' = 2t - 3y$, $0 \le t \le 4$, $y_0 = 4$.

SOLUTION

In the following program, formula (2) is applied n times, with step size $h = (t_1 - t_0)/n$. The graph generated is shown in Figure 5.7.

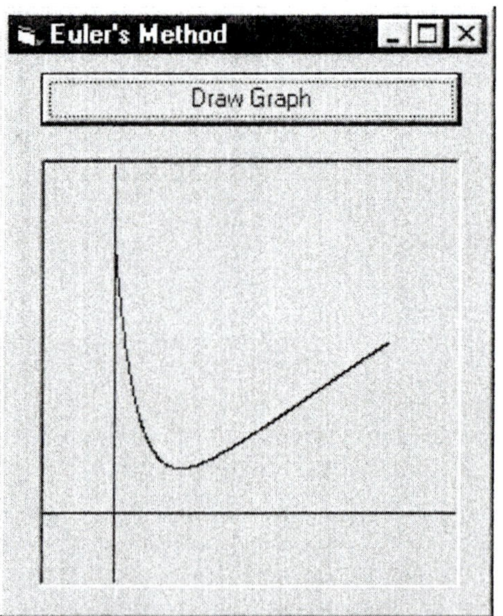

Figure 5.7. Solution to the differential equation of Example 3.

```
Private Sub cmdDrawGraph_Click()
    Dim a As Single, b As Single, c As Single, d As
      Single
    Dim t0 As Single, t1 As Single, y0 As Single, n As
      Integer
    'Graph the solution of a differential equation
    a = -1: b = 5                     'Extent of t-axis
    c = -1: d = 5                     'Extent of y-axis
    n = 1000                          'Number of iterations
    t0 = 0: t1 = 4
    y0 = 4                            'Set initial y value
    Call Initialize (a, b, c, d)
    Call Graph (t0, t1, y0, n)
End Sub


Private Function g(t As Single, y As Single) As Single
    g = 2 * t - 3 * y
End Function

Private Sub Graph(t0 As Single, t1 As Single, y0 As Single,
                  n As Integer)
    Dim h As Single, y As Single, t As Single, i As Integer
    'Draw graph with initial value y using n steps
    h = (t1 - t0) / n
    y = y0
    t = t0
    picOutput.PSet (t, y)
    For i = 1 TO n
        y = y + g(t, y) * h 'Increment y value
        t = t + h
        picOutput.Line -(t, y)
    Next i
End Sub


Private Sub Initialize(a As Single, b As Single,
                       c As Single, d As Single)
    'Set coordinate scales, draw axes
    picOutput.Scale (a, d)-(b, c)
    picOutput.Line (a, 0)-(b, 0)          'Draw t-axis
    picOutput.Line (0, c)-(0, d)          'Draw y-axis
End Sub
```

5.1.3 Comments

1. Here is a technique that can be used to determine a good range of values for a Scale method when graphs with only positive values are to be drawn.

    a. Let r be the x coordinate of the rightmost point that will be drawn by any Line, Pset, or Circle method.

b. Let h be the y coordinate of the highest point that will be drawn by any Line, Pset, or Circle method.

c. Let the numbers on the x axis range from about −[20% of r] to about r + [20% of r]. Let the numbers on the y axis range from about −[20% of h] to about h + [20% of h]. That is, use

```
picOutput.Scale (-.2 * r, 1.2 * h)-(1.2 * r, -.2 * h)
```

2. The graphs drawn in Examples 2 to 4 can also be printed on the printer. Just replace each occurrence of picOutput with Printer, and add Printer.EndDoc as the last statement of the event procedure. Also, the graphs will look best in landscape orientation which is invoked with the statement Printer.Orientation = 2.

3. If one or both of the points used in the Line method fall outside the picture box, Visual Basic draws only the portion of the line that lies in the picture box. This behavior is referred to as *clipping* and is used for the Circle method also.

4. You can use graphics methods in a Form_Load event procedure. If so, you must set the AutoRedraw property of the picture box to True. Otherwise the contents of the picture box will be erased when the event procedure terminates.

5. In Euler's method, certain choices of a and b (and t_0 and t_1) can result in Overflow error messages due to exceptionally large function values. This is especially true for the solutions to differential equations that grow fast. Some knowledge of the graph can help in the choices. Otherwise, experimentation is required.

6. In Euler's method, the value of n should be large to guarantee a good graph. Theoretically, the larger the value of n, the better the graph. If n is too large, however, roundoff errors will invalidate the method.

PRACTICE!

1. Suppose you want to write a program to draw a line from (3, 45) to (5, 80). Use the technique of Comment 1 to select appropriate values for the Scale method.

Solution

1. The largest value of any x coordinate is 5. Because 20% of 5 is 1, the numbers on the x axis should range from −1 to 6 (= 5 + 1). Similarly, the numbers on the y axis should range from −16 to 96 (= 80 + 16). Therefore, an appropriate scaling statement is

```
picOutput.Scale (-1, 96)-(6, -16)
```

5.2 FOUR ADDITIONAL CONTROLS

In this section, we discuss the four controls indicated on the Toolbox in Figure 5.8.

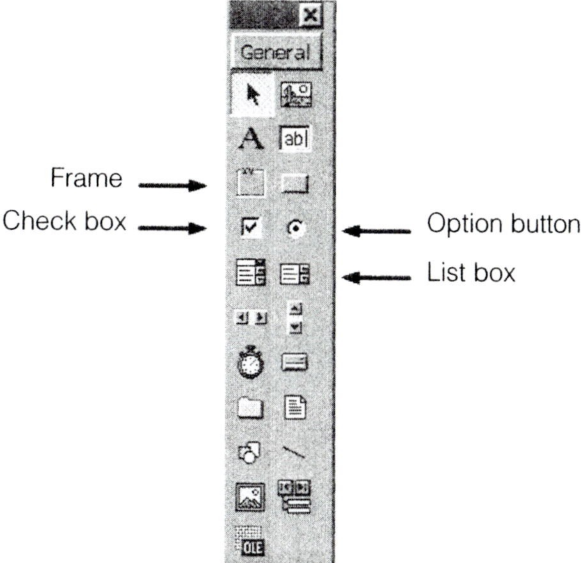

Figure 5.8.

5.2.1 The Frame Control

Frames are passive objects used to group related sets of controls for visual effect. You rarely write event procedures for frames. The frame above has a group of three text boxes attached to it. When you drag the frame, the attached controls follow as a unit. If you hide the frame, the attached controls will be hidden as well.

A control must be attached to a frame in a special way. You cannot just double-click to create the control and then drag it into a frame. To attach a control to a frame, first create the frame. Next, single-click on the control icon to activate it, then move the mouse pointer inside the frame to the point where you want to place the upper-left corner of the control. Finally, drag the mouse to the right and down, and then release the mouse button when you are satisfied with the size of the control. This is referred to as the *single-click-draw technique*.

A group of controls also can be attached to a picture box. The advantages of using frames are that they have a title sunk into their borders that can be set with the Caption property and that they cannot receive the focus. As shown later in this section, the frame control is particularly important when working with groups of option button controls. The standard prefix for the name of a frame is *fra*.

5.2.2 The Check Box Control

A *check box*, which consists of a small square and a caption, presents the user with a yes/no choice. The form in Example 1 uses four check box controls. The Value property of a check box is 0 when the square is empty and is 1 when the square is checked. At run time, the user clicks on the square to toggle between the unchecked and checked states. So doing also triggers the Click event.

The following program allows an employee to compute the monthly cost of various benefit packages:

OBJECT	PROPERTY	SETTING
frmBenefits	Caption	Benefits Menu
chkDrugs	Caption	Prescription Drug Plan ($12.51)
	Value	0 – Unchecked
chkDental	Caption	Dental Plan ($9.68)
	Value	0 – Unchecked
chkVision	Caption	Vision Plan ($1.50)
	Value	0 – Unchecked
chkMedical	Caption	Medical Plan ($25.25)
	Value	0 – Unchecked
lblTotal	Caption	Total monthly payment:
lblAmount	Caption	$0.00

```
Private Sub chkDental_Click()
   Call Tally
End Sub

Private Sub chkDrugs_Click()
   Call Tally
End Sub

Private Sub chkMedical_Click()
   Call Tally
End Sub

Private Sub chkVision_Click()
   Call Tally
End Sub

Private Sub Tally()
    Dim sum As Single
    If chkDrugs.Value = 1 Then
       sum = sum + 12.51
    End If
    If chkDental.Value = 1 Then
       sum = sum + 9.68
    End If
    If chkVision.Value = 1 Then
       sum = sum + 1.5
    End If
    If chkMedical.Value = 1 Then
       sum = sum + 25.25
    End If
    lblAmount.Caption = FormatCurrency(sum)
End Sub
```

[Run, and then click on the desired options.]

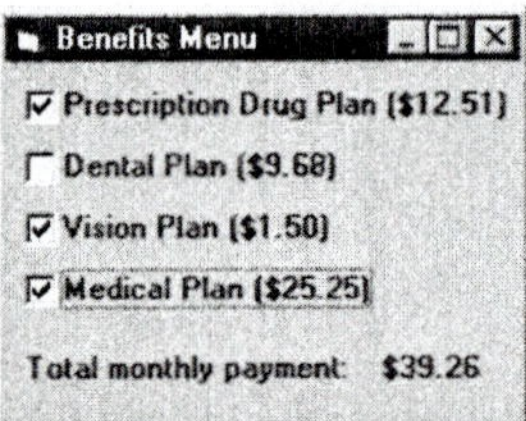

When a check box has the focus, the spacebar can be used to check (or uncheck) the box and invoke the Click event. In addition, the state of a check box can be toggled from the keyboard without first setting the focus to the check box if you create an access key for the check box by including an ampersand in the Caption property. (Access keys appear underlined.) For instance, if the Caption property for the Dental Plan in Example 1 is set as "&Dental Plan," then the user can check (or uncheck) the box by pressing Alt+D.

The Value property of a check box also can be set to "2-Grayed." When a grayed square is clicked, it becomes unchecked. When clicked again, it becomes checked.

5.2.3 The Option Button Control

Option buttons are used to give the user a single choice from several options. Normally, a group of several option buttons is attached to a frame or picture box with the single-click-draw technique. Each button consists of a small circle accompanied by text that is set with the Caption property. When a circle or its accompanying text is clicked, a solid dot appears in the circle and the button is said to be "on." At most one option button in a group can be on at the same time. Therefore, if one button is on and another button in the group is clicked, the first button will turn off. By convention, the names of option buttons have the prefix *opt*.

The Value property of an option button tells if the button is on or off. The condition

```
optButton.Value
```

is True when optButton is on and False when optButton is off. The statement

```
optButton.Value = True
```

turns on optButton and turns off all other buttons in its group. The statement

```
optButton.Value = False
```

turns off optButton and has no effect on the other buttons in its group.

The Click event for an option button is triggered only when an off button is turned on. It is not triggered when an on button is clicked.

The next program tells you if an option button is on.

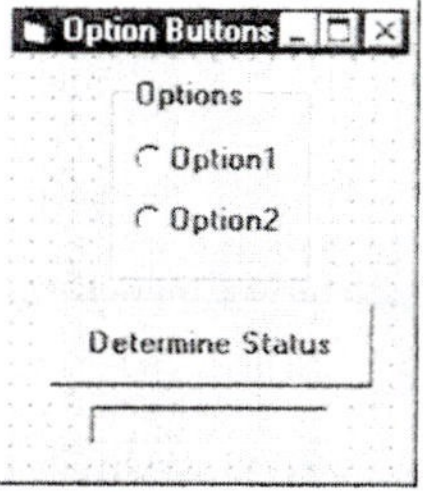

OBJECT	PROPERTY	SETTING
frmOptions	Caption	Option Buttons
fraOptions	Caption	Options
optOpt1		
optOpt2		
cmdStatus	Caption	Determine Status
picStatus		

```
Private Sub cmdStatus_Click()
    picStatus.Cls
    If optOpt1.Value = True Then
       picStatus.Print "Option1 is on."
    End If
    If optOpt2.Value = True Then
       picStatus.Print "Option2 is on."
    End If
End Sub
```

```
Private Sub Form_Load()
     optOpt1.Value = False 'Turn off optOpt1
     optOpt2.Value = False 'Turn off optOpt2
End Sub
```

[Run, click on one of the option buttons, and then click the command button.]

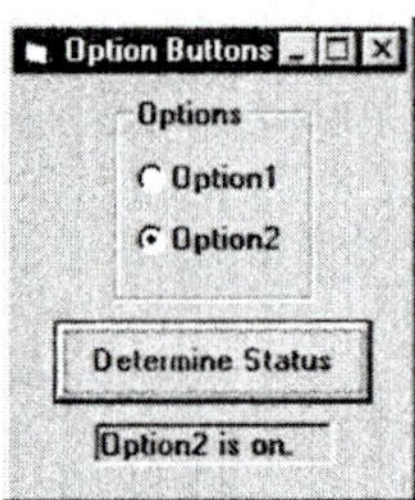

The text alongside an option button is specified with the Caption property. As with a command button and a check box, an ampersand can be used to create an access key for an option button.

The following program allows the user to select the text size in a text box. The three option buttons have been attached to the frame with the single-click-draw technique.

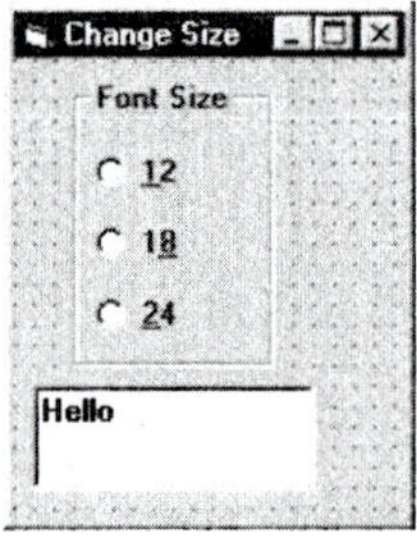

OBJECT	PROPERTY	SETTING
frmSize	Caption	Change Size
fraFontSize	Caption	Font Size
opt12pt	Caption	&12
opt18pt	Caption	1&8
opt24pt	Caption	&24
txtInfo	Text	Hello

```
Private Sub opt12pt_Click()
   txtInfo.Font.Size = 12
End Sub

Private Sub opt18pt_Click()
   txtInfo.Font.Size = 18
End Sub

Private Sub opt24pt_Click()
   txtInfo.Font.Size = 24
End Sub
```

[Run, and click on the last option button (or press Alt+2).]

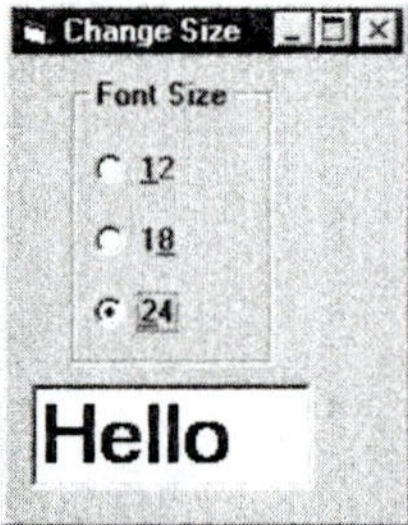

A single form can have several groups of option buttons. However, each group must be attached to its own frame, picture box, or to the form itself.

5.2.4 The List Box Control

The fifth row of the standard toolbox (in most editions of Visual Basic) contains the list box icon on the right. The list boxes discussed in this text will display a single column of strings, referred to as *items*. The items to appear initially can either be specified at design time with the List property or set with code in a procedure. Then code is used to access, add, or delete items from the list. We will first carry out all tasks with code and then show how the initial items can be specified at design time. The standard prefix for the name of a list box is *lst*.

The Sorted property is perhaps the most interesting list box property. When it is set to True, the items will automatically be displayed in alphabetical (that is, ANSI) order. The default value of the Sorted property is False.

If *str* is a string, then the statement

```
lstBox.AddItem str
```

adds *str* to the list. The item is added at the proper sorted position if the Sorted property is True, and otherwise is added to the end of the list. If a list box is too short to display all the items that have been added to it, Visual Basic automatically places a vertical scroll bar on the right side of the list box. The user can then scroll to see the remaining items of the list. At any time, the value of

```
lstBox.ListCount
```

is the number of items in the list box.

Each item in lstBox is identified by an index number ranging from 0 through lstBox.ListCount–1. The value of

```
lstBox.NewIndex
```

is the index number of the item most recently added to lstBox by the AddItem method. During run time you can highlight an item from a list by clicking on it with the mouse or by moving to it with the up- and down-arrow keys when the list box has the focus. (The second method triggers the Click event each time an arrow key causes the highlight to move.) The value of

```
lstBox.ListIndex
```

is the index number of the item currently highlighted in lstBox. (If no item is highlighted, the value of ListIndex is −1.)

The string array lstBox.List( ) holds the list of items stored in the list box. In particular, the value of

```
lstBox.List(n)
```

is the item of lstBox having index *n*. For instance, the statement picBox.Print lstBox.List(0) displays the first item of the list box. The value of

```
lstBox.List(lstBox.ListIndex)
```

is the item (string) currently highlighted in lstBox. Alternatively, the value of

```
lstBox.Text
```

is also the currently highlighted item. Unlike the Text property of a text box, you may not assign a value to lstBox.Text.

The statement

```
lstBox.RemoveItem n
```

deletes the item of index *n* from lstBox, the statement

```
lstBox.RemoveItem lstBox.ListIndex
```

deletes the item currently highlighted in lstBox, and the statement

```
lstBox.Clear
```

deletes every item of lstBox.

An oxymoron is a pairing of contradictory or incongruous words. The following program displays a sorted list of oxymorons. When you click an item (or highlight it with the up- and down-arrow keys), it is displayed in a picture box. A command button allows you to add an additional item with an Input box. You can delete an item by double-clicking on it with the mouse. (*Note:* When you double-click the mouse, two events are processed—the Click event and the DblClick event.) After running the program, click on different items, add an item or two (such as "same difference" or "liquid gas"), and delete an item.

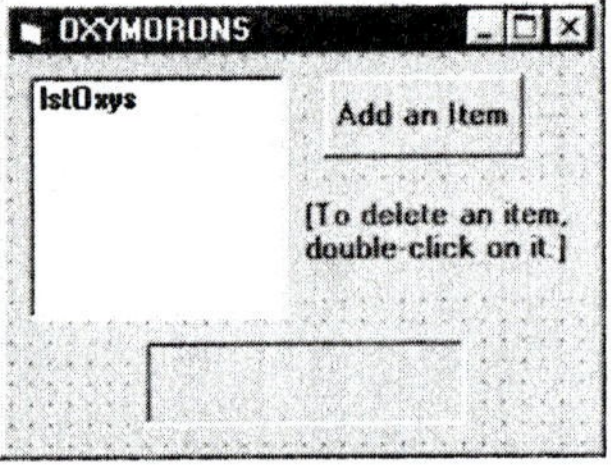

OBJECT	PROPERTY	SETTING
frmOxyMor	Caption	OXYMORONS
lstOxys	Sorted	True
cmdAdd	Caption	Add an Item
lblDelete	Caption	To delete an item, double-click on it.
picSelected		

```
Private Sub cmdAdd_Click()
    Dim item As String
    item = InputBox("Item to Add:")
    lstOxys.AddItem item
End Sub

Private Sub Form_Load()
    lstOxys.AddItem "jumbo shrimp"
    lstOxys.AddItem "definite maybe"
    lstOxys.AddItem "old news"
    lstOxys.AddItem "good grief"
End Sub

Private Sub lstOxys_Click()
    picSelected.Cls
    picSelected.Print "The selected item is"
    picSelected.Print Chr(34) & lstOxys.Text & Chr(34) & "."
End Sub

Private Sub lstOxys_DblClick()
    lstOxys.RemoveItem lstOxys.ListIndex
End Sub
```

```
[Run, and then click on the second item of the list box.]
```

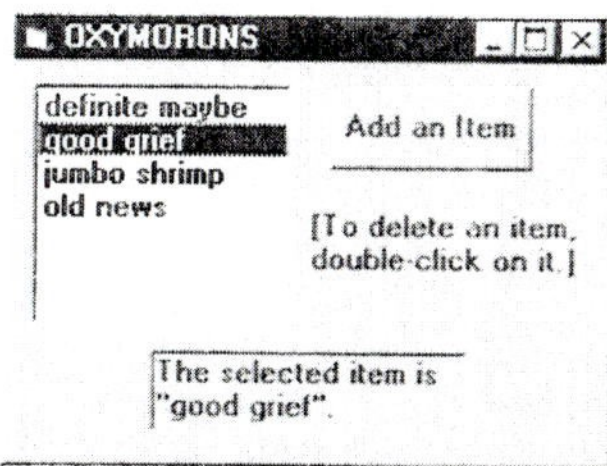

The following steps show how to fill a list box at design time.

1. Select the List property of the list box.
2. Click on the down arrow of the Settings box. (A small box will be displayed.)
3. Type in the first item and press Ctrl+Enter. (The cursor will move to the next line.)
4. Repeat Step 3 for each of the other items.
5. When you are finished entering items, press the Enter key.

When the Sorted property of a list box is True, the index associated with an item will change when a "lesser" item is added to or removed from the list. In many applications it is important to have a fixed number associated with each item in a list box. Visual Basic makes this possible using the ItemData property. The statement

```
List1.ItemData(n) = m
```

associates the number *m* with the item of index *n*, and the statement

```
List1.ItemData(List1.NewIndex) = m
```

associates the number *m* with the item most recently added to the list box. Thus, the List1 list box can be thought of as consisting of two arrays, List1.List( ) and List1.ItemData( ). The contents of List1.List( ) are displayed in the list box, allowing the user to make a selection while the hidden contents of List1.ItemData( ) can be used by the programmer to index records or, as illustrated in Example 5, to set up parallel arrays that hold other data associated with each item displayed in the list box.

Here is a program that uses NewIndex and ItemData to provide data about inventions. When an item is highlighted, its ItemData value is used to locate the appropriate entries in the inventor( ) and date( ) arrays. Assume the file Inventor.txt contains the following three lines:

"Ball-point pen", "Lazlo and George Biro", 1938
"Frozen food", "Robert Birdseye", 1929
"Bifocal lenses", "Ben Franklin", 1784

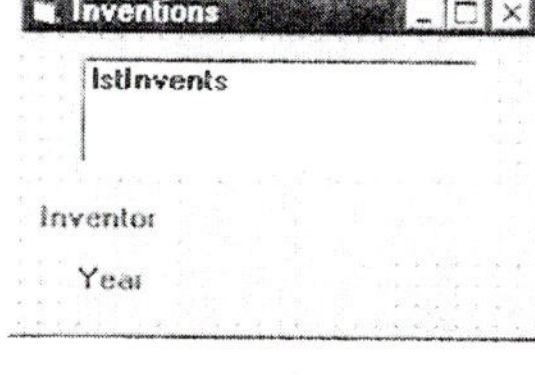

OBJECT	PROPERTY	SETTING
frmInvent	Caption	Inventions
lstInvents	Sorted	True
lblInventor	Caption	Inventor
lblWho	Caption	(none)
lblYear	Caption	Year
lblWhen	Caption	(none)

```
'In the (Declarations) section of (General)
Dim inventor(0 To 10) As String
Dim yr(0 To 10) As Integer
Private Sub Form_Load()
    Dim what As String, who As String, when As Integer, index
       As Integer
    Open "Inventor.txt" For Input As #1
    index = 0
    Do While (index << 10) And (Not EOF(1))
       Input #1, what, who, when
       index = index + 1
       lstInvents.AddItem what
       lstInvents.ItemData(lstInvents.NewIndex) = index
       inventor(index) = who
       yr(index) = when
    Loop
    Close #1
End Sub

Private Sub lstInvents_Click()
    lblWho.Caption = inventor(lstInvents.ItemData
       (lstInvents.ListIndex))
    lblWhen.Caption = Str(yr(lstInvents.ItemData
       (lstInvents.ListIndex)))
End Sub
```

[Run, and then highlight the second entry in the list.]

5.3 VISUAL BASIC DEBUGGING TOOLS

Errors in programs are called *bugs*, and the process of finding and correcting them is called *debugging*. Because Visual Basic does not discover errors due to faulty logic, such errors present the most difficulties in debugging. One method of discovering a logical error is by *desk checking*, that is, tracing the values of variables on paper by writing down their expected value after "mentally executing" each line in the program. Desk checking is rudimentary and highly impractical except for small programs.

Another method of debugging involves placing Print methods at strategic points in the program and displaying the values of selected variables or expressions until the error is detected. After correcting the error, the Print methods are removed. For many programming environments, desk checking and Print methods are the only debugging methods available to the programmer.

The Visual Basic debugger offers an alternative to desk checking and Print methods. It allows you to pause during the execution of your program in order to view and alter values of variables. These values can be accessed through the Immediate, Watch, and Locals windows, known collectively as the three Debug windows.

PRACTICE!

1. Suppose you create a frame and then drag a preexisting text box into the frame. How will this text box differ from a text box that was attached to the frame by the single-click-draw method?
2. What is the difference between a group of check boxes attached to a frame and a group of option buttons attached to a frame?
3. Write code to copy the contents of a list box into a file.

Solutions

1. The text box attached by the single-click-draw method will move with the frame, whereas the other text box will not.
2. With option buttons, at most one button can be on at any given time, whereas several check boxes can be checked simultaneously.
3.
```
Private Sub SaveListBox()
     Dim i As Integer
     Open "Listdata.txt" For Output As #1
     For i = 0 to lstBox.ListCount - 1
        Write #1, lstBox.List(i)
     Next i
     Close #1
End Sub
```

5.3.1 The Three Program Modes

At any time, a program is in one of three modes—design mode, run mode, or break mode. The current mode is displayed in the Visual Basic title bar.

```
Title bar during design time.
Title bar during run time.
Title bar during break mode.
```

At design time you place controls on a form, set their initial properties, and write code. Run time is initiated by pressing the Start button. Break mode is invoked automatically when a run-time error occurs. While a program is running, you can manually invoke Break mode by pressing Ctrl+Break, clicking onBreak in the Run menu, or clicking on the Break icon (located between the Start and Stop icons). While the program is in break mode, you can use theImmediate window to examine and change values of variables and object settings. When you enter Break mode, the Start button on the Toolbar changes to a Continue button. You can click on it to proceed with the execution of the program.

5.3.2 The Immediate Window

You can set the focus to the Immediate window by clicking on it (if visible), by pressing Ctrl+G, or by choosing "Immediate Window" from the View menu. Although the Immediate window can be used during design time, it is primarily used in Break mode. When you type a statement into the Immediate window and press the Enter key, the statement is executed at once. A statement of the form

```
Print expression
```

displays the value of the expression on the next line of the Immediate window. In Figure 5.9, three statements have been executed. (When the program was interrupted, the variable *numVar* had the value 10.) In addition to displaying values of expressions, the Immediate window also is commonly used to change the value of a variable with an assignment statement before continuing to run the program. *Note1:* Any statement in the Immediate window can be executed again by placing the cursor anywhere on the statement and pressing the Enter key. *Note2:* In earlier versions of Visual Basic, the Immediate window was called the Debug window.

Figure 5.9. Three Print statements executed in the Immediate window.

5.3.3 The Watch Window

You can designate an expression as a watch expression or a break expression. Break expressions are of two varieties: those that cause a break when they become true and those that cause a break when they change value. At any time, the Watch window shows the current values of all watch and break expressions. In the Watch window of Figure 5.10, the type of each expression is specified by an icon as shown in Table 5.1.

Expression	Value	Type	Context
num1	5	Single	Form1.cmdButton_Click
num2	10	Single	Form1.cmdButton_Click
num2 > 9	True	Boolean	Form1.cmdButton_Click

Figure 5.10. The Watch window.

TABLE 5-1 Watch type icons

ICON	TYPE OF EXPRESSION
	Watch expression
	Break when expression is true
	Break when expression has changed

The easiest way to add an expression to the Watch window is to right-click on a variable in the code window and then click on "Add Watch" to call up an Add Watch dialog box. You can then alter the expression in the Expression text box and select one of the three Watch types. To delete an expression from the Watch window, right-click on the expression and then click on "Delete Watch." To alter an expression in the Watch window, right-click on the expression and click on "Edit Watch."

5.3.4 The Locals Window

The Locals window, invoked by clicking on "Locals Window" in the View menu, is a feature that was new to Visual Basic in Version 5.0. This window automatically displays the names, values, and types of all variables in the current procedure (Figure 5.11). You can alter the values of variables at any time. In addition, you can examine and change properties of controls through the Locals window.

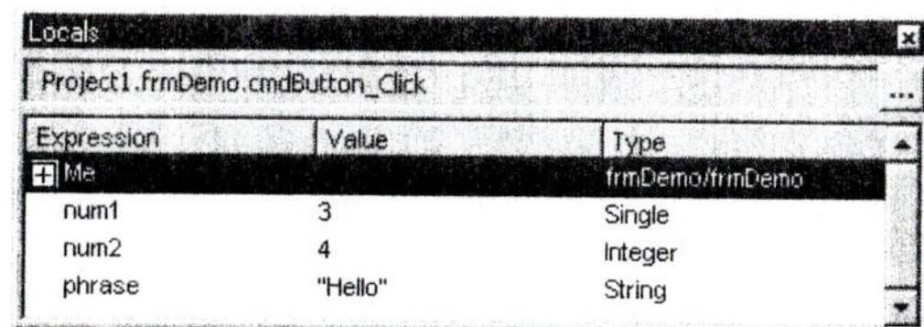

Figure 5.11. The Locals window.

5.3.5 Stepping Through a Program

The program can be executed one statement at a time, with each press of an appropriate function key executing a statement. This process is called *stepping* (or *stepping into*). After each step, values of variables, expressions, and conditions can be displayed from the debugging windows, and the values of variables can be changed.

When a procedure is called, the lines of the procedure can be executed one at a time, referred to as "stepping through the procedure," or the entire procedure can be executed at once, referred to as "stepping over a procedure." A step over a procedure is called a *procedure step*. In addition, you can execute the remainder of the current procedure at once, referred to as "stepping out of the procedure."

Stepping begins with the first line of the first event procedure invoked by the user. Program execution normally proceeds in order through the statements in the event procedure. However, at any time the programmer can specify the next statement to be executed.

As another debugging tool, Visual Basic allows the programmer to specify certain lines as *breakpoints*. Then, when the program is run, execution will stop at the first breakpoint reached. The programmer can then either step through the program or continue execution to the next breakpoint.

The tasks discussed previously are summarized below, along with a means to carry out each task. The tasks invoked with function keys can also be produced from the menu bar.

Task	Means
Step Into:	Press F8
Step Over:	Press Shift+F8
Step Out:	Press Ctrl+Shift+F8
Set a breakpoint:	Move cursor to line, press F9
Remove a breakpoint:	Move cursor to line containing breakpoint, press F9
Clear all breakpoints:	Press Ctrl+Shift+F9
Set next statement:	Press Ctrl+F9
Continue execution to next breakpoint or the end of the program:	Press F5
Run to cursor:	Press Ctrl+F8

5.3.6 Six Walkthroughs

The walkthroughs shown next use the debugging tools with common Visual Basic programming structures.

Stepping Through an Elementary Program The following walkthrough demonstrates several capabilities of the debugger.

1. Create a form with a command button (cmdButton) and a picture box (picBox). Set the AutoRedraw property of the picture box to True. (During the debugging process, the entire form will be covered. The True setting for AutoRedraw prevents the contents of the picture box from being erased.)
2. Double-click on the command button and enter the following event procedure:

```
Private Sub cmdButton_Click()
    Dim num As Single
    picBox.Cls
    num = Val(InputBox("Enter a number:"))
    num = num + 1
    num = num + 2
    picBox.Print num
End Sub
```

3. Press F8, click the command button, and press F8 again. A yellow arrow points to the picBox.Cls statement and the statement is highlighted in yellow. This indicates that the picBox.Cls statement is the next statement to be executed. (Pressing F8 is referred to as stepping. You can also step to the next statement of a program with the Step Into option from the Debug menu.)
4. Press F8. The picBox.Cls statement is executed and the statement involving InputBox is designated as the next statement to be executed.
5. Press F8 to execute the statement containing InputBox. Respond to the request by typing 5 and clicking the OK button.
6. Press F8 again to execute the statement num = num + 1.
7. Let the mouse sit over any occurrence of the word "num" for a second or so. The current value of the variable will be displayed in a small box (Figure 5.12).

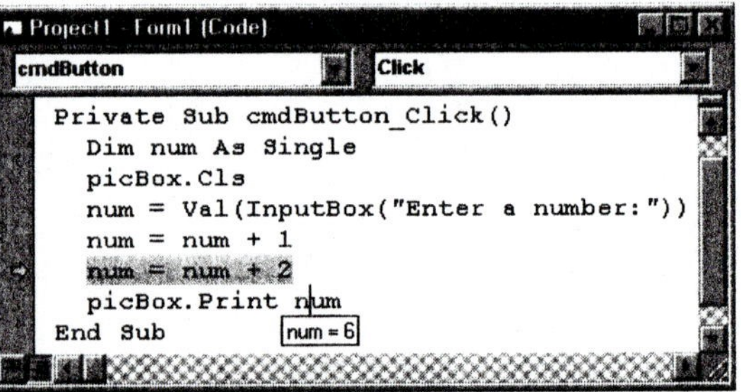

Figure 5.12. Obtaining the value of a variable.

8. Click on the End icon to end the program.
9. Move the cursor to the line

```
num = num + 2
```

and then press F9. A red dot appears to the left of the line and the line is displayed in white text on a red background. This indicates that the line is a breakpoint. (Pressing F9 is referred to as toggling a breakpoint. You also can toggle a breakpoint with the Toggle Breakpoint option from the Debug menu.)

10. Press F5 and click on the command button. Respond to the request by entering 5. The program executes the first three lines and stops at the breakpoint. The breakpoint line is not executed.

11. Open the Immediate window by pressing Ctrl+G. If necessary, clear the contents of the window. Type the statement

```
Print "num ="; num
```

into the Immediate window and then press Enter to execute the statement. The appearance of "num = 6" on the next line of the Immediate window confirms that the breakpoint line was not executed.

12. Press F7 to return to the Code window.

13. Move the cursor to the line num = num + 1 and then press Ctrl+F9 to specify that line as the next line to be executed. (You can also use the Set Next Statement option from the Debug menu.)

14. Press F8 to execute the selected line.

15. Press Ctrl+G to return to the Immediate window. Move the cursor to the line containing the Print method and press Enter to confirm that the value of *num* is now 7, and then return to the Code window.

16. Move the cursor to the breakpoint line and press F9 to deselect the line as a breakpoint.

17. Press F5 to execute the remaining lines of the program. Observe that the value displayed in the picture box is 9.

General Comment: As you step through a program, the form will become hidden from view. However, the form will be represented by a button on the Windows taskbar at the bottom of the screen. The button will contain the name of the form. You can see the form at any time by clicking on its button.

5.3.7 Stepping Through a Program Containing a General Procedure

The following walkthrough uses the single-stepping feature of the debugger to trace the flow through a program and a Sub procedure:

1. Create a form with a command button (cmdButton) and a picture box (picBox). Set the AutoRedraw property of the picture box to True. Then enter the following two procedures:

```
Private Sub cmdButton_Click()
    Dim p As Single, b As Single
    picBox.Cls
    p = 1000 'Principal
    Call GetBalance(p, b)
    picBox.Print "The balance is"; b
End Sub

Private Sub GetBalance(prin As Single, bal As Single)
    'Calculate the balance at 5% interest rate
    Dim interest As Single
    interest = .05 * prin
    bal = prin + interest
End Sub
```

2. Press F8, click the command button, and press F8 again. The picBox.Cls statement is highlighted to indicate that it is the next statement to be executed.
3. Press F8 two more times. The Call statement is highlighted.
4. Press F8 once, and observe that the heading of the Sub procedure GetBalance is now highlighted in yellow.
5. Press F8 three times to execute the assignment statements and to highlight the End Sub statement. (Notice that the Dim and comment statements were skipped.)
6. Press F8, and notice that the yellow highlight has moved back to the cmdButton_Click event procedure and is on the statement immediately following the Call statement.
7. Click on the End icon to end the program.
8. Repeat Steps 2 and 3, and then press Shift+F8 to step over the procedure GetBalance. The procedure has been executed in its entirety.
9. Click on the End icon to end the program.

5.3.8 Communication Between Arguments and Parameters

The following walkthrough uses the Locals window to monitor the values of arguments and parameters during the execution of a program.

1. If you have not already done so, type the preceding program into the Code window.
2. Press F8, and click on the command button.
3. Select "Locals Window" from the View window. Notice that the variables from the cmdButton_Click event procedure appear in the Locals window.
4. Press F8 three more times to highlight the Call statement. Notice that the value of the variable *p* has changed.
5. Press F8 to call the Sub procedure. Notice that the variables displayed in the Locals window are now those of the procedure GetBalance.
6. Press F8 three times to execute the procedure.
7. Press F8 to return to cmdButton_Click event procedure. Notice that the value of the variable *b* has inherited the value of the variable *bal*.
8. Click on the End icon to end the program.

5.3.9 Stepping Through Programs Containing Decision Structures

If Blocks The following walkthrough demonstrates how an If statement evaluates a condition to determine whether to take an action.

1. Create a form with a command button (cmdButton) and a picture box (picBox). Set the AutoRedraw property of the picture box to True. Then open the Code window and enter the following procedure:

```
Private Sub cmdButton_Click()
     Dim wage As Single
     picBox.Cls
     wage = Val(InputBox("wage:"))
```

```
        If wage << 5.15 Then
            picBox.Print "Below minimum wage."
        Else
            picBox.Print "Wage Ok."
        End If
    End Sub
```

2. Press F8, click the command button, and press F8 twice. The picBox.Cls statement will be highlighted and executed, and then the statement containing InputBox will be highlighted.

3. Press F8 once to execute the statement containing InputBox. Type a wage of 3.25 and press the Enter key. The If statement is highlighted, but has not been executed.

4. Press F8 once and notice that the highlight for the current statement has jumped to the statement picBox.Print "Below minimum wage." Because the condition "wage < 5.15" is true, the action associated with Then was selected.

5. Press F8 to execute the picBox.Print statement. Notice that Else is skipped and End If is highlighted.

6. Press F8 again. We are through with the If block and the statement following the If block, End Sub, is highlighted.

7. Click on the End icon to end the program.

8. If desired, try stepping through the program again with 5.75 entered as the wage. Since the condition "wage < 5.15" will be false, the Else action will be executed instead of the Then action.

5.3.10 Select Case Blocks

The following walkthrough illustrates how a Select Case block uses the selector to choose from among several actions.

1. Create a form with a command button (cmdButton) and a picture box (picBox). Set the AutoRedraw property of the picture box to True. Then open the Code window and enter the following procedure:

```
Private Sub cmdButton_Click()
    Dim age As Single, price As Single
    picBox.Cls
    age = Val(InputBox("age:"))
    Select Case age
        Case Is < 12
            price = 0
        Case Is < 18
            price = 3.5
        Case Is >= 65
            price = 4
        Case Else
            price = 5.5
    End Select
    picBox.Print "Your ticket price is ";
        FormatCurrency(price)
End Sub
```

2. Press F8, click on the command button, and press F8 twice. The picBox.Cls statement will be highlighted and executed, and then the statement containing InputBox will be highlighted.
3. Press F8 once to execute the statement containing InputBox. Type an age of 8 and press the Enter key. The Select Case statement is highlighted, but has not been executed.
4. Press F8 twice and observe that the action associated with Case Is < 12 is highlighted.
5. Press F8 once to execute the assignment statement. Notice that End Select is highlighted. This demonstrates that when more than one Case clause is true, only the first is acted upon.
6. Click on the End icon to end the program.
7. If desired, step through the program again, entering a different age and predicting which Case clause will be acted upon. (Some possible ages to try are 12, 14, 18, 33, and 67.)

5.3.11 Stepping Through a Program Containing a Do Loop

Do Loops The following walkthrough demonstrates use of the Immediate window to monitor the value of a condition in a Do loop that searches for a name.

1. Access Windows' Notepad, enter the following line of data, and save the file on the A drive with the name Data.txt.

```
Bert, Ernie, Grover, Oscar
```

2. Return to Visual Basic. Create a form with a command button (cmdButton) and a picture box (picBox). Set the AutoRedraw property of the picture box to True. Then double-click on the command button and enter the following procedure:

```
Private Sub cmdButton_Click()
    'Look for a specific name
    Dim searchName As String, nom As String
    picBox.Cls
    searchName = InputBox("Name:") 'Name to search for in
                                    list
    Open "Data.txt" For Input As #1
    nom = ""
    Do While (nom <> searchName) And Not EOF(1)
       Input #1, nom
    Loop
    Close #1
    If nom = searchName Then
       picBox.Print nom
      Else
       picBox.Print "Name not found"
    End If
End Sub
```

3. Press F8, and click on the command button. The heading of the event procedure is highlighted in yellow.

4. Double-click on the variable *searchName*, click the right mouse button, click on "Add Watch," and click on OK. The variable *searchName* has been added to the Watch window.

5. Repeat Step 4 for the variable *nom*.

6. Drag the mouse across the words

```
(nom <> searchName) And Not EOF(1)
```

to highlight them. Then click the right mouse button, click on "Add Watch," and click on OK. Widen the Watch window as much as possible in order to see the entire expression.

7. Press F8 three more times to execute the picBox.Cls statement and the statement containing InputBox. Enter the name "Ernie" at the prompt.

8. Press F8 repeatedly until the entire event procedure has been executed. Pause after each keypress and notice how the values of the expressions in the Watch window change.

9. Click on the End icon to end the program.

5.4 PROGRAMMING PROJECTS

1. Write a program to draw the graph of the polar coordinates function $r = 3\cos 2\theta$. (*Note:* This graph is called a four-leaf rose.) The program should be written in a style so that it can be easily modified for other functions using polar coordinates.

2. Write a general graphing program for bounded functions that does auto-scaling. The values a and b for the extent of the x-axis should be given as in Example 2. The endpoints of the domain of the function should be passed to a Sub procedure that estimates the highest and lowest function values and uses these to set the values c and d for the extent of the y-axis.

3. Write a program that graphs the derivative of a function specified in a function procedure. The limit definition of the derivative should be used to obtain the values of the derivative function at each point.

4. *Voting Machine.* The members of the local Gilligan's Island fan club bring a computer to their annual meeting to use in the election of a new president. Write a program to handle the election. The program should add each candidate to a list box as he or she is nominated. After the nomination process is complete, club members should be able to approach the computer one at a time and double-click on the candidate of their choice. When a "Tally Votes" command button is clicked, a second list box, showing the number of votes received by each candidate, should appear alongside the first list box. Also, the name(s) of the candidate(s) with the highest number of votes should be displayed in a picture box.

KEY TERMS

Breakpoint	Frame	Procedure step
Check box	List box	Single-click-draw technique
Desk checking	Option button	Stepping (into)

Problems

PROBLEM 5.1

1. Suppose the statement picBox.Scale (−1, 40)–(4, −8) has been executed. Write down the statements that draw the x axis and the y axis.

In Problems 2 and 3, write an event procedure to draw a line between the given points. Select an appropriate Scale method, draw the axes, and draw a small circle around each end point of the line.

2. (2, .5), (4, .3)
3. (3, 200), (10, 150)

In Problems 4 through 9, rewrite the event procedure in Example 2 to produce a reasonable graph of the function.

4. $f(x) = -.01x^3 + x + 1$
5. $f(x) = e^{-.02x}$
6. $f(x) = x\sin x$
7. $f(x) = 3\cos x + \cos 3x$
8. $f(x) = \sqrt{9 - x^2}$
9. $f(x) = \ln(5 - x)$

In Problems 10 through 13, rewrite the event procedure in Example 3 to produce a reasonable graph of the function.

10. $f(x) = 1/(x - 10)^2$
11. $f(x) = 1/(10(x^2 - 5x + 6))$
12. $f(x) = 1/\sqrt{x^2 - x - 2}$
13. $f(x) = \tan 2x$

In Problems 14 and 15, rewrite the event procedure in Example 4 to produce a reasonable graph of the solution of the differential equation.

14. $y' = t - 2y,\ 2 \le t \le 3, y(2) = 3$
15. $y' = y\ (2t - 1),\ 0 \le t \le 1, y(0) = 8$
16. The function in Example 3 has the line $y = 15$ as a horizontal asymptote. Write a Call statement and a Sub procedure to draw this line.
17. Consider the program in Example 2. Write a Call statement and Sub procedure to draw a tick mark on the x-axis of length about 1/4 inch at $x = 1$. (Assume the height of the picture box is about 4 inches.)
18. Write a program to display the graphs of the functions $f(x) = 1 + x + .5x^2$ and $g(x) = e^x$ on the same coordinate system. *Note:* $f(x)$ is the second Taylor polynomial approximation of $g(x)$.
19. Consider the differential equation $y' = -y^2 + 10y - 21, 0 \le t \le 5$. The shape of the solution depends on the initial value y_0. Write a program to display the four solutions for the initial conditions $y_0 = 1$, $y_0 = 4$, $y_0 = 6$, and $y_0 = 7$ on the same coordinate system.
20. Graph the solution to $y' = 2\pi\cos 2\pi t$ with $-1 \le t \le 1, y(-1) = 0$, for $n = 4$, 16, 64, and 256. Notice that the larger the value of n, the more the graph resembles the solution of the differential equation, $f'(t) = \sin 2\pi t$.

PROBLEMS 5.2

In Exercises 1 to 6, determine the effect of setting the property to the value shown.

1. `Frame1.Caption = "Income"`
2. `Check1.Value = 1`
3. `Check1.Value = 0`
4. `Check1.Caption = "&Vanilla"`
5. `Option1.Value = False`
6. `Option1.Caption = "Punt"`

In Problems 7 and 8, determine the state of the two option buttons after the command button is clicked.

7.
```
Private Sub Command1_Click()
    Option1.Value = True
    Option2.Value = True
End Sub
```

8.
```
Private Sub Command1_Click()
    Option1.Value = False
    Option2.Value = False
End Sub
```

9. Which of the controls presented in this section can receive the focus? Design a form containing all of the controls and repeatedly press the Tab key to confirm your answer.
10. Create a form with two frames, each having two option buttons attached to it. Run the program and confirm that the two pairs of option buttons operate independently of each other.

For Problems 11 to 20, suppose that the list box lstBox is as shown and determine the effect of the code. (Assume the Sorted property is set to True.)

Bach
Beethoven
Chopin
Mozart
Tchaikovsky

11. `picOutput.Print lstBox.Text`
12. `picOutput.Print lstBox.List(2)`
13. `picOutput.Print lstBox.List(lstBox.ListCount - 1)`
14. `lstBox.AddItem "Haydn"`
15.
```
lstBox.AddItem "Brahms"
picOutput.Print lstBox.List(lstBox.NewIndex)
```
16. `lstBox.RemoveItem 0`
17. `lstBox.RemoveItem lstBox.ListIndex`
18. `lstBox.RemoveItem lstBox.ListCount - 1`
19. `lstBox.Clear`
20.
```
For n = 0 To lstBox.ListCount - 1
    If Len(lstBox.List(n)) = 6 Then
        lstBox.RemoveItem n
    End If
Next n
```

A form contains a command button, a small picture box, and a frame with three check boxes (Check1, Check2, and Check3) attached to it. In Problems 21 and

22, write a Click event procedure for the command button that displays the stated information in the picture box when the command button is clicked.

21. The number of boxes checked.
22. The captions of the checked boxes.

In Problems 23 to 26, suppose the form contains a list box containing positive numbers, a command button, and a picture box. Write a Click event procedure for the command button that displays the requested information in the picture box.

23. The average of the numbers in the list.
24. The largest number in the list.
25. Every other number in the list.
26. All numbers greater than the average.
27. A computer dealer offers two basic computers, the Deluxe ($1500) and the Super ($1700). In addition, the customer can order any of these additional options: multimedia kit ($300), internal modem ($100), 64MB of added memory ($150). Write a program that computes the cost of the computer system selected.
28. Item 34a of Form 1040 for the U.S. Individual Income Tax Return reads as follows:

    34a Check if: ☐ **You** were 65 or older, ☐ Blind; ☐ **Spouse** was 65 or older, ☐ Blind
    Add the number of boxes checked above and enter the total here→ **34a**. ☐

    Write a program that looks at the checked boxes and displays the value for the large square.
29. Consider the Length Converter in Figure 5.13. Write a program to place the items in the list and carry out the conversion.

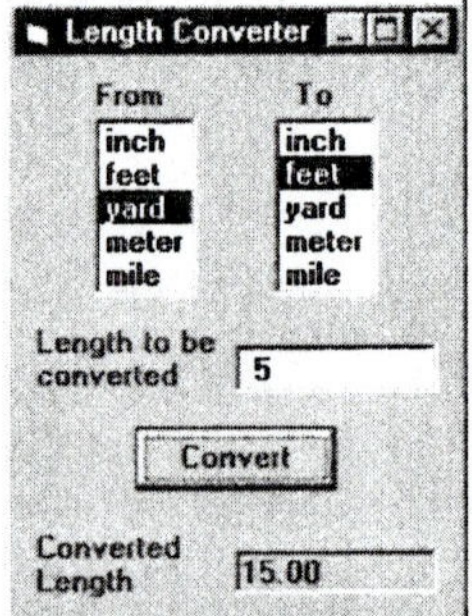

Figure 5.13. Form for Exercise 29.

PROFESSIONAL SUCCESS

OLE Objects

OLE (object linking and embedding) is a method that allows you to run another application from within your Visual Basic project. Applications are incorporated into a form by clicking on the OLE button in the VB toolbox, and choosing from the available options in the *Insert Object* dialog box. This allows you to greatly extend the functionality of your VB projects, with little or no additional programming. For instance, instead of writing code to allow the performance of simple calculations within a form, embedding a Microsoft Excel worksheet automatically allows such tasks to be performed.

Two techniques are available for integrating OLE objects into a VB project. A *linked* OLE object refers to an external file prepared using an outside application. Linked OLE files never become part of the VB code, and can be manipulated both from within VB and the original application. Problems may arise if the linked OLE object is inadvertently modified or deleted. External files are linked to a VB project by choosing *Create From File* in the *Insert Object* dialog box, and checking the *Link* option.

Creating a new OLE object or leaving the *Link* option unchecked places a form containing an embedded OLE object into your VB project. An embedded file is only accessible from within VB, and is stored together with your project. Once an external file has been embedded, any changes made to the file outside of Visual Basic are not reflected in the embedded version of the file. A further drawback of embedded objects is that they can increase significantly the size of your VB project files.

ActiveX ControlsObjects

ActiveX is the name, coined by Microsoft, given to a category of add-in controls that can be used to add functionality to your Visual Basic project. Similar to a Java Applet, an ActiveX control consists of a self-contained software module that can run without modification in many different hardware and software environments. Originally limited to VB applications, the newest ActiveX controls can be incorporated into programs written in languages such as Visual C++ and Visual J++. In addition, ActiveX controls can be added to Word documents and Excel spreadsheets, and implemented as executable macros on World Wide Web pages.

A number of ActiveX controls are included with VB6. They are listed in the *Components* dialog box, which you can display by choosing *Project, Components...* from the menu bar. Any of the listed components can be added to your project by clicking on the appropriate check box, and then clicking OK. For every component chosen, a new button will appear in the VB toolbox. Double-clicking this button will place the ActiveX control in the form window, where it can be manipulated in the same manner as any other VB control.

You are not limited to using only those ActiveX modules included with VB6. ActiveX controls have been written to perform virtually any task you can think of, and are widely available over the Internet. Two sources of downloadable ActiveX controls are www.microsoft.com and www.download.com/PC/Activex. In addition, you can also write your own ActiveX controls using *Visual Basic Professional Edition*, by clicking on the appropriate icon in the *New Project* dialog box.

Visual Basic and Microsoft Office Applications

Visual Basic for Applications (VBA) is a version of Visual Basic that is provided as part of the Microsoft Office package. Within each Office application, VBA is controlled via a five-button toolbar, accessed by choosing *View, Toolbars, Visual Basic* on the menu bar. Clicking the middle button on the toolbar displays the VBA editor, which is similar in appearance to the VB6 editor. Choosing *Insert, User Forms* from the VBA menu bar displays a blank form and the VBA toolbox. Instead of stand-alone applications, VBA is used to design controls and forms that can be incorporated into Office documents. In addition, VBA can be used to customize and add functionality to Microsoft Office itself.

A convenient way of getting started with VBA in Microsoft Office is to record a *macro*, which is a set of command sequences and instructions grouped together and stored for reuse. A macro is recorded by clicking on the *record button* located on the VBA toolbar. During the recording process, each action performed by the user within the Office application is translated into VBA code. Once the macro has been created and stored, its code can be viewed and modified from within the VBA editor by choosing *Tools, Macro, MacrosComponents...* from the menu bar, and clicking *Edit* in the Macro dialog box.

Answers to Selected Problems

A.2 CHAPTER 2

Problems 2.1

1. Command buttons appear to be pushed down and then let up when they are clicked.
3. When a command button is clicked, it appears to be pressed and then released. The left and top borders are temporarily darkened.

(In Problems 7 to 24, begin by pressing Alt/F/N to create a new form.)

7. Click on the Properties window or Press F4 to activate the Properties window. Press Shift+Ctrl+C to highlight the Caption property. Type in "CHECKING ACCOUNT".
9. Double-click the text box icon in the Toolbox. Activate the Properties window and highlight the BackColor property. Click on the down-arrow to the right of the Settings box. Click on the Palette tab. Click on the desired yellow in the palette. Press Shift+Ctrl+T followed by three down arrows to highlight the Text property. Click on the Settings box and delete "Text 1". Click on the form to see the empty, yellow text box.
11. Double-click on the text box icon in the Toolbox. Activate the Properties window and highlight the Text property. Type the requested sentence. Highlight the MultiLine property. Double-click on the highlighted MultiLine property to change its value to True. Highlight the Alignment property. Double-click twice on the highlighted Alignment property to change its value to 2-Center. Click on the form.Use the mouse to resize the text box so that the sentence occupies three lines.
13. Double-click on the text box icon in the Toolbox.

    Activate the Properties window and highlight the Text property. Type "VISUAL BASIC". Highlight the Font property. Click on the ellipsis to the right of the Settings box. Click on "Courier" in the Font box, and click OK. Resize the text box to accommodate its text. Click on the form to see the resulting text box.

15. Double-click on the label icon in the Toolbox. Activate the Properties window and highlight the Caption property. Type "ALIAS". Click on the form to see the resulting label.
17. Double-click on the label icon in the Toolbox. Activate the Properties window and highlight the Alignment property. Double-click twice on the highlighted Alignment property to change its value to "2-Center". Highlight the Caption property. Type "ALIAS". Double-click on the BorderStyle property to change its value to "1-Fixed Single". Highlight the Font property and click on the ellipsis. Click on Italic in the Font Style box and click OK. Click on the form to see the resulting label.
19. Double-click on the label icon in the Toolbox. Activate the Properties window and highlight the Font property. Click on the ellipsis to the right of the Settings box. Click on Wingdings in the Font box. Click on the largest size available (72) in the Size list box. Click OK. As one means of determining which keystroke in the Wingdings font corresponds to a diskette, follow steps a–g.

    a. Click the Start button.
    b. Point to Programs and then point to Accessories.
    c. Click Character Map.
    d. Click on the down arrow in the Font box and click on Wingdings.
    e. Click on the diskette character (fourth from the right end of the first row).
    f. Note in the Status bar at the bottom of the Character map window that the keystroke for the diskette character is a less than sign.
    g. Close the Character Map and return to Visual Basic.

    Highlight the Caption property. Change the caption setting to a less than sign by pressing <. Click on the label, and enlarge it.
21. Double-click on the picture box icon in the Toolbox.

    Activate the Properties window and highlight the BackColor property. Click on the down-arrow to the right of the Settings box. Click on the Palette tab. Click on the desired yellow in the palette. Click on the form to see the yellow picture box.
23. Double-click on the picture box icon in the Toolbox. Increase the size of the picture box so that it can easily hold two standard size command buttons. Click (do NOT double-click) on the command button icon in the Toolbox. Move the mouse to the desired location in the picture box where you want the upper-left corner of the first command button to be. Press and hold the left mouse button and drag the mouse down and to the right until the rectangle attains the size desired for the first command button. Release the left mouse button. Repeat the preceding four steps (starting with clicking on the command button icon in the Toolbox) to place the second command button on the picture box.
25. Create a new project. Change the form's caption to "Dynamic Duo". Place two command buttons on the form. Enter as the caption of the first "&Batman" and of the second "&Robin". Increase the font size for both command buttons to 14.
27. Create a new project. Change the form's caption to "Fill in the Blank". Place a label, a text box, and another label on the form at appropriate locations.

Change the caption of the first label to "Toto, 1 don't think we're in" and of the second label to "A Quote from the Wizard of Oz". Delete "Text1" from the Text property of the text box. Resize and position the labels as needed.

29. Create a new project. Change the form's caption to "An Uncle's Advice". Place a picture box on the form and increase its size to provide plenty of space. Place on the picture box five labels and three command buttons. Change the captions of each label to the appropriate text. Change the BorderStyle property of the last label to "1-Fixed Single". Change the captions of the command buttons to "1", "2", and "3". Resize and position the labels and command buttons as is appropriate. Finally, the size of the picture box and form can be adjusted down as appropriate.

Problems 2.2

1. The word Hello.
3. The word Hello in italic letters.
5. The word Hello in green letters.
7. The word Hello in big, fixed-width letters.
9. The name of the control has been given but not the property being assigned. The line frmhi ="Hello" must be changed to frmHi.Caption = "Hello".
11. Text boxes do not have a Caption property. Information to be displayed in a text box must be assigned to the Text property.
13.
```
lblTwo.Caption = "E.T. phone home."
```
15.
```
txtBox.ForeColor = vbRed
txtBox.Text = "The stuff that dreams are made of."
```
17.
```
txtBox.Text = ""
```
19.
```
lblTwo.Visible = False
```
21.
```
picBox.BackColor = vbBlue
```
23.
```
txtBox.Font.Bold = True
txtBox.Font.Italic = True
txtBox.Text = "Hello"
```
25.
```
cmdButton.SetFocus
```
27.
```
lblTwo.BorderStyle = 1
lblTwo.Alignment = 2
```
29.
```
Private Sub cmdLeft Click()
    lblShow.Alignment = 0
    lblShow.Caption = "Left Justify"
End Sub

Private Sub cmdCenter_Click()
    lblShow.Alignment = 2
    lblShow.Caption = "Center"
End Sub

Private Sub cmdRight_Click()
    lblShow.Alignment = 1
    lblShow.Caption = "Right Justify"
End Sub
```

31.
```
Private Sub cmdRed_Click()
     txtShow.BackColor = vbRed
End Sub

Private Sub cmdBlue Click()
     txtShow.BackColor = vbBlue
End Sub

Private Sub cmdWhite_Click()
     txtShow.ForeColor = vbWhite
End Sub

Private Sub cmdYellow Click()
     txtShow.ForeColor = vbYellow
End Sub
```

33.

Object	Property	Setting
cmdLarge	Caption	Large
cmdSmall	Caption	Small
cmdBold	Caption	Bold
cmdItalics	Caption	Italic
txtShow	Text	(blank)

```
Private Sub cmdLarge_Click()
     txtShow.Font.Size = 18
End Sub

Private Sub cmdSmall_Click ()
     txtShow.Font.Size = 8
End Sub

Private Sub cmdBold_Click()
     txtShow.Font.Bold = True
     txtShow.Font.Italic = False
End Sub

Private Sub cmdItalics_Click ()
     txtShow.Font.Italic = True
     txtShow.Font.Bold = False
End Sub
```

35.

Object	Property	Setting
ftmEx35.	Caption	Face
lblFace	Font.Name	Wingdings
	Caption	K
	Font.Size	24
cmdVanish	Caption	Vanish
cmdReappear	Caption	Reappear

```
Private Sub cmdVanish_Click()
     lblFace.Visible = False
End Sub

Private Sub cmdReappear_Click()
     lblFace.Visible = True
End Sub
```

Problems 2.3

1. 03125
3. 8
5. 3E+09
7. 4E−08
9. Valid
11. Valid
13. 10
15. 9
17.
```
Private Sub cmdCompute_Click()
     picOutput.Cls
     picOutput.Print 7 * 8 + 5
End Sub
```
23. True
25. True
27. 8
29. 1.28
31. 6
37. The third line should read c = a + b.
39. The first line should not contain a comma. The second line should not contain a dollar sign.

Exercises 2.4

1.
```
Hello
1234
```
3. `12 12 TWELVE`
5. `A ROSE IS A ROSE IS A ROSE`
7. `1234 Main Street`
9. The variable phone should be declared as type String, not Single.
11. End is a keyword and cannot be used as a variable name.
13. True
15. True
17. ha
19. 2
21. `$2 BILL`
23. `12,345.00`
25. `$12,346`
27. Tomorrow's date
29. The current year
31. The interest rate is 4.50%
33. The minimum wage is $5.15

35.
```
12345678
2,000
```

37.
```
Private Sub cmdDisplay Click()
    Dim firstName As String, middleName As String
    Dim lastName As String, yearOfBirth As Integer
    picOutput.Cls
    firstName = "Thomas"
    middleName = "Alva"
    lastName = "Edison"
    yearOfBirth = 1847
    picOutput.Print firstName; " "; middlename; " ";
    picOutput.Print lastName; ","; yearOfBirth
End Sub
```

39.
```
Private Sub cmdDisplay Click()
    Dim publisher As String
    picOutput.Cls
    publisher = "Prentice Hall, Inc."
    picOutput.Print Chr(169); " "; publisher
End Sub
```

41.
```
Private Sub cmdCompute_Click()
    picSum.Print Val(txtNum1.Text) + Val(txtNum2.Text)
End Sub
```

43.
```
Private Sub cmdCompute_Click()
    lblNumMiles.Caption = Str(Val(txtNumSec.Text) / 5)
End Sub
```

45.
```
Private Sub cmdCompute_Click()
    Dim cycling As Single, running As Single, swimming As
       Single, pounds As Single
    picWtLoss.Cls
    cycling = Val(txtCycle.Text)
    running = Val(txtRun.Text)
    swimming = Val(txtSwim.Text)
    pounds = (200 * cycling + 475 * running + 275 *
       swimming) / 3500
    picWtLoss.Print pounds; "pounds were lost."
End Sub
```

47.

Object	Property	Setting
frmEx47.	Caption	Net Income
lbl Revenue	Caption	Revenue
txtrevenue	Text	(blank)
lbl Expenses	Caption	Expenses
txtExpenses	Text	(blank)
cmdCompute	Caption	Display Net Income
picOutput		

```
Private Sub cmdCompute_Click()
    Dim income As Single
    picOutput.Cls
    income = Val(txtRevenue.Text) - Val(txtExpenses.Text)
    picOutput.Print "The company's net income is"; income
```

```
End Sub
```

49.

Object	Property	Setting
frmEx49.	Caption	Tipping
lblAmount	Caption	Amount of bill:
txtAmount	Text	(blank)
lblPercentTip	Caption	Percentage Tip
txtPercentTip	Text	(blank)
cmdComputeTip	Caption	Compute Tip
picOutput		

```
Private Sub cmdComputeTip_Click()
    picOutput.Cls
    picOutput.Print "The tip is";
        FormatCurrency(Val(txtAmount.Text)*
        Val(txtPercentTip.Text)/100)
End Sub
```

45.
```
Private Sub cmdCompute_Click ()
    picOutput.Cls
    acres = 30 yieldPerAcre = 18
    corn = yieldPerAcre * acres
    picOutput.Print corn
End Sub
```

49.
```
Private Sub cmdCompute_Click()
    picOutput.Cls
    waterPerPersonPerDay = 1600
    people = 270000000
    days = 365
    waterused = waterPerPersonPerDay * people * days
    picOutput.Print waterUsed
End Sub
```

Problems 2.5

1. `16`
3. `baseball`
5. `Age: 20`
7. `setup`
11. `You might win 180 dollars.`
13. `Hello John Jones`
15. `        1 one        won`
17. `one           two`
19. `1234567890`
21. The Input #1 statement will assign "John Smith" to *str1*, leaving nothing left to assign to *str2*. An "Input past end of file" error will occur.
23. Each line in the file consists of three items, but the Input #1 statements are reading just two. As a result, the second Input #1 statement will assign the numeric data 110 to the string variable *building* and 0 to *ht*. This is not what was intended.

25. The response is to be used as a number, so the input from the user should not contain commas. With the given user response, the value in the variable *statePop* will be 8.

27. Should be Printer.Font.Name = "Courier".

29. Commas cannot be used to format the caption of a label. Also, the value of the caption must be surrounded by quotation marks. The programmer might have intended

```
lblTwo.Caption = " 1            2"
```

31. When assigning properties of the form, the correct object name is Form1 (or whatever the form is named), not Form. Also, Tab(5) and semicolons can only be used with a Print method.

33.
```
Private Sub cmdDisplay-Click()
     Dim activity As String, percent96 As Single,
        percent97 As Single
     'Compute change in political activity
     picOutput.Cls
     Open "Politics.txt" For Input As #1
     Input #1, activity, percent96, percent97
     picOutput.Print "The change in the percentage of
        college freshmen who ";
     picOutput.Print activity; " was "; percent97 -
        percent96
     Input #1, activity, percent96, percent97
     picOutput.Print "The change in the percentage of
        college freshmen who ";
     picOutput.Print activity; " was "; percent97 -
        percent96
     Close #1
End Sub
```

35.
```
Private Sub cmdDisplay_Click()
     Dim begOfYearPrice As Single, endOfYearPrice As
        Single, percentIncrease As Single
     'Report percent increase for a basket of goods
     picOutput.Cls
     begOfYearPrice = 200
     endOfYearPrice = Val(InputBox("Enter price at the end
     of the year:"))
     percentIncrease = 100 * (endOfYearPrice -
        begOfYearPrice) / begOfYearPrice
     picOutput.Print "The percent increase for the year is";
     picOutput.Print percentIncrease
End Sub
```

37.
```
MsgBox "The future isn't what it used to be."
```

39.
```
Private Sub cmdSummarize_Click()
     Dim account As String, beginningBalance As Single
     Dim deposits As Single, withdrawals As Single
     Dim endOfMonth As Single, total As Single
     'Report checking account activity
     picReport.Cls
     Open "2-5-e49.txt" For Input As #1
     '1st account
```

```
    Input #1, account, beginningBalance, deposits,
       withdrawals
    endOfMonth = beginningBalance + deposits -
    withdrawals
    total = endOfMonth
    picReport.Print "Monthly balance for account ";
    picOutput.Print account; " is ";
       FormatCurrency(endOfMonth)
    '2nd account
    Input #1, account, beginningBalance, deposits,
       withdrawals
    endOfMonth = beginningBalance + deposits -
    withdrawals
    total = total + endOfMonth
    picReport.Print "Monthly balance for account ";
    picOutput.Print account; " is ";
       FormatCurrency(endOfMonth)
    '3rd account
    Input #1, account, beginningBalance, deposits,
       withdrawals
    endOfMonth = beginningBalance + deposits -
    withdrawals
    total = total + endOfMonth
    picReport.Print "Monthly balance for account ";
       account; " is "; FormatCurrency(endOfMonth)
    picReport.Print "Total for all accounts = ";
    picReport.Print FormatCurrency(total)
    Close #1
End Sub
```

41.

```
Private Sub cmdComputeAvg_Click()
    Dim socNmb As String, exam1 As Single, Dim exam2 As
       Single, exam3 As Single
    Dim final As Single, average As Single, Dim total As
       Single
    'Compute semester averages
    picOutput.Cls
    Open "2-5-e51.txt" For Input As #1
    '1st student
    Input #1, socNmb, exam1, exam2, exam3, final
    average = (exam1 + exam2 + exam3 + final * 2) / 5
    total = average
    picOutput.Print "Semester average for "; socNmb;
    picOutput.Print "is"; average
    '2nd student
    Input #1, socNmb, exam1, exam2, exam3, final
    average = (exam1 + exam2 + exam3 + final * 2) / 5
    total = total + average
    picOutput.Print "Semester average for "; socNmb; is";
    picOutput.Print average
    '3rd student
    Input #1, socNmb, exam1, exam2, exam3, final
    average = (exam1 + exam2 + exam3 + final * 2) / 5
    total = total + average
    picOutput.Print "Semester average for "; socNmb; is";
    picOutput.Print average
```

```
    picOutput.Print "Class average is"; total / 3
    Close #1
End Sub
```

A.3 CHAPTER 3

Problems 3.1

1. Why do clocks run clockwise?
   Because they were invented in the northern hemisphere where sundials move clockwise.
3. Keep cool, but don't freeze.
   Source: A jar of mayonnaise.
5. 168 hours in a week
   76 trombones in the big parade
7. 24 blackbirds baked in a pie
9. 9
11. 25
13. 203
15. The population will double in 24 years.
17. train
19. moral has the negative amoral
20. political has the negative apolitical
21. There is a parameter in the Subprocedure, but no argument in the statement calling the Subprocedure.
23. The first of the function definition should end with As String, not As Single.
27.
```
Private Sub cmdCalculate_Click()
    picResult.Cls
    picResult.Print "Your BMI is"; BMI(Val(txtWeight),
        Val(txtHeight))
End Sub

Private Function BMI(w As Single, h As Single) As Single
    'Calculate body mass index
    BMI = Round(703 * w / h ^ 2)
End Function
```

Problems 3.2

5.
```
Nope.
He worked with the developer, von Neuman, on the ENIAC.
Correct
```
15. `a = 5`
17. `If j = 7 Then`

```
    b = 1
Else
    b = 2
End If
```

Problems 3.3

1. `17`

7. Program never stops.

11. `While num >= 7`

13. `Until response <> "Y"`

Problems 3.4

1.
```
Pass # 1
Pass # 2
Pass # 3
Pass # 4
```

5.
```
5  6  7  8  9  10  11  12  13
```

7.
```
1  4  7  10
2  5  8  11
3  6  9  12
```

9. Loop is never executed because 1 is less than 25.5 and the step is negative.

11.
```
For num = 1 To 10 Step 2
    picOutput.Print num
Next num
```

13.
```
Private Sub cmdDisplay_Click()
    Dim i As Integer
    'Display a row of 10 stars
    picoutput.Cls
    For i - 1 To 10
        picOutput.Print "*"
    Next i
End Sub
```

15.
```
Private Sub cmdComputeSum_Click()
    Dim sum As Single, denominator As Integer
    'Compute the sum 1 + 1/2 + 1/3 + 1/4 +...+ 1/100
    picOutput.Cls
    sum = 0
    For denominator = 1 To 100
        sum - sum + 1 / denominator
    Next denominator
    picOutput.Print "The sum is"; sum
End Sub
```

A.4 CHAPTER 4

Problems 4.1

1. 3 7 0
3. 6 2 9 11 3 4
5. The Dim statement in the (Declarations) section of (General) dimensions *companies*() with subscripts from 1 to 100 and makes *companies*() available to all procedures. Therefore, the ReDim statement in the Form_Load event procedure produces the error message "Array already dimensioned." First line should be `Dim companies() As String`.
14.

```
Private Sub cmdDisplay_Click()
     Dim i As Integer, total As Single
     'Display names, percentage of total units for top ten
       pizza chains
     Dim nom(1 To 10) As String, units(1 To 10) As Single
     'Read from data file and record names and number of
       units
     'Compute total units
     Open "4-1-e33.txt" For Input As #1
     total = 0                              'Total units
     For i = 1 To 10
         Input #1, nom(i), units(i)
         total = total + units(i)
     Next i
     Close #1
     'Display names and percentage of total units
     picOutput.Cls
     picOutput.Print "Name"; Tab(30); "Percentage of
       units"
     For i = 1 To 10
         picOutput.Print nom(i); Tab(30);
             FormatPercent(units(i)/total)
     Next i
End Sub
```

Problems 4.2

1. No
3. 200 100
5. Sequential, since the array is not ordered
7. 4 swaps
9. $(n - 1) + (n - 2) + \ldots + 1$ or $n(n - 1)/2$
11. Go through the list once, and count the number of times that each of the four integers occurs. Then list the determined number of 1s, followed by the determined number of 2s, etc.

13.
```
Private Sub TripleSwap(x As Single, y As Single, z As
                          Single)
    Dim temp As Single
    'Interchange the values of x, y, and z
    temp = x
    x = y
    y = z
    z = temp
End Sub
```

17.
```
Private Sub cmdCalcAvg_Click
    Dim nom As String, i As Integer
    Dim score(1 To 7) As Integer, sum As Integer
    Dim passNum As Integer, temp As Integer
    'Input student's name and seven test scores
    nom = InputBox("Student's name:")
    For i = 1 To 7
        score(i) = Val(InputBox("Test score " & Str(i) &
                              ":", ""))
    Next i
    For passNum 1 To 6
        For i = 1 To 7 - passnum
            If score(i) < score(i + 1) Then
                temp = score(i)
                score(i) = score(i + 1)
                score(i + 1) = temp
            End If
        Next i
    Next passNum
    picAvg.Cls
    sum = 0
    For passNum = 1 To 5
        sum = sum + score(passNum)
    Next passNum
    PicAvg.Print nom & ":   "; "Average ="; sum / 5
End Sub
```

Problems 4.3

1. Hello
3. Hello
   Aloha
   Bon Jour

9.
```
Private Sub cmdFind_Click()
    Dim search As String, nom As String, yob As Integer
    'Search for a name in Yob.txt
    picOutput.Cls
    search = txtName.Text
    Open "Yob.txt" For Input As #1
    nom = ""
    Do While (search > nom) And (Not EOF(1))
       Input #1, nom, yob
    Loop
    Close #1
    If (nom = search) And (search <> "") Then
       picOutput.Print nom; "'s age is"; 1999 - yob
    Else
       picOutput.Print search; " is not in Yob.txt"
    End If
End Sub
```

11.
```
Private Sub cmdCreateFile_Click()
    'Add initial batting average record to Average.txt
    Write #1, txtPlayer.Text, 0, 0   'Initialize counters
    txtPlayer.Text = ""
    txtPlayer.SetFocus
End Sub

Private Sub cmdQuit_Click()
    Close #1
    End
End Sub

Private Sub Form_Load()
    Open "Average.txt" For Output As #1
End Sub
```

13.
```
Private Sub cmdAddPlayer_Click()
    'Add a player to the end of the file Average.txt
    Write #1, txtPlayer.Text, 0, 0
    txtPlayer.Text = ""
    txt Player.SetFocus
End Sub

Private Sub cmdQuit_Click()
    Close #1
    End
End Sub

Private Sub Form_Load()
    Open "Average.txt" For Append As #1
End Sub
```

A.5 CHAPTER 5

Problem 5.2

1. The word "Income" becomes the caption embedded in the top of Frame1.
3. The Check1 check box becomes unchecked.
5. The Option1 option button becomes unselected.
7. Option2 is selected (True) and Option 1 is unselected (False).
9. Check boxes, list boxes, and option buttons can receive the focus.
11. The currently selected item, Mozart, in 1stBox is displayed in picOutput.
13. The last item, Tchaikovsky, from 1stBox is displayed in picOutput.
15. Brahms is added to the list (after Beethoven) and is displayed in picOutput.
17. The currently selected item in 1stBox is deleted.
19. All items are removed from 1stBox.
21.

```
Private Sub cmdDisplay_Click()
     Dim numChecked As Integer
     numChecked = 0
     If Check1.Value = 1 Then
        numChecked = numChecked + 1
     End If
     If Check2.Value = 1 Then
        numChecked = numChecked + 1
     End If
     If Check3.Value = 1 Then
        numChecked = numChecked + 1
     End If
     picOutput.Cls
     picOutput.Print "You have checked"; numChecked;
                     "check box";
     If numChecked <> 1 Then
        picOutput.Print "es."
     Else
        picOutput.Print "."
     End If
End Sub
```

23.

```
Private Sub cmdDisplay_Click()
     Dim i As Integer, total As Single
     total = 0
     For i = 0 to 1stNumbers.ListCount - 1
        total = total + Val (1stNumbers.List(i))
     Next i
     picOutput.Print "The average of the numbers is";
     picOutput.Print total / 1stNumbers.ListCount
     End Sub
```

25.

```
Private Sub cmdDisplay_Click()
     Dim i As Integer
     For i = 0 to 1stNumbers.ListCount - 1 Step 2
        picOutput.Print 1stNumbers.List(i)
     Next i
End Sub
```

ndex

ɔs function 67, 68
ccess key 23
ccumulator 128
tiveX control 247
ldition 34
lditions 42
gebraic Functions 67
gorithm 7
testing 14
gorithms 4
ignment property 23
ıd 118
ınotation symbol 9
NSI character set 49
ɔostrophe
comment lines 64
p.Path 65
ɔpend option 199
guments 102
communication with parameters 240
ithmetic operations 34
precedence levels 42
ray variable 175
ray variables
procedure-specific 179
two-dimensional 184
rays
and sequential files 197
creating and accessing 175
passing to procedures 187
searching 193
sorting 187
two dimensional 184
vectors and matrices 185
CII characters 49
signment statements 27, 57
arrays 177, 179
strings 44
erisk 35, 43
AN2 function 164
function 69, 71
oRedraw property 226

kColor property 25

BackStyle property 25
Basic 4
bEr 36
Binary search 193
Bisection method for finding 124
Boolean data type
do loops 131
BorderStyle property 25
Box model 148
Boxes 15
Break mode 235
Breakpoints 237
Bubble Sort 189
Bubble sort 188
inefficiency 206
Bugs 234
Built-in Functions 67
Button clicks 6
Buttons 15

C

C 4
Call 42
Call statement 97, 99, 108
arguments 102
Called procedure 99
Calling procedure 99
Caption property
check boxes 229
command buttons 22
frames 227
initial setting 25
labels 23
option button 229, 230
Caret 35
Case clause 114, 120
Check box 227
Click event procedure 31
Clipping 226
Close statement 66
Cls method 35
Code 27
Code window 28
array dimensions 176
disk-saved programs 43
function creation 107
hiding 32
subprocedure typing 97
Code windows
code processing in 34
Color constants 33
Colors 33
Command button
naming 25
setup walk through 22
Command buttons 6, 17
Commas 57
Comment statements 57
subprocedures 101
Comments 64
Computer
computer languages 3
Computers 1
applications 2
Concatenation 46
Condition
relational operators 40
Conditions
decision structure 110
do loops 121, 123
logical operators 118
strings 51
truth value 119
Connector symbol 9
Control variable 132, 139
Controls 6, 15
Form window 17
Cos function 69, 70
Counter 128
Currency numeric variables 73
Currency variables 47

D

Data 44
Debug menu 16
Debug windows 234
Debugging 234
and subprocedures 100
Decision programming construct 14
Decision structure 12, 110
Decision structures
stepping through programs
containing 240
Decision symbol 9

Declaring a variable 47
Declaring variables 54
Default value 47
Delete key 18
Derivatives 127
Design mode 235
Desk checking 14, 234
Differential Equations
  Euler's method 223
Dim statement 47, 72
Dim statements 54
  arrays 186
  arrays of unknown size 182
Dimension, of array 176
Divide-and-conquer method 11
Division 34
Divisions 42
Do loop 121
Do loops
  stepping through programs containing 242
Do statement 121
Double variables 47
Double-click on 26
Double-clicking 24
Double-precision numeric variables 73
Double-subscripted variables 184

E

Edit menu 16
Element 176
Elementary Row Operations 203
Else 113, 119
End 33
End key 20
End-of-file condition 129
Equal to operator 40
Error 43
Errors 33
Euler's Method 223
Euler's method 226
Event 27
Event procedure 27
  creation walkthrough 28
  general procedure contrasted 97
Event procedures 6
  renaming 34
  subprocedures contrasted 109
Events 6
Exp function 67, 68
Exponentiation 34
Exponentiations 42
Exponents 36
Expressions
  as argument 102
  for...next loops 136
  selectors 117

F

F1 key 26
F4 key 18
F5 key 20
False 33
Field 201
File menu 16
Files 197
  reading data from 57
  sequential 197
Fix function 72
Flag 128
Flags
  array search quarry 193
Flowchart 14
Flowchart symbols 8
Flowcharts 8
  use with hierarchy charts 11
Flowline symbol 9
Focus 21
Font dialog box 20
Font property 19, 25
Font.Size property 34
FontSize property 34
For statement 132, 139
For...Next loop 132
For...Next loops
  nested 136
ForeColor property 19
Form 15, 17
Form Layout window 17
Form window 17, 43
Form_Load event procedure 178, 191, 202
  graphics with 226
Format functions 53
Format menu 16
FormatCurrency function 53, 56
FormatDateTime function 54, 56
FormatNumber function 53, 56
FormatPercent function 53, 56
Form-level scope 48, 177
Forms
  as default object 32
  naming 25
  properties 24
Frames 227
Function calls 108
Function procedures 97, 106
Functions 41
  finding zeroes with bisection method 124
  graphing 217
  invoking 109

G

Gauss Elimination Method 204
General procedure 97
General procedures
  getting info on 108
  stepping through program containing 239
  without parameters 108
GotFocus
  event procedure 28, 32
Graph subprocedure 219
Graphical user interfaces 5
Graphics 217
Graphing calculator 218
Greater than operator 40
Greater than or equal to operator 40
Greatest integer function 72

H

Hardware 3
Heap sort 206
Hierarchy Charts 11
Hierarchy charts 8, 14
HIPO (Hierarchy plus Input-Process-Output) charts 11
Home key 20

I

If 42
If block 110, 119
If blocks
  stepping through programs containing 240
If statement 119
Immediate Window 235
Indenting
  for...next loops 138
  If blocks 119
Infinite loops 130
Initialize subprocedure 219
Input 3
  from input boxes 60
  numeric function 41
  text boxes for 17, 48
Input # statement 65

Input box 60
Input boxes
  use-provided data 65
Input option 199
Input past end of file box 66
Input# statement 58
Input# statements 57
  arrays 179
Input/Output symbol 9
InputBox function 122
InputBox statement 60
InStr function 52
Int Function 41
Int function 72
Integer numeric variables 73
Integer variables 47
Internal Documentation 64
Inverse tangent function 69
ItemData property 233

J

Java Applet 247

K

Key field 196
Keywords 14, 33
Kill statement 199

L

Label
  setup walk through 23
Labels 17
  for output 56
  naming 25
Last point referenced 220
Left function 51
Len function 52
Less than operator 40
Less than or equal to operator 40
Line Continuation Character 63
Line statements 221
Linked OLE object 247
List boxes 231
List Properties/Methods 29
List Properties/Methods feature 34
List property 231
Load Picture dialog box 24
Local scope 47, 108
Locals Window 236
Log function 67, 68
Logical error 43
Logical operators 118
  truth values 120
Logical programming construct 14
Long integer numeric variables 73
Long variables 47
Loop 121
Loop programming construct 14
Loop statement 121, 123
Loops
  avoiding infinite 130
Losing focus 76
LostFocus
  event procedure 28, 32
LostFocus event procedure 29

M

Machine language 3
Macro 248
Matrices 185
Matrix Inversion 204
Memory 2
Menu bar 16
Message boxes 6, 57
  using for output 63
Method 35
Microprocessor 2
Microsoft corporation
  support for Visual Basic 7
Microsoft Office 7
Microsoft Windows 5
Mid function 51
Midpoint rule 140
Modeling 147
Modes 199
Module 11
Mouse movements 6
MultiLine property 20, 26
Multiplication 34
  omission of asterisk denoting 43
Multiplications 42

N

Name property 24
  initial setting 25
Name statements 199
Natural logarithmic function 67
Nested If blocks 112
Nested loops 136
New Project window 15, 16
NewIndex property 233
Next statement 132, 139
Not 118
Notepad 57, 197
Numbers 34
Numeric constants 34
Numeric expression 38
Numeric Functions 41
Numeric Variables
  types 72
Numerical integration 139

O

Object box 28
Objects 15
Offpage Connector symbol 9
OLE objects 247
Opening a file for append 198
Opening a file for input 57
Opening a file for output 197
Option buttons 229
Option explicit 55
Or 118
Ordered Arrays 187
Output 3
  formatting with print zones 61
  numeric function 41
  picture boxes for 17
  text boxes for 48
  to printer 64
  using message boxes for 63
Output option 199

P

Parallel arrays 186
  searching 196
Parameter info 108
Parameters 100
  communication with arguments 240
  passing arguments to 102
Parenthesis, in Visual basic expressions 42
Pass 121
  bubble sort 189
Passed by reference 104
Passed by value 109
Passing 99
Personal computer 1
Picture box 217
Picture boxes 17
  frames contrasted 227
  naming 25
  setup walkthrough 23
Picture property 24

Predefined Process symbol 9
Print method 35, 39, 57
Print zones 61, 66
Printer 64
Printer.EndDoc statement 226
Private 27
Problem solving 4
Procedure box 28
Procedure step 237
Processing 3
Processing symbol 9
Program 3
Program documentation 64
Program Flow control
  general procedures 97
Program flow control
  decision structures 110
  do loops 121
  for…next loops 132
  numerical integration case study 139
Program Modes 235
Programmer 3
programming construct 14
Programming Tools 7
Programs
  stepping through 237
Project 6
Project Container window
  changing size 26
Project menu 16
Projects 21
Prompt argument
  input boxes 60
  message boxes 63
Properties 27
Properties window 17, 24
  command buttons 22
  labels 23
  picture boxes 24
  text boxes 18
PSet statement 221
Pseudocode 8, 10, 14
  use with hierarchy charts 11
Push buttons 76

Q

Quarry, array search 193
Quick Info 60
Quotation-mark character 54

R

Range, of array 176
Record 201
Record button 248
ReDim statement 186
ReDim statements 181
Reference number, sequential file 197
Relational Operators 40
Relational operators 51
Rem statements 64
Reserved words 33
Restricted keywords 42
Return, Functions 41
Right function 51
Round Function 41
Rounding of number 73
Run mode 235
running a program 20
Running the program
  running a program 3
Run-time errors 43

S

Save File As dialog box 21
Save Project As dialog box 21
Scale method 219, 225
Scientific notation 36
Scope of variables 47
Searching arrays 193
Select 42
Select case blocks 114
  stepping through programs containing 241
Selected object 17
Selector 114, 117, 119
Semicolons 45
  in Print methods 39
Sequence programming construct 14
Sequence structure 11
Sequential Files
  adding items to 198
Sequential files 197
  deleting item from 199
  sorting 201
Sequential search 193
SetFocus statement 33
Settings box 18
Sgn function 72
Simple variable 175
Simpson's rule 140
Sin function 69, 70
Single-click-draw technique 227, 229
Single-precision numeric variables 47, 73
Single-precision real number 47
Single-subscripted variables 184
Sizing handles 17
Software 3
Sort 188
  algorithm evaluation 206
Sorted property 231
Sqr Function 41
Sqr function 67
Statements 27
Step value 134
  non integer 139
Stepping out of a procedure 237
Stepping over a procedure 237
Stepping through procedure 237
Stepping(stepping into) 237
Str function 55
String 65
  relationships between 51
String array 177
String constant 44
String declaration 100
String expression 46
String functions 51
String variables
  selectors 117
String-related numeric functions 52
Strings
  concatenation 46
  passing to subprocedure 100
Structure charts 11
Structured programming 4, 14
Sub 27, 33, 42
Sub procedure
  passing strings to 100
Sub procedures 97
  calling by other sub procedures 108
  invoking 109
  passing to 99
  passing values back from 104
Subscripted variable 176
Subscripts 176
Substrings 52
Subtraction 34
Subtractions 42
Syntax errors 42

T

Tab Function 62
Tab function 66
Tab key 24
  as event 27
  Focus changing with 22
Table 184
Table lookup 196
Tan function 69, 71
Template, for subprocedures 97

Terminal symbol 9
Text box properties window 18
Text boxes 6, 17
  naming 25
  setup walkthrough 17
  user-provided data 65
  using for string I/O 48
  with option buttons 230
Text files 197
Text propertiy
  initial setting 25
Text property 18
Title argument
  input boxes 60
  message boxes 63
Toolbar 15
Top-down charts 11
Trapezoidal rule 140
Trigonometric Functions 69
Trigonometric functions 73
Trim function 51, 55
True aspect settings 219
Truncate function 72
Truth values 119
  logical operators 120
Two-dimensional arrays 184

U

UBound function 185
UCase function 51, 196
Unconditional branch 14
Underscore character 63
Unequal to operator 40
Until 121, 130
User 3
User-defined function 106
User-defined functions
  returning arrays 185

V

Value property
  check boxes 227
  option button 229
Variable 175
  declaring type 46
  naming 38
Variable names 55
Variables 37
  as argument 102
  declaring 54
  scope 47
  scope in general procedures 108
Vectors 185
View menu 16
Viewing Window, for graphics 217
Visible property 25
Visual Basic
  application development 6
  as a higher level language 3
  built-in functions 67
  code-independent program
    capabilities 20
  debugging tools 234
  graphics capabilities 217
  history of 4
  initial screen 16
  input and output 57
  introduction to 4
  invoking 15
  numbers 34
  program creation steps 27
  program modes 235
  strings 44
  versions 7
  windows in 5
Visual Basic 6.0 7
Visual Basic Events 27
Visual Basic for Applications (VBA) 247
Visual Basic Objects 15
VTOC (Visual Table of Contents) charts 11

W

Watch Window 236
While 121, 130
Window menu 16
Windows 95 7
Windows 98 7
Windows NT 7
Write # statement 197

Z

Zero of a function 124